The men of the 5th Division ('The Pioneers') were among the workhorses of the British Peninsular army. Lacking both the kudos and the wealth of letters, journals and memoirs of divisions like the 3rd and the Light, it is easy to overlook the part they played in the struggle that finally drove the French out of Spain and Portugal. Yet they were the first troops into the streets of Badajoz. They, along with the 3rd Division, played a crucial part in the great victory at Salamanca. And they made up the bulk of the troops that finally took San Sebastian after a protracted and bloody siege. There is also a surprisingly wide range of material that records both their exploits and the experience of serving in the war, extending from the voices of men in the ranks to company and staff officers, brigade commanders, and the journal of the aide-de-camp of the general most associated with the division, James Leith. Looking at one division in detail also allows analysis of the divisional system as it functioned in Wellington's Peninsular Army.

The purpose of this study, therefore, is to retell a familiar story from a less familiar perspective and thus demonstrate the strategic relationship between the parts and the whole while also emphasising that wars are fought by individuals – and no two individuals react in the same way. Each man's experience is his own.

Carole Divall lives in Lincolnshire, and for a long time she was head of English at a local girls' high school. Having retired from the classroom, she now works full-time as a writer, lecturer and researcher. She has a long-standing interest in the period of the Revolutionary and Napoleonic Wars as a time of great social, political and cultural change, as well as for the military aspects. Her particular interest is the British Army of the late eighteenth and early nineteenth century, its organization, the campaigns in which it was engaged and the human perspective. This is Carole Divall's eighth book, and continues her interest in the Peninsular War.

Wellington's Unsung Heroes

The Fifth Division in the Peninsular War, 1810–1814

Carole Divall

 Helion & Company

Helion & Company Limited
Unit 8 Amherst Business Centre
Budbrooke Road
Warwick
CV34 5WE
England
Tel. 01926 499619
Email: info@helion.co.uk
Website: www.helion.co.uk
Twitter: @helionbooks
Visit our blog at http://blog.helion.co.uk/

Published by Helion & Company 2023
Designed and typeset by Mach 3 Solutions Ltd (www.mach3solutions.co.uk)
Cover designed by Paul Hewitt, Battlefield Design (www.battlefield-design.co.uk)

Text © Carole Divall 2023
Cover: Lieutenant Francis Maguire leading the forlorn hope at San Sebastian, 31 August 1813,
© Julia Higgins.
Illustrations © as individually credited.
Maps by George Anderson © Helion & Company 2023

Every reasonable effort has been made to trace copyright holders and to obtain their permission for the use of copyright material. The author and publisher apologise for any errors or omissions in this work, and would be grateful if notified of any corrections that should be incorporated in future reprints or editions of this book.

ISBN 978-1-915113-91-7

British Library Cataloguing-in-Publication Data.
A catalogue record for this book is available from the British Library.

All rights reserved. No part of this publication may be reproduced, stored in a retrieval system, or transmitted, in any form, or by any means, electronic, mechanical, photocopying, recording or otherwise, without the express written consent of Helion & Company Limited.

For details of other military history titles published by Helion & Company Limited, contact the above address, or visit our website: http://www.helion.co.uk

We always welcome receiving book proposals from prospective authors.

Contents

List of Maps and Illustrations		vi
Preface		vii
1	1810	9
2	1811	36
3	1812	72
4	1813	156
5	1814	219
6	Inside the Division	229
Appendix: 5th Division – Battle Casualties		248
Bibliography		251
Index		256

List of Maps and Illustrations

Lieutenant General Viscount Wellington. (The British Library)	10
Lieutenant General James Leith by Charles Picart. (Philadelphia Museum of Art)	13
William Maynard Gomm, engraving by Joseph Brown. (Public Domain)	15
The Battle of Bussaco.	21
The Battle of Buçaco, 27 September 1810, by Richard Simkin. (Public Domain)	25
View towards the Lines of Torres Vedras from the French position at Santarém, from *Views in Spain & Portugal, taken during the Campaigns of His Grace the Duke of Wellington*, by G. Cumberland. (Public Domain)	37
The 1811 Campaign.	40
Guarda, by Andrew Leith Hay. (*A Narrative of the Peninsular War*)	46
Sabugal on the river Coa, by Thomas Staunton St Clair. (Public Domain)	48
The Battle of Fuentes de Oñoro, 3 May 1811.	53
The 1812 Campaign.	74
Badajoz.	81
The 30th Foot escalading the San Vincente bastion.	87
Distant Salamanca, by Andrew Leith Hay. (*A Narrative of the Peninsular War*)	98
The environs of Salamanca.	99
The Battle of Salamanca.	114
The Battle of Salamanca, by J.A. Atkinson. (Anne S.K. Brown Military Collection)	120
The area around Villamuriel.	141
The campaigns of 1813 and 1814.	159
The advance of the 5th Division.	161
The Battle of Vitoria.	169
Fighting in the village of Gamarra Maior, by James Beadle. (Nuneaton Museum and Art Gallery)	175
Victory of Vitoria, by John Massey Wright, illustrating the aftermath of the battle. (Anne S.K. Brown Military Collection)	179
The Siege of San Sebastion.	181
San Sebastian, by Andrew Leith Hay. (*A Narrative of the Peninsular War*)	183
Crossing of the Bidassoa, by William Heath. (Public Domain)	202
The Battle of the Nivelle.	208
The Battle of the Nive, 9 December 1813.	212
The Battle of the Nive, 10 December 1813.	214

Preface

When Napoleon decided in 1807 to interfere in the affairs of the Iberian Peninsula he could never have realised that he was about to create what he himself described as his Spanish Ulcer. It must have seemed a relatively simple matter to take possession of Portugal and thus enforce the Continental System which the Portuguese, as 'England's Oldest Allies' refused to implement. After all, by the recently signed secret Treaty of Fontainebleau, he had gained Spain's agreement to the dismemberment of Portugal. Spain itself, governed by a family riven by discord and a population still trapped in the mores of an earlier time, may well have seemed a less than reliable ally; or did Napoleon believe that the country would be better under French rule? Whatever his motive, the arrival of French troops across the Pyrenees in the autumn of 1807 set in motion the Peninsular War, which would drive both Portugal and Spain into the arms of Great Britain and would continue until the Emperor's abdication in 1814, by which time British, Portuguese and Spanish troops were on French soil, and the drain on French manpower and resources had seriously impeded the French war effort.

The first British army, initially commanded by Lieutenant General Sir Arthur Wellesley, then briefly by Lieutenant Generals Sir Harry Burrard and Sir Hew Dalrymple, arrived in Portugal in August 1808 and was victorious at Roliça and Vimeiro. This led to the evacuation of the French on British navy ships by the terms of the Convention of Sintra, which caused such controversy in Britain that all three generals were summoned home to face an official enquiry. Lieutenant General Sir John Moore was then appointed to the command of the 30,000 British troops, with orders to cooperate with the Spanish in order to rid the Peninsula of the French. At the same time, Napoleon had arrived to sort out the Spanish insurgency, a campaign that resulted in the capitulation of Madrid and the restoration of his brother, Joseph, whom he had made king of Spain. Moore had no choice but to retreat. At Corunna on 16 January 1809, a French army was held at bay long enough for the navy to evacuate the British troops. It was a hollow victory which cost Moore his life.

When Wellesley returned to Portugal three months later, Napoleon had long since departed but the French controlled most of Spain to a greater or lesser degree, and the north of Portugal to the Douro was in their hands. There were Spanish armies ready to fight, if not happily as allies of the British; the partisan bodies, the guerillas, were forming up to fight the invaders in a new type of war; and the Cortes of Cadiz nominally operated as an organ of government. It was obvious that a protracted struggle lay ahead, a struggle which would require a larger army and would thus witness the evolution of a divisional system in place of the brigade system which Wellesley had previously used. Eventually, he would command an army organised in eight infantry divisions, the last of them, the 7th, being formed early in 1811.

In the sense that reputation is everything, some divisions were definitely more equal than others. The Light Division, partly because of its wealth of letter-, journal- and memoir-writers and partly because of its activities, definitely enjoys a distinction that sets it apart from the numbered divisions. Picton's 3rd Division is notable for its fiery, or some would have said vainglorious, commander, which reflects on the battalions of which it was composed, while Hill's 2nd Division, so often acting alone in exposed positions, certainly deserves all the respect that it receives. This begs the question, were the other five divisions merely unassuming but reliable workhorses? The focus of the following study is one of those unsung divisions, the 5th, of whom Andrew Leith Hay wrote that 'there is nothing within the scope of human powers which might not have been accomplished by the 5th Division.'[1]

It would be fair to say that the 5th Division have had no better publicist than Leith Hay who, as aide-de-camp to his uncle, Major General James Leith, knew them very well and had shared many dramatic moments with them, as a reading of his *Narrative of the Peninsular War* makes clear. Beside this can be set the letters and memoirs written by men of the division; particularly the letters, which so often catch the moment and its emotions. From the narrative perspective, the immediate response and the subsequent memories it is possible that even a workhorse division, with its unsung heroes, deserves the respect that Leith Hay gave it.

As ever, I have to thank those who have helped me in a variety of ways to write this study. Particular thanks go to Andrew Bamford and Rob Griffith of Helion, the former having provided the spur for the writing of this book, and Mark Thompson for solving many of the issues relative to San Sebastian, surely the most testing of all the challenges the 5th Division faced in the Peninsula.

---

[1] Andrew Leith Hay, *A Narrative of the Peninsular War* (Edinburgh: Henry Washbourne, 1831) vol.II, p.273.

1

1810

A Fifth Division

When Sir Andrew Leith Hay published his account of the Peninsular War in 1831, he chose the following dedication: 'To Lieutenant-General Sir John Oswald, G.C.B. and the surviving officers and soldiers of the Fifth Division of the Peninsular Army, the following pages are respectfully dedicated by the Author'. For Leith Hay, the 5th Division was as fine as any other division in Wellington's Peninsular army, a judgement he made clear when he reached the point in his narrative where he would mention them for the last time.

> As it is the last occasion on which I shall have to notice the services of the 5th division, it may be permitted me to revert to those deeds which entitled its battalions to as ample a meed of praise, and as just a claim to gratitude from their country, as any portion of the Peninsular army. Whether in defending the heights of Busaco, in scaling the walls of Badajos, in leading the victorious attack at Salamanca, in driving back the pursuing enemy at Villa Muriel, in forcing the passage of the Zadorra at Vittoria, in storming and taking San Sebastian, or in planting the British ensign on the French imperial territory, their conduct was equally conspicuous for gallantry, devotion and discipline. Although many years are now passed since this body of troops have been separated, and it may be supposed mature consideration of what they were, and of their achievements, must be tempered with some degree of moderation as the enthusiastic recollections with which I revert to those scenes, the contrary effect is produced in my mind; and while, with increased feelings of respect, I feel honoured in the good fortune of having served with these gallant soldiers, I at the same time unequivocally record my belief, that, commanded by a general possessing the confidence of his army, as Lord Wellington did, and led as they invariably had been, there is nothing within the scope of human powers which might not have been accomplished by the 5th division.[1]

Although Sir Arthur Wellesley was not the first to use the divisional system as a means of organising a campaigning army, he was certainly the first in the British Army to demonstrate

---

1   Leith Hay, *A Narrative*, vol.II, pp.272–273.

the value of such a system over an extended period. Previously, as in the campaigns of the French Revolutionary Wars, the usual formation was the brigade, composed of two to four battalions, which could then be brought together with other brigades on an ad hoc basis. Frederick, Duke of York referred to columns during the Dutch campaign of 1799, while Sir Ralph Abercromby used the term, lines, in Egypt in 1801. The first time a British army was organised in divisions, as the term was subsequently understood, was against the Danes in 1807. Sir John Moore then used the same arrangement in December 1808, forming his army into a cavalry division, four infantry divisions, each two or three brigades strong, and two flank brigades. In neither case did these divisions exist long enough to acquire any sense of permanence.

Lieutenant General Viscount Wellington. (The British Library)

During his first period of command in the Peninsula (1808) Wellesley had used the brigade system. When he returned in 1809 he was thinking in terms of a right and a left wing, with some staff from the Adjutant General's office attached to each. A general order issued at Coimbra on 8 May, preparatory to the attack on Oporto, demonstrates this point. 'These wings will be formed into two or more lines, as circumstances may require, to form advanced guards and reserves: there is to be no alteration in the order of march tomorrow.'[2] The following day, however, another general order instructed that 'The Divisions under General Sherbrooke, General Cotton, General Hill and General Cameron, will march tomorrow according to the routes already given by the Quarter Master General.'[3] And then on the eve of the crossing of the Douro yet a third general order referred to 'Officers commanding different columns…'[4]

Only on 18 June, at Abrantes, was a general order issued where the use of the term, division, is unequivocal:

---

2   Anon. (ed.), *General Orders*, vol.I, pp.24–25.
3   Anon. (ed.), *General Orders*, vol.I, pp.25–26.
4   Anon. (ed.), *General Orders*, vol.I, p. 26.

4. As the weather will now admit of the troops hutting, and they can therefore move together in large bodies, brigades are to be formed into divisions as follows:

1st Division
Guards
Brig. Gen. Cameron's Brigade
Hanoverian Legion

2nd Division
Major Gen. Hill's Brigade
Brig. Gen. R. Stewart's Brigade

3rd Division
Major Gen. McKenzie's Brigade
Colonel Donkin's Brigade

4th Division
Brig. Gen. A. Campbell's Brigade
Colonel Peacocke's Brigade

Lieutenant General Sherbrooke will take the command of the 1st division; the senior General Officers of brigades will respectively take command of the division in which their brigades are placed, till the other Lieutenant Generals will join the army.

The brigades in divisions are to be formed from the right, as placed in this order:

The divisions will stand in one or more lines, in respect to each other, as will be ordered at the time.
An Assistant Adjutant General will be attached to the Officer commanding the division; an Assistant Provost will also be attached to each division.[5]

This is undoubtedly the genesis of Wellington's divisional system, to which further refinements were added, as will be discussed subsequently in relation to the 5th Division.

When Wellesley wrote to Viscount Castlereagh, the Secretary of State for War, on 12 May to inform him of events leading up to the successful crossing of the Douro, he specifically stated that 'The infantry of the army was formed into three divisions for this expedition'. Just over a month later, on the 17 June, as part of an extended diatribe on the matter of indiscipline and the need for a different approach, he wrote that

> British armies have been in the field before, and that these complaints, at least to the same extent, have not existed; to which I answer – first, that the armies are now

---

5   Anon. (ed.), *General Orders*, vol.I, p.71.

larger, their operations more extended, and the exertions required greater than they were in former periods; and that the mode of carrying on war is different from what it was.[6]

Although he was explicitly addressing the problems of law and order, the divisional system may be thought implicit in his reference to changes in the scope and manner of warfare. In 1808 at Vimeiro, he had commanded no more than 20,000 troops. At Bussaco in 1810 his Anglo-Portuguese forces would be over 30,000 strong, while three years later, at Vitoria, he would command an Allied army of up to 80,000 men.

At Talavera, fought on 27 and 28 July, the British order of battle consisted of the one cavalry brigade, under the command of Lieutenant General William Payne, and four infantry divisions commanded by Lieutenant General John Coape Sherbrooke, Major General Rowland Hill, Major General John Rolland Mackenzie, who was killed on the second day of the battle, and Brigadier General Alexander Campbell. There was also, famously, a light brigade which failed to reach Talavera in time to participate in the battle. This would evolve into the Light Division, being officially recognised as such in February 1810.

After Talavera, Wellesley found himself threatened by an advance south of a force under the command of Maréchal Jean-de Dieu Soult. This was intended to close off the route to Portugal and left the British commander with no choice to abandon Spain.

Wellesley had been given command of the Portuguese army in April 1809, but it was an army that was definitely not battle-ready. Marshal Beresford, however, had been appointed commander-in-chief a month before and given the specific task of creating an army with the organisation, discipline and fighting skills of its British allies, a task he immediately set in motion with impressively rapid results. Upon Wellesley's return to the Peninsula, Beresford was created *Marechal do Exército* (Marshal of the Army). By early 1810 there were Portuguese troops that Wellesley could make use of. He first tried to integrate them into the existing divisions by attaching a Portuguese battalion to each brigade. When this proved unsuccessful, he added a Portuguese brigade to the 3rd and 4th Divisions, while attaching Hamilton's Portuguese to the 2nd. These brigades comprised two line battalions and one of caçadores. He had already increased the presence of light infantry by dispersing the companies of the 5/60th among the four line divisions.

That 1809 had ended in disappointment and frustration after the successes at Oporto and Talavera probably explains why there was so much grousing among the British officers, or 'croakers' as they came to be known. Viscount Wellington (as he now was in acknowledgement of his victory at Talavera) had a more serious problem to consider. Although the French had withdrawn from Portugal after Oporto, there was every reason to believe that the Armée de Portugal, so named by Imperial decree on 10 April 1810, would make a third attempt to establish French control of the whole Iberian Peninsula and drive the British into the sea. Wellington was already taking defensive measures to protect Lisbon, which were known only to his engineers, but there was a more immediate threat, because by mid-March the French were massing men and resources in the vicinity of Salamanca. At this point, the Light Division was holding the area between the two vital fortresses, Spanish

---

6   Gurwood (ed.), *Dispatches*, vol.IV, pp.322, 435.

Ciudad Rodrigo and Portuguese Almeida, which guarded a major border crossing point. At the same time, Wellington had posted the 1st Division at Celorico, the 3rd Division at Pinhel, and the 4th Division at Guarda. This concentration of the bulk of his forces could be easily effected. The 2nd Division, under Hill, however, was further south, in the Alentejo, guarding against a supporting movement by *Général de division* Jean-Louis-Ebénézer Reynier in command of the II Corps, who was in position to threaten Castello Branco and Abrantes.

The newly appointed commander of the Armée de Portugal was the battle-hardened *Maréchal* André Masséna, Duke of Rivoli, Prince of Essling, and heroic veteran of the French Revolutionary Wars. By 1810, however, he was in his 52nd year and those who had known him in his younger days remarked on how much he had aged. Travelling south from France, he reached Valladolid on 11 April, and Salamanca on 28 May. It soon became clear that the first objective, as might have been predicted, was Ciudad Rodrigo. Towards the end of April French troops closed in on the town. By the end of May, the VI Corps, under *Maréchal* Michel Ney, Duke of Elchingen, was in position, either to blockade or to conduct a siege. There was also some skirmishing between French troops, probing the Anglo-Portuguese positions and the Light Division. At the same time, Reynier, with the II Corps, crossed the Tagus at Almaraz. In response, Hill did the same at Villa Velha.

Lieutenant General James Leith by Charles Picart. (Philadelphia Museum of Art)

It was during this period of Allied uncertainty that the nascent 5th Division came into being. On 15 June Wellington informed Hill that he intended 'to attach General Leith to your division. I should give him command of General Tilson's brigade, and of the second division; freeing you, for the present, from the details of that division, and leaving you in command of the whole Alentejo.'[7] Had Wellington implemented these intentions, Leith would have found himself in command of the 1/3rd, 2/31st, 2/48th and 2/66th Foot, and of the 2nd Division, but the brigade was eventually commanded by Major General William Stewart and Hill remained with the 2nd Division.

Major General Sir James Leith, born in 1763, had served at Toulon in 1793, in Ireland during the rebellion of 1798 (when he seems to have behaved with more humanity than

---

7   Gurwood (ed.), *Dispatches*, vol.VI, p.196.

many other officers) and in Lieutenant General David Baird's corps under Moore in 1809. He had also served during the Walcheren campaign, contracting the fever which was to cause him several periods of ill-health during his time in the Peninsula. He had been appointed to the staff of Wellington's force in January 1810. On 11 April, some time after his arrival in Portugal, and also after he had recovered from a bout of the intermittent Walcheren fever, he was named as president of a court martial sitting in Lisbon. Significantly, the members of the court were officers from three newly arrived battalions, the 3/1st (Royals), the 1/9th (East Norfolk) and the 2/38th (1st Staffordshire), which would later form the first British brigade of the 5th Division under Leith's command.[8] Like Leith, two of the battalions, the 3/1st and 1/9th, had been at Walcheren, with its implications for their future health. They had also served in the Peninsula previously, under Wellington and Moore.

At this point, General Orders record a series of appointments to 'the division commanded by Major General Leith'.[9] In other words, this body of troops was not yet recognised as the 5th Division, although it was taking on the form of a division. For example, Captain John Selby Smith of the 3/1st was appointed brigade major of the British brigade, whose composition has already been noted, while Sergeant Richard Newman, also of the 3/1st, was made assistant provost marshal and Captain George Ross (Royal Engineers) was posted to the new unit. Leith also acquired a Portuguese brigade, comprising two battalions of the 3rd Line, and a single battalion of the 15th Line, with the Tomar militia attached, under the command of Brigadier General William Spry.[10]

We have the testimony of Captain William Maynard Gomm of the 1/9th, who was on Leith's staff as Deputy Assistant Quartermaster General, that 'At last the long-expected order has arrived for moving us up country. We march on Thursday. Three out of the four regiments in garrison here – the 4th, 9th, and 38th, – march for Leyria.'[11] This was written in Lisbon on 18 June. Gomm seems to have confused the 4th with the 3/1st. By 6 July Gomm was at Tomar, which was now the headquarters of Leith's command. Interestingly, although Gomm recognised that the Portuguese were raw troops, he did not dismiss them as many of his fellow officers did. Instead, he described them as 'all young, full of spirit, and with discipline enough, even now, to promise everything that ought to be expected from them.'[12] All they needed, he felt, was a chance to gain confidence. It would be useful to know whether Leith shared Gomm's opinion. Time would tell, because it would not be many weeks before he sent them into action.

Leith reached Tomar in mid-July and, to Gomm's amused chagrin, ousted his staff officer from his comfortable lodgings. Also according to Gomm, Leith immediately set about 'reconnoitring the passes of the Zezere, and everything seems to indicate that we shall remain in this neighbourhood for the present. We are to compose part of a division of 6,000 men, and the remainder of our force will arrive shortly.'[13]

---

8   Anon. (ed.), *General Orders: Spain and Portugal* (London: T. Egerton, 1814), vol.II, p.60.
9   Anon. (ed.), *General Orders*, vol.II, p.112.
10 Anon. (ed.), *General Orders*, vol.II, pp.111–117.
11 Francis Culling Carr-Gomm (ed.), *Letters and Journals of Field-Marshal Sir William Maynard Gomm, G.C.B.* (London: John Murray, 1881), vol.I, p.147.
12 Carr-Gomm (ed.), *Letters and Journals*, vol.I, p.154.
13 Carr-Gomm (ed.), *Letters and Journals*, vol.I, p.167.

Gomm anticipated that their task would be to watch the passages of the Tagus around Abrantes, Punhete and Castello Branco. In fact, Leith's command had changed from Wellington's original thinking. A memo to Hill sent on 2 July made clear that, instead of taking command of the 2nd Division, Leith was required to take position 'upon the Zezere as a support to Lieut. General Hill with the corps of troops placed under his orders.'[14] A week later Wellington wrote again to Hill:

William Maynard Gomm, engraving by Joseph Brown. (Public Domain)

> I have formed a corps under General Leith upon the Zezere, with the object of securing the retreat of Le Cor from the mountains; the communication of this army with the Tagus; and of yourself through Abrantes with Punhete. I think these points are tolerably secure, and in a few days will be more so.
>
> But in the situation in which we are, it is necessary to provide for events which are possible, although I hope not very probable.
>
> When Ciuded Rodrigo shall fall, it is probable that the enemy will direct the march of a large detachment, at least, of his army upon Castello Branco, and the mountains between the Tagus and the Zezere. It is not very probable, but it is possible that the Tagus may be fordable at Villa Velha; in which case, if the enemy should be able to cross that river, your march upon Abrantes would be difficult…[15]

This dispatch makes clear that Wellington's dispositions depended on the fate of Ciudad Rodrigo, where the governor, Andrés Pérez de Harrasti, had been conducting a determined resistance to French siege operations, although at the same time urging Wellington to come to his assistance. Unfortunately for the governor, making a foray into Spain, even if just across the border, was not part of Wellington's overall strategy. The French eventually blew a practicable breach in the walls of the much-damaged city and on 10 July launched an

---

14   Gurwood (ed.), *Dispatches*, vol.VI, p.238.
15   Gurwood (ed.), *Dispatches*, vol.VI, p.253.

assault. Beleaguered, and with no hope of succour, Herrasti was forced to surrender, which obliged Wellington to pull in the most forward of his troops. Having already blown up Fort Conception, the Light Division withdrew to Fuentes de Oñoro and Aldea del Obispo.

Hill remained in the Alentejo, and Leith on the Zezere, but for both generals it was necessary to keep a close check on French activities. On 24 July Gomm received orders from Leith to ride to Portalegre in order to discover the strength and movements of the French in that area, and between the Tagus and the Guadiana. He was also to communicate with *Teniente general* Pedro Caro, Marques de la Romana, at Badajoz, and the commander at Elvas. These were the two fortresses that guarded the main southern route into Portugal, and Gomm's orders reflected Wellington's concern that the French in southern Spain might launch an attack in support of Masséna's advance into Portugal.

The Zezere was an uncomfortable position, as some correspondence makes clear. On 31 July Wellington wrote to Hill, approving his movements from Atalaya, in the direction of Castello Branco, but also warning him that with *Général de division* Reynier and the II Corps possibly about to threaten his position, he should take care not to be cut off from Leith, who was in his rear. A week later, in another dispatch to Hill, Wellington wrote: '

> I have heard complaints from General Leith of the inconvenience which he feels from the weather in the occupation of his position on the Codes and the Zezere; and, advertising to the existing state of affairs, I am of opinion that it will be expedient to keep his corps in reserve, rather than throw it in the position which I had allotted to it.[16]

More specifically, Wellington wrote to Leith himself:

> I entirely concur with you in the expediency of keeping the troops under your command under cover as much, and for as great a length of time, as possible. None of the regiments of this army, excepting those which prefer it are now out. All are cantoned in the villages.
>
> I beg of you to dispose of your troops as follows, till you shall receive directions from Lieut. General Hill or from me, to alter this disposition.

Figueiro de Vinhos	The 8th Portuguese regt. infantry
Cabaços	One Portuguese regt. infantry
Thomar	One Portuguese regt. of infantry
	Three battalions of British infantry
	Two brigades of Portuguese artillery
Barca de Codes	One battalion of Portuguese militia
Torres Novas	Two battalions of Portuguese militia
	One regiment of Portuguese cavalry
Santarem	One regiment of Portuguese cavalry

---

16 Gurwood (ed.), *Dispatches*, vol.VI, p.333.

> I shall thus have it in my power to dispose of your corps, either in support of Lieut. General Hill, or to preserve the communication between Lieut. General Hill and this army, or to cover the right and communicate with the Marques de la Romana, as I may think proper.
>
> ...I have written to the Portuguese Government respecting the difficulties in supplying the Portuguese troops under your command, which, adverting to their numbers, and to the stations which they occupy, appear to me most extraordinary.[17]

This communication was written on 7 August. The following day Leith's corps was officially instituted as the 5th Division. (It would be followed a month later by a 6th division.)

The Loyal Lusitanian Legion, under Lieutenant Colonel Sir Robert Wilson was also included in Leith's command, so that he had a preponderance of Portuguese troops. As Gomm had pointed out, the Portuguese had still to prove themselves and it may have seemed more sensible to employ a large number of them as a corps de reserve, as Wellington himself called them. Nevertheless, three days later he instructed Hill to detach Brigadier General George Madden's Portuguese cavalry brigade from Leith and send it to Romana, who was maintaining his watching brief at Badajoz.

How Wellington would choose to use Leith's corps was conditioned by the movements of the French. Having gained possession of Ciudad Rodrigo, Masséna could either begin siege operations against its twin border fortress, Almeida, or bypass this stronghold and strike directly at the main Anglo-Portuguese force. Masséna chose the first option and prepared for another challenging siege. Meanwhile, as he informed Hill, Wellington was still contemplating the possibility of a move by Reynier across the Tagus, using the fords at Villa Velha, in order to cut communications between Hill and the Marques de Romana. This would isolate the Spanish troops, who would then be threatened by the II and V French corps. To counteract whatever Reynier's intentions might prove to be, Wellington presented Hill with several options, one of which concerned the disposition of Leith's troops:

> As soon as you find that the enemy's plan is to turn your right, which their first movement from Niza will show, you will order Leith's corps to Santarem, and with your own will follow the enemy's movements along the Tagus. When your right shall reach Santarem, Leith's corps should move on upon Villa Nova, observing the fords of Salvaterra, below which place there is no ford...The great object for you will be to prevent the enemy's passage at a point below you, which you will be able to effect by Leith's corps; and by the position at Santarem to prevent the enemy from annoying this part of the army on the great road from Leyria to Lisbon, if he should cross on any of the fords above you.[18]

This dispatch was written on 22 August. Three weeks later Gomm informed his sister that:

---

17 Gurwood (ed.), *Dispatches,* vol.VI, pp.334–335.
18 Gurwood (ed.), *Dispatches,* vol.VI, pp.378–380.

> The French under Regnier [*sic*] abandoned the right bank of the Tagus three days ago, moving in the direction of Guarda; he is no doubt going to form a junction with Masséna, and the thunder-cloud will shortly burst. We are prepared with waterproof jackets and conductors for lightning since the unfortunate fall of Almeida. The army are all in the highest spirits.[19]

Gomm was right to anticipate some action, because Masséna had summoned Reynier specifically to strengthen his force.

Wellington had also informed Hill on 22 August that the French had not yet opened fire on Almeida. Just four days later an explosion in the powder store wrecked the town and forced Brigadier General William Cox, in command, to surrender. This disaster required Wellington to rethink his dispositions. Having expected Almeida to hold out for several weeks, he now had to accept that Masséna's immediate objective was to defeat the Anglo-Portuguese army, or at least drive it to Lisbon and embarkation for England. He started drawing back towards Lisbon, while Hill did likewise, moving west of Castello Branco. At the same time, Wellington maintained communications with Leith. On 1 September he commented on the plans of Captain John Williams R.E. for the construction of defensive works on the Zezere, approving them in principle. At the same time, he was aware of the risk of fatiguing the troops. Thus, Leith was to proceed only if the work could be undertaken either with the local peasantry or by the troops 'without any great inconvenience'.[20] He also informed Leith that should the French direct their line of march against the main Anglo-Portuguese army, the Zezere would no longer serve a defensive purpose and he should collect all his troops on the Alva.

Interestingly, the salutation in this dispatch had changed from 'Sir' to 'My Dear General'. This might seem of little significance but there was a clear social implication to the salutations Wellington used.

Five days later, a further dispatch confirmed that the works on the Zezere should be started, under the direction of Captain Williams, with details of the payment rates to the Portuguese peasants who would serve as the artificers and labourers. Wellington continued: 'I have no doubt of the zeal of the troops under your command, nor of their desire to be actively employed.' This may be surmised as a response to a direct request from Leith. The sting was in the tail, however, presumably as a comment on another request. 'In answer to your desire to have more English troops under your command, I must inform you that I class and dispose of the troops of the different descriptions according to my view of the service which will be required of them, and not as a matter of favor to any officer.'[21]

Meanwhile, the French were marching through country devoid of people and resources, thanks to what today would be called a scorched earth policy. This had been initiated by Wellington, and approved by the Portuguese Regency. Masséna decided, therefore, to make for Vizeu, where he confidently expected to find supplies for his hungry troops. He followed a route which would bring him into the Mondego valley, via Guarda. By 15 September he was said to be at Pinhel. Wellington instructed Hill, therefore, to warn Leith to be ready to

---

19   Carr-Gomm (ed.), *Letters and Journals*, vol.I, p.181.
20   Gurwood (ed.), *Dispatches*, vol.VI, pp.398–399.
21   Gurwood (ed.), *Dispatches*, vol.VI, pp.405–406.

move his troops, should it transpire that the troops which had marched through Guarda were Reynier's.[22]

Two days later it became clear that the French were in the Mondego valley, so Leith received orders to commence a march to Espinhal, but to go no further until the head of Hill's column reached the town. Then he was to advance to Miranda de Corvo, where he should stay until further orders arrived. In fact, Wellington was waiting for the detached troops of Hill, Leith and Le Cor to join his right before crossing the Mondego.[23] By 20 September Hill was at Espinhal, while Leith remained at the rear of the main Anglo-Portuguese force but on the march to the Mondego. Masséna's search for supplies had given Wellington time to call up Hill and Leith, and had also allowed him the advantage of choosing favourable ground if he decided to make a stand.

Masséna reached Viseu on 19 September, only to discover that the town was virtually deserted, and there were no supplies for his army other than grapes and lemons. Furthermore, he had been marching into hostile country with unreliable maps and without local guides. The Lopez map that he was using had been produced in 1778 and was notable only for its inadequacies: natural features distorted out of all recognition, towns misplaced, and non-existent roads brought into existence. Nor was it possible to judge whether the roads which actually did exist were suitable for wheeled transport. Reconnaissance would have been the obvious solution to Masséna's difficulties but with the Ordenança haunting the countryside and falling on any scouting parties, even that option was denied to him. He also had to await the belated arrival of his guns before he could proceed further, so not until 23 September did the first French troops leave Viseu. Nor did he have much idea of what lay ahead: the Buçaco ridge where his opponent, more familiar with the country, had chosen to post his army.

On 21 September, having called in all his troops, Wellington was able to write to Lord Liverpool, Secretary of State for War and the Colonies:

> I shall thus have collected in one body the whole of the disposable force in Portugal, and I hope to have it in my power to frustrate the enemy's designs.
>
> I imagine that Marshal Massena has been misinformed, and has experienced greater difficulties in making his movements than he expected. He has certainly selected one of the worst roads in Portugal for his march.[24]

In fact, Masséna should have known just how formidable an obstacle was the Buçaco ridge, since it was a rare point of accuracy on the Lopez map. Convinced as he was that Wellington was concentrating on Coimbra, which he himself needed to reach in the expectation of finding supplies, it seems not to have occurred to him that the position might be defended.

---

22 Gurwood (ed.), *Dispatches*, vol.VI, p.441.
23 Gurwood (ed.), *Dispatches*, vol.VI, pp.450, 453.
24 Gurwood (ed.), *Dispatches*, vol.VI, p.458.

The Battle of Buçaco (Bussaco)

Fought on the 27 September, the Battle of Buçaco was essentially a delaying action in which the Allies made a stand and the French attempted to dislodge them and drive them into precipitous retreat, if not actually to overwhelm them. The Allies were definitely favoured by the ground, which Wellington subsequently described to Liverpool, in a dispatch written on the 30 September, as 'a high ridge which extends from the Mondego, in a northerly direction about eight miles. At the highest point of the ridge, about two miles from its termination, is the convent and garden of Bussaco. The Serra de Bussaco is connected by a mountainous tract of country to the Serra de Caramula…'[25] It rises steeply at its highest point to nearly 2,000 feet and at the time of battle was covered in scrub and gorse. This was the ground that Wellington intended to hold.

The 3rd and 4th Divisions had been on the ridge since 21 September, with the Light Division and Brigadier General Dennis Pack's Independent Portuguese Brigade thrown forward and lower down. Three days later, Ney's VI Corps, leading the departure from Viseu, came up against Pack's troops, first driving in some light cavalry before being checked by allied artillery. The following day Reynier brought up his II Corps and Brigadier General Robert Crauford judiciously ordered a skirmishing withdrawal to the position on the ridge that Wellington had already allotted to his division. Leith arrived on the 25th, having crossed the Mondego at the Peña Cova fords, while Hill was only one day's march away.

With only the 1st and 2nd Divisions still to arrive, Wellington had 40,000 troops. When the whole allied army was in position, this rose to over 52,000 which enabled him to occupy an extended front.[26] Hill was on the extreme right, and slightly behind the rising ground while to his right and forward of his position was a battalion of the Loyal Lusitanian Legion, with two guns. The terrain then became rougher as it dipped for the São Paulo to the Palmazes road, which was straddled by Leith's division, comprising his British brigade, Spry's Portuguese brigade, the other two battalions of the Loyal Lusitanian Legion, the Tomar Militia and the two-battalion 8th Portuguese Line. Major General Thomas Picton's 3rd Division was posted from the San Antonio de Cantaro to Palheiros road onto some rising ground, the highest point of which was occupied by the three British brigades of the 1st Division. To their left were Pack's, Brigadier General Francis Coleman's and Brigadier General Alexander Campbell's independent Portuguese brigades which, with the infantry of the King's German Legion, operated as a reserve. To their front was the Light Division, separated from Pack by a cleft in the ground. Finally, the 4th Division was to the left rear. Sixty guns and four Portuguese batteries were distributed along the line, while two squadrons of the 4th Dragoons were on the summit.

Even without considering the 2nd Division, on the extreme right, nearly a mile separated the right of the 5th Division from the left of the Light Division. Indeed, the southern sector, occupied by Hill and Leith, actually comprised three-fifths of the whole position. Because the French were on lower ground, however, their movements were clearly visible, so the only means for taking the allies by surprise was a night attack; and only a very foolhardy general

---

25 Gurwood (ed.), *Dispatches*, vol.VI, p.471.
26 Oman, *A History of the Peninsular War*, vol.III, pp.544–547. Other sources put the Allied strength as high as 55,000.

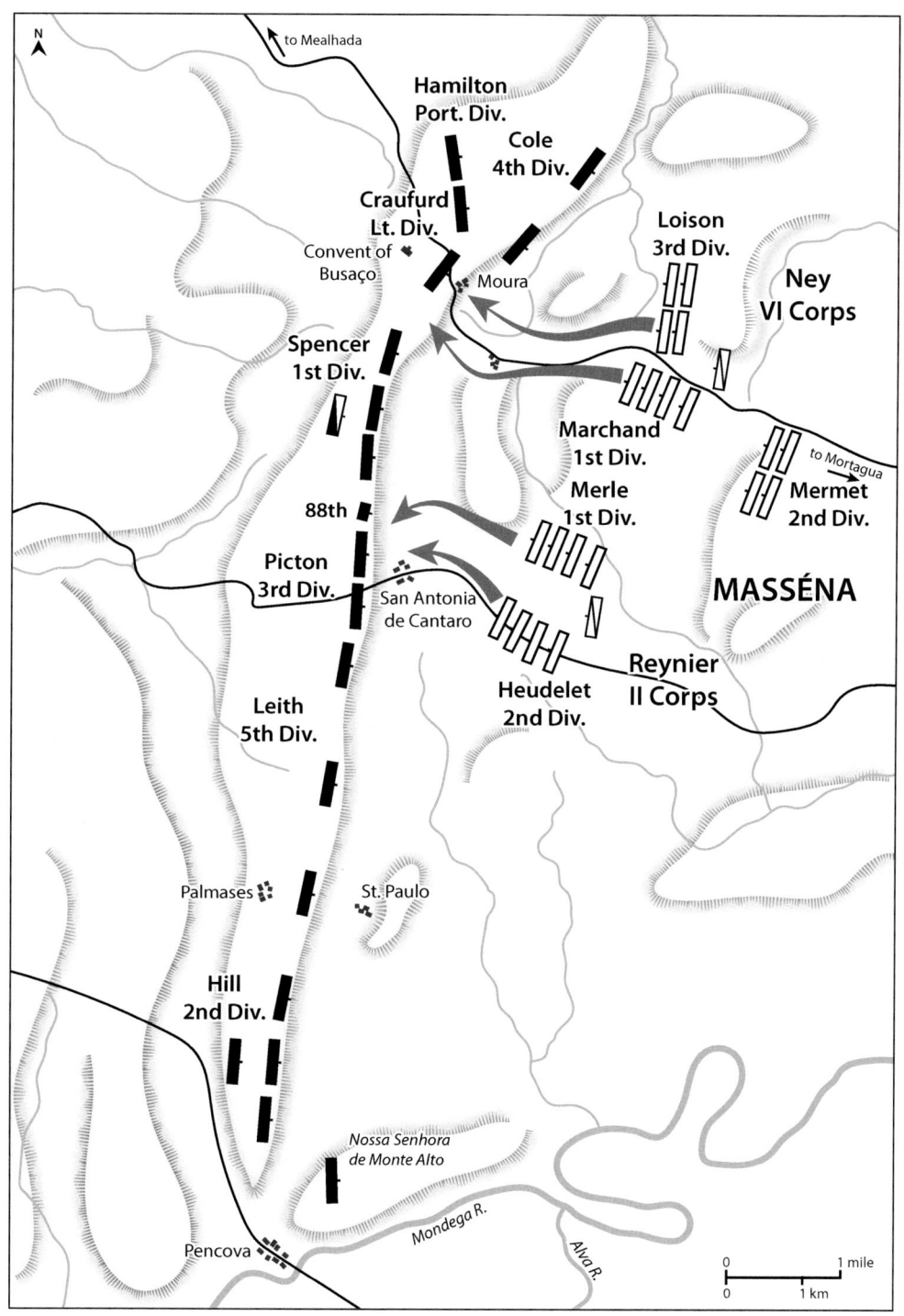

The Battle of Bussaco.

would have taken the risk on such terrain. Furthermore, there was a newly repaired track and flattish ground behind the crest of the ridge, which meant that Wellington could move his troops at will, as could a divisional commander, if he saw the need.

Reynier and Ney were the first corps commanders to reach the ridge, on 25 September. Reynier moved to his left to accommodate the VI Corps, but the fall of darkness made any other movement impossible. At this point, there was no sign of Masséna. The following morning, Ney reconnoitred and came to the conclusion from what he could see that the enemy comprised only the Light and 4th Divisions, their position suggesting that the enemy was heading for Oporto. It was early afternoon before Masséna came up, while *Général de division* Jean-Andoche Junot's VIII Corps, the cavalry and the artillery were still to arrive. They were close enough, however, for Masséna to decide upon a plan of attack, even though he had only examined the ground from the bottom of the ridge. According to orders issued that evening, there would be a two-pronged advance along the most accessible routes, the San Antonio to Palheiros road on the French left and a paved road that led towards a convent on their right. These were to be direct and vigorous attacks, screened by tirailleurs and designed to break the allied line at two different points. Reynier was in command of the left column, and Ney, the right, each with between 13,000 and 14,000 men. As he had what was considered the easier line of advance, Reynier was to move first and Ney was to advance only when Reynier had broken through the Allied line. Junot's corps would act as a reserve, giving support where needed.

On the morning of 27 September Reynier formed his men into two columns, screened by tirailleurs. His target was the 3rd Division. Once the British line had been broken, Reynier would re-form his troops, descend the rear slope and then move to the rear of the allied centre, an order which suggests total ignorance of Leith's and Hill's arrival. Ney's men would also be in two columns and would follow the paved road and a rough path on the Sula spur in order to attack the allied right centre. Once he had penetrated the enemy positions, he would also re-form and support Reynier. Junot's VIII Corps was to stand to at Moura, not only waiting to intervene, but to post the artillery in order to prevent an Allied advance in the unlikely event that either Reynier or Ney failed to overwhelm his immediate opponents.

The night before the battle Wellington's men occupied the ridge in darkness, muskets by their side. This meant that when the French began their advance the following morning they remained ignorant of the exact disposition of their opponents. In contrast, the French positions were clearly illuminated by their campfires.

The morning was misty enough to hide the onset of Reynier's advance. *Général de division* Étienne Heudelet's troops, comprising 15 battalions, was on the left, led by the 31e légèr of Arnaud's brigade, and followed by 17e légèr and 70e de la ligne of *Général de brigade* Maximilien Sébastien Foy's brigade, while Arnaud's other regiment, the 47e de la ligne, was held in reserve. To their right were *Général de division* Pierre Hugues Merle's troops, led by the two regiments of *Général de brigade* Jacques Sarrut's brigade, the 36e de la ligne and the 2e légèr, with the one regiment of Graindorge's brigade, the 4e légèr, bringing up the rear. Both columns had a breadth of one company and were led by a screen of skirmishers. Inevitably, having to ascend over steep, rough terrain meant that formation was soon lost as men scrambled over rocks and forced their way through thick vegetation. But they persevered. Merle's tirailleurs were the first to make contact with Picton's 3rd Division, coming up against the light companies of the 74th, 88th, and 45th, plus three rifle companies of the 5/60th. The skirmish line was pushed back and Merle's men now moved to the left, to the dip in the crest where the San Antonio road passed over the summit. This brought them up against the 45th, and the 8th Portuguese from the right of Leith's command.

Picton had already been alerted to the French advance by the sound of musketry. Although the mist was clearing he still could not fully evaluate the situation. It was actually Heudelet's division which initially pressed in, threatening the 74th and the Portuguese 21st. The fire of the two allied battalions and Captain Karl von Arendschildt's guns held them at bay. Satisfied that the immediate danger had been contained, Picton left Major General Henry Mackinnon to deal with the situation and returned to his other troops on the left. This was timely, because Merle's battalions had finally reached the crest of the ridge. Before they could re-form, however, they were overwhelmed by the 88th and a wing of the 45th, supported by two guns brought up by Wellington and a rolling volley from the 8th Portuguese. Although the pursuing British troops were finally brought to a halt when they came within range of the French guns, Merle's brigade had effectively been driven out of the battle.

Général de brigade Foy had believed that he was in reserve to the rest of Heudelet's division and was now castigated by Reynier for his inaction, before being sent forward. As he neared the summit of the ridge, he encountered the other wing of the 45th, a battalion of the 9th Portuguese, serving with the 3rd Division, and the 8th Portuguese. There followed an unequal struggle between the allied troops and Foy's seven battalions.

Leith had received orders from Wellington to move closer to Picton if it became evident that he himself was not a target. He now saw his moment and moved his division to his left by way of the newly repaired track, leaving Hill to bring the 2nd Division forward. Spry's brigade and the Tomar Militia reached the São Antonio road just as Foy launched his attack. Spry was followed by the Loyal Lusitanian Legion and the British brigade. A Portuguese battery also came into action. Initially Leith held Spry's Portuguese troops in reserve and sent the three British battalions forward.

Lieutenant Colonel John Cameron, in command of the 1/9th, then met Colonel Waller, a staff officer attached to the 3rd Division, who urged him to hasten his march. Cameron wrote:

> I of course continued as I had done all along, and on approaching the scene of action perceived the ridge thickly planted with tirailleurs who, on discovering the brigade, pointed their fire towards us. Our advance was a little impeded by the retreat of a considerable body of Portuguese crossing our front and flying to the rear, I rode among them and requested them to clear my front which they understood and shouted 'Viva los Ingleses', 'Valoroso Portuguesas'. Having received directions from General Leith to wheel up, we formed line, advanced to the charge and drove the enemy from the sierra at the point of the bayonet. When we had gained the ridge, I perceived a strong column of the enemy within 50 yards and charging them, they faced about and retired preserving their formation, down the hill under a heavy fire of musquetry which I opened upon them as far as they retreated, The 9th pursued them some distance down the sierra inflicting a very heavy loss of killed and wounded.[27]

---

27 Gareth Glover (ed.), *The Napoleonic Archive Volume 1: British Line Memoirs* (Godmanchester: Ken Trotman Publishing, 2021), pp.19–20.

In the British ranks, Sergeant John Douglas of the Royals, who were following the 9th, remembered how:

> ... the fire increasing rapidly, we got under arms and marched to the support of the troops defending the centre. Most fortunate it was that we did for just as we reached the ground, which was very rugged, we were obliged to form sections and double quick, which brought us up to the scratch in the nick of time, as the French here forced the hill and the Portuguese having given way were in the utmost confusion; had not our brigade made their appearance, I might say at the moment the consequences might have proved fatal to the Army, as it would have been completely separated. A small opening between the rocks of level ground admitted of a few companies wheeling into line, while the enemy on either side from the rocks kept up a quick and destructive fire.[28]

As Cameron and Douglas indicate, the British brigade had arrived just as Foy's pressure was driving back the 45th, the 8th Portuguese and the Tomar Militia, the militiamen quickly being put to flight while the 8th were withdrawing in reasonable order. Leith's memorialist later wrote:

> On this occasion, Major-General Leith evinced that decision of character which was remarkable throughout his military life. A wavering determination, or a slowly executed attack, by giving the enemy time to take advantage of its temporary success, would have occasioned great loss in regaining the point he was most eager to force, – but which, the rapid movement made by the Major-General deprived him of all hopes of accomplishing; and General Regnier [sic] desisted from any further attack.[29]

On the French right, meanwhile, *Général de division* Louis Henri Loison's troops of Ney's VI Corps had taken their cue from Merle's advance towards the summit of the ridge and begun their own ascent. They were initially successful in overwhelming the skirmishers who had been sent forward but they then, without warning, encountered two concealed battalions of the Light Division, and were quickly overwhelmed by a bayonet charge or, in the case of one battalion that had moved to the right as they climbed, Portuguese fire. Ney's other division, *Général de division* Jean Gabriel Marchand's, was no more successful, being held by four battalions of Pack's Portuguese brigade. At this point, Ney called off the attack.

Masséna could have continued the battle. He still had *Général de division* Julien Mermet's division from the VI Corps and Junot's VIII Corps, but he obviously decided that there was no point in risking more troops against an unassailable position. By now, Hill's corps were in evidence and the 4th Division could be seen more clearly, in close support of the Light Division, so he called off the attack, having learnt a valuable lesson. The Anglo-Portuguese army was a more determined opponent that he may previously have supposed.

---

28 Stanley Monick (ed.), *Douglas's Tale of the Peninsula and Waterloo* (Barnsley: Leo Cooper, 1997), p.17.
29 Andrew Leith Hay, *Memoirs of the Late... Sir James Leith, with a Précis of Events of the Peninsular War, by a British Officer* (Barbados: printed for the author, 1817), p.36.

The Battle of Buçaco, 27 September 1810, by Richard Simkin. (Public Domain)

James Hale of the 9th described their situation after the battle. They were first required to clear the ground, for 'There the dead lay so thick that we could not make it convenient to lie down in any comfort, therefore we set to work, and drew them a little distance away – thirty-two were on that bit of ground that our company was to lie down on.' Only then could they enjoy the rum provided by the commissary and 'a little refreshment'.[30]

Douglas's account contains a reminder of how quickly the animosity of battle could turn into something more amicable.

> That night being on picket we were stationed about halfway down the hill with double sentries close to a rivulet which separated the two armies. The day had been extremely warm and on so elevated a space water scarce, which caused many a longing glance at the brook. However, as night closed in the French sentinel made the first advance towards a refreshment by laying down his firelock and signing for drink. His example was soon followed and, meeting at the brook, we had a

---

30 James Hale (transcribed by Peter Catley), *The Journal of James Hale late sergeant in the Ninth Regiment of Foot* (Windsor: IX Regiment, 1998), pp.57–58.

most delightful draught, shook hands, and resumed our post, just in time, as Major Gordon was field officer and a strict disciplinarian.[31]

As for casualties, the 1/9th and the 2/38th had taken 24 and 23 respectively, killed and wounded, while the Portuguese 8th Line had lost 144 killed and wounded, including one officer killed.[32] They had been in contact with the French for longer than the two British battalions, however.

From Wellington's perspective, it was obvious that Masséna would eventually locate the road to Coimbra, thus enabling him to turn the Anglo-Portuguese position without first ascending the serra. In that case, if he stayed put, he would be forced to offer battle on less favourable ground. Withdrawal was the only rational option. He obviously anticipated no problems with his troops, because, as he wrote to Liverpool on the 30 September from Coimbra, 'Throughout the contest on the Serra, and in all the previous marches, and those which we have since made, the whole army have conducted themselves in the most regular manner.'[33] It remained to be seen whether this would still be the case as the army undertook what looked suspiciously like a retreat. It would certainly seem that Leith was less confident of his troops' good behaviour. On the night of the 29th, 'We were just on the point of scrambling down the mountain when a hogshead of rum was ordered to be staved, the General looking on. A little would have been the greatest service on a bitterly cold night.'[34]

Belated reconnaissance had indeed led *Général de brigade* Charles de Sainte Croix to discover and inform Masséna of the alternative route, not a good road but certainly passable, which led on to the Coimbra road. At the same time, the Allies seem to have been expecting further attacks from the French. Indeed, Gomm reported to his sister that he was twice interrupted from some letter-writing by false alarms. It transpired, however, that 'although they were evidently forming their columns, it was for other purposes than attack; before nightfall [on the 28th] they had almost disappeared from our front, taking principally a direction to our left. The following morning the whole of our army fell back upon Coimbra, and we have been since that time constantly on march.'[35]

To Hale, in the ranks, there was something desperate about the retreat from Buçaco:

> …before it was hardly break of day, we received orders to retreat towards Coimbra with all speed, for the enemy had been on the march several hours, with an intention to out-flank us, with a much superior force. But, however, their intention proved unsuccessful, for we took the nearest way across fields, etc making all speed that possibly we could, till we arrived on the other side of Coimbra, which was about eight leagues.[36]

---

31 Monick (ed.), *Douglas's Tale*, p.18.
32 Oman, *A History of the Peninsular War*, vol.III, pp.550–551.
33 Gurwood (ed.), *Dispatches*, vol.VI, p.475.
34 Monick (ed.), *Douglas's Tale*, p.19.
35 Carr-Gomm (ed.), *Letters and Journals*, vol.I, p.184.
36 Hale, *Journal*, p.58.

As a final word on the Battle of Buçaco, it is worth noting some evidence of battalion rivalry. Wellington had written in his dispatch to Liverpool that 'Major General Leith also moved to his left to the support of Major General Picton and aided in the defeat of the enemy by the 3rd battalion of Royals, the 1st battalion of the 9th, and the 2nd battalion of the 38th regiments.'[37] Gomm commented to his sister in a later letter:

> … the 9th Regiment are out of humour with the despatches. They will have it that they did not *assist* in driving the enemy from the heights, nor had the 38th and Royals an opportunity of doing as they did; but according to their own story they found the French crowning the top of the hill, after having driven whatever had been opposed to them, waving their caps with exultation, and increasing in number every instant; they climbed up at them and hurried them down the hill one over the other, while the alarm was spreading to the right and left that the French had succeeded in breaking our line.[38]

Gomm, whose regiment was the 9th, agreed that the story 'is a true one', which he might even have heard from Cameron. Nevertheless, one wonders how the 2/38th managed to take about the same number of casualties.

Since Wellington had avoided a French attack on his flanks by his precipitous departure from Buçaco, Masséna set his troops towards Coimbra, where the Anglo-Portuguese had arrived on 29 October. To Wellington's annoyance most of the population was still in the city but the realisation that the French were advancing on Coimbra persuaded many of them to join the allied troops as they recommenced their march the following day, a train of desperate civilians that would only grow as more towns were passed.

Having already ordered the 2nd Division, along with Major General John Hamilton's Portuguese, to cross the Mondego and then march towards Lisbon by way of Peñacova, Espinhal and Tomar, he now sent the 3rd Division on a route via Alcobaça and Obidos. He then brought the rest of his army south through Redinho, Leiria and Battalha. To the men in the ranks it seemed that they were making for Lisbon and embarkation to England.

It was a dispiriting aftermath to a notable victory, made worse for many by the suffering of the Portuguese. Douglas was not alone in remembering

> …the unfortunate inhabitants plundered by both friends and enemies… If you could picture to yourselves a family hastily packing up the most valuable of their substance on one or more bullock cards, bidding no doubt a farewell to the spot of their birth; a spot in all probability, if they survived and returned, the naked walls alone pointed to the spot where joy and gladness reigned… Often on this retreat has it happened that urging the poor animals beyond their strength to avoid falling into the hands of the enemy, either the beasts give up, or the cart breaks down, and all is irreversibly lost, while the unfortunate owners wander on destitute of all save the life which they have put into the hands of strangers.[39]

---

37 Gurwood (ed.), *Dispatches*, vol.VI, p.473.
38 Carr-Gomm (ed.), *Letters and Journals*, vol.I, p.188.
39 Monick (ed.), *Douglas's Tale*, p.20

As for Gomm, it made him think of nothing so much as Virgil's description of the flight from Troy. That destitution was to cost the lives of many thousands of Portuguese as they crammed into Lisbon, the cruel cost of a policy needed, and approved by the Regency, to rid the country of the French.

Nor did the good behaviour that had so pleased Wellington survive the frustration of retreat. On 3 October, at which point headquarters were at Leiria, he issued a general order to the effect that '1. The Commanding Officers, of the 3d Battalion Royals, 1st Battalion 9th Regiment, 2d Battalion 38th Regiment, are referred particularly to the General Orders of the 9th May, 1809' which targeted straggling.

> There are more stragglers from these three regiments, than from all the others of the British Army taken together, which must be occasioned either by the neglect of the Officers, or by the soldiers being unable to keep up with the march.
>
> In either case, these regiments are unfit to do duty with the army; and if the Commander of the Forces should observe any more of this straggling on the march, he will send the regiments into garrison, and report their conduct especially to His Majesty.
>
> 2. The Commander of the Forces requests, that Major General Leith will communicate these Orders to the Portuguese troops in his division, of whom, particularly the Lusitanian Legion, there is as much reason to complain, as of the British brigade.
>
> He also requests to have a Return this day of the number of men missing from each regiment, British and Portuguese, in the division, on each day's march, since the 1st instant inclusive.[40]

There were further orders, more generally directed, that each divisional commander should order the provost marshal attached to his division to punish all cases of straggling. There was also to be an inspection of packs, and anything other than the soldiers' necessaries was to be burnt and the owners of what was obviously the reward of plundering were to be punished. As for Picton's division, they were to enter no towns unless necessity absolutely obliged it.

The problems continued. The following day the 5th Division was once again the subject of a general order. Having desired that an officer from each regiment should be sent to find the missing men, and their arrival reported to him, Wellington then published the details of the stragglers. The Loyal Lusitanian Legion returned a drummer and 50 rank and file missing and the British brigade, 36 rank and file. He concluded: 'The Commander of the Forces trusts that, by the attention of the Officers commanding regiments, this disgraceful circumstance will not occur again.'[41]

The French, having reached Coimbra on the 1 October, were running riot rather than pursuing, which allowed Wellington to re-arrange his forces. As a result, 'The 5th Division of Infantry is to be commanded by Major General Leith, and is to consist of Brigadier General

---

40 Anon. (ed.), *General Orders*, vol.II, pp.172–174.
41 Anon. (ed.), *General Orders*, vol.II, p.175.

Hay's Brigade [3/1st, 1/9th, 2/38th], and of a brigade of British Infantry, composed of the 1st Battalion 4th, 2d Battalion 30th, and 2d Battalion 44th, under the command of the senior Officer until further orders; and of Brigadier General Spry's Brigade of Portuguese Infantry' which comprised the 3rd and 15th Portuguese of the Line and the 6th Caçadores.[42] It is interesting to wonder whether the appointment of Andrew Hay to command the existing British brigade was linked to its disciplinary problems, most apparent in the ranks of the Royals. Hay had been their lieutenant colonel, and was, according to Douglas, 'a very strict disciplinarian, and did not bear the best of names among the men'.[43]

The Lines of Torres Vedras

On 8 October, as the weary troops trudged towards Lisbon, the weather broke and the autumn rains set in. The following day, however, the leading troops discovered that the Portuguese capital was not their objective. Instead, they were to withdraw only as far as a defensive system that had been under construction since November 1809, Wellington having given the requisite order in October. They had reached the Lines of Torres Vedras.

It is questionable how many of the allied troops were aware of the existence of the Lines before they actually reached them. Certainly, Masséna had a vague idea of earthworks of some kind. Gomm certainly seems to have had some knowledge of defensive activity taking place because he wrote to his sister on the 9 October: 'You know, of course, that since we have been in possession of the country we have given our attention to strengthening the passes leading to Lisbon, through the chain of mountains running across from Villa France to Torres Vedras and Mafra…'[44] As a strategy, this was nothing new. During earlier wars with Spain similar defensive measures had been taken to protect Lisbon, which had included bringing women and children into the capital and requiring the men to hold the defences.

It is doubtful, however, whether even Gomm was aware of the scope of a thoroughly developed defensive system, initially conceived by Wellington in the autumn of 1809 as a result of studying maps produced by the Portuguese engineer, *Brigadeiro* José Maria das Neves Costa, the year before. Wellington had originally thought in terms of a single line of defensive positions, but time allowed for a more ambitious undertaking. As a result, there were three lines: the outer one extended from Alhandra on the Tagus via Sobral and Torres Vedras to the Zizandre; the second ran from Alhandra to Mafra and Ribamar; and the third, west of Lisbon, protected Fort St Julien to enable a safe embarkation, should it prove necessary. These were not continuous fortifications in the form of a wall. Rather, the most vulnerable points were fortified with redoubts, frequent enough to allow crossfire. The redoubts were to be garrisoned by Portuguese local troops, the Militia and the Ordenança, so that regular troops would be available to counteract any French attack. Lateral roads had been repaired or built to facilitate easy movement. Telegraph stations under naval direction ensured rapid communication along the Lines, while naval gunboats patrolled the Tagus.

---

42 Anon. (ed.), *General Orders*, vol.II, p.177.
43 Monick (ed.), *Douglas's Tale*, p.5.
44 Carr-Gomm (ed.), *Letters and Journals*, vol.I, p.185.

As further discouragement, should the French think to launch an attack from the left bank, the ruined fortress at Almada had also been repaired and strengthened.

The effort required to construct the Lines lies outside the focus of this study, but it is worth noting Captain John Jones R.E.'s comments on the thousands of Portuguese peasants:

> …forced to work, many at the distance of forty miles from their homes while their own lands lay neglected … nevertheless, during a twelve month of this forced labour, not a single instance of insubordination or riot occurred, and the great quantity of work performed should, in justice to the Portuguese, be more ascribed to regular habits of persevering labour in those employed, than to the efficiency of the control exercised over them.[45]

As a result, 'Wellington would make his stand, on ground of his own choosing that had been carefully prepared and heavily fortified. If the British were driven form these positions they would be forced to evacuate the Peninsula. If the French failed to break through the defences they could never win the war.'[46]

The allied troops moved into pre-assigned positions within the first line, the one that Wellington thought might be breached. The 2nd Division was posted at Alhandra and Hamilton's Portuguese, at Vila Franca. With cavalry in reserve and Romana's troops brought up from Badajoz, the left of the line was firmly anchored on the Tagus. The Light Division was in position from Alhandra to Monte Agraço, with the 5th Division to the rear of Monte Agraço, where Pack's Portuguese were at the great redoubt. The 1st and 4th Divisions extended from Monte Agraço to Torres Vedras, where the 3rd Division was posted to watch for any French advance on the Zizandre.

Only when the last of the Anglo-Portuguese troops were behind the Lines could the final stages of the fortifications be completed. This required the destruction of bridges and buildings, the felling of trees, even the damning of some valleys. The bridges which were essential for communications remained in place but they were mined and guarded by Portuguese artillery. The resultant fortifications were sufficient to daunt any advancing force.

On 11 October *Général de division* Pierre Soult, in command of the advanced units of the French cavalry, reached Vila Franca, where he found his progress blocked by Hill's outposts. He pushed them back, only to realise that a considerable force lay beyond Alhandra, protected by fortifications. He passed this information on to *Général de division* Louis-Pierre Montbrun, who was approaching Sobral, which was held by the Allies. Montbrun reported back to Masséna but the *maréchal* persisted in his belief that only earthworks lay ahead. This was based on information given to him by some Portuguese staff officers who had chosen to align their fortunes with the French. They spoke of a rounded plateau which would allow offensive operations.

The following day Junot's VIII Corps, leading the French infantry, reached Alenquer, which subsequently became the French headquarters. Pushing on to Sobral, Junot then

---

45 Anon. (ed.), *Papers on Subjects Connected with the Duties of the Corps of Royal Engineers* (London: Weale, 1839), vol.III, p.40.
46 John Grehan, *The Lines of Torres Vedras: the Cornerstone of Wellington's Strategy in the Peninsular War 1809-12* (Staplehurst: Spellmount, 2000), p.xiii.

clashed with Allied picquets. These he was able to overwhelm, but with only 12,000 men he decided to avoid an all-out attack. Instead, he contented himself with driving in any other outlying troops that he encountered.

Wellington, though, expected a French attack on Sobral and called in all but the 2nd and 5th Divisions, the latter being held in reserve. There was some brisk skirmishing between the recently arrived 71st (Highland Light Infantry) and the 19e de la ligne that lasted several hours but the French did nothing to intensify the conflict. Masséna had now seen the reality of the Lines and realised that he needed reinforcements before he could attack the Allies. As if to confirm this judgement, when Reynier reconnoitred Hill's position he also reported that it was too strong to be attacked.

There were two sources of reinforcements in Spain, Soult in Andalusia and *Général de division* Jean-Baptiste Drouet d'Erlon further north. To force them to assist him, though, Masséna would first have to gain Napoleon's permission. To effect this, he sent Foy to Paris with the message that the army would be compromised if it attacked a defensive system, itself formidable, held by 30,000 English and 30,000 Portuguese, aided by 50,000 armed peasants.[47] On his own initiative, Foy urged d'Erlon, whom he encountered at Valladolid, to bring his IX Corps to Masséna's aid as quickly as possible.

The French now dug in, resigned to a long blockade, but the shortage of food meant that discipline and morale were difficult to maintain. Deserters began to trickle across the Lines and foraging parties quickly became marauders.

On the other side of the Lines Wellington concentrated on his own defensive position. He was still expecting an attack, probably on the right, as a dispatch of 17 October to Brigadier General Crauford makes clear. The 5th Division was part of his plan to counteract this.

> I have brought General Leith's division to the rear of this fort [the great redoubt], where part of it is encamped. General Spry's Portuguese brigade will be cantoned this night in a village in the rear of redoubts Nos. 12 and 13. The Hanoverian legion are in the villages behind No. 11; to all of which the British brigades in General Leith's division will be in reserve.
>
> If the enemy should make his attack between this and Arruda, I think these arrangements will make us tolerably secure, and will give time to make further movement of troops to the right. On the other hand, if he should make his attack upon the centre or left wing of the army, with all the troops in front of this place, I shall be able to transfer General Leith's division to be the reserve of the right, for which I originally intended him.[48]

This not only places Leith's troops but also notes the arrival of the battalions which would comprise the second British brigade. The 2/30th (Cambridgeshire) and 2/44th (East Essex) had arrived in Lisbon from Cadiz on 6 October and reached divisional headquarters at Enxaro de Cavaleiros a week later. By 16 October they were encamped with the rest of the division on Monte Agraço. Both battalions had served in Gibraltar before moving to Cadiz,

---

47 Maurice Girod de L'Ain, *Vie Militaire de Général Foy* (Paris: E.Plon, Nourrit et Cie, 1900), p.343.
48 Gurwood (ed.), *Dispatches*, vol.VI, p.517.

where they formed part of Graham's defence. Thus, they were acclimatised. Neither had been at Walcheren. The 1/4th (King's Own), which joined the division on 8 November, had been at Walcheren, however. Despite this, they struck the adjutant of the 30th, Lieutenant William Stewart, as a remarkably fine battalion. The second British brigade was completed on 11 and 12 November when Major General James Dunlop arrived to take command. Two companies of the Duke of Brunswick's Oels Corps, recently arrived in Portugal, were attached to the two British brigades to bolster the light companies and caçadores.

Gomm, writing on the 1 November, felt that everything now favoured the allies. The French

> are still encamped along our front, but whether, according to the reports of deserters, they are waiting for reinforcements or have other objects in view, it is plain they do not intend to attack us immediately. Whether they expect reinforcements or not, we shall certainly receive a very powerful one in the rainy season, which is fast approaching, and which will be an equivalent, at least, for any addition of force they can hope to receive.

As for the allied position,

> We begin now to feel a little settled in our quarters. A great part of the division I belong to is encamped and watching over a most important part of the position. I am myself living in a village close to the rear of this encampment, called Dubaço. You will look for it in vain upon the map, but we are indebted to it for shelter from a great deal of cold and some wet weather lately. Our troops continue very healthy, but whenever the rain sets in for a continuance we must contrive to get them under shelter less equivocal than that they are at present enjoying.

Gomm was also well pleased with his divisional commander. '…I am living with a most excellent man, General Leith, and a higher gentleman or a better soldier I believe is not to be found among us. I am very much indebted to him, and fortunately I find him every day more and more worthy of the respect which I feel inclined to pay him on this account.'[49]

Gomm added a postscript to this letter in which he postulated that the French were on the point of retreat. This proved over-optimistic, since Masséna held his ground until 14 November. Then he withdrew to Santarém, which lay on high ground above the Rio Maior. He had previously given orders that boats and pontoons were to be constructed there, and had sent back his artificers and other craftsmen for the purpose, being convinced that if he could control both banks of the Tagus he would be able to defeat the Allies. The withdrawal began at 8:00 p.m., covered by dense fog which not only hid the French from the allied picquets but also muffled the sound of their departure. The deception lasted until mid-morning the following day, when French sentries were discovered to be straw-stuffed dummies.

---

49   Carr-Gomm (ed.), *Letters and Journals*, vol.I, pp.187, 189.

As the French pulled back, the 5th Division moved into Sobral. Lieutenant William Stewart of the 30th congratulated himself on finding

> a good Stable with plenty of sweet Straw & our Mess contrived to get a middling Room for our accommodation. It had however one very great fault, namely, that the Doors and Windows were surrounded with dead Bodies not buried more than a few Inches under Ground. The Enemy must have lost great numbers in this place, as every Garden contained heaps of their dead & even amongst the rubbish in the Houses many unfortunate Wretches were found by our Soldiers in the same state.[50]

Masséna now attempted to implement his plan by putting his pontoon bridge into place but he was thwarted by allied counter-measures. With Brigadier General Henry Fane's cavalry already on the left bank and naval gunboats ready to intervene, the French had little chance of success. Fane had artillery, including rockets, and Santarém came under fire, without much effect, except to convey a clear message to the French.

Wellington was now ready to venture from the Lines and attack the French in their new position. The 1st, 5th and Light Divisions and Pack's Portuguese were brought forward. They reached Cartaxo on the 20 November, the attack being planned for the same day. Santarém was protected not only by the Rio Maior but also by a marshy flood plain, making a narrow causeway the only feasible approach. According to Leith Hay, 'A sharp abattis, lined with tirailleurs, formed the French advance post along the road, and the height, close to the end of the causeway on the Santarém side, was armed with artillery, which swept the whole extent of it.'[51]

Wellington's orders required one brigade of the 5th Division and Pack's Portuguese to ford the Rio Maior to the west of Santarém, while the Light Division did the same to the east. The rest of the 5th Division and the 1st Division were to storm the causeway. There had been heavy rain, however, which had flooded the fords, while the flood plain was a morass. There had been some suggestion that many of the French were behind the Zezere but news now arrived that they were still concentrated in strength in Santarém. The planned attack was aborted.

Stewart wrote in his journal that the 30th:

> Marched out with Lord W. an Hour before Day light & after passing over two Leagues of a deep & swampy Road, arrived within a short distance of Santarem. Here we halted on a Common the entire Day under the most incessant Rain I ever beheld & every Moment expecting to be ordered to the attack. In the Evening however the Division was ordered back to Cartaxo supposed owing to the Floods which had so swelled the River as to make it impossible to throw a Bridge across a Ford fix'd upon by his Lordship. The main Bridge at Villa Valle was to have been stormed & the Town of Santarem entered at two different points & thus turn the

---

50 The National Army Museum (NAM): 6112-33: Journal of Captain William Stewart, 16 November 1810.
51 Leith Hay, *A Narrative*, vol.I, pp.42–44.

Enemies [sic] left Wing. Saw along the road this day the Bodies of some Peasants who had been murdered by the French.[52]

Wellington lingered for a few days more but on 23 November he ordered his troops into winter quarters. For the 5th Division, this initially meant Alcoentre, but when sickness set in they were moved to Torres Vedras.

The two armies were now experiencing very different conditions. Masséna was fretting about reinforcements, while his troops continued their desperate search for food, much of what they found having been inexpertly hidden by the Portuguese. D'Erlon's IX Corps finally joined Masséna towards the end of December, accompanied by a detachment under *Général de brigade* Claude Matthieu Gardane, bringing ammunition. Masséna had little expectation of breaching the Lines without yet more reinforcements, however, and he still had no food.

According to Douglas, the Allies were 'pretty regularly rationed', although the lack of firewood created problems.

> …it was rare to bring the meat to the boil. We used to eat it as thin as possible, and if you could bring the water to a good heat so as to take the red colour out of it all was right. But this kind of steam soup without salt was, in my opinion, not very nourishing and indeed many men got fluxed by it.

He also noted that 'those regiments who had come from Walcheren were ordered tents, which was very acceptable, but for the fact of being so small and so crowded.[53]

Before the French withdrew to Santarém the Allied troops had been under arms, in marching order, two hours before daylight. Now there might still be battalion and brigade drill, even a field day, as well as all the usual soldier's duties, but for a man in the ranks like Hale life was 'comfortable and peaceable until after Christmas'.[54] Indeed, the greatest excitement seems to have been caused by an earthquake in the middle of the night.

For officers there was a far greater variety of activities beyond their duties, as the minutiae of daily life recorded in William Stewart's journal makes clear. Entertaining or being entertained took up a lot of time. One might dine with officers of one's own battalion or from other regiments in the division, including British officers in the Portuguese service. But socialising might also be a chance to catch up with officers whom one knew from previous service. For a more active life, there was fowling and coursing, riding and walking. In Stewart's case there was a great deal of walking, usually with other officers of the 30th. Somewhat bizarrely, he also mentioned a leaping match, as well as the more predictable racing on the drill ground. On a quieter note, there was the pleasure of writing letters home and receiving replies (although Stewart frequently complained about the lack of replies). British newspapers were sometimes available, out of date but still better than no news. At the very least, it gave them something to talk about. Nor was Stewart likely to be the only officer who dedicated so much time to learning Portuguese. The ultimate treat, of course,

---

52 NAM: 6112-33: Journal of Captain William Stewart, 21–22 November 1810.
53 Monick (ed.), *Douglas's Tale*, pp.23–24.
54 Hale, *Journal*, p.61.

was a period of leave in Lisbon. Although decried as filthy, there were still plenty of sights to see and a night at the theatre to enjoy.

Thus 1810 drew to a close with hungry but resilient invaders held at bay by allied defences behind which their opponents lived in reasonable comfort. Yet there were problems for Wellington too as even the most acclimatised units began to show a disturbingly high incidence of sickness, a problem that would return every winter, a combination of the excessive rain and the curse of Walcheren.

2

1811

The French Retreat

Masséna continued to occupy central Portugal into the new year, still confident that reinforcements would eventually join him, while also expecting Wellington to challenge the French position. The allied commander, however, preferred to rely on General Famine to do the business for him. During this stalemate, the first French reinforcements began to arrive. Yet the foraging activities of the French were constrained by the proximity of Allied troops, including the irregular forces of Brigadier General Nicholas Trant and Wilson's Loyal Lusitanian Legion, so that extra mouths would only add to Masséna's problems unless they came with their own supplies. Nevertheless, he was still focused on taking Lisbon and he knew himself to be in command of troops who could uncover even the most deviously hidden cache of food.

Although d'Erlon's IX Corps had joined Masséna in mid-December, it was made up of drafts from the newly raised fourth battalions of 24 regiments, variously attached to the different French corps, including those with Soult. In addition, d'Erlon was seriously short of transport and staff since his original orders had merely been to get the drafts to their regiments. He was also under orders both to maintain contact with Almeida and to join Masséna. This could only be achieved by dividing his forces, so he had left one division in the Celorico-Trancoso area and brought the rest to Leiria. These were new foraging grounds, but they were soon exhausted.

It is interesting to note that both the French and the Allied commanders were waiting on the actions of *Maréchal* Soult. Masséna still hoped that he would move into the Alentejo to threaten the allied position. Wellington recognised the same possibility but he was depending on the Spanish under *Teniente General* Gabriel de Mendizábel, the 2nd Division and the 30,000-strong garrison at Elvas to hold Soult at bay. In fact, Soult's objective was Badajoz and he had no intention of sending troops into the Alentejo.

On 2 February, Foy arrived back from Paris with 1,800 men and new orders from Napoleon, dated 22 December. These required Masséna to hold his position until detachments from the Armies of the South and the Centre arrived. Then he was to go on the offensive. There was little chance of the detachments arriving, however. *Maréchal* Édouard Mortier, designated to join the Army of Portugal, was fully engaged in the siege of Badajoz. And the 8,000 men from the Army of the Centre marched as far as Plasencia, where they ran out of provisions and withdrew. Masséna was on his own and it could only be a matter of time before his position became untenable.

View towards the Lines of Torres Vedras from the French position at Santarém, from *Views in Spain & Portugal, taken during the Campaigns of His Grace the Duke of Wellington*, by G. Cumberland. (Public Domain)

For the 5th Division a particular source of satisfaction was the return of Major General Leith on 4 January from a short period of leave in Lisbon. Unfortunately, his stay proved of short duration. The effects of post-Walcheren fever were as debilitating for him as for so many of his troops. Although the weather was on the turn, the cold, wet conditions of the past weeks had put many men on the sick list. Yet Stewart of the 30th (who had not been at Walcheren) took the view that it was possible to avoid sickness. On 4 February he noted that

> The Day was fine and the walk as usual was of the greatest service to us, for at this time it was observable that all those who took no exercise, but had a sedentary life amongst the filth of the Town & moist and unwholesome Atmosphere of so low a situation were the first Victims to Fever – disease of all kinds.[1]

There were other complaints, though, from officers like Gomm and Stewart, both of whom lamented the absence of letters from home. Stewart assumed his trusted correspondents were simply not writing. Gomm had a different view. In a letter to his sister, written at Torres Vedras on 30 January he decided that there must be 'letters flying about at this moment in search of me, and which will in the end reach me, for we are here so completely out of the world that they do not seem to think us entitled to the same attention as the rest of the army, so that letters are sent to us in all sorts of ways.'[2] As would become clear when the allies finally moved from behind the Lines, the 5th Division was definitely a reserve force.

---

1 NAM: 6112-33: Journal of Captain William Stewart, 4 February 1811.
2 Carr-Gomm (ed.), *Letters and Journals*, vol.I, pp.201–202.

Before the Allies could advance, however, the French needed to withdraw. On 19 February Masséna summoned his corps commanders and other senior officers to Golegão for what he obstinately refused to call a council of war. He gave his opinion that there were just two choices: retreat, or attack the allies prior to an advance into the Alentejo in order to join forces with Soult. Inevitably, Ney and Reynier had their divergent views but Masséna over-ruled them. He had already decided that, having held out for as long as possible, they were now to withdraw to the Mondego, where he expected to maintain a new position in central Portugal for as long as two months. If nothing else, the army would benefit from rest and recovery in a more favourable situation.

At the end of February, as Wellington awaited the arrival of the newly landed battalions which would form the 7th Division, Masséna accepted that he would receive no help from Soult. The first orders were issued for a withdrawal on 3 March. Two days later a column comprising Ney's infantry and Montbrun's cavalry, was heading towards Coimbra while Reynier's corps made for Ponte de Murcella. There were more straw dummies to confuse the allied picquets. Although Wellington had brought forward all but the 5th Division and Campbell's independent Portuguese brigade in anticipation, the French movements still took him by surprise.

The following day it was clear that Santarém had been abandoned, and Wellington set his own troops in motion, including bringing up the 5th and Campbell's men. The French, having reached Coimbra, discovered that the bridge across the Mondego was broken and Trant's Portuguese were in possession of the city. At the same time, the 5th Division were following the 3rd and 6th on a route that took them towards Pernes, about 15 miles north of Santarém. Stewart recorded that they had

> Very fine weather. The Division marched from Torres Vedras to Cadaval [omitted] Leagues. The Road for the most part tolerably good, but in bad weather many parts of it must be unpassable. Within three miles of Torres Vedras we march'd thro' a small mean Villiage call'd ------ & a little beyond it pass'd thro' another rather larger call'd ------. Most part of the Days march lay across a moor – near to Cadaval we pass'd through a small Villiage & saw another a little to our left where the Portuguese Brigade was sent. Heard of the Enemy having retired from their Lines on our arrival at this place. In our billet we met a most sensible & Gentlemanlike Priest, as also a very humane Padrone who in the midst of his own Sufferings & Calamities paid the most strict & unceasing attention to the wants & miseries of the innumerable sick & poor in his Villiage. Whilst we remained in his House he was constantly employed in giving Medicens [sic] to the diseased.[3]

Even in these early stages of dogging the footsteps of the French, it was obvious that they were pursuing a demoralised army venting its spleen in wanton acts of destruction. This was behaviour that would only get worse, as the enemy took comfort in simple spite. Gomm blamed this on one man. For him Masséna had

---

3 NAM: 6112-33: Journal of Captain William Stewart, 7 March 1811.

> ...descended upon the land like a fiend, commanding the destructions of towns, countenancing the massacre of the peasantry.
> ...The French generals give orders for the burning of towns and the French soldiers talk of the massacre of peasantry and women and children with as little concern as if they had been ridding the world of monsters.

This was no exaggeration. It was understandable that the French were stripping the areas they passed through of every morsel of food and inevitable that they would kill in their determination to find it, but the firing of towns and the murder of children and babies did indeed suggest, as Gomm told his sister, that they would have 'degenerated by the close of this campaign in Portugal into something worse than Huns.'[4]

As for the French, Reynier with 11,000 men was marching eastwards along a bad road towards Espinho, while Junot's 16,000 men were following an easier route towards Pombal. Ney had the strongest corps, with 20,000 men. Frustrated at Coimbra, he left Montbrun to repair the bridge and get into the city and marched his VI Corps to Leiria. He was now following d'Erlon who, like Jordan, was marching for Pombal.

Based on what he could deduce from these initial movements, Wellington decided to focus on Ney. He committed the 3rd and Light Divisions, along with Pack's Portuguese, to the pursuit. The 5th Division and Campbell's Portuguese were still well to the rear, so that Wellington would need two days to concentrate his whole army. By 11 March, though, there had been some closing up. Stewart wrote that their march that day started at 6:00 a.m.

> in company with General Pictons Division towards Pombal. Met 26 French Prisoners about a League from Leirra & heard that the Enemy were in force & meant to dispute the Heights of Pombal with us.' This proved an accurate supposition. 'Arrived on a Common above that Town and saw some sharp skirmishing & the Enemy driven back into Pombal. Our Division encamped for the night in three Lines. From this place we saw the advance of most of the Divisions of our Army in every direction. It was one of the Grandest Military Spectacles I had ever witnessed.[5]

Ney, with what was now the French rearguard, had first held up his pursuers and then managed to withdraw under cover of night. The pursuit continued to Redinha, where he had taken up a new position.

The following afternoon the 5th Division passed through Pombal, which proved a harrowing experience for Stewart.

> The Enemy left in & near the Town of Pombal a great number of their killed & wounded & it was disturbing to see in the Streets of this dirty Town the mangled Remains of our Fellow Creatures bruised & blended with the Mud by the trampling of Horses & Mules as well as the Passage of Guns, Waggons etc over them, until

---

4   Carr-Gomm (ed.), *Letters and Journals*, vol.I, pp.205–206.
5   NAM: 6112-33: Journal of Captain William Stewart, 11 March 1811.

The 1811 Campaign.

these once valiant Heroes could no longer be distinguished from the filth of the Road.⁶

It is interesting to note that, even after witnessing the atrocities of the French, Stewart could still feel pity for the enemy. After an action at Redinha, which did not involve the 5th Division and again saw Ney conducting an effective rearguard action before retiring to Condeixa, the division passed through the town, where they found scenes similar to Pombal. They then:

> Ascended the side of a Mountain and passed thro' an extensive Wood in which & along the entire Road of this Days Route lay <u>killed</u> & <u>wounded</u> left by the Enemy – I also saw one poor Fellow who excited the liveliest feelings of pity in the Breast of every Officer who beheld him – This Man had swell'd Limbs from Dropsy & the Blood really gushed through the Skin from the excess of the Disease – in this State & with little life left from Hunger he discovered the British Columns marching near to him – He lay at the foot of a Tree & clinging to it, he made a last exertion to raise his feeble Frame from the Ground.

Nothing could be done for him according to the physician who was called to him.

> In this melancholy situation therefore was the suffering Soldier left casting such looks after us as I can never forget – he was scarcely able to [illegible], but still sustained a lively expression of Countenance – I fear the Portuguese soon put an end to his pitiable state, as they were known to have murdered many of the wounded whom they met; nor would they be deserving of much blame for almost the commission of any act of cruelty, after all they had suffered from the invaders of their rights of liberty.⁷

Masséna now had to decide on his next move. Condeixa offered routes west to Coimbra and east to Almeida. If he marched to the latter, it would clearly signal that he was abandoning Portugal. In a despatch to *Maréchal* Louis-Alexandre Berthier, Napoleon's chief of staff, he explained that he had been forced to retreat because Wellington outnumbered him, which was untrue. More pertinently, he was short of ammunition while still struggling with the problem of feeding his troops. Then there was the likelihood that Wellington would simply retire to the Lines in response to French aggression. Consequently, even as he wrote the despatch, he had already set all but Ney's corps on the march to Celorico, where d'Erlon was already in position. Ney was once again left to hold up the allied advance.

Ney failed to remain at Condeixa for as long as Masséna had anticipated, thanks to a turning movement by Wellington. Masséna, however, blamed Ney and this led to an intensification of the bad feeling between the two *maréchaux*. On the same day, Montbrun finally withdrew from Coimbra, having been tricked by a Portuguese *sargento* into believing an

---

6 NAM: 6112-33: Journal of Captain William Stewart, 12 March 1811.
7 NAM: 6112-33: Journal of Captain William Stewart, 13 March 1811.

exaggerated version of Trant's strength. It is fair to say that matters were not going well for the French.

So far, the Allies had maintained a successful pursuit. The day after Ney had been forced from Condeixa, however, they came close to their first setback when Major General Sir William Erskine, in command of the Light Division, led the division, along with Pack's Portuguese and Arendschildt's cavalry, into an early morning attack despite the French position being masked by thick fog. The rear of the VI Corps, under *Général de division* Jean-Gabriel Marchand's command, was holding a strong position at the village of Castel Nova. The Allied advance came up against French picquets, whereupon Erskine ordered some of the 52nd to clear them away. The resultant struggle drew in more and more of the Light Division. Then the fog cleared to reveal the guns of 11 enemy battalions. Fortunately, Picton's arrival forced the French to abandon this position and others they tried to take up, but not before the Light Division had taken heavy losses.

The 5th Division arrived late. Stewart wrote in his journal:

> The Action still continuing, our Columns moved forward at an increased pace, & at some short distance beyond Condaxo [sic] we met several wounded Officers & Men carried on Bearers from the Scene of the Action; amongst the former was Col. Stewart 95th Regt. & Capt Nappier [sic] 52nd etc. The Enemy were retiring from their last position, just as our Divisions arrived, having been already driven from several very strong & commanding ones – Our success in this respect was highly owing to a wise precaution taken by Lord W: the Evening before, of detaching Brigr Genl. Nightingale with his Brigade so as to turn the Enemies left Flank by the time our Troops approached their Positions – It had the intended effect, for they no sooner observed the advance of this small Column down the high Mountains, than they retired leaving a great number of killed & prisoners as before – on our part the loss was rather severe, as only the Light Troops were heavily engaged & had to fight very superior numbers.[8]

The advance continued somewhat belatedly the following morning on account of the thick mist. When it cleared, Stewart witnessed another example of French brutality.

> We pass'd through the Village of Pudentes [Podente] which was in Flames & filled with dead French and murdered peasants. In one house which was on fire I saw a poor old Woman of upwards of 70 Years with her Arm broken - She told me it had been done by a French Soldier & pointed to a Room where she said her Husband was hanging, having been left so, previous to their retreat – I found it but too true, & instantly sent in some Soldiers to remove the poor Wretch & the remains of her murdered Husband to some other place![9]

---

8   NAM: 6112-33: Journal of Captain William Stewart, 14 March 1811.
9   NAM: 6112-33: Journal of Captain William Stewart, 15 March 1811.

The division marched on to Miranda de Corvo, having passed the wreckage of gun carriages, as well as private vehicles, and found buried ammunition, all of which suggested that the French were desperate to speed up their retreat. As for Miranda de Corvo itself, the scene was only too familiar; dead and dying, every building on fire so that passing through required great caution. This meant that they were still marching when darkness fell. As the result of what Stewart describes as 'an error in the usual manner' they were misdirected through a vineyard instead of keeping to the road.

> This gross want of a knowledge of the Country was the means of retarding our march at least two hours! during which time Col. Offley of the Lusitanian Legion & myself waited on the Road & saw the Troops pass in true Indian [single] File, for they could not be made to march otherwise.
>
> Such of the mounted Officers as were with the Column, had very narrow escapes from breaking their Necks over old Walls & Stumps of Vines etc. Our march now lay considerably to the right of the Ponte de Marcella [Murcella] Road, & over Mountains & bye Roads; this circumstance joined with the unpleasantness of a long & most tedious night march rendered our sufferings by no means trifling, indeed, many of the Offrs & men virtually were sleeping at intervals as they walked, & for my own part I nearly fell off my Horse seven or eight times.

Worse lay ahead, a scene that lived in the memory for Stewart, 'We saw on the Road Clusters of dead & dying Asses & Mules left by the Enemy after a sharp Skirmish which they had [illegible] this Day with our Light Division & Genl. Pictons.'[10] In fact, as part of his attempt to march light, since the route ahead was mountainous, Masséna had given orders that all unnecessary baggage and carriages should be destroyed, including the waggons for the wounded, and surplus animals should be hamstrung so that the allies could make no use of them. To the British this was an act of unnecessary cruelty. As Hale remarked in his memoirs: 'had they shot them, they would have been out of their misery.'[11] But that would have been a waste of ammunition.

It was the early hours of the 16 March before the 5th Division were able to get some sleep. That day there was no marching, a welcome rest after 14 hours spent covering just two leagues, according to Stewart. Meanwhile, the French had reached Foz de Arouce, where the main army took position on high ground beyond the village, while Ney was posted in front of the village to hold off the Allies. He had been ordered to bring his corps beyond the Ceira but had chosen to leave part of it on the other side of the bridge. Wellington had again been forced to delay the day's march because of yet more fog, so that it was 4:00 p.m. before the 3rd and Light Divisions made contact with the French. Ney was initially taken by surprise and his troops south of the river were soon in danger of being overwhelmed. He managed to extricate them, and the Army of Portugal continued its retreat.

---

10   NAM: 6112-33: Journal of Captain William Stewart, 15 March 1811.
11   Hale, *Journal*, p.64.

The 5th Division did not approach Foz de Arouce until the following day, by which time only the French rearguard was still in touch with the Allies. Wellington was forced to call a halt, however, because his army had outmarched its supplies. Stewart commented on the shortage, particularly of biscuit, and on the failure of the Portuguese Regency to feed their troops. He also lamented the fact that on St Patrick's Day they 'Had no opportunity of drowning our Shamrocks excepting in the heavy Dews of the Night as we lay without covering of any kind.'[12] No doubt the large proportion of Irish in the 5th Division and elsewhere in the army shared his regret.

From his headquarters at Lousão, Wellington gave orders for the 4th Division, Major-General Alexander Hamilton's Portuguese Brigade and Colonel George de Grey's cavalry to join Marshal William Beresford, who had been sent to relieve Badajoz. By 10 March, Wellington knew that Badajoz was in French hands and was now determined to protect Campo Maior and Elvas. He also gave orders not only for the Portuguese garrisons to leave their posts on the Lines but also for the disbandment of the Ordenança and leave for the Militia. With the French retreating out of Portugal and the new 7th Division battalions expected any time, he could dispense with the Lines.

The 5th Division remained on the fringes of the action, while the misbehaviour of one of the battalions in the division was unlikely to recommend them to Wellington. During this brief respite

> the 38th Regiment plundered a village in the neighbourhood of the camp… of 112 alquiers of Indian corn.
>
> The Commander of the Forces desires that the Rolls of the 38th Regiment may be called every hour, every Officer being present, till further notice.
>
> The obedience of this Order must be reported daily to Head Quarters.
>
> The Commander of the Forces will not allow the soldiers to plunder, which they ought to know by this time.
>
> If Indian corn or any other article is wanted from the Country, the General Orders of the army point out the mode in which it is to be procured without plunder or violence, or without loss of property of the inhabitants.
>
> Sergeant James Johnston of the 1st Battalion, 9th Regiment, is appointed an Assistant Provost Marshal, and is attached to the 5th Division of Infantry.[13]

This last point is actually a separate order but its proximity to the misbehaviour of the 1/38th makes a point. Wellington was determined that his troops should not imitate the French. As for the hourly roll calls, these lasted until the 30 March and, presumably, held up the rest of the division.

Masséna, having now recognised that he could not hold a position in central Portugal, decided to establish himself in Almeida and Ciudad Rodrigo. By 17 March his troops were on the Alva, where they took up another strong position. Later the same day he became aware that some allied cavalry had crossed the Ceira at Foz de Arouce while the 6th and

---

12   NAM: 6112-33: Journal of Captain William Stewart, 17 March 1811.
13   Anon. (ed.), *General Orders*, vol.III, p.60.

Light Divisions were approaching Ponte de Murcella. At the same time, the 1st, 3rd and 5th Divisions were following an easterly route to the upper Alva, where there were fords. In response, Masséna sent Jourdan's VIII Corps to Galegos, closer to Reynier, while Ney maintained a position at Ponte de Murcella. The following day, though, the VI Corps was driven across the river. At the same time, the 1st Division crossed at Pombeiro, which forced Reynier into a retrograde movement. All three corps were marching towards Spain along mountainous roads, the VIII Corps leading the II and VI.

The whole Allied army now crossed the Alva, whereupon the Light, 3rd and 6th Divisions continued the pursuit while the 1st and 5th Divisions, along with Pack's and Major General Charles Ashworth's Portuguese brigades, spent several days near Venda de Vale. On 21 March, the 5th Division 'march'd over a Mountain & Hutted in some Woods near to the Villiage [sic] of Venda de Vale, which is close to the great Road leading to Celerico etc…This part of the Country is very fruitful & in view of our Ground were many neat Villiages – It is distressing to see the Corn Fields made a Pasture for Horses etc, but we have no alternative –' The following day, 'Great Pains taken in improving our Hutts, as it now became necessary to halt a few Days until Provisions come up from the rear –' while on the 23rd, 'Rolls ordered to be instantly call'd and all Absentees confin'd on their return to Bivoac [sic], in consequence of maurauding.'[14] Presumably, this fruitful countryside offered temptations some soldiers could not resist, particularly while waiting for the arrival of provisions.

By 22 March all the French units were at Celorico except for Reynier's corps, which was at Guarda. At this point Masséna could congratulate himself that the Allied army had been held at bay. For the Allies, though, things looked rather different. Their advance had so far determined the route the French had been obliged to follow. At noon on the 22nd, however, Masséna issued new orders which demonstrated his determination to take the initiative. Rather than establishing themselves in the area around Almeida and Ciudad Rodrigo, the French forces would venture into the mountains towards Coria and Plasencia, where there would be food, supplies and the chance to rest. After a period of recuperation, they would then be able to launch an attack on central Portugal. It must be assumed that there had been no reconnaissance because this new route would have seriously challenged even an army that was not exhausted and demoralised.

At this point Ney, who had been fulminating against Masséna at every opportunity, finally pushed the boundary of insubordination too far. As soon as he heard of the change of plan, he wrote a series of angry letters, the last of which threatened downright disobedience. Instead of following the new route, he would take his corps to Almeida. Masséna had no choice but to dismiss probably the most talented of his corps commanders, sending him to Valladolid to await Napoleon's further pleasure. *Général de division* Louis Henri Loison now took command of the VI Corps.

---

14 NAM: 6112-33: Journal of Captain William Stewart, 21–23 March 1811.

Guarda, by Andrew Leith Hay. (*A Narrative of the Peninsular War*)

Action at Sabugal

On 23 March, while d'Erlon was taking the sick and wounded to Almeida, Junot was on the road to Guarda, followed by Loison. The march continued for five days, although Reynier, who had reached the Serra de Estrela, was in serious difficulties after only three days. At the same time, Junot, at Belmonte, was reconnoitring what lay ahead in the hope of finding a passable road. On the 27th Reynier wrote to Masséna that further progress was impossible, a view which Junot supported. Masséna had no choice but to change his orders, justifying himself by claiming that the garrisons at Almeida and Ciudad Rodrigo were facing difficulties. Reynier was ordered to Sabugal, there to await Junot's arrival, while Loison was to remain at Guarda. He was, however, to send one of his brigades towards Sabugal.

Meanwhile, on 24 March Allied cavalry had reported that the French had left Celorico, although their objective was impossible to ascertain. Wellington sent the 3rd, 6th and Light Divisions to Celorico. Supplies arrived the following day, enabling the 1st and 5th Divisions to follow, while the 7th were finally in touch with the allied army.

Further reconnaissance by the cavalry established a general movement towards Guarda, but this did not clarify Masséna's ultimate intentions. Wellington, however, assumed the French were still making for the border, By 29 March, with his forces all in close contact, he felt able to move against them. He sent the Light Division and Sir John Slade's and Arendschildt's cavalry brigades towards Guarda, while the 3rd Division targeted the town from the west and the 6th Division advanced between them. Picton was the first to arrive, taking Loison by surprise. The latter then became aware of the advance of the Light Division and immediately withdrew towards Sabugal. It was a hasty retreat which enabled the pursuing troops to seize prisoners and animals.

On the same day, when the 5th Division was a league from Guarda, Gomm wrote an optimistic letter to his sister, which concluded:

> We are all exceedingly healthy, and ready at this moment for any enterprise. We may now expect a continuation of fine weather. The equinox has just passed over us. We crossed the Estrella mountain the day before yesterday in the middle of it. You will, therefore, not be surprised when I tell you I rode in a whirlwind the whole day. We climbed like so many Titans. I shall write again as soon as we ascertain the direction we are moving in. We are living now in a crazy house, which the French did not think worth burning. But the valley of the Mondego is as delightful as ever.[15]

When Masséna halted his three corps, who were now some distance apart, Wellington seized the opportunity to pick one of them off. He sent the 1st, 5th and 7th Divisions to join the three advanced divisions so that he could deliver a parting shot to drive the French out of Portugal. He intended to hold the VI Corps on the Coa while turning the French at Sabugal. As he subsequently wrote to Lord Liverpool:

> The 2nd corps were in a strong position with their right upon a height immediately above the bridge and town of Sabugal, and their left extending along the road to Alfayates, to a height that commanded all the approaches to Sabugal from the fords of the Coa above the town… It was intended to turn the left of this corps, and with this view the Light division and the cavalry, under Major General Sir William Erskine, and Major General Slade, were to cross the Coa by two separate fords upon the right; the cavalry upon the right of the Light division; the 3rd division, under Major General Picton, at a ford on their left, about a mile above Sabugal; and the 5th division, under Major General Dunlop, and the artillery, at the bridge of Sabugal.[16]

Wellington was confident that the II Corps would be overwhelmed by such an attack before other French units could intervene, even though Reynier was in communication with Junot. As for Loison, he would be held by the 6th Division, with support from the 7th Division. Timing was obviously crucial, though, if the allied attack was to succeed. The 3rd and 5th Divisions were to move only once the Light Division had crossed the Coa. It was important, however, that they did so before Reynier could bring his full force against Erskine.

Such was the plan and, had the 3 April not dawned to thick fog, all should have been well. Although fog was obviously beneficial in concealing allied positions and movements, it made co-ordination difficult. This problem was obvious to Picton and Dunlop, causing them to exercise caution and send to Wellington for further orders. Erskine, in contrast, exhibited the same rashness as at Castel Nova. He ordered the Light Division to march to the Coa and commanded Lieutenant Colonel Thomas Beckwith to lead his brigade across the river. The same order was sent to the cavalry.

---

15 Carr-Gomm (ed.), *Letters and Journals*, vol.1, p.209.
16 Gurwood (ed.), *Dispatches*, vol.VII, p.431.

Sabugal on the river Coa, by Thomas Staunton St Clair. (Public Domain)

The result of this rashness was predictably catastrophic. Beckwith advanced but soon lost his way in the fog. He eventually found a crossing point, although it was hardly a ford since the men were up to their armpits in water. It was also closer to Sabugal than the chosen ford. Even as the troops crossed, they came under fire from French picquets. These they were able to drive back as soon as they reached the far bank. Then they blindly continued their advance uphill, only to find themselves confronted by French troops already under arms. Beckwith's brigade had actually made a frontal attack and now found itself facing the left of *Général de division* Pierre Merle's battalions. As for Erskine, he was with the cavalry as they wasted time trying to find their ford.

After they had driven in a screen of French sharpshooters, Beckwith's two battalions of the 95th were able to rally on the 43rd, but their position was perilous. Fortunately, there were stone walls which offered shelter, and they held this position until the arrival of Lieutenant Colonel James Drummond's brigade, which had been following an even more circuitous route than Beckwith's. Drummond had actually been told by Erskine to do nothing, but acting on his own initiative he joined Beckwith in driving back Merle's brigade. The French re-formed, however, and, with cavalry support, attacked the Light Division, who again took refuge in a stone-walled enclosure.

All this was happening in mist, followed by torrential rain. Significantly, in his dispatch Wellington makes no reference to Erskine's rashness when briefly summing up this first stage of the action. Nor does he criticise him hereafter, a reminder of his tendency to protect the reputation of a senior officer, a characteristic with which the 5th Division would subsequently become acquainted. Fortunately, Picton and Dunlop now intervened, the former, it must be admitted, to the greater effect.

> The enemy were making arrangements to attack them again in this post, and had moved a column on their left, when the light infantry of Major General Picton's division, under Lieut. Colonel Williams, supported by Major General the Hon. C. Colville's brigade opened their fire upon them.
> At the same moment the head of Major General Dunlop's column crossed the bridge of the Coa, and ascended the heights on the right flank of the enemy, and the cavalry appeared on the high ground in rear of the enemy's left; the enemy then retired across the hills towards Rendo…[17]

The light companies of the 5th Division were actually the first troops into Sabugal castle and enjoyed some unexpected spoils, as the historian of the 30th relates:

> The French brigade in Sabugal, ignorant of the fact that the head of Dunlop's column was on the other side of the river and only prevented by the fog from crossing, had spent a peaceful morning in cooking their dinners, which had not been a thing of everyday occurrence lately: their interest in this occupation seems to have interfered with their watchfulness, and when the fog lifted the light company of the 44th ran across the bridge at Sabugal, the 30th and the other light companies splashed through the river where they could, and at the same time the order came from Reynier for the French to fall in and double to the rear. There was no help for it; they had to be off and leave their dinners to be eaten by the light companies.[18]

Although the division had performed its part in Wellington's plan, there was clearly a sense of frustration at once more playing a supporting role. As Gomm commented, the 5th Division 'could only show what it was ready to do if they [the French] chose to wait for it.'[19] If Douglas is to be believed, at least one brigadier thought it was a case of too little too late. While the division waited to attack,

> General Hay rode up in a rage to General Dunlop, who commanded the Division, and demanded why he did not attack the enemy. His reply was, 'I am waiting for a guide.' 'There's the enemy, there's your guide,' exclaimed Hay. He then wanted his own Brigade to lead the attack but, 'No,'; on which sheathing his sword with madness, he exclaimed in front of the Division, 'I shall report your cowardice to Lord Wellington this night,' and I believe he was as good as his word, as the General went off to England in a few days and did not make his appearance for several months.[20]

---

17 Gurwood (ed.), *Dispatches*, vol.VII, p.432.
18 Neil Bannatyne, *History of the Thirtieth Regiment now the First Battalion East Lancashire Regiment 1689-1881* (Liverpool: Littlebury Bros, 1923), pp.252–253.
19 Carr-Gomm (ed.), *Letters and Journals*, vol.I, pp.209–210.
20 Monick (ed.), *Douglas's Tale*, p.28.

Certainly, Erskine was appointed to command the division on 22 April, but a direct accusation of cowardice to a senior officer within the hearing the troops seems unlikely, even for Hay.

It is no surprise that while the Light Division took 123 casualties and even the 3rd Division, 25, the Fifth Division took none. The French suffered even more severely with losses estimated at 760.[21]

From Sabugal to Fuentes de Oñoro

On 3 April, even before learning of events at Sabugal, Masséna finally took the decision which marked his failure in Portugal. His army was to retire from the Coa into Spain. The following day the French troops made a forced march towards the border, seemingly because their commander believed if he lingered any longer Wellington would force a general action which the French troops were in no condition to fight.

He now took position with the II Corps at Fuentes de Oñoro, the VI Corps at Fuente Guinaldo and the VIII Corps between the two at Campilla de Azaba, all still close to the Portuguese border. This enabled him to re-establish contact with d'Erlon's IX Corps, which withdrew from its vulnerable position at Almeida. The new alignment could only be temporary, however. The countryside offered little in the way of food and other supplies, while further into Spain were fertile sources of both. Masséna also believed, with some justification, that Wellington would not advance into Spain while Almeida remained in French hands. The defences had been repaired and strengthened since the explosion of the previous August; the garrison of 1,300 men were sufficiently supplied to hold out against a blockade; and the governor, *Général de brigade* Antoine François Brenier, could be relied upon not to capitulate. On 8 April, the French resumed their retrograde march, finally establishing themselves in and around Salamanca, with the IX Corps at San Muñoz.

These movements came as no surprise to Wellington. The testimony of French prisoners had made clear that their army was in desperate need of rest and recuperation. Masséna had been correct, however, in his supposition that Wellington would not pursue him. Not only was there the problem of Almeida, but the allies were also in need of the supplies which were being transported across Portugal from Coimbra. And the state of the Portuguese troops was becoming desperate. They were short of food, despite the Regency's promises, and this inevitably led to sickness and straggling. In the 5th Division, for example, Spry's brigade, in which the three battalions each had a notional strength of 1,400 rank and file now mustered just 1,841 men.[22]

While he waited for Masséna's next move and for supplies to arrive from Coimbra, Wellington ordered Trant to maintain pressure on Almeida. Once the army had been supplied, he intended to send the 6th Division and Pack's Portuguese to conduct the blockade. Beyond Almeida, he had already identified Ciudad Rodrigo as his next objective and, with this in mind, he was relying upon Julian Sanchez' irregulars to prevent the

---

21 Oman, *The History of the Peninsular War*, vol.IV, p.616.
22 Gurwood (ed.), *Dispatches*, vol.VII, p.424.

garrison from receiving supplies. The Light Division and Arendschildt's light cavalry were then close enough to intervene should it prove necessary. Unfortunately, on 13 April, and again two days later, Erskine, still with the Light Division, was slow to react when a convoy approached the town.

On 15 April Wellington decided on a rapid ride down to Elvas to inspect the situation at Badajoz. He left Lieutenant General Sir Brent Spencer in command with instructions not to provoke the French to action or reaction. Not that Wellington believed the enemy troops were yet in a condition to offer battle, or even launch a more limited action.

During Wellington's absence the general order already noted was issued on 22 April. 'Major General Sir William Erskine, Baronet, will assume command of the 5th division of infantry.'[23] It remained to be seen whether he would function more effectively with troops who were being used more circumspectly than the Light Division. To Gomm, at least, this appointment must have seemed an improvement. He had written to his sister a fortnight before: 'You regret in one of your letters, for my sake, that General Leith's health did not permit him to remain here. You cannot regret it more than I do, particularly as I dislike the person I am with exceedingly.'[24] This person was, of course, Major General Dunlop.

With supplies of food arriving only intermittently and no movement from the French, the allies now went into cantonments. The 5th Division were at Fort Concepcion, in support of the Light Division, which was 'to defend the passages of the Agueda, viz., the Bridge of Barba del Puerco, the ford of Val de Espino, the ford of Cismiro, the ford of Molina de Fores.' Should the French make a movement to raise the blockade of Almeida, the 5th Division would advance to Alfaiates. If further withdrawal became necessary, they 'and the Light division, and the cavalry, would fall back as circumstances would render necessary.'[25] There was no threat from the French, however, and the 5th Division remained peaceably quartered at Aldea del Obispo, which Gomm described as a delightful Spanish village and Stewart considered 'the only clean & tolerably comfortable Quarters we had seen from our leaving Torres Vedras on the 7th March' Writing on the day they arrived, he added, 'It snowed very fast this Day, & we were kept out under it by Genl D. for some Hours whilst a distribution was making of about 150 houses!'[26] This, no doubt, added to Dunlop's unpopularity.

Masséna may have seemed quiescent but he was, in fact, preparing to relieve Almeida, thus burnishing his damaged reputation before he surrendered command of the Army of Portugal. (Napoleon had already appointed *Maréchal* Auguste Frédéric Marmont in his place.) Although Marchand, who had commanded the second convoy into Ciudad Rodrigo, had reported that the allies were strongly positioned, Masséna reasoned that with the drafts and reinforcements which he could now call upon, there being 18,000 troops stationed around Salamanca, he could make a foray into Portugal which would sweep the Allies aside and strengthen the French at Almeida. His army lacked nothing except horses, which were still in short supply. With 40,000 men, plus a thousand extra cavalry and supporting

---

23 Anon. (ed.), *General Orders*, vol.III, p.76.
24 Carr-Gomm (ed.), *Letters and Journals*, vol.I, p.211.
25 Gurwood (ed.), *Dispatches*, vol.VII, pp.432–433.
26 NAM: 6112-33: Journal of Captain William Stewart, 9 April 1811.

artillery reluctantly brought by *Maréchal* Jean-Baptiste Bessières, commander of the Army of the North, he believed his intentions were viable.

Having received information from Brent Spencer that alerted him to the signs of renewed activity by the French, Wellington undertook another of his rapid rides and was back with his army by 29 April. Although his forces were outnumbered by the French, he was still prepared to make a stand. Surprisingly, the one arm in which the Allies surpassed the French was artillery, by a ratio of almost three to two.

The Battle of Fuentes de Oñoro

As at Buçaco, Wellington was able to choose his ground. The disposition of his troops would follow the line of the Dos Casas stream from Fort Concepcion on the left, where it flowed between steep banks before becoming passable, to Fuentes de Oñoro on the right. This was a village of stone houses and small, stone-walled enclosures situated on rising ground. Continuing right, beyond the village, the terrain towards the hamlets of Porto Velho and Nave de Haver was more undulating, thus permitting cavalry and infantry manoeuvres, before reaching a morass in front of the latter village. Some seven or eight miles further back was the river Coa, which was fordable at Castello Bom but otherwise impassable except by bridge, so that an army in retreat would struggle to cross it.

On 2 May the French left Ciudad Rodrigo in two columns along parallel roads, while the Light Division and the light cavalry were still in their outlying positions. The French advance forced the Allied troops to retire to Fuentes de Oñoro, although not without some skirmishing. Wellington set about positioning his troops. The 5th Division were on the extreme left of the Allied line, in front of Fort Concepcion, with some Portuguese on the left flank to prevent a French turning movement. The 6th Division was on the right of the 5th Division, fronting the hamlet of San Pedro. The 1st, 3rd and 7th Divisions, along with Ashworth's Portuguese, occupied the ground behind Fuentes de Oñoro, with the lately arrived Light Division as a reserve, while the light and rifle companies of the 1st and 3rd Divisions were in the village itself.

Masséna, for his part, placed Reynier's II Corps on the right, more or less opposite Fort Concepcion and separated from the 5th Division by the declivity through which the Dos Casas flowed. On Reynier's left was *Général de division* Jean-Baptiste Solignac's division from the VIII Corps Loison's VI Corps lay before Fuentes de Oñoro, with d'Erlon's IX Corps behind him and *Général de division* Louis-Pierre Montbrun's and *Général de brigade* François Fournier's cavalry to his left. This concentration of 30,000 men suggested that Masséna expected to encounter the bulk of the allied army in Fuentes de Oñoro, and that the village would need to be taken before the French could claim a victory.

Wellington was initially suspicious of Reynier's intentions and sent the Light Division to intervene, should the II Corps launch a serious attack. Reconnaissance had convinced Reynier, however, that even if he moved further to his right, the Dos Casas would remain impassable. He stayed where he was and the Light Division was brought back to its former position.

The first serious assault occurred in the early afternoon when *Général de brigade* Claude François Ferey's troops of the VI Corps launched a frontal attack on Fuentes de Oñoro, only

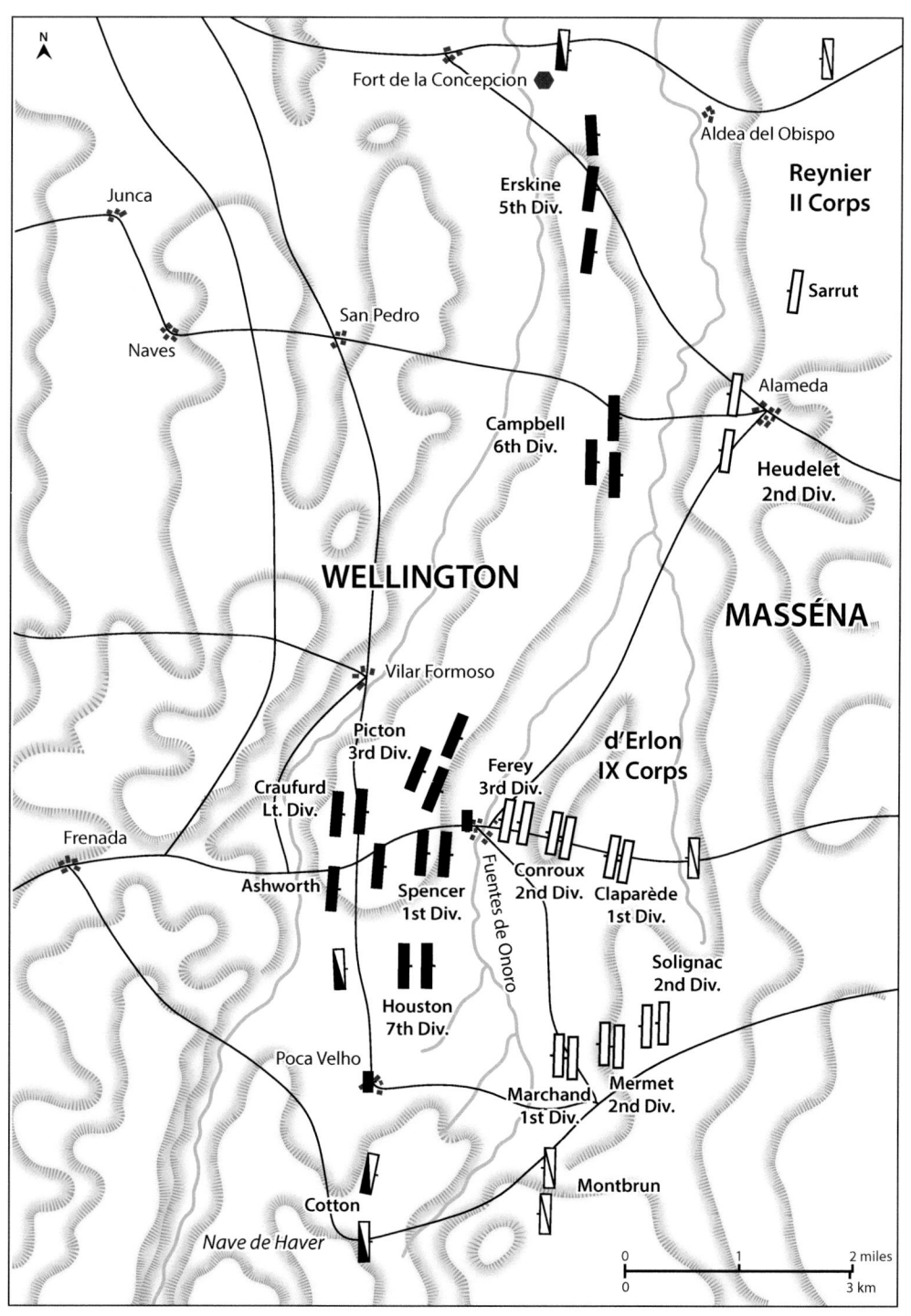

The Battle of Fuentes de Oñoro, 3 May 1811.

to come under allied fire. Undaunted, the French maintained their advance, crossed the Dos Casas and occupied the lower part of the village. What followed was a rare event, fierce hand-to-hand fighting with bayonets in enclosed spaces, including the houses themselves. Eventually, the French were driven back across the stream, They attempted a counter-attack but were unable to hold a position on the Allied side of the river, although they occupied buildings on their side.

It was soon obvious to Masséna that a different approach was needed. On 4 May, while both sides kept up some desultory firing, Montbrun reconnoitred the area around Porto Velho and Nave de Aver. He reported that the allied position was more vulnerable on its right. Julian Sanchez's irregulars were at Nave de Haver; a battalion was holding Porto Velho; and a thin line of cavalry acted as a screen. He also suggested that cavalry could operate between the two hamlets, while infantry could assault Porto Velho. Masséna now planned to turn the allied right, using the open ground as far out as Nave de Haver, while another assault on Fuentes de Oñoro would distract Wellington from his actual intentions. To further confuse the allied commander, Reynier on the French right would demonstrate against the 5th Division. During the night the French took up new positions to facilitate this plan, when three infantry divisions, 17,000 strong, would advance into the open ground.

Wellington, however, was in a good position to interpret the implications of these nocturnal movements and respond appropriately. More cavalry was sent to strengthen the covering force already in position. There were not enough of them, though, to secure the allied right, so the 7th Division moved towards Porto Velho to reinforce the detached battalion that was already there and occupy the surrounding area. The 1/71st and the 1/79th from the 1st Division were in Fuentes de Oñoro, with the 2/24th in support. Meanwhile, the 5th Division remained on the far left.

At daybreak on 5 May the French cavalry made a threatening movement on Nave de Haver, driving off the Spanish guerillas and the 14th Light Dragoons. The French then turned their attention to Porto Velho, driving in more of the allied cavalry. At this point the French infantry made an appearance and the hitherto untested 7th Division was soon under intolerable pressure. Wellington sent in the Light Division, under Brigadier General Crauford's command since the previous evening, to rescue the 7th, and there followed one of the most notable moments of the battle. The Light Division, supported by horse artillery, retreated in square against cavalry attack while protecting the 7th Division. At the same time, the 1st and 3rd Divisions created a new line *en potence*. Under normal circumstances the angle created by the new alignment would have been vulnerable to artillery fire, but, as noted, on this occasion Wellington was able to outgun the French.

Two hours after daybreak, Ferey's division, preceded by grenadiers from the IX Corps launched a frontal attack on Fuentes de Oñoro and enjoyed immediate success when the 71st and 79th were driven out. The two Highland battalions quickly rallied and counter-attacked with the support of the 24th. They forced the desperate French to take refuge in the houses by the Dos Casas. D'Erlon responded by ordering *Général de division* Nicholas François Conroux's and *Général de division* Michel Clarapède's battalions, 10,000 strong, to retake the village. Again, the French enjoyed some initial success, although the fighting was desperate, but when Wellington sent in Major General Henry Mackinnon's brigade from the 3rd Division the extra manpower swung the balance in favour of the allies. The 74th led the final charge which drove the French back to the stream and beyond. By 2:00 p.m. the fighting was over.

As for the 5th Division, they might be regarded as on the scene but not of the scene. Reynier's instructions were to make 'a general demonstration all along his line, to support the attack of the main army'.[27] Only if Wellington brought the troops on his left closer to Fuentes de Oñoro should Reynier move in parallel. The demonstration amounted to nothing more than the 31e légère of *Général de division* Étienne Heudelet's division skirmishing with the support of two guns on the edge of the steep bank of the Dos Casas. This fire was returned by the light troops of the 5th Division.

Gomm summed up the day's activity in another of his letters to his sister:

> More to the left they cannonaded for a short time where the 5th Division was posted. We occupied the left of the line, from Fort Concepcion to the point where the great road from Ciudad Rodrigo to Almeida crosses the ridge. This was done merely to engage our attention in this quarter, while the main attack was carrying on against our right.
>
> Our light troops in this quarter were engaged during the greater part of the day with trifling loss on both sides.'[28]

And trifling it was when compared with the total losses suffered by both sides. The 31e légère had four officers and 48 men killed or wounded against a French total of 2,844. The light companies of the 3/1st (9), 1/9th (4), 2/30th (4), 2/44th (4) and 8th Caçadores (6) lost a total of 27 men wounded. As for the Black Brunswickers, it is possible that the man killed in action and two posted missing belonged to one of the companies attached to the division. The allies lost 1,804 in total.[29]

Almeida

At daybreak on 6 May the two armies still occupied the ground they had held the previous afternoon, although the allies had entrenched some of their positions during the night. Masséna, however, had abandoned the idea of relieving Almeida. His intention now was to extricate the garrison, having reluctantly come to the conclusion that he could no longer maintain even this small presence in Portugal. First, he needed to warn Brenier that he could expect no relief, and then instruct him to effect his escape as soon as possible. With a reward of 6,000 francs in the offing, three volunteers agreed to carry a message to Almeida. Brenier was to follow a northern route to Barba del Puerco where Reynier's II Corps would be waiting on the far side of the river Agueda at San Felices to cover the crossing of the bridge. To signal that the critical message had been received, Brenier was to fire three salvoes, which were duly heard by both the French and the Allies. As Masséna began his withdrawal on

---

27 Oman, *A History*, vol.IV, p.339, citing Masséna's orders.
28 Carr-Gomm (ed.), *Letters and Journals*, vol.I, p.214.
29 Oman, *The History of the Peninsular War*, vol.IV, pp.623–624.

8 May, Brenier spiked the guns in Almeida. This created a disturbance that attracted some allied attention, only for it to be misinterpreted as signals to Masséna.

Wellington re-established the blockade once Masséna withdrew. Major General Campbell, now in command of the 6th Division, posted his troops and Pack's Portuguese so that they ringed the town, although, somewhat surprisingly, the strongest concentrations were to the south and west, not the most likely route that an escaping force would take. A Portuguese force was posted at Junça, more than three miles south of the town. Major General Richard Hulse's British brigade, to the west, might also have been considered too far removed to prevent an escape. Only the 2nd Foot from Brigadier General Robert Burne's brigade, posted a mile from Almeida, and the southern flank of Pack's Portuguese were anywhere near the town. Campbell also failed to post night picquets close to the walls. Indeed, he would later be criticised for delegating to officers in command of the picquets the decision on how to respond in face of the enemy.

At 6:00 p.m. on 9 May, George Murray, the Quartermaster General, sent orders to Erskine, who was still in command of the 5th Division. Leith was on his way back and, in the light of subsequent events, the whole division, particularly the 4th Foot, must have wished that he had travelled faster. Erskine was now required 'to push one Battalion of infantry to your left to the distance of two or three miles beyond Fort Conception. This battalion should place pickets at the passes over the Dos Casas riverlet which lead from the side of Villar de Ciervo and Barba del Puerco towards Malpartida.'[30]

Further instructions stressed that the movements of the chosen battalion should commence at dusk and be made with all possible concealment so that the French would not be aware of it. Pack was then to be informed of the battalion's final position and communication was to be maintained by means of the Portuguese dragoons already in the area. Erskine handed over the choice of battalion to Dunlop, who selected the 1/4th under Lieutenant Colonel Charles Bevan for the task. The 4th was the senior regiment in the second brigade and enjoyed a positive reputation. The position Bevan took up lay two or three miles from Fort Concepcion in wild and wooded ground, which offered good cover but was not ideal for rapid movement. The focal point was the bridge over the Dos Casas, a possible escape route for the French. On the other hand, it was more than seven miles from Barba del Puerco, an equally likely crossing point.

The following afternoon Erskine received another order, this time from Wellington, who had been reconnoitring the area and now appreciated that the bridge at Barba del Puerco was the probable escape route. Consequently, the position taken by the 4th Foot would need to be extended northwards in order to obstruct this route. It was this order upon which a later tragedy hinged, so it is significant to note that whereas Major General Campbell reported late in the afternoon of the 10th that his troops were in position around Almeida, no such message was received from Erskine.

The men of the garrison in Almeida were now ready to make their escape and at about 11:30 p.m. they slipped out, undetected. They were already close to Campbell's picquets when, at midnight, the mines they had set detonated.

Gomm subsequently wrote his soldier-brother,

---

30 National Library of Scotland (NLS): Adv 46-4-16-126 & 127: Murray Papers.

The walls presently exploded. Those who slept most like the dead were startled, and indeed everything, animate and inanimate, seems to have been in motion – but the pickets. They seem to have made it a point of honour to take care of the town, as nobody else would, and the French had greatly the start, before it seems to have been clearly understood that the town could not run away, but the tenantry could.[31]

Best placed to intervene were the 2nd Foot, but although Lieutenant Colonel William Iremonger, their commanding officer, had sent out patrols, he then remained inactive even when those patrols reported the flight of the French. The first to react was Pack, who went in pursuit with a small force of Portuguese and also sent a warning message to Campbell. A troop of the Royal Dragoons also went into action, although there was little 50 men could do against the two French battalions. Most frustratingly, Lieutenant Colonel James Douglas had brought the 8th Portuguese towards Barba del Puerco in immediate response to the explosions but then moved on because there was no sign of the French.

By 6:00 a.m. the two French columns were at the bridge. Hale of the 9th was puzzled by this.

> …where our second brigade was, the while the enemy were making their escape, I cannot ascertain, but however as soon as they were apprized of the enemy's movement, they proceeded on their march in pursuit of them with all speed towards St Felice in Spain. Our brigade not being far off, we soon got intelligence, and in consequence of that, the light companies of the brigade were immediately dispatched off in pursuit of them, with all possible speed…

Hale then exaggerates somewhat, claiming that the struggle at the bridge lasted five hours.

> At length, it was thought necessary to show them the point of the bayonet and give them a charge, which we did with great vigour, for having no knapsacks, we could out-run the enemy, as they were loaded with the plunder of Almeida. The enemy seeing what was our intention, they turned their backs to us and ran as fast as they possibly could, and in a few moments they came to the brink of a hill, a place that they were not very well acquainted with, for in one place was a very steep rugged rock, between twenty and thirty yards in length, and a considerable distance to the bottom, and in consequence of their retreating so rapidly, many of them were not able to make a stop so sudden, but went headlong down the rock, by which some met with present death, and some with broken arms and legs.[32]

Hale was remembering the gist of the event. In fact, as the second column neared the bridge, the first having already crossed, they came under fire from the 36th from Burne's brigade, who were on higher ground. The 4th were closer to the actual bridge but not in a good firing position. Lieutenant Colonel Basil Cochrane of the 36th now brought his troops down and

---

31 Carr-Gomm (ed.), *Letters and Journals*, vol.I, pp.216–217.
32 Hale, *Journal*, pp.68–69.

joined with the 4th to fall on the second of the two French battalions. The result was a fierce encounter, as Hale describes, the two British battalions being reinforced by the light companies of the 5th Division. But it was not a one-sided struggle because Reynier's covering fire inevitably produced casualties. There were 18 Allied casualties and an officer and 17 men were taken prisoner. The 1/4th lost two men killed and 11 wounded, which certainly places them on the scene.[33] Nor could it be claimed as a victory, since so many of the garrison had escaped. Nevertheless, as Gomm informed his brother, 'Several hundred [French] were killed and nearly three hundred taken, and I believe they lost at least one third of their number.'[34]

This was no consolation to Wellington. His response was extreme, possibly coloured by the fact that Brenier owed him a considerable sum of money from his time in London as a paroled prisoner of war. He wrote to Beresford: 'I think the escape of the garrison of Almeida (although we have taken and destroyed a lot of them) is the most disgraceful military event which has yet occurred to us.'[35] He had given specific orders that the bridge at Barba del Puerco should be guarded. The blame, therefore, rested with the battalion that had failed to expedite the order. Yet the question remains, why were the 4th Foot not at the bridge? According to Wellington, he had sent his order to that effect at about 1:00 p.m., although it is interesting to note that many years later, in conversation with Stanhope, he claimed to have sent it direct to Lieutenant Colonel Bevan rather than to Erskine, or even Dunlop. This protestation, though, may well have been coloured by later events. Erskine was dining with Lieutenant General Sir Brent Spencer when the order probably reached him, at about 4:00 p.m. Other accounts suggest Erskine must have received it an hour or two earlier, unless the messenger rode out to the 5th Division and then had to come back to Vila Formosa to find Erskine.

For his part, Erskine claimed that he forwarded the order to the 4th Foot, who were still some seven or eight miles from Barba del Puerco. Lieutenant Colonel Bevan, however, subsequently insisted that he had not received it until midnight, by which time the garrison was making its escape from Almeida. Every contemporary opinion, and many were expressed, inclined towards Bevan's account, the consensus being that Erskine, dilatory at the best of times, had put it into his pocket and forgotten about it until many hours later. It is interesting that two intelligent officers unconnected to the 5th Division, George Simmons of the 95th and William Tomkinson of the 16th Light Dragoons, both defended Bevan in their respective journals.[36]

Bevan was anxious to defend himself. He wrote a letter to Dunlop, which was to be forwarded to Erskine. Having made the point that he did not reach the bridge until 6:00 a.m., timing which suggests that he must have set out at about 3:30 a.m. at the latest, he continued:

33　TNA: WO12/2205: 1/4th Muster Book.
34　Carr-Gomm (ed.), *Letters and Journals*, vol.I, p.217.
35　Gurwood (ed.), *Dispatches*, vol.VII, p.533.
36　William Willoughby Verner (ed.), *A British Rifleman* (London: Greenhill Books, 1986), p.174 and James Tomkinson (ed.), *The Diary of a Cavalry Officer in the Peninsular War and Waterloo Campaign 1809-1815* (London: Swan Sonnennschien & Co., 1895). p.102.

And further, as a reason for my not having marched last night, that, although I had ascertained that one party of the enemy's troops had crossed the river, I was by no means certain that others were not moving in the same direction. I therefore thought it might be more essential to retain my position at the bridge [over the Dos Casas] and march in the morning, which I accordingly did, having sent a patrol from the Portuguese to reconnoitre Barba de Puerco.[37]

Wellington had already chosen to blame Bevan. He told Liverpool that the garrison escaped because the 1/4th lost its way, which was Erskine's explanation, and the one Lieutenant Stewart of the 30th recorded in his journal, suggesting that it quickly became the 'official' version. In the later conversation with Stanhope, he even suggested what can only be described as a calumny, that Bevan had stayed put on the advice of his junior officers. Neither of these explanations has any supporting evidence, Indeed, one diarist specifically denied the 'lost its way' claim. Captain William Tomkinson of the 16th Light Dragoons maintained that it was merely offered by Erskine 'to cover himself, when required to explain by Lord Wellington.' Nor did Wellington take the trouble to question Bevan directly. 'Lord Wellington was much enraged at this, and would never allow the thing to be inquired into, or admit of any excuse from Colonel Bevan, 4th regiment, who was the person condemned as having erred.'[38] Bevan's own belief, that the garrison might follow different routes to effect their escape, explains the initial delay. He was also posted in difficult ground and to advance across it in the dark without a guide would be foolhardy. It has been suggested, therefore, that he delayed while a guide was found. Alternatively, he might have waited for the first glimmers of daylight for the same reason.

Only two men were censured for the debacle: Cochrane for getting into an unequal struggle that caused unnecessary casualties; and Bevan for not expediting a specific order. The later now had to live with the threat of a court martial for dereliction of duty. This, for a man who took pride in his competence and who would now probably be described as bipolar, was to prove a burden beyond bearing. In contrast, Campbell, and Erskine both emerged unscathed. Nor was Iremonger castigated for his culpable lack of action. As a result, the army was left with the conviction that the more junior officers would always be sacrificed to protect the reputation of their seniors.

It is worth noting that Napier put the blame on Campbell and Erskine, while Oman held Erskine and Iremonger responsible, and Fortescue maintained that Campbell was principally to blame. Not one of them blamed Bevan.

While the main army had been occupied in driving Masséna out of Portugal, Marshal Beresford, in command of the troops posted beyond the Tagus, had led an expedition into Estremadura, initially, as already noted, to relieve Badajoz. When the town fell into French hands on 11 March, Beresford could do little without a siege train. Having made a flying visit to Badajoz and inspected the defences for himself, on 23 April Wellington ordered Beresford to commence siege operations as soon as the guns arrived, even though orders had been given for the formation of a siege train of heavy Portuguese guns only five days

---

37 NLS: Adv 46-2-12-220: Murray Papers.
38 Tomkinson (ed.), *The Diary of a Cavalry Officer*, p.102.

before. Consequently, it was 6 May before Beresford could commence siege work, which was then interrupted by the advance of *Maréchal* Soult from Andalusia, seemingly unaware that Beresford had been joined by the Spanish army of *Teniente General* Joaquín Blake y Joyes. Soult had 24,000 troops against the 35,000 of the Allied force. The result was an action at Albuera on 16 May, generally regarded as the bloodiest battle of the Peninsular War. The Allies claimed victory but only after a hard-fought and very costly struggle, which forced Soult to withdraw to Andalusia.

Wellington now decided that the siege should continue under his direction. His chosen troops were the 3rd and 7th Divisions, who were to join Hill's 2nd Division and Major General the Hon. Lowry Cole's 4th Division. There was a danger that such a move might lead to the junction of the Army of Portugal, now under Marmont's command, and Soult's Army of the South, which would obviously threaten the Allied position. Nevertheless, on 10 May Wellington began his advance to Badajoz, leaving Brent Spencer in command of the remaining troops, comprising the 1st, 5th, 6th and Light Divisions, Pack's and Ashworth's Portuguese, cavalry and artillery.

Spencer was ordered to adopt a defensive stance in readiness to repel any advance by Marmont. He was to hold a line, with his troops cantoned from Almeida to Nave de Haver, the 5th Division being at Nave de Haver. Should Marmont threaten, Spencer was to abandon Almeida and withdraw south to Alfaiates. If the pressure continued, he was to take up a position behind the Coa, or even as far as the Zezere.[39]

Wellington, however, did not expect that such movements would prove necessary, since Marmont was short of supplies and had dispersed his troops. A memorandum which Wellington sent to Brent Spencer five days later suggested that Marmont still presented no threat to the Allied troops, since all the indications were that the *maréchal* was either moving south towards Badajoz or withdrawing deeper into Spain. Spencer, therefore, was to send Major General Kenneth Howard's brigade of the 1st Division and Ashworth's Portuguese to Badajoz, with the proviso that should he be threatened by Marmont, he could recall them.[40]

Even with extra manpower, the siege of Badajoz was unlikely to end successfully, however, because resources were inadequate: artillery firepower was insufficient, and there was a serious dearth of artificers. Furthermore, the engineers miscalculated when deciding how to attack the town, choosing to continue Beresford's strategy of attacking the two strongest points, San Cristobal and the castle. As a result, at noon on 10 June Wellington decided to raise the siege, partly because it was obvious that success was becoming increasingly unlikely and partly because Marmont was on the move.

Moves and Countermoves

It had been clear by the end of May that the Army of Portugal was preparing to advance south. In accordance with another of Wellington's orders, that he should shadow any such movement on Marmont's part, Spencer initially brought the 1st and Light Divisions

---

39 Gurwood (ed.), *Dispatches*, vol.VII, p.553.
40 Gurwood (ed.), *Dispatches*, vol.VII, p.558.

towards Sabugal. He subsequently realised that he had been misinformed and sent the two divisions back to their previous positions. This was on 27 May. The following day certain news arrived that Marmont was concentrating his troops in two bodies. Wellington now instructed Spencer to be ready to move once Marmont's intentions became clear, whereupon he should send the right of his force to Penamacor and the left to Sabugal, leaving just a screen in front of Ciudad Rodrigo. Two days later the thrust of Marmont's movements was revealed. The previous day he had brought Foy's division towards Almeida as a demonstration to keep Spencer in position, while a further two divisions under Reynier were moving south. Unsure of the strength of Marmont's advance, Spencer played safe by pulling back the Light Division and Slade's cavalry from their advanced positions and sending the other three divisions to Sabugal. Pack, at Almeida, blew up what was left of the town's defences and then moved west.

There was some cavalry skirmishing in response to Marmont's advance. Otherwise, Spencer continued to retire without offering any resistance, reaching Alfaiates by 6 June, even though his troops comfortably outnumbered the force Marmont had sent against them. This became evident when one of Wellington's exploring officers, Colonel John Waters, reported that a larger French force was at Puerto de Baños, 30 miles to the east. Spencer had effectively been duped, although he now realised he could safely bring his troops towards Badajoz in parallel with the French. Also, the position he had taken up meant that he could cross the Tagus at Villa Velha while the French would have to pursue a more circuitous route.

On 11 June Gomm wrote to his sister from Sabugal, noting that they had withdrawn behind the Coa in response to the threat of Marmont's supposed advance against them. Two days later he continued the letter with the news that

> Our army of the north has, in conformity with the movements of the enemy, extended itself from hence towards Peñamacor, Castel Branco, and the Tagus; and the greater part of it, I should think, would be in march at this moment, directing its course towards Badajos… We are directed to move to-morrow to Capinha; it is a league nearer to Castel Branco than Belmonte on the Guarda road. Upon my word, I like anything better than fighting for fighting's sake; but while we are in the world we like to live in it, and fighting seems to be the order of the day here.[41]

Spencer had been ordered to hold the 5th Division back, which explains why, when the column led by Anson's cavalry reached Vila Velha by 11 June, Gomm was writing from Sabugal. Six days later, only Slade's cavalry and the 5th Division had yet to cross the Douro. This allowed Wellington to consolidate his position before Marmont could reach him. He also intended to send Blake's Spanish force to threaten Seville in order to dissuade Soult from moving against him. With Marmont coming closer, though, there was every possibility of a battle. If Soult advanced further, he could use one of his divisions to turn the Allied line with a flanking movement while bringing the rest towards Albuera. Marmont could then march along the Guadiana to join him.

---

41   Carr-Gomm (ed.), *Letters and Journals*, vol.I, p.225.

Only on 19 June did the Marmont realise that the siege had been raised and the Allies had withdrawn behind the Guadiana. He probed to establish the new Allied position and by the 22nd he had discovered the appropriate positions that they now occupied. With the last of the allied troops coming in the following day, it was clear that Wellington was ready for action. He was in a strong position and one that precluded a surprise attack. No attack came, however. The French were deterred by the discovery that Spencer's force had joined Wellington's. Nor was Soult prepared to commit the whole of his troops to a joint enterprise when such a move could endanger his hold on Andalusia. Four days previously he had learnt of Blake's move against Seville and that was enough to draw him back to Andalusia, as Wellington had anticipated. The two French commanders decided to part company.

Wellington, however, continued to prepare against the possibility of an attack. On 27 June, the French blew up the walls of Olivenza and retired to Valverde but it was not immediately clear whether they were concentrating or preparing for a retreat. The following day, it seemed that the latter was more likely, based on what appeared to be Soult's withdrawal, he having first sent one of his divisions and 500 cavalry to Marmont against the chance of a renewed allied attack on Badajoz. Marmont concentrated on making sure that Badajoz was fully supplied to withstand another siege, which took him until the middle of July. Then he withdrew the Army of Portugal to northern Estremadura in order to find food to feed them.

As for the 5th Division, by the beginning of July they were as far south as Portalegre where, according to Gomm, 'we continue to remain, much to our satisfaction, and I believe I may add, the object of envy of the whole army besides.' There was the threat that headquarters would soon be in the town, which meant, of course, that the officers would be turned out of their comfortable quarters, '…but we do not despair of being suffered to keep hiding-places in the town, even should this awful visitation come upon us.' Other factors in favour of remaining as long as possible in Portalegre were its beauty and that it was healthy in all seasons.[42]

Despite this, however, there had been a tragedy, for

> Our sunshine has been clouded for some days past by the self-murder of an amiable man, in command of one of the regiments of our division, thinking (at variance, I believe, with all the world besides) that a slight had been thrown upon his character in one of the late dispatches relating to Almeida. He was young, ardent, full of military qualifications, universally esteemed, and married to a young wife, with a family to which he was tenderly attached. What has he not left us to regret in this dreadful act, unjustifiable in any age of the world, in any condition or season of life, under any calamity short of madness – and then only pardonable – how much more unjustifiable, then, in the times and in the belief we live in.[43]

The officer who died by his own hand was Lieutenant Colonel Charles Bevan. Although he suffered intermittently from periods of depression, Gomm's comments make clear that since Almeida Bevan had been unable to shake off what he himself called the Blue Devils.

---

42   Carr-Gomm (ed.), *Letters and Journals*, vol.I, p.228.
43   Carr-Gomm (ed.), *Letters and Journals*, vol.I, p.229.

He was a man with a keen sense of honour, who felt that the castigation he had suffered affected not only him but reflected adversely on his regiment. On 8 July, alone in his quarters, he put a gun to his head and ended his anguish.

There was never any question of his not being allowed the full honours of a military funeral. On the 10th, at midday, the 1/4th was on parade, while the officers assembled at the senior major, John Piper's quarters and a firing party stood ready under the command of the second major, Alured Dodsworth Faunce. The other officers of the division had been invited to attend, and in response every officer in the division made a point of being present. If it were reported to him, Wellington might have recognised that it was a tacit comment on his treatment of Bevan but even so, having made a judgement, it is unlikely that he would have changed his mind.

On 18 July, the Allies began to withdraw from the malarial Guadiana, leaving only Hill's 2nd Division, strengthened with Howard's brigade which had been transferred from the 1st Division, and Hamilton's Portuguese, in the area around Elvas. By the 25th the 5th Division was at Quinta de Alameira, having been kicked out of Portalegre, as Gomm termed it. They were now living '"under the canopy of birds and beasts" a week since; wild ones, too, for the woods we inhabit are the ancient inheritance of wolves and wild boars and serpents.' Fortunately, these creatures were either too afraid or too few in number to trouble them. Although tongue in cheek, Gomm did seem to feel that his division had been slighted.

> ...we find it difficult to lessen our misfortune in the eyes of the world, and we are doing all we can to lessen the disgrace. Like all heroes of old, we would magnify the prowess of our vanquishers, and comfort ourselves that, at least, we fall by no ignoble hand. Headquarters, with the 1st division at their heels, are not found to be stout enough; but they must call on Castaños the Great, and all that is worthy to be called Spanish, to complete the overthrow.[44]

In fact, as Gomm goes on to admit, he is actually still 'living under a roof' because of his staff position.

He may well have meant a roof of a temporary nature, because Lieutenant John Allen of the 3/1st noted in his diary (which he sent to *The Military Chronicle* for publication) that they were 'Very busily employed in constructing a hut &c. This place we called Vauxhall, from the wooded scenery and our bands reminding us of that place [Vauxhall Gardens, London].'[45]

The Army of Portugal was now holding positions along the Tagus, at Palencia and in the area around Ávila, while *Général de divison* Paul Charles Thiébault's division from the Army of the North was stationed at Salamanca. Marmont's first concern was to build defences at Almaraz in order to create a stronger and more convenient crossing point of the Tagus which, in turn, would create a more secure French presence in the central Tagus area. Wellington was fully aware of this activity, thanks to the spies who provided him with information and intercepted dispatches. He also appreciated that the Army of Portugal was

---

44 Carr-Gomm (ed.), *Letters and Journals*, vol.I, p.229.
45 John Allen, 'Journal of an officer of the Royals in the seat of war', *The Royal Military Chronicle*, November 1811, p.9.

sufficiently dispersed to prevent rapid concentration. Furthermore, Soult was fully occupied in Andalusia. Yet he made the decision to leave Badajoz alone, since Marmont, an energetic general, would undoubtedly respond as quickly as possible and could descend on the Allies within 10 days. As experience had proved, that was not time enough to take the place. Instead, Ciudad Rodrigo now became a possible target, although Wellington himself recognised that with the strength of the Army of Portugal similar to his own, the situation remained unpredictable.[46]

During the first week of August the allied divisions took up new positions on the Azara and Agueda. The Light Division marched to the left bank of the Agueda near Ciudad Rodrigo and established a blockade with the 3rd Division, which was on the right bank of the river. The 1st Division was at Penamacor, and the 4th, 20 miles north east of Castello Branco. As for the 5th Division, having reached Castello de Vide at the end of July, they then crossed the Tagus at Vila Velha, were at Castelo Branco on the 5th, and reached Sabugal five days later. Nor was the march without incident, although the enemy on this occasion was not the French, as Allen noted.

> While bivouaced at Atalaya, many of our officers were robbed, particularly the quarter-master and two others. They had their uniform coats stolen, and the epaulettes being stript off, they were thrown away. One officer lost above a hundred dollars. The robbery was committed while there were three officers sleeping in the same hut, and their servants outside. A soldier of the 32d was detected with a part of the property, and his brother, belonging to our regiment, was implicated.[47]

Allen does not reveal what happened to the thieves, nor how a soldier of the 32nd, who were in the 6th Division, could have been involved. Yet a general order of the 30 August refers to the trial of John Marsland of the 32nd, who was accused of having 'aided and assisted in committing a robbery, in the tent occupied by Lieutenant Rea, Lieutenant Ingram, and Lieutenant Balfour of the Royal Regiment, at the camp near the village of Attalya, on the night of the 5th, or the morning of the 6th of August last.' He faced a second charge of 'having in his possession various articles' which were taken from the three lieutenants' tent. Having been cleared of the first charge, he was found guilty of the second charge and sentenced to a thousand lashes, the sentence 'to be carried into execution tomorrow evening, the 31st instant…in the presence of the 32d regiment and the troops in the same cantonment, to be paraded for the purpose.'[48] Receiving was a capital crime in civil law, but soldiers were less expendable than the general population.

By the middle of the month the division was watching the passes of the Sierra Gata against a French division posted at Plasencia. The 6th and 7th Divisions had also come up, the former now positioned between the Coa and the Agueda and the latter near Sabugal and Fuente Guinaldo, where Wellington had established his headquarters. In addition, *Teniente General* Francisco Javier Castaños had sent Spanish troops under Carlos de España to Ledesma, while the irregular troops of Julian Sanchez troubled Thiébault in Salamanca.

---

46   Gurwood (ed.), *Dispatches*, vol.VII, p.177.
47   Allen, 'Journal', pp.10–11.
48   Anon. (ed.), *General Orders*, vol.III, pp.171–172.

The light companies of the 5th Division, including the caçadores and the Brunswickers, were posted in advance at Valverde, watching for any French movement, with one or other battalion of the division in support, hutted to provide some protection against the cold of the night. The light companies were turned round week by week and it seems that a definite rivalry developed between them as to who could cover the 12 miles to the forward position the quickest. Allen reported that on 15 September he was 'On the Valverde picket. Running with the advance above two hours.'[49] Unfortunately, he does not say whether this was a good time. The competition probably provided some respite for the men from the boredom of their situation, while for the officers there was the distraction of hunting the wolves that not only roamed the hills but occasionally approached the bivouacs.

Nevertheless, the situation of the advanced troops was increasingly uncomfortable. On the 17th, 'The weather very wet and cold, and our huts as miserable and wretched as a grave. We have had neither wine or spirits for the last ten days', while three days later 'The rain and wind were incessant; but there was no defence against the pityless storm.' A commanding officer could make a difference to the situation, however. 'And here allow me to pay my mite of gratitude to our commanding officer, Colonel Barnes, who, though we are in front of the enemy, has never harassed us by unnecessary duty.'[50] Nor could Allen resist the temptation of expressing his complaints poetically:

…No bed, no blanket here our bones defends
From cold, or damp, disease, aches and stitches,
Pale shivering ague with her train attends,
No lining here to regimental breeches!!…

My once gay coat in tatters hangs about,
With many vary coloured pieces patch'd,
From ghosts of shoes, my wounded feet peep out,
Thro' threadbare gaiters, how my legs are scratched…[51]

No wonder Allen wondered why he had 'left the Town'.

The French made little response to the Allied movements. Although Marmont appreciated that Ciudad Rodrigo had, in effect, been cut off, he knew the place to be well supplied and also thought that Wellington lacked a siege train. This degree of confidence, however, was disabused when Marmont learnt in mid-September that there was indeed an allied siege train at Villa da Ponte. It did occur to him, however, that Salamanca might also be a target, so the Sierra de Gata passes were probed to establish whether there was a strong allied presence in the area, which at least explained to the light troops why they had been posted with a watching brief.

Some alterations Marmont made to his dispositions further north led Wellington on 27 August to change the position of some of his own troops. He brought the 1st and 4th

---

49 Allen, 'Journal', *The Royal Military Chronicle,* December 1811, p.124.
50 Allen, 'Journal', p.125.
51 John Allen, 'The Subaltern's Complaint', *The Royal Military Chronicle,* March 1812, pp.341–343. This is merely a short extract.

Divisions closer to Fuente Guinaldo because he anticipated that Marmont was about to make an attempt to raise the blockade of Ciudad Rodrigo. This assumption was based on an intercepted dispatch from Foy at Truxillo to *Général de brigade* Étienne Gerard, commanding a brigade in d'Erlon's IX Corps. This suggested Foy was about to move forward and cross the Tagus. When Foy failed to move, however, Wellington concluded that there was no immediate danger of a French concentration.

At the beginning of September another threat became apparent. *Général de division* Jean-Marie Dorsenne, now in command of the Army of the North, was reported to have brought supplies to Salamanca in order to revictual Ciudad Rodrigo, for which purpose a supply train was being prepared. Then on 17 September news arrived that Foy had finally left Truxillo two days previously, while further information established that the supply train would be ready to make its way to Ciudad Rodrigo by the 21st. It also became clear that at least part of the Army of the North was about to unite with the Army of Portugal, a combined force which would outnumber the Allies, particularly as the many Walcheren units, which included most of the recent reinforcements, were suffering the effect of the intermittent fever caught during that campaign. In terms of numbers, the Allies mustered 46,000 fit men against the combined French of 55,000-60,000.[52] Wellington had no intention of offering battle under those circumstances. Instead, he planned to remain as close to Ciudad Rodrigo as was safe while being prepared to take up a defensive position from Fuente Guinaldo to Alfaiates. In preparation, the 4th Division had already started to fortify the former place. Picton and Crauford were instructed to hold their positions unless the French attacked in force, in which case Crauford was to withdraw beyond the Agueda and Picton to El Bodón and Pastores.

On 18 September Allen of the 1st Foot had written in his journal: 'Received intelligence that the French were again advancing, and about to occupy the towns on the other side of the sierra de Gato. If so we may expect an immediate attack.'[53] No attack took place, although on 22 September, when Marmont brought up the Army of Portugal to relieve Ciudad Rodrigo, he left Foy's division at the Sierra de Gata with an order to demonstrate against Plasencia; that is to say, against the 5th Division. At the same time, Dorsenne brought part of the Army of the North to San Muñoz. Wellington could not risk a battle on the open plain, but he was also unsure of Marmont's intentions, whether his objective was merely to relieve Ciudad Rodrigo or rather, to attack the Allies. In such a moment of uncertainty, he abandoned his usual caution. Unwilling to give ground, he kept the 3rd and Light Divisions in position, yet failed to call up any other troops in support.

By the 23rd the leading French cavalry units were approaching the town. The British cavalry, which had been blocking the road from Salamanca, was ordered to draw back. The next day it became clear that Marmont was bringing a large force to Ciudad Rodrigo, while Dorsenne was also advancing. For his part, Marmont had recognised that Wellington was not concentrating his forces. Two reconnaissance parties were sent out and the one that was exploring the lower Agueda encountered some Allied cavalry but was driven off when some infantry came forward. A more serious engagement took place at El Bodón where the 3rd Division had

---

52   Oman, *The History of the Peninsular War*, vol.IV, p.536.
53   Allen, 'Journal', p.125.

taken position on poor ground, which Picton was now instructed to maintain as Marmont prepared to attack. Although a French frontal assault was held off, Wellington realised that the troops must be withdrawn. The French pursued strongly but were eventually repulsed, leaving only enemy artillery to continue the attack. Then, as the 3rd Division neared Fuente Guinaldo, other allied troops came up in support. The 3rd Division had been brought off, and the Light Division had already been able to withdraw, by an indirect route, but the outcome could have been a disaster. Nor was the danger over, although it would seem that Marmont had reservations about attacking when Wellington was in a strong position and offering battle. It is also possible that Dorsenne was reluctant to attack. In his memoirs Marmont offered a different reason: he was not prepared for either a battle or an advance into Portugal, but he had succeeded in resupplying Ciudad Rodrigo, which had been his objective all along.[54]

The Allied force at Fuentes Guinaldo now retired to a position in front of Alfaiates, with the 1st and 6th divisions in touch at Bismula and Rendo. At the same time, Marmont had begun his own withdrawal, but then changed his mind and decided to pursue the Allies, although not to press them. On 27 September Montbrun, along with *Général de division* Joseph, Comte Souham, from the Army of the North, encountered the Light and 5th Divisions, and Alten's cavalry in position in front of Alfaiates. The Allies were considered too strong to attack, however. Then *Général de division* Pierre Watier, in conjunction with Thiébault, both from the Army of the North, met the 4th Division and Brigadier John Slade's cavalry at Aldea da Ponte. Wellington was determined to hold this position but when Montbrun and Souham arrived at dusk and Souham attacked, the Allies were driven from their position. Wellington accepted this reverse, not wanting a fight in the dark.

Having called in all his divisions except the 2nd, Wellington intended to hold a line which extended for seven miles, with the Coa on each flank because of a wide loop in the river's course. Once all the troops were in position, the 5th Division would be on the right, posted on a steep slope at Aldeia Velha. To their left would be the Light and 4th Divisions in front of Alfaiates, then Pack's and Lieutenant Colonel Thomas McMahon's Portuguese at Nave, with the 1st and the 6th Divisions were on the left. The 3rd and the 7th Divisions were in reserve, and the cavalry was posted as appropriate.

Allen sent an account of the 5th Division's advance to join the rest of the Allied army. On the 25 September they 'Heard a heavy cannonade in the direction of Ciudad Rodrigo, and found that it was an attack of a prodigious force of cavalry and infantry on Feunte [*sic*] Guinaldo.' This, of course, was the action at El Bodón. The following day, the division was under arms from 4:00 a.m. and on the 27th marched to Aldeia da Ponte,

> ...when just in the midst of our cookery the alarm was given that the French were approaching, in great force, on the other side of the town, and which was confirmed by an instantaneous discharge of cannon and musquetry. The beef and soup were thrown in every direction, and we stood to our arms. Two companies were ordered to a stone wall in front, to protect the movements of the division in their formation. In this position we waited for the approach of the enemy... The attention of the enemy was, however, called off by a division to the left of ours [the Light Division], and General

---

54 Auguste de Marmont, *Mémoires de Maréchal Marmont, Duc de Raguse* (Paris: Perrotin, 1856), vol.IV, p.64.

> Dunlop thought it advisable to remove to a more advantageous position, and more protected from cavalry. We therefore moved to a hill on the left, and formed in close column, to support the division then engaged, if necessary… We had here an opportunity of calmly beholding a field of battle as spectators, and a most unpleasant spectacle to my feelings it was: not a man but anxiously wished that it might become general.

After nearly two hours of skirmishing, the French launched what promised to be a more purposeful advance, but when they took casualties from Allied shells they went right-about and the skirmishing continued. All this while,

> Our men, though fatigued and hungry, and without even wine or spirits, were anxious to engage, and were hammering their flints, and making all the usual preparations. There were some Irish lads, whose conversation was truly laughable. An officer of the 3d Portuguese was leading on his men in fine style (the grenadiers) and was haranguing them, apparently with great effect: he began with 'O valorosos Portugueses.' The Portuguese all stood to their arms most gallantly, and, I am confident, would have done their duty; that regiment was 900 strong and good men.

On the 28th, they 'marched, at 1 P.M. through Coito, towards Sabugal, as bad a march, I think, as ever was undertaken, extremely dark, and the road broken, craggy and rocky: such a road as I never before witnessed, through a perfect valley of stones. I really could not have rode, if any one had given me the best horse in the division.' When they reached Coito,

> The poor inhabitants lifted up their hands and eyes to heaven, and were very much affected by our retreat. From Sabugal they were flying. In every direction, to the woods and mountains, and carrying their pitiful shreds with them. A very heavy rain, during which we halted for three hours, and afterwards slept in a wood. On the 25th, all our baggage had been ordered to the river, so that not one in ten had even a great coat – nothing but their uniforms. Spent another miserable night…

The following day they finally reached Sabugal, where they encountered two other divisions and some cavalry, on their way to join Wellington. They also discovered that their baggage had been sent to Guarda. As a result, because they had not been able to wash or shave since the 24th, 'some of us began to resemble our allies, the Portuguese, as to mustachios and whiskers, and smoky complexion.' On the 29th, though, they finally reached Guarda, not only to be reunited with their baggage but also to have roofs over their heads. As Allen somewhat ironically commented,

> For the first time in my life I became the proprietor of a freehold, and, to say truth, the prospect of being detained here for a little while is pleasing: some rest, too, for the men, is absolutely requisite. My chateau, however, is, I fear, by no means weather proof: there are, too, no windows or fireplaces, and, as is usual, the lower part of the house is a stable, and miserably dirty and damp.[55]

---

55 Allen, 'Journal', *The Royal Military Chronicle*, April 1812, pp.419–421.

Wellington was confident that he could hold the line he planned on the Coa, but it was never put to the test. Marmont, already critical of Souham's and Thiebault's conduct on the 27th, decided against accepting the clear invitation Wellington was offering him. He recognised that the Allies were in a stronger position than at Fuente Guinaldo and gave the order to withdraw.

The following morning Wellington was once more planning to disperse his troops because the crisis had passed. This view was justified when, on 1 October. Dorsenne began a march north, to take up the unending struggle against the guerrillas, while the Army of Portugal went into cantonments. Just to add to what was happening during the final days of September, on the 28th Foy, who had been occupying the foothills of the Sierra de Gata, began to ascend the heights, only to discover the following day that Marmont was retreating. Foy then made a precipitous return to Plasencia. His diversion had come too late. If the 5th Division had still been in their earlier position they would have had to stay put, which would have weakened the situation for the Allies.

Into Cantonments 1811

Wellington now dispersed his troops, confident that the campaigning season was over. The 1st, 5th and 6th Divisions were cantoned about Guarda, Celorico and Freixadas; the 7th Division was at Penamacor; the 3rd, 4th and Light Divisions were posted at the Spanish frontier, the Light Division across the Agueda, the 4th Division at Gallegos and Barba del Puente, the 3rd Division at Aldea da Ponte and Fuente Guinaldo. Three light cavalry brigades covered these three divisions, while other cavalry units blacked the road between Ciudad Rodrigo and Salamanca. Julian Sanchez and Carlos de España were also in forward positions beyond the Agueda, and Sanchez had the satisfaction of stealing the herd of cattle belonging to the garrison of Ciudad Rodrigo.

As for the Army of Portugal, its various divisions were dispersed in central Castile, although it was obvious that Ciudad Rodrigo would need revictualling, since Marmont's and Dorsenne's troops had eaten into the supplies intended for the garrison.

The situation was now stalemate, Wellington waiting for an opportunity to move against Ciudad Rodrigo, Marmont waiting upon Wellington's movements and Dorsenne too preoccupied with more immediate problems to join Marmont in any joint operation. And then Napoleon, not for the first time, interfered to create a situation that Wellington could use to his advantage.

The orders that reached Marmont as the year was drawing to a close came from Berthier but they were, of course, the Emperor's orders. The first plan was that Marmont should march towards Elvas in an attempt to draw Wellington out of position. This carried the obvious risk that Wellington would take the opportunity to attack Ciudad Rodrigo. Since Marmont now knew of the Allied siege train, he definitely did not intend to move south. Then came a second set of orders, and these created the opportunity that Wellington had been hoping for. Marshal Louis-Gabriel Suchet, operating on the east coast, had decided upon an attack on Valencia with his Army of Aragon. The Army of the Centre, nominally under the command of Joseph Bonaparte, the *soi-disant* King of Spain, and posted around Madrid, was to march east in support, which required Marmont to send some of the Army of Portugal to fill the vacated ground. In a dispatch from Paris written on 21 November, Marmont learnt that he was to send 12,000 men to Valencia and depute another 3,000 to maintain communications. This deliberate weakening of the Army of Portugal was based on the assumption that 20,000 of the allied troops were sick. Sickness certainly was a problem for Wellington, but he still had 38,000 fit British troops, plus the Portuguese, whom Napoleon never considered in his calculations. Yet, as Allen remarked, many of them were 'good men'.

By the end of the year, thanks to Napoleon's interference, Marmont had lost one cavalry and two infantry brigades. The road to Ciudad Rodrigo was now open. As for the 5th Division, as the year drew to a close they were posted at Oliveira do Hospital, Medões and Travanca. It was from the last of these places that Lieutenant Peter Le Mesurier of the 1/9th, a Guernsey man who had recently come from England, wrote to his family on the 23 December.

> …nothing very particular has happened. For want of Real Fighting we go out Sham fighting, which is not very pleasant. Last week we had to March about two Leagues from this Place for a Sham fight. We were out from half after Eight till Six in the Evening for Genl: Hay's amusement and came home with voracious appetites. We do not require very nice Bits after a day's work of that kind; a tough Beef Steak with a Musty loaf & a little Grog satisfies our appetite. Everything here is getting dearer & dearer every day. Eggs, which we got at half a penny a piece, have now trebled in Price. A loaf, which in England would cost one penny, we pay 41/2d for patatoes – 11/2d per pound.

His messmate, however, had gone to a fair about two leagues away in order to get something for a Christmas dinner 'as we intend to regale ourselves on the Day with something extraordinary.'

There were further tribulations. 'We have but a bad Quarter here, having but one Room for cooking, Dining, &c:, and two little places to sleep which are filled with Mice. I awoke a few mornings since & found something working very hard about my neck, and on turning saw a Rat scampering off.' Against this, though,

> My spirits are much better than when I wrote last. I had then about 8 Dollars to pay to Different persons which I was unable to pay from the scarcity of money. I have therefore availed myself of your kindness and drawn £10 which has enabled me to clear myself and to procure little triffles which I wanted. I shall give you a sample of our way of living; Breakfast: Coffé, Bread and butter and a few Pilchards or, if we expect any extra Drilling, eggs. Dinner: Soup, Beef & Patatoes or Rice, after which we smoke a Pipe and take a glass of Grog or some time a Glass of Mulled Wine. We seldom have any extra articles for Dinner except a Heart which cost us One Shilling.

Even with his father's generosity, he was still short of money, being owed £13 in pay while still having to meet expenses like the cost of 'Washing, Shoe Mending, &c:' as well as his mess bill.[56]

---

56 Adrian Greenwood (ed.), *Through Spain with Wellington: the Letters of Lieutenant Peter Le Mesurier of the 'Fighting Ninth'* (Stroud: Amberley, 2014), pp.83–86.

Hale, also of the 'Fighting Ninth', had been absent from the battalion for two months, which he spent at Belem, recovering from the effects of a virulent fever. Upon his return at the end of the year he learnt that his colleagues

> …had been very comfortable the whole time that I had been away, having nothing but their own regimental duty to do; and also good provisions and very regular. But a short time after I joined the regiment, we received orders from Lord Wellington for a party of different trades, such as masons, carpenters, and miners, to go on a working party to Ciudad Rodrigo.[57]

There would be an early start to campaigning in 1812.

---

57 Hale, *Journal*, p.74.

3

1812

Ciudad Rodrigo

By the beginning of 1812, the initiative for any new campaign lay with Wellington, Napoleon's orders to Marmont having weakened the *maréchal*'s position to the point where it was impossible for him to act aggressively against the Allies. Wellington, in contrast, had positioned four of his divisions close to the border between Portugal and Castile and León, or, in the case of the Light Division, covering Ciudad Rodrigo. The 5th Division was posted in the rear of the rest of the army, still at Oliveira do Hospital, Midões and Travanca. Even more detached were Hill's troops in Estremadura, where they had continued to probe the positions of the Army of the South. Of particular concern was d'Erlon's IX corps, and there had already been an action when Hill worsted *Général de division* Jean-Baptiste Girard's division at Arroyomolinos on 28 October.

Wellington's primary objective for the forthcoming campaign was to take possession of the two border fortresses, Ciudad Rodrigo and Badajoz. Having suffered two setbacks at Badajoz the previous year, his immediate target was Ciudad Rodrigo, which he initially hoped to starve into submission. For this to succeed, he relied on the Light Division and Julian Sanchez's lancers to frustrate any French attempt to revictual the town. The governor of Salamanca, however, *Général de division* Paul Thiébault, managed to get a supply train, along with a new governor, *Général de brigade* Jean Léonard Barrié, into the town, the previous governor having been seized in a raid by Sanchez.

A revictualed town would obviously not be forced into surrender by pangs of hunger; and Barrié was a more determined opponent than his predecessor. Wellington accepted that there would have to be a regular siege, which he anticipated would take 25 to 30 days. The nearest four divisions were set to work making fascines and gabions, while a siege train had already been assembled at Almeida. Then Wellington issued a general order that called in the men with the skills needed for the actual siege. This would be laborious and potentially dangerous work, but there were still men from the 5th Division who chose, or were persuaded, to volunteer. In the 1848 General Service Medal Roll eight men from the six British battalions in the 5th Division claimed a bar for Ciudad Rodrigo.[1] All of these

---

1   TNA: WO 100/6: Military General Service Medal Roll, 20th to 43rd Foot.

survivors, incidentally, were in the 2/30th, but it is unlikely this was the only battalion that provided men for the working parties.

The general order of 3 January also called for the names of any officers disposed to act as assistant engineers. Among the volunteers was Lieutenant Percy Parke Nevill of the 2/30th, who 'became first employed to act as an assistant engineer, and was set to work in making gabions and fascines for the batteries', perhaps not what he had expected would be required of him.[2] According to the medal roll, he was joined by three officers of his own battalion, Lieutenants Andrew Baillie, Robert Smith and Lorraine White, and an officer from the 2/44th, Lieutenant Thomas Peacocke. Again, it may be assumed that others also volunteered their services but did not survive until 1848 to claim a General Service Medal

The investment of Ciudad Rodrigo was completed by 8 January. The 5th Division, meanwhile, remained in the same quarters. The men and the young officers, like Ensign John Carter of the 2/30th, were subject to regular drill, starting at 7:00 a.m. on cold winter mornings, while the senior and seasoned officers performed their normal duties. All the officers were then able to pursue a more leisurely social life. Indeed, Carter makes clear in his journal that he was very much involved in the lively, and sometimes drunken, conviviality of his battalion officers, which was unlikely to be very different from the way the officers of other battalions passed their leisure time.[3]

John Allen did not blame alcohol for his mishap on New Year's Day in the account he wrote for *The Royal Military Chronicle*, but it may well have played a part. He described how he

> ...went to dine with a friend at Galizes, a league from Oliverez de Hospital, and returned early, but was directed wrong by a Portuguese, and did not reach home till midnight: indeed was three hours finding my way out of a wood. At last saw a light, and, after a steeple hunt of two hours, found myself at Bruendelis, the quarters of the 4th regiment.

The experience had been made worse by the awareness that he was 'in a country abounding with wolves, and where it is not unusual for them to attack men, oxen, or horses, in mid-day.' Nor did his pleasant existence last much longer. The following day he was ordered to take all the division's sick and convalescents to Celorico. Once there, after a three-day march, he was given further responsibility for the sick who were already in Celorico, about a thousand men. This duty required him to make frequent visits to the hospitals, with all the attendant risk of infection. He would eventually be required to take a detachment to Ciudad Rodrigo to join their regiments, which would involve a long march across difficult country.[4]

Le Mesurier, according to a letter written to his family on 12 January, had come to the conclusion that an order to leave their present position, which everyone was anticipating, would not be issued, so they were unlikely to be involved in whatever was happening a

---

2   Percy Parke Nevill, *Some Recollections in the Life of Lieut.-Col. P.P. Nevill* (London: Cox & Wyman, 1864), p.10.
3   Gareth Glover (ed.), *Ensign John Carter's Journal 1812* (Huntingdon: Ken Trotman, 2006).
4   Allen, 'Journal', p.424.

74 WELLINGTON'S UNSUNG HEROES

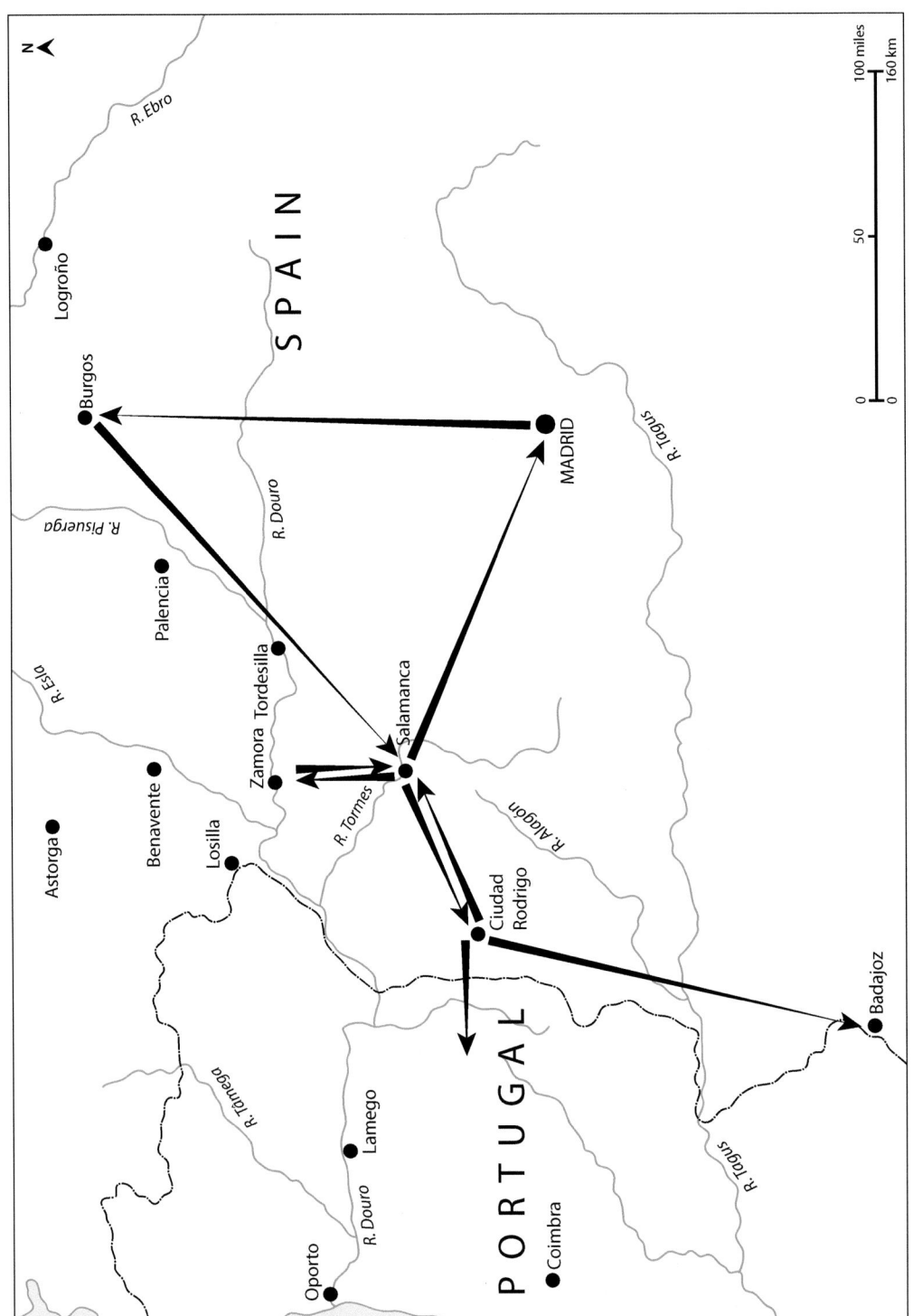

The 1812 Campaign.

hundred miles away at Ciudad Rodrigo. There were other matters of concern to an officer, however trivial:

> We have been making ourselves Comfortable in our Huts building Chimneys, etc: I am now writing by the light of a window of our own making. We cut holes in the Shutters & put oil'd paper in them. The Portuguese are not very partial to our improvements, not even of our Fire places. Whilst we were building a very elegant one in this place, the Landlord came in and did not appear greatly pleased. On our enquiring the cause, he said it was not the custom to have chimneys in their houses and that he would have the trouble of pulling it down when we were gone, or people would laugh at him for having two Kitchens.[5]

For Nevill, though, life was becoming more interesting.

> In a few days [after the investment] we carried a fortified convent which annoyed us, and our parallels were constructed with such good will that in a week we had made an advanced breaching-battery before the work on the hill, which we had already captured, and mounted our guns, from which we battered in a breach. Here we had twenty-two 24-pounders and a smaller battery on the left to breach a flank work destined for the Light Division to storm.[6]

The convent was San Francisco and the hill, the Teson redoubt that the Light Division had taken under cover of darkness on the night of the 8th. This pleasing progress suggested that Ciudad Rodrigo would fall well before the four weeks that Wellington had anticipated.

According to Carter it was after church parade on the 12th, the same date as Le Mesurier's letter, that the division learnt they would finally be on the march to Ciudad Rodrigo the following day. By the 15th they were at Guarda, which Carter, at least, was pleased to reach after 'a very long & fatiguing day, had not the weather been very fine, it would have knocked up one half of the men. We were prevented going over the mountains on account of the snow; Guarda hill was covered with ice that they found great difficulty in getting the baggage up.'[7] Two days later they were at Aldeia da Ponte, only to find the town full of dragoons which necessitated their marching another league and a half to Casillas de Flores. Carter and his messmate, Assistant Surgeon John Evans, 'felt very dry and hungry. We did not stomach the march further, we ran into town & bought some bread & wine, the wine was very good & put us in famous spirits.'[8] Presumably, this was the same wine which the previous day had left a private dead drunk. If that were not bad enough, he had also broken the cock of his firelock and vomited over the new clothing he had received only a few days before.

The first brigade seems to have been more fortunate. The 9th arrived at Albergaria on 17 January and then enjoyed a day's rest on the 18th, while the second brigade moved to within five leagues of Ciudad Rodrigo. The next day both brigades were on the march to Fuente

---

5   Greenwood (ed.), *Through Spain with Wellington*, pp.87–88.
6   Nevill, *Some Recollections*, pp.10–11.
7   Glover (ed.), *Ensign John Carter's*, p.12.
8   Glover (ed.), *Ensign John Carter's*, p.17.

Guinaldo and Carter, for one, was expecting that they would be required to take their turn in the trenches. By the 18th the sound of the guns at Ciudad Rodrigo could be clearly heard and Gomm also had some hope of action, although not in the trenches or even in a final assault. On the same day he wrote home:

> We are within twenty miles of the town, and hear the cannon distinctly. It has been incessant during the night and continued at intervals throughout the day… The 5th, 6th, and 7th Divisions have nothing to say to all this; they are taking too good care of us. We expect General Leith to join us this evening or to-morrow; and we hope, through his merits, to be brought forward, should Marshal Marmont get over the Gata with the intention of disturbing us.[9]

Marmont, at Valladolid, heard about the siege on the 14th, too late for him to intervene. Even Thiébault, at Salamanca, was unaware how close Ciudad Rodrigo was to falling into Allied hands.

At Fuente Guinaldo the 5th Division received the news that the town had been taken the previous evening, as Nevill recalled:

> On the 19th both breaches were ready. The great breach in our front was immediately stormed and taken by the 3rd Division and General Pack; whilst the Light Division stormed the small breach on the left. Both were gallantly taken, but we unfortunately lost one of the best officers of our army – General Crawford, commanding the Light Division. General Mackinnon and several men were blown up by a mine on entering the great breach; but our loss, though heavy, was not so very great, considering the result.[10]

Nevill, of course, was an eye-witness to the storm, and to the disorder that followed, although he made no reference to it in his memoirs. Le Mesurier, however, wrote a week later that, although the sacking of the town 'will certainly add no credit to those who had the management of the business…This the Inhabitants, however, deserved in some degree, for Don Carlos de Hispania warned them before the French entered this place that it would be given up to the Soldiers when retaken, if the Inhabitants remained in it.'[11] There was some suspicion that many of the inhabitants favoured the French, which seems to be confirmed by their willingness to stay in the town despite the threat of an Allied assault.

As the 5th Division approached the town, they encountered 'the Light Division which we met returning from the town loaded with plunder of every description. When we got within two miles of the town we met about 1600 French prisoners.'[12] The sight that confronted those who ventured into the town was a distressing one, as Hale remembered:

---

9   Carr-Gomm (ed.), *Letters and Journals*, vol.I, p.244.
10 Nevill, *Some Recollections*, p.11.
11 Greenwood (ed.), *Through Spain with Wellington*, p.91.
12 Glover (ed.), *Ensign John Carter's*, pp.17–18.

> ...it was a most miserable place to behold, for the enemy's dead were lying about in all directions, and the buildings beat to pieces by our cannon shot in a frightful manner, and several houses were then on fire, in consequence of which, we were immediately set to work to extinguish the fire, and fortunately, by much exertion, we got the upper hand of it in a short time. The next thing that was thought most necessary for us to do, was to put the dead bodies under ground.[13]

Le Mesurier was most disturbed by the effect of the magazines blowing up.

> Some unfortunate wretches were buried under the Ruins and a few of them taken up alive, with their Faces burnt, Arms and Legs broken. Immediately on our arrival, going round a corner, I was almost horror struck at the scene that discovered itself – about Twenty Men laying dead, Five or Six Wounded that had not yet been taken to the Hospital, & a house on fire from a mine which had blown up.

He added later in this letter of the 26 January, 'Such, my Dear Mother, are the scenes we have witnessed this last week. You may then judge how requisite it is to have the common feelings blunted to bare these Scenes. I must confess mine are so far blunted that I have borne them like a Philosopher.'[14]

The Pioneers

The 5th Division was now given the laborious task of restoring Ciudad Rodrigo to a defensible state, ready for a Spanish garrison to occupy it. Gomm sardonically wrote to his sister: 'We are promised that our labours in the army shall not continue long. If we display as much industry in repairing as others have shown vigour in destroying, we shall do well.' He added, somewhat optimistically, 'I hope the Division next on the list will soon take the spade and shovel out of our hands, although I fear there is little chance of more interesting employment at present.'[15]

In the letter referenced above, Le Mesurier explained why the 5th Division had been given a particular nickname: 'We have acquired the most honourable name of Pioneers to the Army, having always been employed in cleaning Quarters, etc: in the rear of the Army. I am now in hopes there may be an end put to that kind of work.'[16]

There was one sobering distraction from all this hard labour, the funeral of Major General Crauford on 25 January, the day after he finally died from the wound he had received during the assault.

> General Crauford was buried, the procession was grand, our division opened file and rest[ed] on their arms whilst the funeral past betwixt us. The 52nd, 95th Regiments & caçadores marched in front, in the rear came the corpse followed by

---

13   Hale, *Journal*, p.76.
14   Greenwood (ed.), *Through Spain with Wellington*, pp.91–92.
15   Carr-Gomm (ed.), *Letters and Journals*, vol.I, p.245.
16   Greenwood (ed.), *Through Spain with Wellington*, p.92.

Lord W, Marshal B & several other great men, their staff followed. He was buried at the foot of the lesser breach which he himself wanted. Something moved the colonel and he ordered the ensigns to the colours on the march…[17]

A duty which certainly did not please Ensign Carter.

The rest of the army remained around Ciudad Rodrigo, while the 5th Division toiled to repair breaches, fill in trenches and construct new works to prevent an enemy from approaching the town by the Upper Teson. Their efforts were not without reward, however. By orders of the 29th the officers received four shillings a day and the men, 8d, which must have been some compensation for finding themselves general cleaners to the army. Their progress was noted by Allen when he finally rejoined the division on the 26th. From the outside the town did not look as if it had so lately sustained a siege and an assault. He was particularly struck by how little damage the cathedral had suffered, having only been grazed by some few balls, despite being close to the greater breach. Closer to the breaches there were clearer signs of 'hot work, as the blood and mangled remains of bodies sufficiently evinced. I counted above seventy French caps of the infantry in less than fifty yards.' This suggests that although Hale might have laconically referred to the need to bury the dead, the division did not regard it as their duty to clean the place of their remains. Allen also reported that 'The inhabitants took a very active part, and deserved to have suffered more severely.'[18]

Not that the 5th Division, for all their efforts, escaped without censure from Wellington. In a general order of 16 February, by which time he was focusing on Badajoz, he took them to task because he had

> …frequently had occasion to notice the misconduct of the soldiers in destroying the houses and other buildings in or near which they may be quartered, by burning, as firewood, the beams and other timbers of which they are built, to the great inconvenience of themselves, of the soldiers of other regiments, and of service in general, and to the injury of the property of the inhabitants of the country.
>
> The Commander of the Forces is concerned to have to observe that the regiments in the ----- division of infantry have been frequently guilty of this practice. They burnt the town of Alcoentre in December 1810; they destroyed the cantonments of the 3rd Division at Aldea da Ponte when the army were closed up in November, 1811; and they have lately burnt the timbers in the roof of the convent of S. Francisco to the great inconvenience of the service.

Interestingly, none of these conflagrations are mentioned in the various letters, journals and memoirs.

Wellington did then concede that the 5th Division was not alone in this, since 'the Commander of the Forces has received complaints of the conduct of the British soldiers on this subject from all parts of the country.' He placed the blame firmly of the non-commissioned officers, for it was

---

17 Glover (ed.), *Ensign John Carter's*, p.18.
18 Allen, 'Journal', *The Royal Military Chronicle*, May 1812, pp.42–43.

> ...impossible that a soldier, or any number of soldiers, can take down the large beams of the roof of a convent, or even of a house, and burn them, without the knowledge of the non-commissioned officers of their companies, and even of the officers, if the latter do their duty, and attend to their men as they ought, not upon the parade only, but in their quarters, at various hours of the day and night.[19]

Henceforth, he decreed, troops guilty of such depredations would have to pay for the repairs.

Whatever the feelings of the division in response to this reproof, there was one event which more than made up for having provoked Wellington's displeasure and that was the return of Major General Leith. John Allen had been the first to encounter him on the way to Ciudad Rodrigo.

> Just descending the side of a mountain, and my detachment straggling more than they had done during the day, I observed the approach of a general officer, with his orderly and retinue, and, to my great surprise, found that it was General Leith, the general of my division, and, of course, I fully expected to be goosed, but, with all the affability and goodness that mark a really great man, after several enquiries, and my informing him that I had divided a two days march into three, I was gratified by his expressing his approbation... With the 5th Division the arrival of General Leith will be greeted as a most auspicious omen, as it may lead to the reaping of some laurels in the ensuing campaign.[20]

This hope was soon to be fulfilled, but even before the arrival of the orders that would set the 5th Division on the road to Badajoz it became clear that when Leith was present a different spirit infused both men and officers alike. Gomm commented that Leith was 'quite renovated, and, if I may use the expression, more himself that ever.'[21] The same comment could be made about the division he commanded. Le Mesurier, for one, noted that 'Genl Leith has joined us and taken command of the Division to the great satisfaction of all the Division. We are in expectation of moving every minute.' He and his fellow officers had even more reason to be pleased.

> We have been particularly gay lately. Three or four days ago Genl Leith gave a Ball & Masquarade at which, being a Curious Bird, I went. Lord Wellington & the Prince of Orange were there and appeared to enjoy the sport very much. Refreshments were very scares [sic] and an Uglier collection of Ladies I never saw. Partners were not to be had except for the Staff Gentlemen, therefore I was obliged to perch on a Chair and be a looker-on...[22]

This was followed by another ball on Shrove Tuesday, given by de España, who was now governor of Ciudad Rodrigo.

---

19 2nd Duke of Wellington (ed.), *Supplementary Despatches, Correspondence and Memoranda of Field Marshal Arthur, Duke of Wellington K.G. Peninsula 1810-1813* (London: John Murray, 1860), vol.VII, p.294.
20 Allen, 'Journal', p.39.
21 Carr-Gomm (ed.), *Letters and Journals*, vol.I, p.248.
22 Greenwood (ed.), *Through Spain with Wellington*, pp.92, 95.

Badajoz

While Wellington remained in the vicinity of Ciudad Rodrigo with all but one of his eight divisions to hand, Marmont was left to anticipate the next Allied move. Initially, he expected Salamanca to come under threat before deciding that Badajoz was a more likely objective. Whatever proved to be the target, however, Marmont had problems of his own, emanating from Napoleon's determination to control affairs in the Peninsula from Paris. Not only was the *maréchal* ordered to send 6,000 men to the Army of the North; he was also instructed to invade Portugal, should Wellington make a move that threatened the south of Spain. The Emperor reasoned that such a threat to his supply lines would force Wellington to retrace his steps but Marmont knew that no French army could survive long in Portugal

Badajoz was indeed the Allies' next target, as already noted, although this was not immediately evident to Marmont. By early February powder and shot were being sent up from Oporto and instructions had been issued for the transportation of howitzers from Almeida to the Portuguese border further south, while 24-pounders would be brought upstream from Oporto; but the presence of seven divisions on the border effectively masked these preparations for yet another siege.

Wellington began to move his divisions south from the middle of February, but again, with the 5th Division so clearly in possession of Ciudad Rodrigo, these movements were not obvious to the French. As early as 10 February Gomm wrote home:

> Badajos the proud is already upon the horizon in our imaginations, and will probably soon be so in our senses. The battering train is on the move, part from this quarter, and part, at the moment sliding up the Tagus to Abrantes. The army is ready. Badajos, besieged for the third time, will hardly withstand the insolence of our attack, so lately crowned with complete and rapid success; and its impetuosity will be increased by recollection of the double disappointment it has already experienced before her own wall.

Gomm believed that the previous failures occurred because the attempts were 'clumsily carried on'. As a result, the engineers 'worked here as if they had a character to retrieve. They had better continue in this humour'. There was one other matter than concerned him, however.

> I had rather have nothing to say to the trenches. I shall be better pleased if it falls to our lot to compose part of the covering army. Soult is a saucy fellow, and will certainly come down from Seville. I have already told you General Leith is with us. I shall be disappointed if you do not find us in some of these matters. Our work here will soon be completed and part of the Spanish will be here tomorrow.[23]

Castaños had already arrived and received approval from Gomm, despite what he identified as the British requirement 'for heroes and thunderbolts of war', which Castaños certainly

---

23 Carr-Gomm (ed.), *Letters and Journals*, vol.I, pp.249–251.

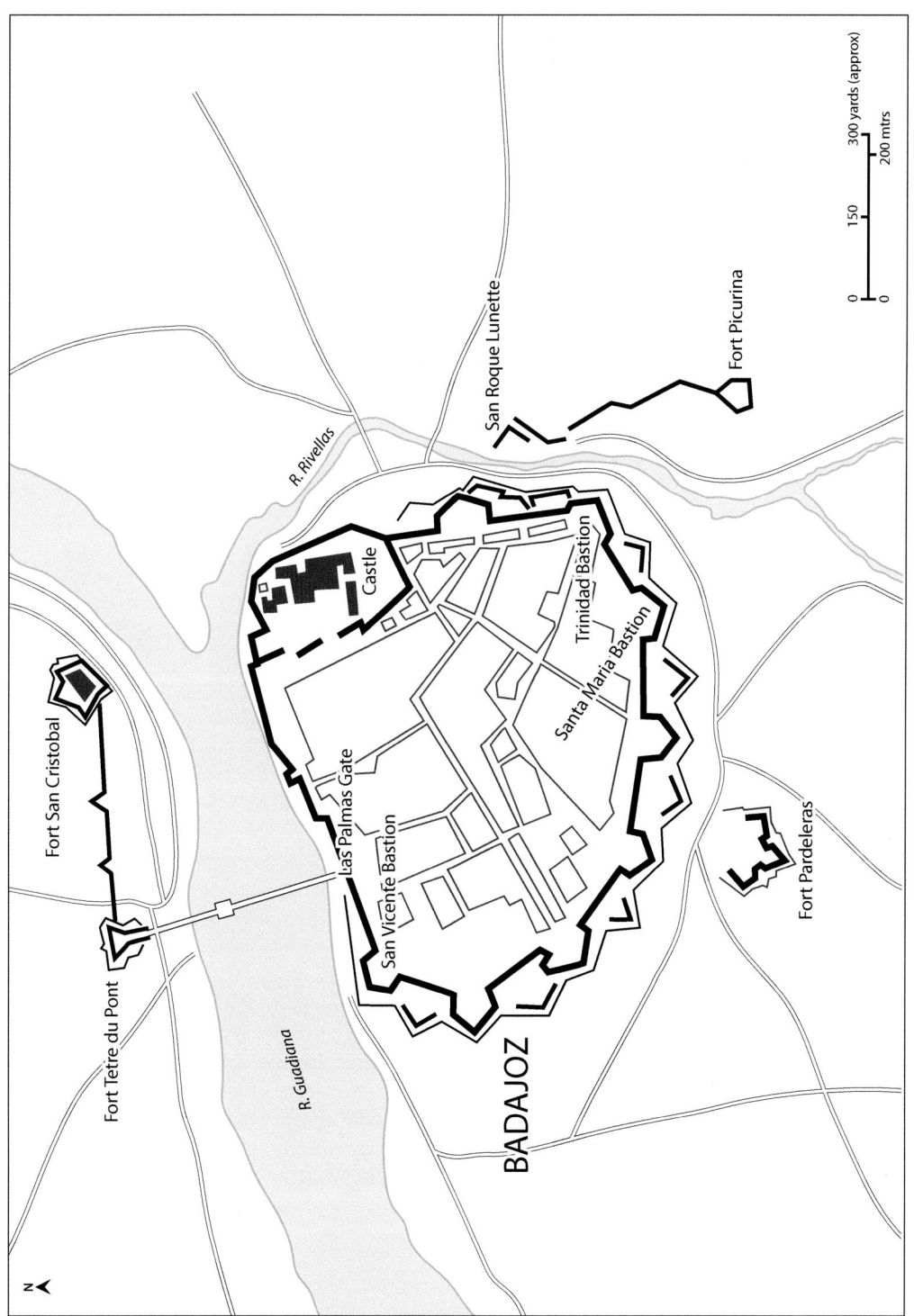

Badajoz.

was not. But he had other virtues, the most important being that he was 'friendly to the English, not only from principle, but evidently from inclination.' Gomm made clear that in his opinion too many British officers did not treat the Spanish with due respect. In contrast, 'General Leith is certainly the very best man in the world to act the part that is required of him on this occasion: but I declare that I have never seen the Spaniards other than conciliating when we ourselves have known how to behave.'[24]

Once the Spanish had arrived to garrison Ciudad Rodrigo, the 5th Division was able to march to Badajoz. Departing on the 9th and 10th,

> ...we made regular stages and took up our quarters in the different towns and villages every night, taking our route, the first day to Aurela, next to Calagas, and so on to St Vincent, and then to Castle Branco, (which is a large town), and from thence to Vila Velha, and crossed the river Tagus. Near that place a floating bridge was made by our engineers, for there was no established bridge near that place. From thence to Niza, and halted there two nights, and from there to Portalegre, which is a large town, from there to Arronches, and next to Campo Maior, which is a small garrison town just on the borders of Portugal.'[25]

This was a distance of over 300 miles, but the route was well-known and well-prepared for the reception of Allied soldiers.

The division spent a week in and around Campo Maior, where torrential rain eventually gave way to sunshine. They were still about 12 miles from Badajoz, which could be seen

> ...very plain... but sometimes the town was almost hid in a cloud of smoke that ascended from the enemy's guns, for they kept up almost a continual fire, with shot and shells, on our working parties from morning till night, by which many were killed and wounded; and, likewise, a great quantity of our works was destroyed, some days, more than we could put together in a whole night.[26]

Hale, who wrote the above and outlined the route, was obviously not involved in the siege at this stage and may well, like Gomm, have been pleased to find himself merely a spectator. In a letter to his sister on 26 March, Gomm updated her on the wider situation. The siege

> ...goes on as well as it possibly can, and with every prospect of ultimate success. Yesterday morning our batteries opened upon one of the principal outworks of the place, and it was in our possession by the evening. The main attack is carried on against the defences on the left bank of the Guadiana, three divisions of the army, the 3rd, 4th and Light, are encamped before the town. General Hill has pushed on his advance as far as Almaraz and Merida. General Graham, with the 6th, 1st, and 7th Divisions, is occupying Salvatierra, Villa Franca, etc. The Guards are at Zafra. Our share of the business is to occupy the attention of the garrison as much as

---

24 Carr-Gomm (ed.), *Letters and Journals*, vol.I, p.251.
25 Hale, *Journal*, p.77.
26 Hale, *Journal*, p.78.

possible on the right bank of the river. For this purpose we made a close reconnaissance of San Cristoval, and the redoubt on this side, the day before yesterday, and we have since closely invested them. Part only of the division is employed in this service, and the remainder in this town [Campo Maior] … Not only the Guadiana, but the smaller rivers, have been so swollen by the rains that our communication with the camp has hitherto been very circuitous. I hope we shall be able immediately to become more familiar with it. We know from the best authority in the world that the place is ill supplied with ammunition.

So late as the 20th Marmont was idle at Salamanca. Soult can do nothing without him for the relief of the town. It must fall shortly…

6 o'clock evening – We have just received the authentic account of the Picurina Fort, the work I have already spoken about, having been carried by storm last night, with some loss on our side, and considerable loss on that of the French. We shall establish our batteries here immediately, and breach the main wall, I hope, in the course of a very few days. The cannonade continues steadily. On our side we are going to raise a redoubt in front of the Fort Mon Coeur, to engage the attention of this and St Cristoval still more clearly.[27]

To elaborate on the information that Gomm gave his sister, Wellington intended that Hill's and Graham's troops, as covering forces, would deal with any advance by Soult and Marmont. Furthermore, the maverick Spanish general, Francisco Ballesteros, would threaten Seville and thus deter Soult from moving to the relief of Badajoz. What might be termed the siege army was at Elvas by 13 March. Two boats were then moored across the Guadiana to create a flying bridge before the engineers constructed a pontoon bridge. This allowed the materiel for the siege to be brought across the river. On the 16th, the 3rd and 4th Divisions crossed to invest Badajoz under the direction of Marshal Beresford. The next day they were joined by the Light Division. As well as the 5th Division, the independent Portuguese brigades of Pack and Brigadier General Thomas Bradford and Major General George Anson's cavalry brigade were still to come up.

Badajoz was held by a garrison no more than 5,000 strong under the command of *Général de brigade* Armand Philippon, who was once again depending on the intervention of Soult. He had also written to Marmont, in anticipation that he would intervene before the garrison's supplies ran out. He had calculated that he had 25 days of ammunition and 30 to 40 days of food. He also instructed the inhabitants to leave the town unless they had their own food supplies. Philippon had also been repairing and strengthening his defences, including flooding the Rivillas stream in front of the La Trinidad, San Pedro and San Antonio bastions, strengthening the ravelin in front of the four bastions from San Vincente to San Juan and improving the defences of the Pardeleras outwork. As the siege progressed, he used his guns at San Cristoval, on the opposite bank of the river, to enfilade the besiegers.

This was the reason for the reconnaissance of San Cristobal referred to by Gomm. The whole Division was then brought forward ready to invest San Cristobal and thus complete the encirclement of the town. Gomm informed his brother, however, that though they were

---

27   Carr-Gomm (ed.), *Letters and Journals*, vol.I, pp.255–256.

first employed in drawing the enemy's attention to the right bank of the Guadiana while the main attack was continuing on the left, this diversionary tactic failed to convince the French that San Cristobal was a target. Before the breaching batteries opened fire, therefore, they were brought across the river and took up their bivouac about a league from the town, on the Valverde road.[28]

The eventual assault was to focus on the Santa Maria and La Trinidad bastions and the stretch of wall between them. Taking the Picurina fort had been a preparatory step because 'the counterguard in front of the right face of the bastion of La Trinidad being left in an unfinished state, the main scarp of the bastion might be sufficiently low down from the hill on which Fort Picurina stands, to be breached from thence.'[29] Within days of the batteries opening fire, there was a breach wide enough for three men to pass through. Inevitably, the French worked to repair the damage under cover of darkness, but it was also noticeable that their fire was slackening, as supplies of gunpowder ran low. Then came news of Soult's advance, meaning that time was no longer with the Allies. The *Maréchal* had forced Ballesteros to withdraw, and he now obliged Graham to do the same. It was little consolation to know that Marmont, rather than proving a threat from the north, had obeyed Napoleon's orders and on 30 March had led a short-lived foray into Portugal. By 5 April, however, the breaches were judged practicable. All was set for the assault.

The 5th Division's part in the fall of Badajoz was destined to extend beyond their activities on the right bank. Yet some members of the division had been involved from the beginning of the siege. As at Ciudad Rodrigo, Wellington had called for volunteers, both officers to act as assistant engineers and other ranks to serve as artificers. General orders issued on 22, 26 and 27 March name all the officers who had been appointed as assistant engineers, and the lists include Lieutenants O'Neil and Rea of the 3/1st, Lieutenant Ross Lewin of the 1/9th, Lieutenant Nevill of the 2/30th and Ensign Stanley of the 2/44th. As for how many men may have served as artificers, this number is difficult to ascertain as there is no list of them and, unlike Ciudad Rodrigo, it is impossible to differentiate between artificers and those involved in the assault.

Young Lieutenant Nevill had obviously enjoyed his experiences at Ciudad Rodrigo sufficiently to volunteer again. Of course, he could have been thinking of that issue which was present in every young officer's mind, promotion. He tells us that he

> …found himself under orders to act as assistant-engineer, and attached to a brigade for that purpose.
>
> We commenced our parallels on the 17th of March, and continued them under torrents of rain, which deluged the trenches, the camp, and everything about us. This weather continued several days, and we were often above our knees in water; but our men worked with an ardour beyond all praise – the Royal Engineer officers and their assistants had only to tell them what to do, and it was done.
>
> At length the weather became fine and warm, which soon enabled us to clear the trenches of water, and we were able to get up some batteries to keep down the

---

28   Carr-Gomm (ed.), *Letters and Journals*, vol.I, p.261.
29   John T. Jones, *Journals of Sieges Carried on by the Army under the Duke of Wellington in Spain between the Years 1811 and 1814* (London: T. Egerton, 1827), vol.I, p.153.

enemy's fire, which galled us very much, particularly from the Picurina and the ravelin of San Roque. Both of those advanced works were stormed in very gallant style, which enabled us to advance our parallels, and at length to establish our breaching-batteries. We had the guns used at Ciudad Rodrigo and some others, and when all was ready opened fire on the bastion of La Trinidad and curtain of St. Maria, and on the breaches becoming practicable they were ordered to be stormed...[30]

The attack was originally intended to take place on the night of 5 April but was delayed in order to counteract French defensive activity; the construction of an inner entrenchment and strengthening of the breaches. During the night of the 5th the guns were directed at what the Spanish reported was a weak point in the curtain wall between the two bastions. The original orders had intended an attack at 7:30 p.m., but this was changed to 10:00 p.m. because, according to Wellington's own memorandum, the arrangements required some delay. Three points were to be attacked: 'the castle, the face of the bastion of La Trinidad, and the flank of the bastion of Sta Maria. The attack on the castle to be by escalade; that of the two bastions, by storm of the breaches.' The 3rd Division was to escalade while the 4th and Light Divisions would storm La Trinidad and the flank of Santa Maria.

These basic orders were then amplified with more precise details. For the 3rd Division, a significant instruction required that 'The troops for this attack must have all the long ladders in the engineers' park, and six of the lengths of the engineers' ladders. They must be attended by 12 carpenters with axes, and six miners with crow-bars &c.'

Finally, there were orders for the 5th Division.

> The 5th Divisions must be formed, one brigade on the ground occupied by the 48th regiment [of the fourth Division]; one brigade on the Sierra del Viente; and one brigade in the low ground extending to the Guadiana, now occupied by the piquets of the Light division.
>
> The piquets of the brigades on the Sierra del Viento, and that in the low ground towards the Guadiana, should endeavour to alarm the enemy during the attack by firing at the Pardeleras, and at the men in the covered-way of the works towards the Guadiana.
>
> In other words, the division would once more serve a diversionary purpose; they would have no share in the glory of the night, if glory there were. This memorandum, however, contains an amendment which demonstrates Leith's power of persuasion.
>
> A plan has been settled with Lieut-General Leith for an attempt to be made to escalade the bastion of San Vincente, or the curtain between that bastion and the bridge, if circumstances should permit. The commanding officer of the Light division will attend to this.[31]

---

30   Nevill, *Some Recollections*, pp.12–13.
31   Gurwood (ed.), *Dispatches*, vol.IX, pp.32–37.

Escalade and into the Town

Possibly implicit in the change of orders was Leith's irritation that once again his division was being denied the opportunity to play a significant part in a forthcoming action. And if the intention was to keep French troops away from the other points of attack, then an escalade would prove even more effective than a mere display. There was further cause for annoyance, however. The attack on the castle had originally been intended as another diversionary tactic, but Picton's insistence led to it being converted into a real attack. Leith and Picton had been at odds since Buçaco, as already discussed, and there was also a clash of personality, the firebrand Welshman with his command of scatological language versus the quietly spoken Scotsman.

The memorandum concludes with what would prove an ironic request:

> The Commander of the Forces particularly requests the General Officers commanding divisions and brigades, and the Commanding Officers of regiments, and the Officers commanding companies, to impress upon their men the necessity of their keeping together and formed as a military body after the storm, and during the night. Not only the success of the operation, and the honor of the army, but their own individual safety, depend upon their being in a situation to repel any attack by the enemy, and to overcome all resistance which they may be inclined to make, till the garrison are completely subdued.

It is clear from what happened later that Leith had already decided upon a real attack, circumstances permitting. Major General George Walker's second brigade would ascend the ladders, with the 2/38th from Hay's brigade in support. The other two battalions of the first brigade would be onlookers, with the 1/9th serving as Wellington's bodyguard or, as Le Mesurier explained, they would 'take pot shots at the enemy as a diversion.'[32]

The atmosphere as the Allied troops waited for the commencement of the assault is effectively conveyed by William Napier, himself a participant:

> The night was dry but clouded, the air thick with watery exhalations from the rivers, the ramparts, and the trenches unusually still; yet a low murmur pervaded the latter, and in the former, lights were seen to flit here and there, while the deep voices of the sentinels at times proclaimed, that all was well in Badajos. The French, confiding in Philippon's direful skill, watched, from their left station, the approach of enemies, whom they had twice before baffled, and now hoped to drive a third time blasted and ruined from the walls; the British, standing in deep columns, were as eager to meet that fiery destruction as the others were to pour it down; and both were alike terrible for their strength, their discipline, and the passions awakened in their resolute hearts.[33]

---

32 Greenwood (ed.), *Through Spain with Wellington*, p.100.
33 W.F.P. Napier, *History of the War in the Peninsula and in the South of France* (London: Constable, 1993), vol.IV, p.419.

The 30th Foot escalading the San Vincente bastion.

Although the attack had been timed to commence at 10:00 p.m., as a result of several mishaps the attack on the castle was launched half an hour early, and at San Vincente, an hour late. In the case of the 3rd Division their advance was discovered by the light of burning carcasses, while Leith's troops were delayed when 'the officer, conducting the party with scaling-ladders from the engineers' park to the bivouac of the 5th Division, lost his way.'[34] This may have been First Lieutenant Thomas Lascelles, the engineer officer attached to the division (who would be the first casualty when he fell into the ditch while directing the troops), Lieutenant Nevill, now attached to Walker's brigade, or an officer of the 4th, although none from the regiment is named in the list of volunteers.

Le Mesurier, as a spectator, could only wonder at the sight he beheld from the high ground at Sierra del Vienta as the assault began in earnest.

> ...the description of the sight then, it is beyond my power to give you. C'etois un beau terrible, the light Balls, Shells, Guns, musquetry, all at the same time playing on the Town, was almost Beautiful, but the Idea of the Heroes that fell during the time was dreadful. Our Regt:, with the Royals, was kept as a kind of reserve, in case anything happened. Lord Wellington was close to us the whole night, so that we had early intelligence of all that passed. The pleasing intelligence that Genl: Picton

---

34   Leith Hay, *A Narrative*, vol.I, p.293.

had got into the castle with his Division was counterbalanced in some degree on hearing that the assault at the Breaches had failed.[35]

Although the 3rd Division had gained possession of the castle after a hard struggle, they could go no further.

> To form and march down on the rear of the force defending the breaches, was immediately determined upon; but it was discovered that the enemy had built up or barricaded the gates in so substantial a manner, as to prevent their being forced, without considerable delay, and the assistance of other implements for removing the obstructions than those in possession of the 3d division. General Picton consequently established the troops under his orders in the captured portion of the fortress, and waited for daybreak.[36]

An officer in the 4th Foot, Captain Peter Bowlby, actually described this as a defeat, but he was undoubtedly biased.[37]

In his account, Leith Hay had already described the brave, increasingly desperate and ultimately hopeless attempts of the 4th and Light Divisions to overcome the equally brave and determined resistance of the defenders. He then concentrated on the actions of the 5th Division, in which he played an active part. After his reference to the delay occasioned by the non-appearance of the ladders, he continued:

> General Leith … had the mortification of being delayed until past eleven o'clock, before he could move to carry the escalade of the bastion of San Vincente into execution. During the interval he attracted the enemy's attention by a false attack on the Pardeleras outwork. The 8th Portuguese caçadores, employed on this service, kept up a galling and incessant fire from the very glacis of the work itself. At length, the ladders having been delivered to the division, the columns moved forwards towards the northwest angle of the place. General Leith, having received instructions to escalade the bastion of San Vincente with one brigade, and to support the attack with the other regiments of his division, ordered General Walker, with the 4th, 30th, and 44th, to mount the wall, the difficulty of which service may be estimated, when it is explained, that the face of the bastion had an escarpe thirty-one feet six inches in height, flanked by artillery – that the palisades of the covered way were entire, – the counterscarp wall nearly twelve feet deep, and in the ditch, a cunette, five feet six inches in depth, by six feet six inches in breadth, had been excavated. The troops were discovered when on the glacis [because they were suddenly flooded by moonlight], and a heavy fire opened upon them before they had forced the barrier gate, but nothing could check the progress of General Walker and the battalions under his orders, until they reached the lofty wall, at the summit of which the enemy, aware of their intentions, and fully prepared, were extended, deliberately and obstinately to resist men ascending singly,

---

35 Greenwood (ed.), *Through Spain with Wellington*, pp.100–101.
36 Leith Hay, *A Narrative*, vol.I, p.293.
37 Glover, Gareth (ed.), *The Napoleonic Archive Volume I: British Line Infantry Memoirs* (Huntingdon: Ken Trotman Publishing, 2021), p.237)

and on ladders upwards of thirty feet high. This does not appear the description of a situation where defence would be difficult, or entrance practicable to ordinary men. At first, few of the ladders could be placed, some of them, after being raised, were thrown from the walls back into the ditch. Others, constructed of green wood, opened and separated, or were not of sufficient length, consequently the troops forced in by three or four only of the number originally appropriated to the service; but force in they did, and General Walker formed his brigade on the ramparts. He had been instructed to move forward, and by making a circuit of the interior of the works, to come in the rear of the enemy's troops defending the breaches.

There are no means of destruction more alarming in the contemplation of mankind than mines, nor any warlike engine or preparation calculated to have the same appalling ideal effect on the minds of the soldiery. There is also the darkness of night, and the treading hostile ground, supposed to have been prepared for every species of obstruction, something so uncertain, that it is no wonder at, nor considered inconsistent with their general bearing, that, under such circumstances, the bravest troops should be seized with irresolution from the most trivial causes. The flame of a port-fire struck a momentary terror into the minds of the men, that artillery, musketry, walls, and the bayonets of French infantry, had failed to daunt. Part of General Walker's brigade, mistaking this appearance for the forerunner of the explosion of a mine, broke, and were bayoneted back to the spot where they had previously surmounted difficulties which could be no discredit in failing to overcome. Fortunately, General Leith had advanced part of the right brigade of his division in support of that already in the town. The second battalion of the 38th regiment, under Colonel Nugent, had ascended, and were formed on the ramparts when the circumstances above occurred, that corps, being prepared, received the pursuing enemy with a volley and bayonet charge that speedily terminated all contest. In the course of this short reverse, General Walker was dangerously wounded, and Lieutenant-Colonel Grey, of the 30th regiment, a very gallant officer, died in consequence of profuse bleeding, before assistance could be procured.[38]

Once Leith was sure his troops were in possession of the ramparts, regimental tradition ascribing to the 2/44th the honour of being the first to plant their colours, he sent a message to Wellington that the 5th Division were in the town. This enabled the 4th and Light Divisions to return to and carry the breaches, where the defenders were also being attacked from the rear. According to Bowlby, the 4th Foot, having led the brigade in the storming, formed the principal force in the great square and their bugles, particularly one bugler of the name of Cox who had tremendous lungs, contributed much to the retreat of the French.'[39] Interestingly, the 44th claimed it was one of their buglers, 18-year-old Muchian, who sounded the advance.[40] Whatever the truth, there could be no doubting that the 5th Division were the first troops into the town.

---

38 Leith Hay, *A Narrative*, vol.I, pp.293–296.
39 Glover (ed.), *The Napoleonic Archive Volume 1*, p.237.
40 Thomas Carter, *Historical Records of the Forty-Fourth or the East Essex Regiment* (Chatham: Gale & Polden, 1887), p.61.

It is no surprise, therefore, that both Gomm and Leith Hay believed the escalade at San Vincente was crucial to the fall of Badajoz. As the former wrote to his brother on the 15th April:

> ...we were admitted to so much more agreeable a share in this enterprise than in most of those that have been lately undertaken, and the part we played proved to be of so much more consequence to the result than was at first imagined it could have been, that our vanity leads us to trumpet our exploits to the world with all their circumstances.

He then explained the practical difficulties which he believed to be more challenging of themselves than those encountered at the castle, although he conceded that San Vincente had not been so strongly defended, in terms of manpower, as the other defences. Nevertheless,

> The rampart at the point was surrounded by a regular ditch, into which there was no descent but with the assistance of the ladders we carried, and the rampart itself nearly 30 ft. high, with *revetement*. Our 24 ft. ladders, therefore, of which we were supplied about twenty, had nearly played us a trick; but the parapet above the cordon was climbable on such an occasion to such as were not interfered with from above. It was some time before we could establish our footing upon the rampart, but, through General Walker's exertions, it was at length effected, and we had thrown, or rather lifted, four regiments into the town before midnight.[41]

This alone, in Gomm's opinion, led to the breaches being abandoned by the enemy, and the governor surrendering. Leith Hay posited that 'After considering the various events of this most important night, and comparing the periods at which it is authenticated that the different services were performed, it appears consistent with truth to arrive at the following conclusions.

> In the first place, had Lord Wellington alone relied upon the ordinary mode of assault, that of storming the breaches, the town would not have been taken. Had General Leith received the ladders, and escaladed soon after 10 o'clock as was intended, he would have been equally successful, and have saved the divisions contending for entrance at the breaches, upwards of an hour of continued and tremendous loss. Had he not escaladed at all, Badajos must have fallen in consequence of the castle being caried by the 3d division, but not until the following day, when the enemy might have given further trouble. It was consequently the escalade of the bastion of San Vincente that occasioned the immediate reduction of the fortress.[42]

Gomm and Leith Hay were obviously eager to sing the praises of the division to which they were attached. It is interesting, therefore, to look at the opinion of a neutral observer who

---

41 Carr-Gomm (ed.), *Letters and Journals*, vol.I, pp.261–262.
42 Leith Hay, *A Narrative*, vol.I, pp.297–298.

was himself involved in the siege, and who came to a similar conclusion, while still giving due respect to the other three divisions involved in the assault. In his journal John Jones R.E. wondered whether future generations would credit the events that led to the fall of Badajoz, 'particularly the escalade directed by General Leith…not as being an undertaking generally to be followed, but marking what it is possible for brave men to effect.'[43]

Although the assault was successful, the butcher's bill was high. In the official return for the siege and assault of killed, wounded and missing, The totals, including Portuguese casualties, were 1,035 killed, 3,787 wounded and 63 missing. Oman broke these down as 521 casualties in the 3rd Division, 925 in the 4th Division, 536 in the 5th Division and 919 in the Light Division, while the Portuguese suffered 730 losses. A further 47 were taken by the general staff, artillery and engineers, and 35 by the detached Brunswick Oels companies.[44] Obviously, these figures did not allow for those who subsequently died of wounds. It is no surprise that the 4th and Light Divisions at the breaches took the highest casualties. It is interesting, however, to compare the 3rd and 5th Divisions, since they were both engaged in an escalade. They are superficially similar, but it is significant that the 3rd Division sent eight British battalions up the ladders and all eight battalions took casualties, while the 5th Division sent only four, thus suggesting a higher casualty rate per capita. Indeed, the 1/4th suffered more losses (230) than all but one of the 4th Division's four battalions and all but two of the Light Division's four battalions, but they were the first up the ladders.

Gomm and his family were friends of Walker, and a letter of 7 April informed them of the general's condition:

> Poor General Walker, I fear I must add, dangerously wounded. Yet I do not, I pray, think there is no room for hope. I saw him an hour ago, easier than he had been, and from the beginning he has been in good spirits… A musket shot has entered his chest, and may possibly have affected the lungs, but it is thought very slightly. He has besides bayonet wounds about him which are none of them serious.[45]

Although none of these later wounds was life-threatening, they occurred after Walker had fallen, as the defenders sought to rob him of his epaulettes and rifle his pockets. He was saved by a French soldier who loaded his musket and, and instead of putting paid to Walker's existence, held off his fellow soldiers. Then he helped one of the British soldiers carry him to safety. Walker had made the mason's sign and that had saved him.

Captain James Macarthy of the 50th, and formerly with the 30th, shared lodgings with Wallker as they both recovered from their wounds. He later described Walker's as 'of a most extraordinarily strange nature – a musket shot cut him across his stomach, grazed the main arteries, which continued oozing for many weeks, hourly threatening hemorrhage: and also detached several ribs from the breast-bone.'[46]

---

43 Jones, *Journals of Sieges*, vol.I, p217.
44 Oman, *A History*, vol.V, pp.394–395.
45 Carr-Gomm (ed.), *Letters and Journals*, vol.I, pp.256–257.
46 James Macarthy, *Recollections of the Storming of the Castle of Badajos* (London: W. Clowes & Son, 1836), footnote, p.63.

Leith Hay described how 'General Leith narrowly escaped being precipitated into the ditch by the fall of a soldier shot dead on the upper part of the ladder he was mounting.'[47] One of several narrow escapes according to Gomm, but few had not experienced a near miss. Gomm himself had been

> ...suffered to escape with a slight bruise upon my left arm from the ricochet of grape-shot. I pique myself on my good fortune on these occasions, and fates have never threatened me nearer that in my horse and in my arm...but the friends I have to regret, and whose fate I am still anxious about since the sun last set, are numberless.[48]

Unfortunately for the reputation of the British Army, the fall of Badajoz was not the end of the story. As if Ciudad Rodrigo had been a dress rehearsal, once the troops were in the town they gave way to their most basic instincts to a degree that the northern fortress had not witnessed, running amok for three days. Order was only restored when, on the third day, Wellington ordered a gallows to be erected in the main square and gave the Provost Major the power of summary execution. In the event, no man was hanged, although satiety rather than the threat of immediate execution may have played its part in bringing the men to their senses.

That the disorder started almost as soon as the first Allied troops were in the town is suggested by Lieutenant Nevill's experience. He believed the men to be

> ... infuriated to madness by their losses; and alas! No tongue could tell the atrocities committed on that terrible night. I witnessed one just entering the town. I intended to join the 30th, my duty of engineer being over, when I met my servant coming from the arsenal, where he and others had conveyed our commanding officer, poor Lieut.-Col. Grey, who was mortally wounded. He had his haversack seemingly well filled with plunder. I asked him where the regiment was; he answered that he did not know, but that he would conduct me to the camp, as I appeared to him to be wounded, having some clotted blood on my face. I certainly was hit in the head, but in the excitement of the escalade did not mind it, neither did I feel a slight wound in my leg; but as I began to be rather weak I took his advice and he assisted me to the bastion we had escaladed.
>
> In passing what appeared to be a religious house, I saw two soldiers dragging out an unfortunate nun, her clothes torn to pieces: in her agony she knelt and held up a cross. Remorse seized one of the soldiers who appeared more sober than the other, and he swore she should not be further outraged; the other soldier drew back and shot his comrade dead. Immediately after, some Portuguese soldiers appeared; they ordered us to halt, and presented their muskets. I said to my servant, 'Throw them some of your plunder;' he instantly took off his haversack and threw it amongst them, when several dollars and other silver rolled out, and they let us pass. Had

---

47   Leith Hay, *A Narrative*, vol.I, p.297.
48   Carr-Gomm (ed.), *Letters and Journals*, vol.I, p.257.

he not done this I am sure those ruffians would have shot us, for the Portuguese troops, I later heard, murdered everyone they met.[49]

By a general order of 7 April, 'The regiments of the 5th division are to return to their bivouacs, by regiments, as soon as Lieutenant General Leith will think proper, excepting the Royal Scots, and 9th regiment, which are to remain in Badajoz, as late this day till all soldiers will have been turned out of the town, and order will be restored.'[50] The two battalions, which had not been involved in the assault, would then be replaced by Brigadier General Sir Manley Power's Portuguese brigade of the 3rd Division.

According to Douglas, 'To attempt anything in the hope of a description of the scene that was going on would be a task not easily performed, and even could it be delineated no one (unless an eye-witness) would credit the tale…' Nevertheless, he made the attempt.

> Fancy so many thousand soldiers let loose, unrestrained by any authority, mad after such slaughter, and I might say doubly so with brandy and rum. The excesses committed were horrible, nor could it be avoided, as any officer who would recall them to a sense of duty ran the hazard of his life. An officer of the 30th Regiment lost his life in attempting to save a young woman from violation. But the principal scene of drunkenness took place in the bread and rum-store, which appeared to be a vault. Here the soldiers of all regiments were making themselves at home, sitting on the bent baskets which contained the biscuits… They were roaring and singing while others were employed in drawing up rum in casks from an underground store. Those below not being too well versed in slinging them dropped them when the casks were perhaps within a few feet on the surface; down they went and got staved. In this manner the floor of the vault became a sea of wine and those who went down perfectly sober got drunk without drinking.[51]

Douglas's reference to an officer of the 30th is inaccurate. Ensign Purefoy Lockwood was certainly said to have saved a woman from violation, but he survived. The scene in the vault, however, appears to have been replicated all over the town, with some French soldiers, even though prisoners, being invited to join the bacchanalia.

On his way back to camp Douglas came across the aftermath of the escalade of San Vincente. 'The very rungs (or steps of the ladders) by which the troops descended into the ditch were literally shot to atoms with musket balls, while underneath the dead and dying lay in heaps; some calling for a drink for God's sake while their drunken comrades were selling their booty without taking the least notice.'[52]

A further general order of the 7th conveys something of Wellington's growing annoyance with the misbehaviour of his troops:

---

49 Nevill, *Some Recollections*, pp.14–16.
50 Anon. (ed.), *General Orders*, vol.IV, pp.51–52.
51 Monick (ed.), *Douglas's Tale*, p.38.
52 Monick (ed.), *Douglas's Tale*, p.39.

> It is now full time that the plunder in Badajoz should cease, and the Commander of the Forces requests that an Officer and six steady Non-commissioned Officers may be sent from each regiment, British and Portuguese of the 3rd, 4th, 5th, and Light Divisions, into the town tomorrow morning, at five o'clock, in order to bring away any men that may be straggling there.[53]

Unfortunately, matters were made even worse by the misconduct of Power's brigade. According to another general order, issued at 11:00 p.m. on the 8th, 'the Brigade in Badajoz, instead of being a protection to the people, plunder them more than those who stormed the town.'[54] As a result, rolls were to be called in camp every hour. Full attendance was required, and only those with a passport from a field officer were to be allowed into Badajoz.

Since the 5th Division had returned to their camp by the time these strictures were delivered, it is possible that Wellington had picked them out as particular offenders, perhaps specifically the officers of the 1st and 9th, since they had been given the specific task of sending men back to their units. Whether or not this was the case, the rebuke caused Lieutenant Colonel John Cameron of the 9th to take up the issue with his own officers.

> [Cameron] called the Offrs: together & told them their Conduct at that place was bad, for instead of paying any attention to their men they had gone about plundering. He did not want their favour or affection, but he would have the Duty done in a very different way in future.
>
> This would have been very right had that been the case, but, with the exception of One or Two, I can safely say none went to plunder. They were so fatigued that they sought a shady place to sit in (the heat being excessive), and there remained until they got their Quarters. In consequence he has put three times the number of Offrs: on Duty than their [sic] used to be. Since his most Gentlemanlike speech none of the Offrs: have spoken to him, except on Duty.[55]

This was written on 20 April, which suggests that what Le Mesurier considered an injustice still continued to rankle. On the other hand, when Wellington wrote his dispatch to Lord Liverpool on the 7th, he gave due attention to the events at the San Vincente bastion and subsequently commented:

> Lieut. General Leith's arrangements for the false attack upon the Pardeleras and that under Major General Walker, were likewise most judicious; and he availed himself of the circumstances of the moment, to push forward and support the attack under Major General Walker, in a manner highly creditable to him. The gallantry and conduct of Major General Walker, who was wounded, and that of the officers and troops under his command, were conspicuous…

---

53 Anon. (ed.), *General Orders*, vol.IV, p.52.
54 Anon. (ed.), *General Orders*, vol.IV, p.53.
55 Greenwood (ed.), *Through Spain with Wellington*, p.103.

> In the 5th division I must mention Major Hill of the 8th Caçadores, who directed the false attack on the fort Pardeleras. It was impossible for any men to behave better than they did.
>
> I must likewise mention Lieut. Colonel Brooke of the 4th Regiment, and Lieut. Colonel Carleton of the 44th, and Lieutenant Colonel Grey of the 30th, who was unfortunately killed. The 2nd battn. 38th regiment under Lieut. Colonel Nugent, and the 15th Portuguese regiment under Colonel Luiz de Rego, likewise performed their part in a very exemplary manner.[56]

The 5th Division remained in camp near Badajoz for several days while Wellington assessed Soult's movements. The *Maréchal* had advanced as far as Villafranca and Wellington hoped he would stay there long enough for the whole Allied force to be brought against him. Soult, however, chose to withdraw once he realised that Badajoz had fallen. At the same time a message arrived from de España that Ciudad Rodrigo, which was under French blockade, was running short of provisions, while Marmont was known to be marching south, reaching Guarda on 13 April. He had yet to hear that Badajoz had fallen and remained in ignorance for several days. Even when he learnt of the Allied advance, he believed for some days that they were still beyond the Tagus. By the 22nd, however, he was fully aware of the threat he faced and ordered a rapid retreat to Salamanca.

Manoeuvres

Gomm offered his sister an evaluation of Marmont's activities in a letter written early in May:

> ...we were not without hope of bringing Marmont to a stand, for want of something better to do. But he built good bridges (better, I think, than we would have contrived to make in the same situation), and put on longer legs for the flight than it would have suited us to adopt for the pursuit. He certainly did some harm, and carried off, I believe, a great deal of plunder; but did not desolate the country so much *à la Française* as we had reason to expect. And had he shown a little more enterprise in attempting, at least, to destroy our bridge at Vila Velha, I should have thought his movement able and well conducted. In a military point of view, as it was, he did us more injury than we had a right to calculate upon, owing to the dastardly behaviour of ten or twelve thousand Portuguese militia, posted at Guarda... who ran away.[57]

Wellington had commenced his march north on 11 April, leaving only Hill in Estremadura. The 5th Division, along with the 4th, followed the road to Campo Maior, and then marched on to Castello Branco, which they reached on the 20th. Here Le Mesurier took the opportunity to write to his father, a letter that conveys the difficulties of a long march.

---

56   Gurwood (ed.), *Dispatches*, vol.IX, pp.40–41.
57   Carr-Gomm (ed.), *Letters and Journals*, vol.I, p.265.

> We came at the rate of Four Leagues a day, except yesterday; we came Six Leagues in a deluge of rain, the whole day. We started at ¼ past Five yesterday morning and were in Quarters at Five in the evening (Croté jusqu'en Genoux). [muddy up to the knees]
>
> Abrm: says he attributes my preserving my health so well to living Regularly and Temperately. The latter, well and good, but as to the former, I do not agree with him; sometimes up at Three in the Morning & breakfasting at that time; sometimes at Eight, and my Dinner as uncertain, so that I cannot attribute preserving my health to regularity.[58]

Nor was Le Mesurier the only one to comment on the weather. It was a permanent interest of Gomm, who wrote in the letter quoted above:

> We crossed the Tagus in a tempest, and at Castel Branco, I told you, the sun began to shine. At Alpedrinha, I lay under a tree all day, reading Ariosto, and the scenery about me was almost what Ariosto fancied. At Guarda and Trancoso I was pelted with hail and snow, and all the artillery of winter; and we have been enjoying all the luxuries that an English or even a Portuguese November can furnish ever since we came here.[59]

The vagaries of the Iberian climate would continue to make life uncomfortable for the Allied troops throughout the year.

Once it was clear that Marmont, like Soult, could not be brought to battle, Wellington put his troops into cantonments while he decided on his further course of action. For the 5th Division, headquarters were at Moimento de Beira, about four leagues from Lamego. The 9th were stationed at Leomil, from where Le Mesurier wrote in a very different frame of mind. His present quarters, although 'cold and decayed', afforded him the pleasure of 'a nice little Garden behind the house where I study Spanish. When the weather is fine the Trees about it are filled with Nightingales that sing most delightfully.' This contrasted with the experiences of the past couple of. months. 'You will see by the Map that our marching has been (I may call it) severe, for since the 1st: March to this present time we have hardly had any rest; always up an hour before Daylight that we might have a cup of Coffé & a piece of Bread & butter, ere we marched.' Nor was he expecting this rest period to last long.

> The orders are for Soldiers to be provided immediately with Shoes and the Public Mules to be inspected to see if they are fit for active service. Some imagine we shall make a Dash in Spain shortly. I wish something decisive may be done one way or the other, that we might not be kept here much longer, for I think the people of the country begin to be very tired of the war.[60]

The army made a protracted stay in Portugal, despite the obvious preparations for another campaign. This may well have been forced on Wellington. As Napier wrote: 'the Walcheren

---

58 Greenwood (ed.), *Through Spain with Wellington*, p.104.
59 Carr-Gomm (ed.), *Letters and Journals*, vol.I, p.266.
60 Greenwood (ed.), *Through Spain with Wellington*, p.106.

expedition was still to be atoned for! the sick were so numerous amongst the regiments which had served there, that only thirty-two thousand or a little more than half of the British soldiers were under arms.'[61] This observation was as true for the 5th Division as for the other divisions.

On 10 May, welcome reinforcements arrived in the form of the 2/4th, from Gibraltar, who joined the senior battalion in Walker's brigade, as it was still called. Major General William Pringle would take command at the end of June. Then, 10 days later Wellington wrote to Lord Liverpool

> …respecting the arrival of the 1st battalion 38th regiment in the Tagus, and the proposed disposal of that regiment when it will arrive. As the 2nd battalion 38th regiment is in this country, and as I know that the 1st battalion is composed of a fine body of men, I think upon the whole it would be expedient to allow the battalion to join the army, and then to send home the 2d battalion.[62]

Gomm, meanwhile, enjoyed himself exploring a part of Portugal with which he was unfamiliar. He explained why in a letter of 12 May.

> General Leith is gone to Lisbon, to visit Lady Augusta, who is just arrived, and is very desirous that I should make myself acquainted with some of the country beyond the Douro during his absence. So am I. People who know as little about the matter as myself, assure me I shall find the roads very bad, and I believe them; but if they are sufficiently good for my purposes, I mean to take the following course.

Having given his route, he continued, 'This is a circuit of about a hundred leagues, which I allow myself a fortnight to accomplish; and this is, perhaps, more than I ought to allow myself, for the army will certainly be in movement the moment the magazines at Almeida and Rodrigo are complete.'[63]

Gomm was actually back at divisional headquarters six days later, having learnt at Lamego that the magazines would be completed earlier than expected. Nevertheless, he explored as far as Braganza and Chaves on the northern border before returning by a direct route and had seen enough to make a judgement that would become crucial the following year.

The Salamanca Campaign

By early June Wellington was ready to take the offensive against the Army of Portugal. He knew Marmont's situation had been made more difficult by Hill's brilliant victory at Almaraz on 19 May and subsequent destruction of the pontoon bridge there, thus effectively severing direct communication between him and Soult.

---

61 Napier, *History of the War*, vol.V, p.107.
62 Wellington (ed.), *Supplementary Despatches*, vol.VII, p.334.
63 Carr-Gomm (ed.), *Letters and Journals*, vol.I, p.267.

Distant Salamanca, by Andrew Leith Hay. (*A Narrative of the Peninsular War*)

The Allies now began to concentrate around Fuente Guinaldo and Ciudad Rodrigo. The 5th Division left their cantonments on 5 June, a sad moment for the 1/9th. 'Our departure caused many tears in Leomil. The Ladies declared they had never passed such an agreeable Month as the time we were there, and the lower class praised the good conduct of our Soldiers, so that you cannot wounder [*sic*] that we felt something like regret at leaving this place.' Le Mesurier was not expecting a pleasant march:

> …if I can prognosticate from the looks of our Com. Offr: …I shall take good care and not come under his Clutches, for since our pleasant conversation at Castel Branco we have had no other confab save when duty obliges me to go to him, and then he is civil enough. I am more inclined to pity his temper than hate the Man, for when he is well and not on a March he sometimes tries to please the Offrs…[64]

Le Mesurier did at least concede that Cameron's health was poor.

By 8 June the whole division had reached Trancoso, after which they marched on to Castelo Mendo, high above the Coa, then to Poço Velho, which they reached on the 10th and where they camped in a tree-shaded valley. The following day they were on the left bank of the Agueda, where they were joined by the 4th Division, and two cavalry brigades; Major General Viktor Alten's 14th Light Dragoons and KGL 1st Hussars, and Major General Eberhard Bock's KGL 1st and 2nd Dragoons. These units, along with the Light Division, formed the centre column under Beresford's command, while on the left were the 3rd Division, Pack's and Bradford's Portuguese and Le Marchant's heavy dragoons, under Picton's command, and on the right, the 1st, 6th and 7th Divisions and Anson's cavalry, under the command of Lieutenant General Sir Thomas Graham, who had recently come up from Cadiz.

According to Leith Hay, the state of the army and the mood of the troops were exceptionally good.

---

64 Greenwood (ed.), *Through Spain with Wellington*, pp.109–110.

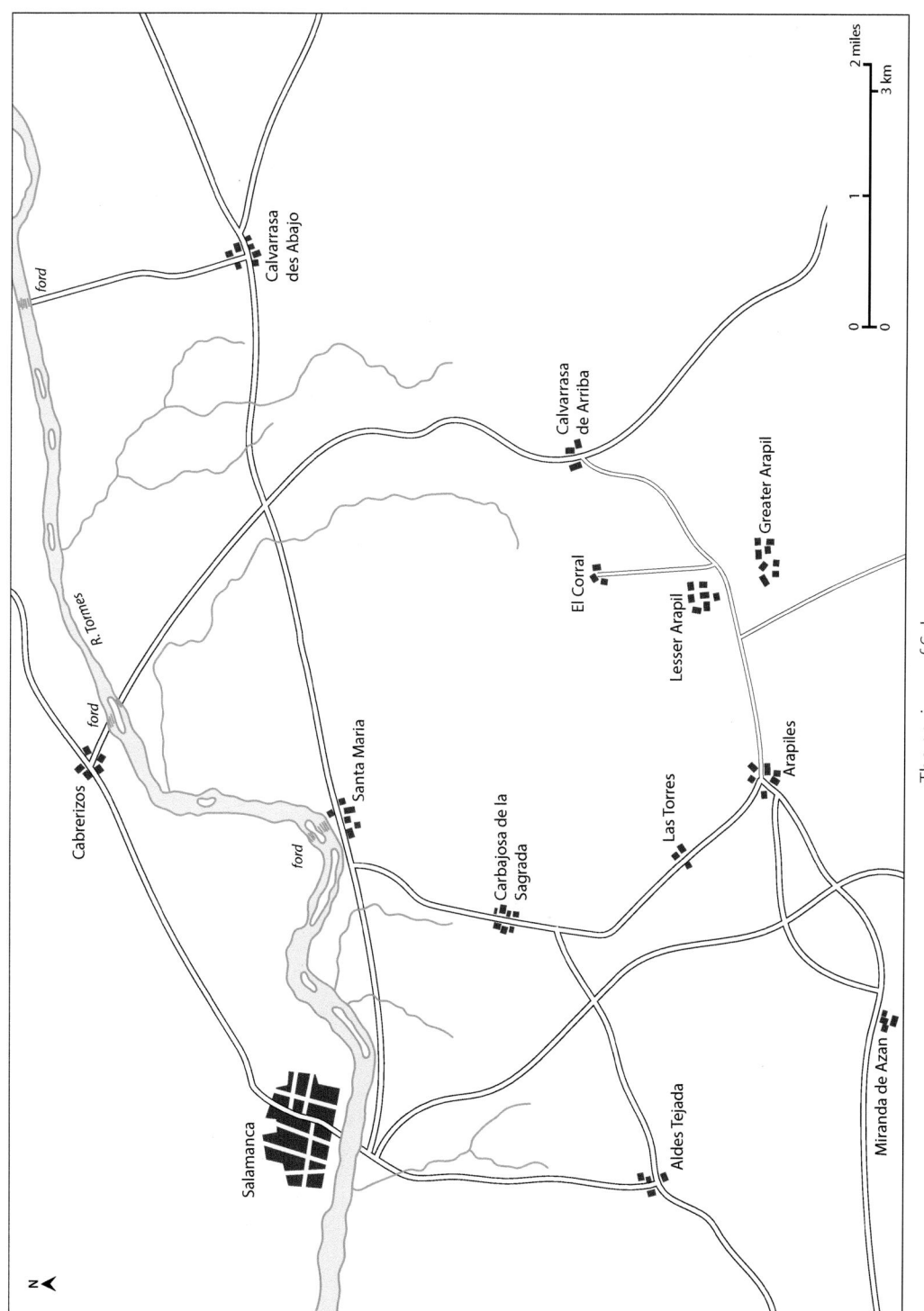

The environs of Salamanca.

Upon no occasion had the allied army taken the field in a more efficient state; every description of force composing it was serviceable and well appointed. The cavalry had recovered their condition. Experience taught the practical minutiæ of active warfare. The weather was beautiful. Confidence in their leader and themselves occupied the minds of the troops; while presages of success and anticipated variety of scene imparted gaiety and buoyancy of spirit.[65]

The first objective was Salamanca, although Le Mesurier, for one, believed it would not be too long before they were in Madrid. He was in a particularly optimistic state of mind. Leith had joined the division at Trancoso and his presence always improved the mood of officers and men alike. Furthermore, Le Mesurier's relationship with Cameron had definitely improved, with his commanding officer finally addressing him by name!

Wellington had already made arrangements designed to distract Marmont. With the support of *Teniente General* Castaños, who was *capitán-general* of both Estremadura and Galicia, he was able to persuade the Spanish Army of Galicia to lay siege to Astorga. At the same time, *Tenente-general* Francisco da Silveira, in command of four Portuguese militia regiments, was to create a diversion at Zamora with the support of Brigadier General Benjamin D'Urban's Portuguese cavalry. The first of these distractions was particularly significant because it should have prevented *Général de division* Jean Pierre Bonnet, currently operating in the Asturias against the local guerrillas, from re-joining the Army of Portugal. When Marmont learnt on 14 June that Wellington had crossed the Agueda, however, he immediately summoned Bonnet to join him. He also warned Joseph Bonaparte and *Maréchal* Jean-Baptiste Jourdan in Madrid that he was in danger of an Allied attack, but they were initially disinclined to believe him, while *Général de division* Marie-François Caffarelli, in command of the Army of the North, ignored his call for reinforcements.

The Allied centre column commenced its march to Salamanca on 13 June across country that seemed perfect for military operations: 'beautifully wooded, and admirably adapted for the encampment of troops, there being great abundance of water, while the trees afforded shelter from the scorching sun.'[66] On the 16th the enemy finally made an appearance. Leith Hay rode out with the early patrols of Alten's hussars: 'About two leagues from Salamanca we encountered the advance of the French cavalry, and proceeded to drive them back. The enemy stood firm, and exchanged shots with the hussars, only retiring when the main body of that regiment debouched from the woods. He then retreated by several roads leading to the town.' As more Allied cavalry came up,

> The scene now became very animated and interesting. Parties were observed firing or charging in all directions. Repeated attacks were made by either force, as circumstances warranted, or as they became more numerous at particular points. In one direction was to be seen a troop or squadron charging half their number of opponents, who, by a precipitate retreat, fell back on others, until their strength

---

65   Leith Hay, *A Narrative*, vol.II, p.4.
66   Leith Hay, *A Narrative*, vol.II, p.6.

became superior, when, in turn, they for a time carried with them the successful tide of battle.[67]

The French were eventually forced back to within two miles of Salamanca. Leith Hay does not make clear whether it was his own love of adventure or a direct command from Leith that caused him to accompany the hussars.

The following day, as the troops commenced their march, Leith Hay again rode forward, this time to gather information. The most important thing he learnt, signalled by artillery fire, was that the French had fortified three convents. He also encountered Major Thomas Brotherton of the 14th Light Dragoons, who had been into Salamanca, as well as being prominent in the previous day's skirmish. Brotherton informed him that the French had abandoned the town during the night, leaving a garrison in the convents. Returning to the 5th Division, Leith Hay met Wellington and passed on his information. Wellington then told him to return to Leith with an instruction to halt until he received further orders.[68]

Marmont had not only abandoned Salamanca, he had also called in all his troops, including an optimistically anticipated detachment from the Army of the North. He had already chosen a point 20 miles north of Salamanca to concentrate his forces.

The three Allied columns now crossed the Tormes by various fords, then marched round the city to meet up on the Heights of San Cristoval, with the 1st and 7th Divisions on the right of the Allied position, the 3rd, 4th and Light in the centre, and Pack's and Bradford's Portuguese on the left. The 5th Division, posted at Aldea Seca, was acting as a reserve along with one brigade of the 6th Division, de España's Spanish and the two heavy cavalry brigades. The light cavalry was in line with the other divisions. The other brigades of the 6th Division were destined to invest the three convents, the defences of which Marmont had been strengthening before his departure.

On 17 June Wellington rode into Salamanca, to receive a rapturous welcome which Leith Hay witnessed.

> Lord Wellington entered Salamanca about ten o'clock in the forenoon: the avenues to it were filled with people clamorous in their expressions of joy; nothing could be more animating than the scene…the streets were crowded to excess; signals of enthusiasm and friendship waved from the balconies; the entrance to the plaza was similar to a triumph; every window and balcony was filled with persons welcoming the distinguished officer to whom they looked up for liberation and permanent relief.[69]

Later there would be a *Te Deum* in the cathedral, to seal the sense of victory.

Despite the celebratory mood, there remained the serious business of taking the three forts, which proved to be more challenging than Wellington had anticipated. Furthermore, Marmont was preparing to march back to Salamanca with four infantry divisions and a brigade of cavalry in order to relieve the besieged garrisons. By 20 June he was in position to drive in the light cavalry vedettes before advancing on the Allied positions on San Cristoval.

---

67   Leith Hay, *A Narrative*, vol.II, p.7.
68   Leith Hay, *A Narrative*, vol.II, pp.8–9.
69   Leith Hay, *A Narrative*, vol.II, pp.9–10.

Wellington interpreted these movements as an offer of battle, and warned his commanding officers to that effect. As a result, the 5th Division left Aldea Seco the following morning 'and formed part of the alignment on the fine position covering Salamanca. The enemy appeared in force, bivouacking directly in front of the allies; some slight affairs were the consequence of the very proximate situation of the two armies, but nothing indicated an intention on either part of immediately proceeding to more serious conflict.' At daybreak on the 22nd, however, it was clear that Marmont's priority was to relieve or withdraw the garrisons, which still held out.

> The ammunition for the heavy ordnance with the allied army had been nearly expended in two days' firing, without having sufficiently damaged the defences to render an assault advisable. The commander of the forces had, therefore, no other alternative left than to watch the motions of his opponents, offer him battle, and mask the works in Salamanca, until additional means of reducing them were procured form the depots.[70]

After some reconnaissance on the morning of the 22nd which almost led to his being taken by the 12th Light Dragoons (with Leith Hay in attendance), Marmont moved to his right, sending some of his troops across the Tormes. In response, Graham's two divisions were sent to take up a position between the French and the town and Wellington, already troubled by shortage of ammunition for the artillery, decided to risk an assault. The detached brigade of the 6th Division had already been called in to strengthen the investment and men from the divisions would make the attack, which was planned for the 23rd, at 10:00 p.m. It ended in complete failure, at the cost of 126 officers and men of the 300 stormers either dead or wounded, including Major General Barnard Foord Bowes, in command of the operation. It was obvious that different tactics were required.

When Marmont, now with two more divisions to hand, continued to manoeuvre, the Allies responded in kind, and all the while there was keen anticipation of a battle. On the 26th Gomm wrote to his sister that Marmont

> ...has 35,000 men within a league of us at the moment, and is expecting to be joined immediately by 10,000 more under Bonnet. They say the King is coming too. Our numbers will be as nearly equal as possible, and the result of a pitched battle should be glorious to us. What a moment of anxiety this is! But it is of a delightful kind, believe me, it is tinctured with more of hope than of fear as to the result of these operations. The whole army is in position. The weather is still settled and not so hot as it might be.'

Having referred to the unsuccessful storm of the forts and news that Soult was advancing on Hill, Gomm concluded, 'On our side, I can assure you, we shall have the hearts of a whole people fighting with us. Nothing can exceed the enthusiasm with which we have been received in Salamanca or the confidence with which they look forward to the approaching contest.'[71]

---

70 Leith Hay, *A Narrative*, vol.II, pp.15–16.
71 Carr-Gomm (ed.), *Letters and Journals*, vol.I, pp.273–274.

The Battle of San Cristoval never happened, however. On the same day that Gomm wrote his letter, powder and shot finally arrived and two of the forts became the gunners' targets. The larger, San Vincente, was to be attacked with red-hot shot and the other, San Cayetano, with artillery fire. The results were as desired. San Vincente was soon burning and by the following day San Cayetano had been breached. Both defending commanders initially cavilled at surrendering but first San Cayetano and then San Vincente offered no resistance when stormers advanced on them. The third fort, La Merced, was quickly taken by escalade. Marmont, still lacking Bonnet and the detachment from the Army of the North which Caffarelli had finally agreed to send him, withdrew towards the Duero.

About this time, Douglas had an unexpected encounter with Wellington.

> Being on picket duty with part of the 38th Regiment, amusing ourselves, as the day was fine, with passing our remarks and conjectures, as a result of our being so convenient to each other, up gallops his Lordship with a few of his staff. Taking out his telescope he viewed their lines for a few minutes. Then, rolling himself in a boat cloak, he lay down on the ground and was soon asleep. The glass he handed to an Aide-de-Camp, telling him to have a look out and if he observed any movement to let him know. He had not lain more than half-an-hour when the Aide-de-Camp shook him soundly. Staring up and rubbing his eyes Wellington seizes the tube and views them a short time, 'Yes, they'll be off tonight,' he exclaimed. So, mounting his horse, off he went.'[72]

Wellington actually had some cause for concern. He was yet to discover whether Commodore Home Riggs Popham's operations on the Biscay coast, or those of the guerrillas in Galicia, would suffice to keep the Army of the North occupied. Soult and Joseph might not have made any definite moves to aid Marmont, but the advance towards the Tagus of d'Erlon's corps, which had been detached further south for some months, could well prove a threat, should Hill fail to hold his position in Estremadura. Nevertheless, he brought his troops forward so that they covered a 15-mile front. On the left were the 3rd Division, the two independent Portuguese brigades, de España's 3,000 troops and the two heavy cavalry brigades. They were stationed south of the Duero, covering the ford at Pollos. On the right the 4th, 5th, 6th and Light Divisions were also south of the Duero, within striking distance of Tordesillas and its undamaged bridge. The 1st and 7th Divisions acted as a reserve at Medina del Campo, although Graham was no longer in command, having had to return home because of eye problems. Picton, still not recovered from his Badajoz wound, had also returned to Britain.

On 7 July the 5th Division was at Torrecilla de Medina. According to Gomm,

> The country we are now making war in is of different a character from that we have for some time past been accustomed to, as the mode of warfare we are carrying on is new. It is a rich luxuriant country, covered with corn, and immediately in this neighbourhood producing a quantity of excellent wine. But the whole of Castile

---

72   Monick (ed.), *Douglas's Tale*, p.40.

may be called a perfect plain, in common language; very elevated, but scarcely a tree to be seen, and water by no means in plenty. The villages are numerous and large; but an army situated as ours is at this moment must not inhabit them merely as a matter of convenience, so that our troops are exposed to as much sun and dew as chooses to light on them… Among our officers the sandiness of the soil and the constant glare are the means of bringing a number of green shades into play.[73]

It was at this point that Major General William Pringle arrived to take command of the second brigade of the 5th Division after a difficult journey upcountry:

I was delayed a long time at Lisbon waiting for my horses which I was obliged to leave behind in England, and after they arrived I had a march of 300 miles to join the army, which, with mules and baggage over I suppose the worst roads, I suppose in Europe, was by far the most tiresome journey I ever experienced.

As he explained to his friend, Aylmer Haly,

Lord Wellington was so good as to consult my wishes in appointing me to a Brigade. I chose that in which the 2 battalions of the 4th were which was then vacant. My brigade now consists of the 2 battalions of the 4th, the 30th and 44th regiments, which is as strong a brigade as most in the army. I am in the 5th division under General Leith who is an old friend of mine and a pleasant man to serve under. We have been this last week moving from Salamanca to the river Douro, which the French have crossed and their army is posted on the opposite banks, their headquarters, I believe, at Valladolid. They have broken down some of the bridges and the others are strongly defended. Whether Lord Wellington means to pass the river or not I am perfectly ignorant as all his plans are kept a profound secret. I really believe he consults nobody. We have got possession of an amazing fine cork country between Salamanca and the Douro and now the harvest is begun it will be of great advantage to us. For the other operations of the army I must refer you to the newspapers which will give you a better account than I can of what we are doing…

I am now extremely glad I have come out and begin to find myself at home in my command as I like the A.D.C. I have got very much, Captain [George David] Wilson of the 4th, and I feel myself very comfortable with my brigade. Our living is not the best. But I have got a pretty good cook, an Italian, who has been accustomed to campaigning and can dress our ration of beef, which is the chief of what we can get, in 20 different ways so that I never yet have wanted a comfortable dinner, and the vin du pays is pretty good about here. I have been unlucky with my horses, two of them lame and one mule died on the march, which if you were to see the roads you would not wonder at. There is a quantity of game in this country which I purpose to attack when the French get a little further from us as I have brought my gun and a brace of dogs. One officer yesterday killed 32 wild duck just by the

---

73   Carr-Gomm (ed.), *Letters and Journals*, vol.I, p.275.

camp… This will find you just about the beginning of your harvest which I know is a busy time with you, but I will not take any excuse for your not writing to me… This is a very fine country all corn and vineyards and the crops are good in general, but they appear very bad farmers, indeed they seem to leave all to nature.[74]

By 9 July, the division was at Nava del Rey and fully experiencing the discomforts Gomm referred to and which Pringle seems not to have noticed. Hale remembered how

…in consequence of the weather being so extremely hot at the time we marched into Navadelrea during the heat of the day, each brigade leaving a strong piquet to watch the enemy's manoeuvres, and then at sun-set in the evening, we marched out of camp, in order to be ready should the enemy make any movement. Some part of the night we were allowed to wrap ourselves up in our blankets and lie down, but not to take off our accoutrements on any pretence whatever, and should we be allowed to lie still four or five hours, (as by chance we were sometimes), our blankets would be almost as wet outside, merely with the dews of the night, as if it had been a storm of rain, for in that country, and likewise in Portugal, the dews of the night are in general very heavy, and I think, the warmer the weather, the heavier the dews.[75]

Gomm referred to 'fine wine', and therein lay a predictable problem, which Napier commented upon in his later account:

The weather was fine, the country rich, and the troops received their rations regularly; wine was so plentiful, that it was hard to keep the soldiers sober; the caves of Rueda, either natural or cut in the rock below the surface of the earth, were so immense and so well stocked, that the drunkards of two armies failed to make any sensible diminution in the quantity.[76]

Whether the men of the 5th Division succumbed to the temptation is impossible to establish, but regimental courts martial records certainly indicate that drunkenness was as much a problem in this division as in any other, as is made clear in the inspection returns for January 1813.[77]

The French were now holding a position on the right bank of the Duero that extended from Toro, where Foy was stationed, to the ford of Pollos, some seven miles to the southeast. Six divisions were covering Tordesillas and its all-important bridge. When Bonnet finally arrived, early in July, Marmont sent him to join Foy, having recognised that the Allies could turn his position. With Bonnet's arrival, the strength of the infantry was now 48,000, sufficient to take the offensive should the *maréchal* so choose.

---

74 Pringle to Aylmer Haly, 6 July 1812, private collection.
75 Hale, *Journal*, pp.85–86.
76 Napier, *History of the War*, vol.V, p.142.
77 TNA: WO 27/112: Inspection returns 1813.

He was helped in this respect by Wellington's caution, which in turn was caused by Marmont's somewhat cavalier attitude to the Galicians at Astorga. This diversion, instead of restricting his options, led him to respond with a diversion on his own, calculated to persuade Wellington that his left was under threat, prior to an attack on the Allied right. Foy was ordered to repair the bridge at Toro, drive in the Allied cavalry and then cross the bridge to distract from the movements of two of the divisions at Tordesillas, which would march to the ford at Pollos. Wellington would surely interpret this as the start of an advance on Salamanca and would react accordingly. First, though, he had to be convinced that his left was under threat.

On the morning of 17 July, curious 'to ascertain the operations of the enemy at Toro', Leith Hay left the camp of the 5th Division,

> …and rode to within half a mile of the bridge then under repair. The French, accompanied by a number of Spanish peasants, were actively employed in laying planks across the chasms that had been formed by the explosion of its two centre arches. The work, apparently, was in a state of great forwardness; nor did it seem improbable that the reports of the enemy's intentions to cross the Duero on the following day, would be realized. The quiet, uninterrupted manner in which I was permitted to overlook this operation, induced me to commit to paper the position of the city, with the river and bridge. No French soldier appeared on the left bank; nor did I meet with the slightest obstruction during the course of a rather protracted sojourn in the enemy's immediate view. The repair, so elaborately bestowed on the bridge at Toro, was, as subsequently proved, for the purpose of deceiving the British general in the line of march by the enemy's troops; consequently, there could be no jealousy created by the circumstances of an officer sketching the position.[78]

Writing to Bathurst on the 21st, Wellington summarised the events that followed.

> It was totally out of my power to prevent the enemy from passing the Duero at any point at which he might think it expedient, as he had in his possession all the bridges over that river, and many of the fords; but he recrossed that river at Toro in the night of the 16th, moved his whole army to Tordesillas, where he again crossed the Duero on the morning of the 17th, and assembled his army that day at La Nava del Rey; having marched not less than ten leagues in the course of the 17th.
>
> The 4th and light divisions of infantry, and Major General Anson's brigades of cavalry, had marched to Castrejon on the night of the 16th, with a view to the assembly of the army on the Guareña, and were at Castrejon under the orders of Lieut. General Sir Stapleton Cotton on the 17th, not having been ordered to proceed further, in consequence of my knowledge that the enemy had not passed the Duero at Toro, and there was not time to call them in between the hour at which I received the intelligence of the whole of the enemy's army being at La Nava del Rey and daylight of the morning of the 18th. I therefore took measures to provide for their

---

78 Leith Hay, *A Narrative*, vol.II, pp.28–29.

retreat and function, by moving the 5th division to Torrecilla de la Orden; and Major General Le Marchant's, Major General Alten's, and Major General Bock's brigades of cavalry to Aleajos.[79]

Wellington praised the admirable order in which the troops retired to Torrecilla de la Orden and then to the Guareña, threatened the whole way by the French in force as Marmont first managed to turn to Allied left at Aleajos and then manoeuvred to turn the right. He might have given more specific details, including his own narrow escape, but to do so would have suggested how effectively Marmont had misled him. Further orders had already been sent to the other divisions, the two independent Portuguese brigades and most of the cavalry to take up positions beyond the Guareña, although the heavy cavalry had soon been ordered back.

The 5th Division, brought back to Torrecilla de la Orden while on their way to Canizal, were now covering the 4th and Light Divisions, who had been kept forward to watch the French.

Leith Hay had his own interpretation of Marmont's intentions.

> As was to be expected, the French marshal advanced with rapidity and determination; either the movement on Toro was perfectly useless, or, if otherwise, his only chance of deriving the slightest advantage from it, was pressing on the allies before the different corps of the army were collected on his line of march, which, he had reason to hope, would be in some measure abandoned.

Having been seen forward to examine the French advance, Leith Hay rode to Castrejon, where Cole, in command of the 4th Division, was watching 'a warm affair' between the cavalry of the two armies, that of the French being supported by infantry and artillery. '… everything indicated the commencement of a very serious affair.' Wellington then arrived and 'much anxiety prevailed to learn what movement he would direct; the enemy was pressing rapidly forward on both flanks, thereby rendering an immediate change of position necessary. The whole French army was in movement.'[80]

Picking up at the point where the 5th Division was ordered back from Canizal to Torrecilla de la Orden, Douglas recalled, if not quite the very serious affair that Leith Hay anticipated, what certainly proved a lively one.

> We continued to retire until daylight, when we were ordered back to check the advance of the enemy, who were considerably outflanking some of our Division, putting their guns and baggage in danger. We advanced about a league when we came in full view of the enemy, and formed line for action with the usual examination of arms; not looking for burnished pieces, but blew down the barrel to see if the touchhole was clear, flints fast and all's well.

---

79 Gurwood (ed.), *Dispatches*, vol.IX, pp.294–295.
80 Leith Hay, *A Narrative*, vol.II, pp.32–33.

> Our position retarded their progress for some time, until they had examined our strength. We retired again and halted on the side of a gentle declivity with a small rivulet in front and formed line, from line into square, for the purpose of keeping their cavalry in due bounds. Our squares were scarcely formed when Arthur and all his staff came galloping down the hill, his head going like a weather cock while the French 9 pounders whizzed about fiercely. We could see, by the clouds of dust, the march of the enemy, when just in our front a French officer rode to the top of the hill which his Lordship had just descended, and fired a pistol. We were pretty well aware of the signal, for in the space of 5 minutes 7 artillery pieces opened fire upon us. 'Twas lucky that Leith had deployed us into line so that the round shot could not do the execution which it would have done had they caught us in square. The first gun shot told near the colours, which carried away a poor fellow's leg and his boot flew into the air. The adjutant says, 'There's one man down.' After remaining about half an hour under this fire without returning the compliment, the guns ceased and on came the cavalry. Each regiment now formed square double quick... On came the cavalry, but the menacing appearance of the squares rather cooled their courage.[81]

Despite the enemy guns, the 5th Division took only one casualty, as Douglas noted, and the Light Division, which had suffered more attention than the 5th, two. The 4th Division, however, being closer to the enemy, suffered about 200 losses.

After a brief rest, the three divisions had to march through vineyards and fields of wheat, in the heat of the day and lacking water. The 5th Division finally reached the Guareña and their original objective, Canizal, although not before the 4th Division, along with Alten's light cavalry and the 3rd Dragoons had to push back yet another French advance that *Général de division* Bertrand Clausel launched on his own initiative and which threatened the Allied left.

Wellington was now holding a defensive position on the left bank of the river while Marmont was on the right bank, strongly posted on some higher ground. Since Wellington seems to have been hoping for a defensive battle, he might well have stood and fought had Marmont pushed the issue. The French, though, had been on the move since the night of the 16th, a point the *maréchal* made when later justifying his inaction, although he may also have been cautious about attacking Wellington when the Allies were already in position. Wellington's dispatch to Bathurst described Marmont's subsequent movements.

> On the 19th, in the afternoon, the enemy withdrew all the troops from the right, and marched to the left by Tarazona, apparently with the intention of turning our right. I crossed the Upper Guareña at Vallesa and Elmo, with the whole of the allied army, in the course of that evening and night; and every preparation was made for the action which was expected on the plains of Vallesa on the morning of the 20th.

Again, there would be no battle.

---

81 Monick (ed.), *Douglas's Tale*, pp.40–41.

…shortly after daylight the enemy made another movement, in several columns, to his left along the heights of the Guareña, which river he crossed below Cantalpiedra, and encamped last night at Babila-fuente and Villoruela; and the allied army made a corresponding movement to its right to Cantalpico, and encamped last night at Cadeza Vellosa, the 6th division and Major General Alten's brigade of cavalry being upon the Tormes at Aldea Lengua.

During these movements, there have been occasional cannonades, but without loss on our side.[82]

Wellington did not comment on the peculiarity of the march on the 20th, but Leith Hay considered it worthy of notice that

When the two armies were thus put into motion, they were within cannon-shot of each other; the French occupying higher ground than the allies: but the space between them was lower than either of the routes, and nothing intervened to obstruct a view of the columns of enemies, that thus continued to pursue their course without the least obstacle to prevent their coming into instantaneous contact; for the slightest divergement [sic] from either line of march towards each other, would have brought them into musketry distance. I have always considered this day's march as a very extraordinary scene. Only to have occurred from the generals opposed commanding highly disciplined armies.

There was some skirmishing, either between the cavalry guarding the flanks of their respective armies

…or the anxiety of French and allied stragglers to obtain undisputed right of pillage in the unfortunate villages that lay in the indeterminate space between the armies; otherwise no spectator would have imagined the two immense moving columns that filled the whole country, and seemed interminable, being lost to the eye in dust and distance, comprised two armies actuated with earnest desire for the destruction of each other, but who, although possessed of numerous artillery and cavalry, were persevering on their way as if by consent refraining from serious hostility, until arrived at the arena destined for the great trial, to which either was now advancing with confidence, and without interruption.[83]

The nearest the two armies came to turning this unusual advance into something more serious occurred as they approached the village of Cantalpino, which lay on the Allies' line of march. Marmont had veered somewhat to his right, bringing the French closer to the Allies. Some of the Allied troops had already passed through the village when Marmont ordered a number of his guns to open fire. The 4th Division was the target but Wellington refused to return fire, simply adjusting his own line of march to open up more distance from

---

82   Gurwood (ed.), *Dispatches*, vol.IX, p.296.
83   Leith Hay, *A Narrative*, vol.II, pp.38–40.

the French. This meant the Allies were now marching in the direction of the Heights of San Cristoval, while the French were heading for the fords at Huerta.

Leith Hay made no reference to the French artillery fire at Cantalpino but he did relate how, at about midday, the rear of the Allied column was an extended line of commissariat stores and private baggage, which was unguarded and straggling. Leith Hay suggests that Bonnet wanted to seize 'these dilatory followers of the troops'. Marmont refused to give permission, but 'At the same moment some French voltigeurs entered a village about equidistance from the lines of march: it was not considered advisable to permit their quiet possession of this point. The fifth division was ordered to halt, and the 8th Portuguese Cazadores [sic] being sent into town, they soon dislodged the enemy; and a great proportion of the persons for whose safety some apprehension had been entertained, being now advanced in the line of the column, the infantry again moved forward.'[84]

By the end of the day the Allies were posted on higher ground in the vicinity of Cabezabellosa and Aldea Rubia, on the route to San Cristoval. As a precautionary measure Wellington sent the 6th Division and Alten's cavalry to the Aldealengua fords. Meanwhile, the French had marched for Babilafuente and their position then extended to the Huerta fords. Marmont was now in position to turn the Allied right, which led Napier to conclude that Wellington had been outmanoeuvred: 'Wellington was deeply disquieted at the unexpected result of this day's operations which had been entirely to the advantage of the French general. Marmont had shown himself perfectly acquainted with the country, had outflanked and outmarched the allies, had gained command of the Tormes…' which gave him the opportunity to effect a junction with the Army of the Centre, King Joseph having decided to bring troops from Madrid to join up with Marmont. Furthermore, Napier was of the opinion that it was becoming less likely Wellington would be able to fight and gain a decisive victory.[85]

The troops must have hoped for an undisturbed night before continuing their march. Instead, 'The men had scarcely had time to compose themselves in their bivouacs or the staff of the respective divisions to occupy the indifferent accommodation which the town afforded, when reports arrived that some French light cavalry were approaching. This appeared a very extraordinary crusade for French cavalry to set out upon…' Nevertheless, Leith Hay was sent to check and, upon nearing the camp, spotted the approach of cavalry. He also noticed that the 3rd Division's guns had been drawn out.

> Having seen the Portuguese cavalry in the morning, I had little doubt, from every circumstance, it was General D'Urban's brigade that now appeared on the plain; they were dressed very similarly to the enemy's chasseurs à cheval, and had not been previously seen by the officers of the infantry bivouac. From whatever cause it proceeded, they advanced with great caution; everything tended to increase the delusion. In the act of riding forward to ascertain their identity, having approached sufficiently near to perceive General D'Urban, I was returning with the information, when a discharge from the artillery of the 3d division was poured into the

---

84   Leith Hay, *A Narrative*, vol.II, p.40.
85   Napier, *History of the War*, vol.V, pp.159–160.

centre of the supposed enemies, and several men and horses rolled on the earth. I galloped back, making signals to General Pakenham [commanding in Picton's absence] that it was General D'Urban and his brigade, rode forward to the latter, who appeared astonished at the unexpected reception he had received.[86]

After this unfortunate friendly-fire incident, the troops did indeed enjoy a quiet night.

Wellington informed Bathurst that by the 20th he had little choice but to march on to Salamanca or attack the French when they were holding a position which gave them every advantage. He also stated categorically that 'unless forced to fight a battle, it is better that one should not be fought by the allied army, unless under such favourable circumstances as that there would be reason to hope that the allied army would be able to maintain the field, while those of the enemy should not.'[87]

One step he had already taken was to send one of de España's battalions to Alba de Tormes in order to deny Marmont use of the bridge there. If Marmont were forced to use the Huerta fords, his troops would be closer to the Allies and strung out, making them more vulnerable to attack. Unbeknown to Wellington, however, de España had withdrawn his troops when the French reached Babilafuente for fear that they would be cut off by any further French advance. Not surprisingly, Marmont had reconnoitred further upstream on the 21st, and soon discovered that Alba de Tormes was undefended, which meant he could cross the Tormes by both the Huerta fords and those at Encinas without the risk of attack on either of his flanks.

Since Wellington had decided that his only option was to march on Salamanca in order to preserve his communications with Ciudad Rodrigo and Portugal, the Allies continued their advance to the San Cristoval Heights while Marmont was preparing to cross the Tormes. Douglas recalled how 'The 21st was spent manoeuvring, taking up positions and leaving them to others. How easy it might appear to some, changing positions, but be assured, it's not easily done.'[88] This was also the day when the 1/38th finally arrived from Lisbon.

The day's manoeuvring brought the Allies to the Tormes, downstream from the French. Leaving the 3rd Division and d'Urban's cavalry north of the river, Wellington brought the rest of his troops to the south bank, using the fords at Aldealengua and Santa Marta. The detached troops, however, were given the task of watching a similar detachment from *Général de division* Jacques Sarrut's division, which was supported by artillery. These troops had been positioned to prevent any Allied interference as the French crossed the river (which lasted into the early hours of the 22nd). Once all were across, the French position stretched from Calvarasa de Arriba on the left to Machecon on the right, with the cavalry posted closest to the river and the infantry behind them. Similarly, the Allied cavalry lay in front of the infantry. In the case of the 5th Division, this was Major General John Gaspard Le Marchant's brigade. The left was closest to the river at Santa Marta, with the cavalry at Calvarasa de Abajo, while the right extended towards the village of Arapiles. Although this position covered Salamanca, the French could still sever Allied communications with

---

86 Leith Hay, *A Narrative*, vol.II, pp.41–42.
87 Gurwood (ed.), *Dispatches*, vol.IX, p.297.
88 Monick (ed.), *Douglas's Tale*, p.42.

Ciudad Rodrigo. To make matters worse, it was now certain that 2,000 cavalry and 20 guns from the Army of the North were fast approaching.

Marmont's intentions were clear enough: to drive Wellington back to Ciudad Rodrigo, with the chance of forcing a battle, even if only with the Allied rearguard.[89] Wellington made his intentions equally clear in his long dispatch of the 21st to Bathurst. He was still determined 'not to give up our communication with Ciudad Rodrigo, unless under very advantageous circumstances, or it should be come absolutely necessary.'[90]

The night that followed proved memorable, as both Hale and Douglas recorded.[91] According to the latter,

> The thunder rolled in awful peals, the glare of the broad sheets of lightning, with the rain that fell in torrents, seemed as if the angry heavens were making their displeasure felt at the scene about to take place. The 5th (or Green Horse) were lying on our right. The awfulness of the night caused numbers of their horses to break from their picketing and run through our ranks as we lay drenched to a skin but unwilling to rise lest we should lose our berth in the ranks and miss a comfortable nap.[92]

Leith Hay, having observed that the men of the 5th Dragoon Guards (the Green Horse) were either sitting or lying, holding their horses, hence the ease with which the animals broke free, continued:

> …nor was the situation in which we were placed one of great brightness. For days past the enemy appeared to control our movements, and to force us back without an effort; we were now, in the darkness of the night, close to him – but where, or in what direction, was known only to the head-quarters, in search of whom officers were constantly passing and re-passing.[93]

Ensign George Freer of the 1/38th later recorded in his memoirs how, having reached Salamanca, they

> … remained under arms until dark, when we received orders to join the main body of the army, through a soaking rain for another league and a half that night. Heaven, as though forbidding the blood that was to be shed the next day, showed its anger by the most awful thunder and vivid lightning I ever witnessed. It was about midnight when we arrived at our position, and not a covering had I or my messmate, Captain Willshire, from the pitiless storm.[94]

---

89 See Marmont, *Memoires*, vol.IV, pp.237, 443.
90 Gurwood (ed.), *Dispatches*, vol.IX, p.298.
91 See Hale, *Journal*, p.89.
92 Monick (ed.), *Douglas's Tale*, p.42.
93 Leith Hay, *A Narrative*, vol.II, p.46.
94 William J. Freer, *The Thirty-Eighth Regiment of Foot, now the First Battalion of the South Staffordshire Regiment* (London: Harrison & Sons, 1915), p.294.

Forty Thousand Men Defeated in Forty Minutes

After the storm, the morning of the 22nd promised a fine day. The troops of the 5th Division had already stood to arms an hour before daybreak. Once the sun had risen, 'the wood and water parties were paraded and marched off to set about cooking, we had for a wonder some days of advance rations.' So far, so normal apart from the plentiful rations, but the previous evening the outlying pickets had been pushed forward as close as possible to the enemy. As a result,

> the pickets began to pop at each other and so smartly that [Douglas] climbed a tree to look into the valley to see how the play went. Scarcely was I mounted when the bugles called us in. The wood and water went to wreck while we double quicked it into the line, on with the accoutrements, fell in and moved to our right not far from the Arapiles.[95]

An action might have seemed inevitable, but as Gomm subsequently wrote home,

> Not a soul ever doubted the issue of the contest, could a battle be brought on; but it was feared that if Marmont continued to pursue the policy he had observed hitherto, he might force us to withdraw from Salamanca, and lay it open, at best, to insult, if not to permanent possession of the French. By mid-day, however, it appeared evident that he was meditating an attack upon us, and the comment was common in the mouth of every one, 'At length Marmont is going to give us what we could have hardly have forced upon him.'[96]

Gomm later commented: 'The country was such that the fifty thousand men of either army could move in all directions, and from many points be in view almost at the same moment.'[97] What was to prove the battlefield of Salamanca is essentially an open, undulating plain, lying a few miles south of the city. There are several salient points: the Greater and Lesser Arapiles face each other across the shallow valley; Nostra Señora de la Peña, held by the 7th Division on the morning of the 22nd, was to prove the furthest point left of the Allied line; the French side of the valley that separated the two armies, was essentially a plateau, with the highest ground to their right, at Calvarrasa de Arriba. It was from this point, early on the 22nd, that Marmont, accompanied by Foy, tried to make out the Allied dispositions. Because of the undulating ground, all that could be seen was the baggage train and the 7th Division, to the left of the Lesser Arapile. Wellington had a clearer view of the French, who were concentrated around Calvarrasa de Arriba and towards the Heights of Nostra Señora de la Peña. The proximity of the 7th Division to the French led to an early morning encounter between voltigeurs from Foy's brigade, who had been sent forward to test the enemy, and the advance troops of the Allied division. Although Wellington sent the 68th and the 2nd Caçadores to hold off the attack, French artillery stopped their advance.

---

95 Monick (ed.), *Douglas's Tale*, pp.42–43.
96 Carr-Gomm (ed.), *Letters and Journals*, vol.I, p.277.
97 Carr-Gomm (ed.), *Letters and Journals*, vol.I, p.278.

The Battle of Salamanca.

The skirmishing continued, intensifying as the light improved, and the 7th Division were eventually replaced by the 95th from the Light Division, who continued to block the French.

It was only belatedly that the significance of the two Arapiles became clear to the Allied command. According to Leith Hay,

> The nearest of the Arapiles, although considerably higher, connected with the ridge on which we now stood, had been occupied by the allies on the preceding night: the other hill of that name, of greater altitude, more isolated, and rising from the plain at the angular point formed by the receding of the heights, had not been considered as important. Early in the morning, however, troops were sent to take possession of it; but the enemy had anticipated this movement, and part of the brigade of General Maucun [sic] already crowned the summit, no effort then being made to dislodge him.[98]

Possession of the Greater Arapile allowed Marmont to extend his left and form his troops behind it. According to Leith Hay again,

> Large bodies of the enemy's troops were perceived marching to their left; forming in rear of the Arapiles, and on the skirts of the wood extending towards Alba de Tormes. These columns were considered by General Leith to be within the range of the artillery of his division, which he ordered in advance to a height in front of his position from whence was obtained a better view of the formation taking place under cover of the Arapiles. Having reached this eminence Captain Lawson opened his fire with such effect that the nearest of the enemy's troops made. a rapid, and not very orderly, change of position, proceeding to a distance greatly out of reach of the point where the British artillery were annoying it.

The French soon brought some of their own guns to bear on Captain Robert Lawson's guns, immediately causing casualties, and Leith Hay was sent down to direct the artillery and the covering troops of the 16th Light Dragoons to retire. This was effected without the losses that might have been anticipated, 'and they soon regained the ground on which the division had been unwilling spectators of their noisy fray.'[99]

As Marmont continued to extend to his left, it could be surmised that his intention was to turn the Allied right and gain possession of the road to Ciudad Rodrigo. In response, Wellington adjusted his own position, as he explained in his post-battle dispatch to Bathurst.

> In the morning the light troops of the 7th division, and the 4th caçadores belonging to General Pack's brigade, were engaged with the enemy on the height called Nuestra Señora de la Peña, on which height they maintained themselves with the enemy throughout the day. The possession by the enemy, however, of the more distant of the Arapiles rendered it necessary for me to extend the right of the army *en potence*

---

98 Leith Hay, *A Narrative*, vol.II, p.47.
99 Leith Hay, *A Narrative*, vol.II, pp.47–49.

> to the height behind the village of Arapiles, and to occupy the village with light infantry; and here I placed the 4th division, under the command of Lieut. General the Hon. L. Cole: and although, from the variety of the enemy's movements, it was difficult to form a satisfactory judgement of his intentions, I considered that upon the whole his objects were upon the left of the Tormes. I therefore ordered Major General the Hon. E. Pakenham, who commanded the 3rd division in the absence of Lieut. General Picton, on account of ill health, to move across the Tormes with the troops under his command, including Brig. General D'Urban's cavalry, and to place himself behind Aldea Tejada; Brig. General Bradford's brigade of Portuguese infantry, and Don Carlos d'España's infantry having been moved likewise to the neighbourhood of Los Torres, between the 3rd and 4th divisions.[100]

Although Wellington made no reference to the 5th Division, it seems that they and the 6th Division also extended to the right, the 5th Division on the right of and slightly back from the 4th Division, with Bradford and de España behind, and the 6th Division behind the 4th. Marmont, who had ascended the Greater Arapiles, now had a clear view of these Allied dispositions. He recognised that Bonnet's troops, behind the Greater Arapile, were vulnerable to attack. What he did not know was that Wellington had given an order to Lieutenant Colonel William Howe de Lancey, the adjutant general, to be prepared for a managed withdrawal.

Marmont continued to extend his left, thus narrowing the gap between the two armies. He had sent first *Général de division* Antoine Louis de Maucune's division forward, as already noted, followed by *Général de division* Jean Guillaume Thomières' and Clausel's. *Général de brigade* Taupin (commanding Brennier's division) was occupying the high ground in front of the wood, while Bonnet had sent one of his regiments forward to occupy a knoll between the village of Arapiles and the Greater Arapile. Three of *Général de division* Pierre François Boyer's dragoon regiments were sent to Clausel, to support an attack on the Allied left, while the light cavalry was in position to attack the Allied right.

Maucune now chose to attack the village of Arapiles, whether by Marmont's order or on his own initiative is not clear, although Marmont claimed in his memoirs that it was the latter. The light troops holding the village comprised those of the Guards brigade from the First Division, the fusilier brigade of the Fourth Division, a company of the 5/60th and one company of the Brunswick Oels light infantry. They soon found themselves under attack, although the combination of a charge and the Allied guns forced the French back. Maucune then sent a stronger force forward. This too was eventually repulsed, although skirmishing continued until either an order from Marmont or a forward movement of the 5th Division caused Maucune to retire.

Even before the attack on the village, Le Mesurier reported in a subsequent letter home that

> After waiting some hours under Arms, we received the welcome intelligence that our general intended to bring them to action, and about Two o'Clock we were ordered (the 5 division) to support some Artillery towards our Right which opened

---

100 Gurwood (ed.), *Dispatches*, vol.IX, p.301.

on the Enemy. This was not a very pleasant position as the Enemy's shot came thick about us and killed and wounded many of our Men.[101]

To pick up on Le Mesurier's reference to an unpleasant position, Leith Hay explained the situation in more detail, although he timed it differently.

> About three o'clock, a force of not less than twenty pieces of artillery were assembled by the enemy on the heights directly opposite to the 5th division. The ground upon which the division stood, was flat, and the troops without any means of shelter. It became consequently advisable to make the regiments recline on the field, and, by so doing, avoid in some measure the effects of what was evidently to become a very heavy cannonade. For at least an hour did those brave soldiers immovably support the efforts made to annihilate them by the showers of shot and howitzer shells that were either passing over or ricocheting through the ranks.
>
> General Leith, on horseback, passed repeatedly along the front of his division, speaking to and animating the men, who anxiously expressed a desire for permission to attack the enemy…[102]

According to Gomm, Leith addressed his troops with the eloquence of Caesar, while Douglas included a recollected taste of his words: 'This shall be a glorious day for Old England, if those bragadocian rascals dare to stand their ground, we will display the point of the British bayonet, and where it is properly displayed no power is able to withstand it.'[103] Douglas was also impressed by how calmly Leith exposed himself to French fire, even though being on horseback made him an obvious target.

Encountering Leith for the first time, 18-year-old George Freer was impressed by the way the general addressed each of the regiments as he passed. The message he gave the 38th was a simple commendation. '"As for you, Thirty-eighth, I have only to say, behave as you always have done."' It had the desired effect because Freer believed that 'never were the coolness, the intrepidity, and the bravery, together with the discipline of the. British soldier so evidently portrayed as on this occasion.'[104] This was a view he maintained, despite having seen the British soldier in action on a further 15 occasions.

Thomières, covered by *Général de brigade* Jean-Baptiste-Théodore Curto's light cavalry, had continued to march his troops forward during Maucune's attack on the village, consequently passing behind Maucune's division and advancing about another three miles. Clausel initially followed but then halted his division, leaving Thomières dangerously exposed. From the Greater Arapile Marmont would have had a clear view of what was happening but made no attempt to intervene. Although he later took pains to emphasise that it should not have happened, it is probable that at the time it appeared to suit his purposes.

This was just the mistake that Wellington had been hoping for. His own account of how he reacted to the dangerously extended French line, famously while eating a delayed lunch,

---

101 Greenwood (ed.), *Through Spain with Wellington*, pp.117–118.
102 Leith Hay, *A Narrative*, vol.II, p.52.
103 Monick (ed.), *Douglas's Tale*, p.45.
104 Freer, *The Thirty-Eighth*, p.295.

describes how he recognised that Marmont's objective was to threaten the Allied position by extending to his left, then attacking and either breaking the Allied line or making any movement to the right impossible to implement.

Although the French continued to occupy good ground and had the guns to defend it, Wellington saw an opportunity to attack. He might have added that he received a message from Leith informing him that Maucune was now stationary, which meant the gap between his and Thomières' division was increasing. He ordered Pakenham, with the 3rd Division and D'Urban's cavalry, supported by two squadrons of the 14th Light Dragoons, to advance in four columns and turn the French left on the higher ground. At the same time the 4th and 5th Divisions, along with Bradford's brigade and the heavy cavalry were to make a frontal attack, with the 6th and 7th Divisions and de España's Spanish in support. On the left of the 4th Division, Pack's brigade was to attack the Greater Arapile. The 1st and Light Divisions, holding ground on the left, remained in reserve.[105]

A skirmish line had already been sent forward, made up of the light companies of the 4th and 5th Divisions and Pack's troops.

> At length the welcome intelligence was imparted, that we were no longer to be cannonaded with impunity. Lord Wellington arrived from the right and communicated to General Leith his intention of immediately attacking the enemy.
>
> It is impossible to describe the energetic exultation with which the soldiers sprung to their feet; if ever primary impulse gained a battle, that of Salamanca was won before the troops moved forward![106]

Wellington specifically ordered that the division should be formed in two lines, and should advance as soon as the 3rd Division became visible, although Leith was also to wait for Bradford's brigade to come up so that he could pivot on its left before marching towards the heights and attacking the French columns. As a reversal of the situation at Badajoz, the first brigade, comprising the 3/1st and the 1/9th, with the two battalions of the 38th between them and commanded by Lieutenant Colonel James Greville in Hay's absence, would form the first line. In order to equalise the lines, the 1/4th joined the first brigade, while the rest of Pringle's brigade, the 2/4th, 2/30th and 2/44th, and the whole of Spry's Portuguese brigade were in the second line. According to Douglas,

> The 3rd brigade on coming down did not please Sir James [Leith]. He marched them back under the whole fire in ordinary time and back again to make them do it in a more soldier-like manner. The Brigade, on coming to its ground, the centre sub-division of the 15th Portuguese was struck with a shot (I mean cannon shot) which did fearful execution. It scarcely left a man standing.[107]

The first blow to the French was felt by Thomières' division. The initial head-on attack came from d'Urban's cavalry and the two squadrons of light dragoons. This was quickly followed

---

105 Gurwood (ed.), *Dispatches*, vol.IX, pp.301–302.
106 Leith Hay, *A Narrative*, vol.II, pp.52–53.
107 Monick (ed.), *Douglas's Tale*, p.45.

by the fire power of the 3rd Division, which proved superior to that of the French, who were already disordered by the Allied cavalry. The infantry then charged and, despite a counter-charge by Curto's light cavalry, soon had Thomières' troops running back in total confusion, while their commander was killed trying to rally them. To make things worse, Marmont was wounded at some point during this initial debacle. Command devolved on Bonnet, who would also be wounded soon afterwards, leaving Clausel to rescue the situation.

Despite the appearance of Pakenham's division, there was some delay before Leith and Cole could set their own troops in motion, Leith waiting for Bradford to come forward from Los Torres and Cole waiting for Leith to move. Once the advance began, however, Leith directed his division towards Maucune's stationary troops. On the Allies' right, Le Marchant's heavy brigade was preparing to join the attack.

> General Leith gave the signal, and the whole advanced in the most perfect order. Previously to this movement, he had dispatched his aides-de-camp, Captain Belsher and Captain Dowson, to different parts of the line, in order to restrain any effort at getting more rapidly forward than was consistent with the important object of its arriving in perfect order close to the enemy, and at all points making a simultaneous attack. In ascending the heights on which the French army was placed, the division continued to be annoyed by the artillery fire from the summit; the ground between the advancing force and that to be assailed was also crowded with light troops in extended order, carrying on a very incessant tiraillade. The general desired [Leith Hay] to ride forward, make the light infantry press up the heights to clear his line of march, and if practicable make a rush at the enemy's cannon. In the exertion of the service, I had to traverse the whole extent of surface directly in front of the fifth division: the light troops soon drove back those opposed; the cannon were removed to the rear; every obstruction to the regular advance of the line had vanished. In front of the centre of that beautiful line rode General Leith, directing its movements, and regulating its advance. Occasionally every soldier was visible, the sun shining brightly upon their arms, while at intervals all were enveloped in a dense cloud of dust, from whence, at times, issued the animating cheer of the British infantry.[108]

Even obstacles that might have caused disorder were quickly overcome. '…while advancing, the village of Arapiles met [the 1/38th's] centre, and to have moved either to the right or left would have wrought confusion, when Colonel Greville, calling me by name, said "Take them over the wall."'[109] Despite being struck on the arm by spent grape shot, Ensign Freer continued to lead the grenadiers over the wall and beyond.

Douglas claimed that

> … the advance of the British at Salamanca never was exceeded in any field. Captain Stewart of our company, stepping out of the ranks to the front, lays hold of Captain

---

108 Leith Hay, *A Narrative*, vol.II, pp.54–55.
109 Freer, *The Thirty-Eighth*, p.297.

The Battle of Salamanca, by J.A. Atkinson. (Anne S.K. Brown Military Collection)

Glover and cries, 'Glover did you ever see such a line?' I am pretty confident that in the Regiments that composed our lines there was not a man 6 inches out of his place. The French seemed to be taken by surprise as the 1st Royal Dragoons, the 5th Green Horse and a regiment of Heavy Germans advanced with us on our right. Some of the Greens sung out, 'Now boys, lather them and we'll shave them.' As we approached the enemy their skirmishers retired, followed by our boys and the Portuguese [8th Caçadores] to within a few yards of their lines for seeing the British advancing through the tempest of balls, they kept advancing in like manner to within a few yards of the enemy's pieces, crying out, '*Fogo me felias*' or 'away my sons.'[110]

The 5th Division, having outpaced the 4th, were now in position to attack. Leith Hay, on horseback, was able to observe that Maucune had drawn up his troops

> ...in contiguous [sic] squares, the front rank kneeling, and prepared to fire when the drum beat for its commencement. All was still and quiet in these squares;– not a musket was discharged until the whole opened. Nearly at the same moment General Leith ordered the line to fire, and charge: the roll of musketry was succeeded by that proud cheer that has become habitual to British soldiers on similar occasions – that to an enemy tremendous sound, which may without exaggeration be termed the note of victory.[111]

---

110 Monick (ed.), *Douglas's Tale*, p.45–46.
111 Leith Hay, *A Narrative*, vol.II, pp.56–57.

Gomm offered a lively description of the same moment to his family.

> The advance was, as Tasso describes it on another occasion: '*rapide si, ma rapide con legge,*' [swift yes, but swift with order] under the destructive fire of the French artillery, which grew more deadly as we approached it. But the spirit of our people rose in proportion, and when they reached the enemy's solid columns, which opened a fire like a volcano upon them, there was not a moment's hesitation: no check along the whole line, but a general shout of exultation was echoed from all quarters. The enemy wavered, retired from height to height; until at length it was impossible to withstand the ardour of our soldiers, which seemed to increase with every fresh assault, and complete rout ensued.[112]

As for the 9th Foot, they

> …pushed forward before the Brigade, the Enemy about Two hundred yards in our front. When we came within a hundred yards they faced to the Right about and moved off in ordinary time, which, however, they quickened as we advanced on them till such a time that, finding us too close, ran as fast as they could put leg to ground, and we followed them, cheering. We had lost the Division, then, and, after advancing over Two Hills, we were ordered to halt, as our men could hardly draw breath and were almost choked with dust.[113] According to Lieutenant Colonel Cameron, the battalion had encountered so many 'fugitives from the enemy in front of the 5th Division that they were compelled to bring up their right shoulders and advance along the high part of the position. In their march they met several bodies of the enemy who gave way with very little resistance.'[114]

If the attack of the 5th Division were not enough to throw Maucune's troops into confusion, 'the heavy cavalry, coming up on the right increased the consternation of the enemy, who fled with precipitation; and to add to their defeat, they were joined by the remains of the extreme left of the French army, flying before the victorious 3rd division, led by the gallant Major General Pakenham.'[115]

It was not only Maucune's and Thomières' divisions that were reduced to a panic-stricken mob. Brennier, posted behind the Greater Arapile, brought his troops forward to support Maucune. They quickly fell into disorder under the assault of the two Allied divisions, although two of Brennier's regiments bravely tried to make a stand. The pressure of the Allied infantry and heavy cavalry was inexorable, however.

The Allied right sustained their attack but the battle was by no means over. A French victory by this stage might have been extremely unlikely but both Pack's brigade, making an attempt to take the Greater Arapile as ordered, and the 4th Division, following a parallel movement to the 5th Division, but some way further back, were forced to retreat. This must

---

112 Carr-Gomm (ed.), *Letters and Journals*, vol.I, p.278.
113 Greenwood (ed.), *Through Spain with Wellington*, p.118.
114 Glover (ed.), *The Napoleonic Archive Volume 1*, p.26.
115 Leith Hay, *Memoirs*, p.91.

have suggested to Clausel that a fight-back was possible. It was his own division that had forced the leading brigade of the 4th Division to retire, while Bonnet's troops had swept the Portuguese away as they clambered towards the summit of the Arapile, driving them back across the valley. Before the French could gain any real advantage, however, the advancing 6th Division effectively checked any further French forward movement. Nor was this the totality of Allied reserves. Nevertheless, Clausel was determined to strike back. He brought Sarrut's division forward to act with his own and Bonnet's troops. This left Foy to continue a desultory engagement with the Light Division.

Clausel's attempt to force the Allies back on themselves was frustrated by the intervention of the 1st Division, while the 7th Division, and Bradford's and de España's brigades were also close to hand. The 3rd and 5th Divisions, meanwhile, were still driving the French along the higher ground, together with Anson's, Arendschildt's and D'Urban's light cavalry. There was some determined resistance but the sustained Allied assault was unassailable. Clausel realised that it was a case of retreat or rout.

The time had come to call in the only unengaged troops, *Général de division* Claude François Ferey's, who would have to make a stand to cover the withdrawal of the rest of the army. This included Foy's division, which was now under threat from both the 1st and the Light Divisions. Ferey posted his troops on a steepish incline, so that every man's fire power could be brought into play. The division formed three ranks deep, with a square at the end of each line to avoid being turned by cavalry. In this formation, Ferey's men were attacked by Henry Clinton's 6th Division but when Ferey gave the order to fire the Allied troops were brought to a halt. There then ensued a musketry encounter that lasted about an hour. As Ferey began to withdraw, the Allied attack was taken up by a Portuguese brigade, the 6th Division having suffered heavy casualties. The Portuguese were also held at bay and it was not until the 5th Division, which had been reforming, attacked Ferey's left flank and created panic in the ranks of the 70e de la ligne that Ferey's battalions finally broke and fled the battlefield. Their stand, however, had enabled the rest of the French army to extricate itself. Sadly, in acknowledgement of his brave determination, Ferey himself was mortally wounded in these final moments of the conflict.

Wellington now sent the 6th Division in pursuit, but tired and battered by their encounter with Ferey, they were too exhausted to harry the French. Foy's division, amongst the freshest on the battlefield, took up the task of covering the French retreat, making a stand at several points to hold back any Allied pursuit. Wellington, still seemingly unaware that there was no Spanish force to prevent the French from availing themselves of the bridge at Alba de Tormes to facilitate their escape, could anticipate total catastrophe for his opponents, despite Foy's resistance.

The divisions that had been most hotly engaged in the conflict, particularly the 3rd, 4th and 5th, now had the opportunity to relax and reflect on what they had achieved; and to feed themselves. The Royals

> …sent out parties for water, having nearly 5 miles to travel before it was found, and then it was as green as the water you may have seen during the heat of summer in a stagnant pond. However, it went down with a fine relish. The only piece of plunder either [Douglas or his] comrade had got happened to be a leg of mutton off a Frenchman's knapsack, which I put down in a kettle to boil, having made a fire of French flintlocks.

> I was sitting on a stone watching the fire, musing over the day's work, when, rising up to look into the kettle, one of the pieces went off, the ball passing between my legs. This was the nearest visible escape I had, for if providence had not so ordered it that I rose at that instant, the contents would have been through my body…

Later, 'having regaled ourselves with whatever we could muster, [we] lay down to rest our weary blackened frames, and in a sound sleep forgot the toils and dangers of the day.'[116]

Like Douglas, Hale of the 9th's first concern was to satisfy the needs of his stomach. Indeed, food seems to have been on his mind rather earlier in the day. Having realised that the French were well supplied, 'in the course of this day most of us got loaded with what they had left behind, for some found small bags of biscuits, about ten or twelve pounds weight, some small bags of flour, about the same weight, and some joints of mutton and goat's flesh…' A veritable feast, in fact.

> So when camp was formed, and our picquets posted, the remaining part were very soon busily employed in providing for the belly, some making hard dumplings with the flour, some getting wood, and others searching for water for our cooking, which by chance was found about one mile distant from the camp. Therefore, towards the middle of the night, we enjoyed ourselves over a most able supper, and after a little conversation over what had passed during the day, we wrapped ourselves in our blankets, with accoutrements on, and lay down in the hopes of getting a few hours' good rest, for we were then getting very much fatigued for want of sleep.[117]

As for Freer and his mess-mate, they were invited 'most respectfully to partake of their meal', which was a mixture of raw meal and bacon dumplings and dough cakes.[118]

Oman put the Allied losses at 4,702 and those of the French at 14,000 killed, wounded and taken prisoner, the 5th Division alone having taken 1,500 prisoners. The breakdown of the 5th Division's casualties gives a total of 506 for the British troops, comprising four officers and 58 men killed, 25 officers and 411 men wounded, and eight men missing, while Spry reported 62 Portuguese killed, 180 wounded (plus three officers returned as 'bruised'), and 23 missing. Examining the figures at battalion level reveals that the heaviest losses were taken by the 3/1st and the 1/38th, the latter having joined only on the morning of the battle, of course. These were the two strongest battalions but proportionately they still suffered more losses than the other two battalions in the brigade. In the second brigade, three battalions took similar losses, while the 1/4th suffered rather fewer proportionately.[119] For the Portuguese, the 15th Line took by far the highest casualties. Having a large number of men 'who never before had been exposed to fire, it is no wonder if some confusion occurred, but they showed every disposition to attack and none to avoid the enemy.'[120]

---

116 Monick (ed.), *Douglas's Tale*, pp.47–48.
117 Hale, *Journal*, pp.91–92.
118 Freer, *The Thirty-Eighth*, p.297.
119 Oman, *The History of the Peninsular War*, vol.V, p.597.
120 Moisés Gaudêncio and Robert Burnham, *In the Words of Wellington's Fighting Cocks* (Barnsley: Pen & Sword, 2021), pp.46–47.

The most serious of the losses suffered by the battalion was that of Major General Leith. Gomm wrote home that

> We should have been too happy had he escaped altogether; but after the most important advantage had been gained, he received a musket shot in the arm, which shattered the bone; and when he grew faint with loss of blood, I tied up his arm as well as I could, and sent him in good hands to the rear. He is since gone into Salamanca, and I rejoice to learn that there is every prospect at present of saving his arm.[121]

Leith seems to have been wounded as his division was about to overwhelm Maucune's troops, while his nephew was also wounded, at about the same time.

> General Leith and myself remained the night of the battle in the village of Las Torres, and were the following day conveyed to Salamanca, where we became residents in the house of the Marques Escalla.
> The gratitude of the inhabitants of Salamanca on this occasion was not confined to empty expressions, or wild ebullitions of patriotic feeling, but far more substantially and usefully evinced by sincere and zealous exertion to provide for the wants of the wounded, and assistance in furnishing the large hospitals, of necessity established after such an action, with every requisite for the comfort of their deliverers, as they designated the troops of the allied army.[122]

A week after the battle Gomm was able to report that there was every hope Major General Leith would make a speedy recovery. 'At headquarters they are full of his praises… The wits say that while he was advancing he looked like the presiding spirit of this tempest; his division the thundercloud that he rolled after him; and his staff were flashes of lightning that he scattered about him.'[123]

Both Gomm and Leith Hay referred to another of Leith's staff, Captain William Dowson, whose foot was shattered by a shot, and who then suffered the misfortune of spending the whole night on the battlefield without receiving any assistance. He was certainly not alone.

Wellington had every reason to praise his army, and he did so in his post-battle dispatch. Having referenced the heavy losses suffered by the French in both men and materiel, he made a comparison with his own, which had not been 'of a magnitude to distress the army, or to cripple its operations'. He then continued:

> I have great pleasure in reporting to your Lordship that, throughout this trying day, of which I have related the events, I have every reason to be satisfied with the conduct of the General Officers and troops.
> The relations which I have given of its events will give a general idea of the share which each individual had in them; and I cannot say too much in praise of the conduct of every individual in his station.[124]

---

121 Carr-Gomm (ed.), *Letters and Journals*, vol.I, pp.278–279.
122 Leith Hay, *A Narrative*, vol.II, p.64.
123 Carr-Gomm (ed.), *Letters and Journals*, vol.I, p.280.
124 Gurwood (ed.), *Dispatches*, vol.IX, p.305.

There follows a long list of Allied senior officers and staff, as well medical officers, officers of the civil departments and senior Spanish officers, to all of whom he felt 'much indebted.' It is interesting to note, therefore, that in a general order issued on 23 July, he struck a somewhat more menacing tone. Having thanked the army for its conduct the previous day, he then added that he 'trusted the events of yesterday have impressed all with a conviction that military success depends upon troops obeying the orders which they receive, and preserving the order of their formation in action, and that upon no occasion they will allow themselves to depart from it for one moment.'[125]

Gomm, having reflected on the charmed life he seemed to lead, remarked that, 'I do not thank Heaven with half so much fervour for having suffered me to pass without injury through this day, as for having suffered me to bear a part in one of the most important of this day's feats. I believe the division will be well spoken of.' In later life he was more specific. 'Salamanca was the prettiest battle that ever was. The fifth division won it; we turned the left flank of the French under a hail of grape and canister.'[126]

Leith Hay shared this view, although ascribing the victory a little more widely. In his memoir of his uncle, published in 1817, he wrote: 'The attack above detailed, added to that of the third division, decided the fate of the day: the left of the enemy were in the greatest confusion, and flying all directions'.[127] Later, in his 'Narrative' he elaborated thus:

> Thus in the short space of less than an hour the battle was decided; the defeat of the French army became inevitable. Other divisions and corps of troops participated in the glory of the day, suffered seriously, and nobly upheld the reputation they had previously acquired; but the battle of Salamanca was in reality won by the 3d and 5th divisions, General Bradford's Portuguese brigade, the squadrons of the 14th dragoons, and the heavy cavalry.'[128]

A few months later, when Madrid could be added to Wellington's laurels, Ensign Thomas Woodward of the 2/4th wrote enthusiastically to his brother,

> …this has been a great year for Lord W--- for in the beginning of the Year he took two of the Principal Fortifications in Spain and Entered as far as Madrid the Capital & things looking very prosperous for the French will never stand against us again after the drubbing they got on the 22nd July they can fight us only by overpowering us in Numbers & if Russia would hold out any time & we could get reinforcements we should drive them out of the Country by this time next year.[129]

This was to prove a prescient prediction but, more significantly, it suggests the optimism which was probably widespread at this time.

---

125 Wellington (ed.), *Supplementary Despatches*, vol.VII, p.360.
126 Carr-Gomm (ed.), *Letters and Journals*, vol.I, p.279.
127 Leith Hay, *Memoirs*, p.92.
128 Leith Hay, *A Narrative*, vol.I, pp.57–58.
129 Thomas Woodward, unpublished letters, Arevalo 1 September 1812.

It was not until the following day that Wellington discovered just how successfully the French had extricated themselves from the battlefield. The Light Division had been sent to the Huerta fords on the evening of the battle, but had found only dead and wounded. Nor were there any signs that an army in flight had passed that way. Still unaware that the Spanish detachment had been ordered to abandon Alba de Tormes, he concluded that the French had been forced to use the fords further upstream, but by that time it was too late to pursue them. Anson's and Bock's cavalry was sent to investigate early on the 23rd, the former to Alba de Tormes and the latter to the Encina fords. Anson discovered Foy holding the bridge, having successfully covered the retreat of the rest of the army. He offered no opposition to the Allied troops but brought his division off to follow the rest of the French who were on the march to Arevalo and Peñaranda.

As for the Allied infantry, according to Hale

> …between two and three o'clock in the morning we were alarmed by the sound of the enemy's trumpets, at which time they began to retreat into Spain again, towards Valladolid; and before four o'clock in the morning our army began to advance in pursuit of them with all speed, leaving the dead on the ground for the inhabitants to bury…[130]

Douglas agreed that 'We were pretty early on our limbs, as the bugles called us to arms to pursue the foe. We started to the march, the day being uncommon warm.'[131] Wellington, however, used the 1st and Light Divisions to spearhead the pursuit, since they had not borne the brunt of the previous day's action, with those that had, spared the pressure of a forced march.

Douglas was ordered to bring up a man who had fallen out, too weak to march. As a result, he became

> …intermixed with the stragglers of the army and followed in the wake of the Division. The day was intensely hot and we were glad to find shelter in a wood. The ground fortunately proved to be marshy. Here you might observe the sick, parched creatures, kneeling down and scraping the mud away 'till they obtained a little water, then sucking it to the dregs. Hunger is bad, and not easily borne, but is nothing in comparison to thirst.'[132]

He and his charge finally caught up with his battalion after they had formed camp near the bridge at Alba de Tormes, which certainly demonstrates that the 5th Division had enjoyed a relatively easy march. Nor was Douglas's timing at fault. He arrived just as the wine was being served out. He also remarked that at this point they were required to get their arms and accoutrements in order, so that they would be ready to resume the pursuit on the following day.

---

130   Hale, *Journal*, p.92.
131   Monick (ed.), *Douglas's Tale*, p.48.
132   Monick (ed.), *Douglas's Tale*, p.48.

The French had a head start, however. Although on the 23rd some of Foy's units had suffered from the attack of the KGL heavy cavalry at Garcia Hernandez, the army still reached its first objective, Peñaranda, that day, and left at daybreak on the 24th, some hours before the arrival of the Allied advance troops. On the 25th they were at Arevalo and three days later, at Valladolid which, as one of the main French depots, had been Clausel's objective from the start of the retreat.

The Allies reached Arevalo on the 27th and Olmedo on the 28th. Anson's and Arendschildt's light cavalry were in the van and were able to report a continuing state of chaos in the Army of Portugal. The evidence was everywhere: wounded men had been abandoned; stragglers, left to fend for themselves; and villages, devastated as the French passed through. As for the main army, as soon as Clausel had resupplied it from the stores at Valladolid, he continued his onward march towards Palencia and Burgos, although this was not immediately clear to the Allies. Writing on 31 July while camped about two leagues from Valladolid, Gomm posited that 'the remains of Marmont's army are marching upon Aranda, where it is supposed they expect to give the meeting to Joseph Bonaparte with a force from Madrid.'[133]

Wellington received a warm welcome in Valladolid, despite its reputation as the most pro-French of the Duero towns. He also learnt something of Clausel's intentions, which persuaded him that he could leave the Army of Portugal to its own devices and focus on Joseph, who had indeed brought troops from Madrid. He was now at Segovia. Gomm continued his letter, 'I think it is probable that we shall be of the party. We march at three tomorrow morning, I believe, in that direction. Joseph will clear our way to Madrid, if he waits for us, depend upon it.'[134]

Three days later Le Mesurier wrote from camp near Cuellar that

> His Excellency seems much out of humour, occasioned, I believe by Sickness in the Army which is very great at present. Our Regt: is not Four hundred Strong, which Two Months ago was over Seven hundred. But the fatigues of the Campaign have been very great. I have been better within the last two or three days than I have been for some time before. Our Rations, on which we have lived for the last month, have not kept us in high condition. We are as lean as Whipping posts.[135]

There was good news, however: an extra two ounces of rice, flour, wheat or barley to thicken their soup and a month's back pay. Other matters were also attracting Le Mesurier's attention, and may in part explain why Wellington was out of humour. The women who followed the army were a constant problem to him and he had now issued a severe order with regard to their plundering. Having declared that women were 10 times worse than men, Le Mesurier then instanced how 'A few days ago the Provost of the Division desired one of them to walk out of a Field where the Industrious Lady was busy digging Patatoes else he would punish her. With a tremendous Oath she replied "You may Flog me every day for a Meal of Pratties", and went out well loaded.'[136]

---

133 Carr-Gomm (ed.), *Letters and Journals*, vol.I, p.280.
134 Carr-Gomm (ed.), *Letters and Journals*, vol.I, p.280.
135 Greenwood (ed.), *Through Spain with Wellington*, pp.120–121.
136 Greenwood (ed.), *Through Spain with Wellington*, p.121.

On to Madrid

To return to more important events, Joseph had reached Segovia on the 27th, and lingered there for several days, in expectation that Clausel would call in the Madrid reinforcements. As Gomm had anticipated, Wellington then gave his attention to the Army of the Centre. He first sent D'Urban to reconnoitre, and once D'Urban had learnt details of the strength of Joseph's force from French deserters, he added Bock's cavalry and a battalion from the 7th Division to D'Urban's command. Having driven in the French cavalry screen, D'Urban then reached Segovia, only to discover that Joseph had withdrawn that very morning in response to Clausel's assertion that even with the king's reinforcements, the Army of Portugal was in no condition to make a stand.

Wellington now brought in the 1st and Light Divisions, which were somewhat detached. Once they had joined, orders were given for a general advance on Segovia, and on to Madrid. Major General Henry Clinton was left to hold a position on the Duero near Cuellar with the 6th Division, which had taken by far the heaviest losses at Salamanca, and five recently arrived battalions, including the 2/4th and the 1/38th. All five were Walcheren regiments and were already suffering the health problems associated with that campaign. Anson's cavalry was still well forward, but was to join Clinton, should Clausel threaten. Since the garrisons in Toro and Zamora were holding out against the Galicians under José María Santocildes, there was certainly a possibility that Clausel might attempt their relief or threaten the Galicians. With the exception of the 2nd Division, which was still operating independently under Hill, Wellington could then bring the rest of the Allied troops against Joseph.

On 7 August D'Urban's and Bock's cavalry and a Royal Horse Artillery troop advanced along the road to Madrid but found no sign of the French. The infantry began their advance over the next two days, and Gomm later sent home a rather facetious account of their march.

> Our late rambles have been such as an amateur who came for the sole purpose of seeing the country would have chosen to follow, step for step. From Valladolid we visited the fine town of Segovia; the Palace, magnificent, I must call it, of San Ildefonso; the Guadarrama mountains; the Escurial, Madrid. How shall I trace out the future? Aranjuez, Toledo; I should be sorry to fix a boundary to the amateur's exploits, yet my pencil is not bold enough to trace out for him further at this moment. A piece of singular good fortune, and in which the amateur is generally more favoured than we are who make a military excursion, has been that we have had time allowed us to give to each of these objects the attention they merit: unless I except San Ildefonso, for I should like to live there. But we have an advantage over all the amateurs who have ever gone before us, or perhaps of all who will ever follow us, in a visit to these places, in that we have had the satisfaction of driving before us as we entered them a band of detestable fellows, with the king of them at their head; and this circumstance has given us an additional pleasure in beholding them, similar to that which one feels in beholding a beautiful and valuable possession of one's own. The poor fugitive king (for I believe he is not a bad man) marched from Madrid in the direction of Aranjuez with a few French and several thousand Spaniards, who, if truly reported of, are at this moment more false to him than they have hitherto been to their country.[137]

---

137 Carr-Gomm (ed.), *Letters and Journals*, vol.I, pp.282–283.

Joseph had been reluctant to leave Madrid, despite Jourdan's urging, since to abandon his capital was to renege on his duties as king. He tried to convince himself at first that Wellington would not come to Madrid, although he also sent 2,000 cavalry and an Italian division (from Suchet's command), to make contact, should the Allies be advancing, and to take prisoners in order to discover Wellington's intentions. As a result, the only action during the Allied advance was a clash between these troops under *Général de division* Anne-François-Charles Treillard and D'Urban's. Although the Portuguese cavalry were quickly overwhelmed, the French were then checked by Bock's German dragoons and the light troops of the 7th Division. They were finally persuaded to retire by the arrival of the remainder of the Allied heavy cavalry (now under the command of Lieutenant Colonel William Ponsonby) and the rest of the 7th Division.

The advance of the Allies and the lack of support from either Soult or Suchet convinced Joseph that he would have to abandon his capital. He left a garrison at the Retiro Palace, which had been fortified and also served as an arsenal, believing that it would be able to hold out until Soult finally obeyed the royal summons to abandon Andalusia and come to Madrid. Then he departed with the Army of the Centre and those Spanish who had aligned themselves with the French cause, making first for Toledo.

Although the 5th Division were under no pressure during the advance, for the men in the ranks the heat proved a powerful natural enemy, sometimes to the point of suffocation. Makeshift tents provided some respite. These were simple affairs, consisting of

> …2 blankets, two firelocks and 4 bayonets. At each corner of the blanket a hole was worked similar to a buttonhole, and in the centre another. A firelock stood at each end to serve as poles. The bayonet of these firelocks passed through the corner holes of both blankets, a ramrod secured the top, and a bayonet at each end fastened in the ground competed our house.

Although this arrangement protected them from the burning intensity of the sun, Douglas added that a cause of discomfort remained because 'the heat inside was intolerable.'[138]

When they reached the highest ground of the Guadarrama mountains they finally had their first, distant glimpse of Madrid. Then it was down to the plain and on to a welcome on 13 August that must have surpassed all expectations, particularly when it was bestowed on the foreign commander of a foreign army. For Douglas it was 'our triumph as it exceeded all the exhibitions perhaps ever witnessed by a British army.'[139] And for Gomm, reflecting on the experience, 'If I live to be a thousand years I shall never pass such another day as yesterday, so full of delirium that the only assurance I have this morning that it was not all a dream, is that everyone I meet has dreamed the same dream with myself; and I then dispose myself to believe that all was real.'[140]

The first crowds were encountered in the suburbs and grew ever larger as the troops marched closer to the heart of the city. Eventually, it became well-nigh impossible for them to make any progress. Everyone was there, from the highest to the lowest. The cheering

---

138 Monick (ed.), *Douglas's Tale*, p.49.
139 Monick (ed.), *Douglas's Tale*, p.50.
140 Carr-Gomm (ed.), *Letters and Journals*, vol.I, p.281.

was deafening, with shouts of 'Vive Ingleses', 'God save King Ferdinand' and 'glory to the English nation'. There were even some vivas for the Portuguese! Every window and balcony was crowded with eager spectators, anxious to get a glimpse of the hero and his brave soldiers. The balconies themselves were hung with silk and velvet in honour of the moment, while massive candles in equally massive candlesticks stood ready for when darkness fell. The ladies above were waving their white handkerchiefs, and those in the street were almost pulling the officers from the saddle in their eagerness to shake hands, a dozen at a time. Flowers, fruit and victors' laurels were presented to the passing soldiers, and some ladies even grabbed the colours and pinned laurel leaves to them. As if that were not enough, they also embraced the young ensigns with the greatest enthusiasm. Madrid was a city simply mad with joy. Towards evening the new, liberal constitution was read out with great solemnity at four different sites and was greeted with shouts of applause. Then the city was ordered to be illuminated for three nights and the candles were lit. Le Mesurier, wandering the streets, not only commented on the illuminations and fine hangings but also on how the crowds of people parading the streets exuberantly embraced every allied soldier they came upon.[141]

There remained the garrison in the fortified Retiro. Gomm, fretting to explore Madrid, felt that 'the attention we are obliged to give to the Retiro at such a moment is extremely annoying. It is not of sufficient importance as a military objective to counter-balance, in our own estimation at least, the privation it occasions us.' As he finished this letter, written on the 14th, he was able to conclude: 'One o'clock. The Retiro has this moment surrendered, and I am going into Madrid. Adieu.'[142]

The governor of the Retiro had boasted, with some justification, that he had the firepower to flatten Madrid. Wellington made his intentions clear when, on the evening of the 13th, detachments from the 3rd and 7th Divisions drove in the French outposts. The following morning crowds gathered to see the spectacle when the Allies attacked. No such attack proved necessary, however. The governor had changed his mind and, instead of offering resistance, sent one of his aides to negotiate surrender terms. As a result, Le Mesurier was able to report that 'at Four in the afternoon, the French marched out of the Retiro and laid down their Arms on the Glacis. A finer Body of men, 1700 in number, were seldom ever seen. They appeared to be a set of picked Men. The stores in the Retiro are, I am informed, beyond conception.'[143]

Gomm could enjoy his sightseeing, while Le Mesurier went to the theatre, where he witnessed Wellington being acknowledged with yet more vivas. As for Douglas, the following night he was involved in darker deeds. 'My comrade, being on guard there [at the Retiro], the day after its surrender, came to the outer wall about midnight, and giving the concerted signal, which was instantly obeyed, threw down about a bushel of tobacco, with half a dozen good linen shirts and some shoes, which was no affront.'[144] It is unlikely that the men of the Royal Scots (their official title since February) were alone in raiding the stores.

---

141 This is a composite account drawn from those serving in the 5th Division who experienced the occasion, with some additions from other eye-witnesses.
142 Carr-Gomm (ed.), *Letters and Journals*, vol.I, pp.282–283.
143 Greenwood (ed.), *Through Spain with Wellington*, p.125.
144 Monick (ed.), *Douglas's Tale*, p.50.

The 5th Division was not destined to remain long in the immediate vicinity of Madrid and Le Mesurier was probably not alone in rueing the order which sent them away. What Madrid offered, particularly to officers, is suggested by the need he felt to

> ...take my last ride in the place and, after buying a few things our Mess wanted, I went to the Prado, the grand public walk of the Capital, and enjoyed the sight for about one hour. Immense crowds of Spaniards that seemed delighted at having the English among them, were promenading in a Beautiful Piece of Ground with Two or Three Rows of Trees on each side, and Bands of some of the Regts: Quartered in Madrid played in different parts. I could have amused myself here much longer, but we were to March at day break the next morning and I was oblige[d] to quit it with regret.[145]

The intense heat in Madrid could be dangerous, however. One of those who succumbed to it, dying of heatstroke, was young John Carter of the 2/30th.

On the 18th the division marched to Escorial, followed by the 1st, 4th and 7th Divisions. Le Mesurier described it as 'a solitary place with few inhabitants' so that 'Men and Officers were crowded', particularly when the other divisions joined them, leading him to take his quarters in a field a mile from the town.[146] Gomm believed that they had been moved to reassure the Spanish that there would be no permanent possession of Madrid. Only Douglas felt that the palace 'furnished abundance of fine quarters for the whole of the British and Portuguese troops and to spare', although he did confess that there might have been some pilfering of the treasures within.[147]

Wellington's next move now depended upon the French. If Soult came to Madrid, as ordered, the Allied commander's decision would be an obvious one. Otherwise, he needed to decide between attacking Soult in Andalusia, moving to the east should Soult join Suchet, whom Joseph had already joined, or dealing with the Army of Portugal, for Clausel had moved south again as the Allies marched for Madrid. By mid-August he was at Valladolid, while Foy had relieved the French garrison in Toro and was about to do the same at Zamora. As a result, Anson crossed the Duero at Tudela and Santocildes, at Torrelobaton. Clinton, inactive at first, then withdrew to Arevalo.

By the time the 6th Division arrived, the 5th Division were already there, having marched from Escorial on 22 August. Arevalo proved more uncongenial than any other place. It was certainly not to Le Mesurier's liking because 'They are completely a Frenchified set in the Town and are as rude as they probably can be without absolutely insulting us, so I hope we shall not stay any lenth [sic] of time among them.' The implicit antagonism extended beyond the town and eventually developed into something worse when, on the 29th,

> ...a forage party of the 44th: Regt: was terribly beaten by the inhabitants of a neighbouring village. The Alcalde [mayor] began the battle by knocking the Offr: off his Horse, & it is reported the Spaniards killed a man of that Regt: When this was

---

145 Greenwood (ed.), *Through Spain with Wellington*, p.126.
146 Greenwood (ed.), *Through Spain with Wellington*, p.126.
147 Monick (ed.), *Douglas's Tale*, p.50.

reported to the Genl: he ordered an Armed party of 60 men to go for the Alcalde, who, conscious of having done wrong, had fled, & in his place they brought back the Chief Inhabitants of the Village who had given security for the appearance of the Magistrate, who most probably will swing for it, if he can be found. I do not hear from any person that the party behaved anyways ill.[148]

On 1 September Wellington finally departed from Madrid, secure in the knowledge that Soult had left Andalusia to join Joseph, that Lieutenant General Thomas Maitland, in command of the Sicilian expedition, had finally reached the east coast, which would keep Suchet busy, while in the north-west Popham and the guerrillas were continuing to keep Caffarelli occupied. Wellington chose to divide his force. He left the 2nd, 3rd, 4th and Light Divisions under Hill's command, along with de España and D'Urban's cavalry, who were at Seville. The gadfly, Ballesteros, was to check the French troops in the east, of which Soult's were the biggest potential threat. Wellington then brought the remaining divisions, as well as Pack's and Bradford's Portuguese and the rest of the cavalry, to join the two divisions at Arevalo.

Burgos

In letters home both Le Mesurier and Gomm reported the progress of the advance, the purpose of which was to force the Army of Portugal back to Burgos, if not further north. Gomm, now enjoying army rank of lieutenant colonel (a promotion he ascribed to Leith's natural liberality and influence), wrote somewhat tersely on 17 September, 'My military news is very little. I think I wrote last from the Escurial. We have since driven the remains of Marmont's army through Valladolid, and are now within two leagues of Burgos which we shall presently take.'[149] For a reason which is not difficult to identify, he omitted any reference to what happened on 6 September and which did not reflect well of the 5th Division.

Le Mesurier, however, gave more detail, since he carried no responsibility. That lay with Major General Pringle and his staff, including his quartermaster, Lieutenant Colonel Gomm.

As the Allies approached Valladolid, they discovered the French posted on the Heights of Casterniga.

> [They] had taken a position with a view, apparently, of making a Stand. Owing to some negligence of the Staff of our Division, our Artillery was delayed some hours, the necessary Orders not having been given, which were to follow the 6th: Division over a Ford where Carriages might pass, whereas in the place where we crossed Horses could with difficulty pass, on account of the Steepness of the Banks on both sides. It was reported that the Marquis [Wellington's recent promotion in the peerage] gave these Gents a severe lecture for their negligence, as we were to have attacked immediately after crossing with another Division, and when the

---

148 Greenwood (ed.), *Through Spain with Wellington*, pp.126–127.
149 Carr-Gomm (ed.), *Letters and Journals*, vol.I, p.286.

Artillery came up it was too late in the Evening, and the next morning the Gent'n: retired from Valladolid, blowing up the Bridge which crossed the Pisuerga River.[150]

It is interesting to read the view of another officer, the censorious Ensign John Aitchison of the 3rd Foot Guards. According to his interpretation, there were only about 6,000 of the enemy on the heights and they were unaware of the Allies. Consequently,

> …notwithstanding their position, which was strong, we had no doubt of success – three strong divisions of Infantry and two brigades of cavalry were up but from some mistake the guns of the 5th Division, which was to have led, missed their way and the attack in consequence was delayed – before they arrived and the other divisions had taken their stations, the enemy had assembled and encircled themselves with vedettes – they also had strong bodies of Infantry on the heights flanking the roads to their position. It was then so late, nearly 5 in the evening, and Wellington then judged it advisable not to attack – we returned to the river and began cooking.
>
> The unhappy result to our expedition, which had every prospect of succeeding, has caused great disappointment in the whole army and an inquiry, it is said, has been ordered into the cause of it, at present it appears to have been originated with Maj.-Gen. Pringle, who commanded the 5th Division (in the absence through illness of General Hulse)[151] in not sending *explicit orders* and a guide to the Artillery attached to it.[152]

Men like Douglas had more immediate matters to think about than the failings of generals and their staff. For them, the fact that 'The harvest was now in its prime. Wheat, grapes etc were more than abundant' meant that the basic diet could be supplemented. At Arevalo they had already taken advantage of the wheat and the flagstones, both of which were plentiful. The flagstones

> …served as the nether millstone, while a piece just as large as a man could conveniently work formed the upper one. It must not be expected that we produced meal of the best quality, but to men having good appetites, and the tenor of the Commissariat far in the rear, it was, you may depend upon it, not to be despised. There were a few Coffee mills in the Regiment which were of infinite use and produced excellent meal.

As for the grapes, they 'were in the height of perfection, and in the fields (or rather the plains) we were under the necessity of encamping. At all times we were as far removed from

---

150 Greenwood (ed.), *Through Spain with Wellington*, pp.126–127.
151 Major General Richard Hulse had been given command of the Fifth Division after Salamanca. He died of typhus on the 7 September.
152 W.F.K. Thompson (ed.), *An Ensign in the Peninsular War: the Letters of John Aitchison* (London: Michael Joseph, 1981), p.197.

those tempting articles as possible, but in this instance it was out of their power to avoid our eating them.'[153]

Although the planned attack on the 6th failed to happen, by the following morning it was apparent that the French had withdrawn under cover of darkness. The Allies took up the abandoned position on the Cisterniga Heights, from where they could see enemy cavalry passing through Valladolid and also that the French were preparing to blow up the bridge across the Pisuerga. The town was

> ...in great confusion as the French had not been gone above two hours. The People did not say much on our entering; I understand they are greatly in the French interest. We halted here on the 8th: & 9th: The new Constitution was proclaimed and the Town was Illuminated, if putting a Candle in front of a large House, or two or Three in a Street can be so called. As I am no great amateur of that kind of Illumination, I went to the theatre which was honoured by the Great Lord in his uniform as Captn: General of the Spanish Armies.

After describing the uniform in some detail, including the Star of the Order of the Golden Fleece, which was reputed to have cost a million dollars, Le Mesurier referred to the play, the subject of which was Christopher Columbus. When the disgraced protagonist bewailed his fate, 'some Spaniards Roared out "Viva Duque de Ciudad Rodrigo!" and it was a long time before silence was restored, and not till after His Lordship had come forward and made some low bows.'[154] Obviously, there were some in Valladolid who had recognised which way the wind was blowing.

To keep pressure on the French, Wellington sent forward the 6th Division and the two independent Portuguese brigades to join the light cavalry, which was about seven miles in front of Valladolid. Clausel was at Dueñas, but when on the 10th the Allies threatened his vedettes, he withdrew further north. On the same day Wellington left Valladolid with the rest of the Allied troops. Clausel had been joined by Foy and by a detachment from the Army of the North, which meant there was less chance of catching and overwhelming him. A forward movement, however, would sustain pressure, although it could not be a rapid one because Wellington was waiting for Castaños and the main Galician army to join him, as well as for Santocildes to come in.

It was soon clear that the French were on the road to Burgos. By 16 September the Allies were at Torquemada, where they were finally joined by 10,000 'men badly clothed and equipped & still worse in discipline. The men themselves were in general, fine stout looking fellows, but had the appearance of not being more than half-fed.'[155] The French were still within reach, and preparations were made for an Allied attack, including sending the baggage to the rear. 'The numbers of the French were about 30,000 men, as Clausel had been joined by general de division Joseph Souham, who brought with him 10,000 [from France]... Up to a late hour of night, the enemy shewed no disposition to abandon his positions & Ld.

---

153 Monick (ed.), *Douglas's Tale*, pp.50–51.
154 Greenwood (ed.), *Through Spain with Wellington*, p.130.
155 Roger Norman Buckley (ed.), *The Napoleonic War Journal of Thomas Henry Browne 1807-1816* (London: The Bodley Head for the Army Records Society, 1987), p.185.

Wellington resolved to attack them at day-break.'[156] The 5th Division was to be in the main line of attack. The whole Allied force, including the Galicians, was under arms by 4:00 a.m., but once again the French had slipped away under cover of darkness, leaving their campfires burning, and hurried on their way to Burgos when the 6th Division turned their position. According to Le Mesurier, on the 16th and the 17th 'the enemy seemed inclined to make a stand but retired after a little skirmishing in which a few men on both sides were killed and wounded.'[157]

Souham, having returned from leave in France, had taken command of the Army of Portugal, being senior to Clausel. He discovered Caffarelli at Burgos, checking the defences. The commanders of the Armies of the North and Portugal then moved on to Briviesca, but not before they had installed a garrison of 2,000 men under the command of *Général de division* Jean-Louis Dubreton, who was to prove a wily and determined opponent of the Allies.

As at Ciudad Rodrigo and Badajoz, Wellington called for volunteers to serve as assistant engineers, and at least three officers from the 5th Division responded: Lieutenant Nevill from the 2/30th and two officers from the 1/9th, Captain Courtney Crowe Kenny and Lieutenant Henry Dumaresque. Nevill included in his memoirs a clear description of the castle, which was

> ...situated on a height above the town and is extremely strong. On the height was placed a battery of twelve heavy cannon. It was nearly surrounded by three lines of field works, the lower line embracing a scarp wall at the base of the hill, very difficult of access. At intervals, between these works were *flèches,* built of masonry, and armed with cannon. The whole was admirably constructed for defence, and amply supplied with stores, ammunition, and provisions.

He also commented on Wellington's determination to take 'this formidable castle', despite having inadequate means and being under time pressure. Most notably inadequate was the number of Royal Engineer officers present, only five of them, with Lieutenant Colonel John Burgoyne in command. There were also few artificers and Wellington would once again have to call upon men with the appropriate artisan skills. Nevill cited a letter he subsequently received from Burgoyne: 'Sir John states, in a few lines to me of recent date, how wretchedly we were then off in everything necessary for a siege.' And what could be more necessary than siege guns? Yet 'The artillery consisted of three 18-pounders and five 24-pounder howitzers of iron, and those cannon not of the best order, having been much used and knocked about, and the supply of ammunition very deficient.'[158]

The actual progress of the siege would not directly involve the 5th Division, since Wellington chose to conduct operations with the 1st and 6th Divisions, sending the 5th and 7th several leagues forward along the road to Vitoria as covering troops in the expectation of a French counter-attack (hence Nevill's reference to time pressure). As it happened, Wellington was allowed rather more time than he expected. With the addition of the 10,000

---

156 Buckley (ed.), *The Napoleonic War Journal*, p.185.
157 Greenwood (ed.), *Through Spain with Wellington*, p.131.
158 Nevill, *Some Recollections*, pp.20–21.

reinforcements which Souham brought with him from France, the strength of the Army of Portugal had risen to 44,000. Furthermore, Caffarelli initially lingered at Vitoria with 9,000 men and 16 guns. Souham, however, an instinctively more cautious commander that Clausel, believed that the Allied strength was 60,000. He also thought that the four divisions under Hill's command were on their way to join Wellington. It would be some time before he realised the true situation, that the Allies under Wellington amounted to only about 30,000, including the Galicians, and Hill was not on the move.

There were also problems with the Allied force which undermined even that numerical imbalance. Le Mesurier lamented that the 2/9th remained in Gibraltar and wished that some of the junior battalion's subalterns might join them in Spain because they now had only 19 officers against a paper strength of 43, and of the 19 only three captains and 11 subalterns were present and fit for duty.[159] The 1/9th were certainly not alone in this respect.

Nor was the shortage of officers the only problem. According to Gomm, the troops had been very sickly, although there had been some improvement recently, presumably as they were relieved from the exigences of marching. The weather had now broken for the worse, however, and the men were without tents, which was not conducive to good health. Douglas noted that

> The number of killed and wounded at Salamanca, with sickness, had so thinned the ranks that out of 6 Sergeants and as many Corporals, there was not one present with the company but myself. Often at daylight, at which time the liquor was served out, I have drawn my company's allowance in two mess-tins, so that it may easily be conjectured we were not very strong; not more than 25 fit for duty in a company, if all were present, numbered 100.

Nor were uniforms in better shape. 'My poor old tattered trousers and coat were no way improved by these excursions and in many cases it would have taken no mean judge to determine the original colour; perhaps a piece of stocking covered a few holes on one sleeve while a piece of biscuit bag covered the other.'[160] If Douglas had but known it, the state of the uniforms would contribute to the heavy losses taken later in the year.

Food was the only consolation. 'Our rations were very good and pretty regular. I think the Spaniards, particularly around Burgos and Biscay, make the best bread in the world. I am much of the opinion they put a quantity of honey in it, and that article is plentiful here.'[161] Le Mesurier was also satisfied with the performance of the commissariat, but he could not resist noting that a newly appointed commissary, 'my Old play mate S.Dobree' was 'just as stout and rosy as ever.' The implication of a well-fleshed commissary would be understood by all who were familiar with their reputation. Like so many officers, Le Mesurier was also able to improve his diet with his gun. The area was full of wild pigeons, and he had the satisfaction of bringing five back to camp 'which made a Capital stew.'[162]

---

159 Greenwood (ed.), *Through Spain with Wellington*, p.132.
160 Monick (ed.), *Douglas's Tale*, p.53.
161 Monick (ed.), *Douglas's Tale*, p.52.
162 Greenwood (ed.), *Through Spain with Wellington*, p.135.

As for the day-to-day routine of the covering troops, Hale described their predictable routine:

> …we encamped in a regular way, but without tents, and about one hour before break of day, we stood to our arms in the usual manner, and continued under arms till it was quite broad day light, and as soon as our general officers were fully satisfied that the enemy were making no movement, we were dismissed, and parties immediately sent out for wood and water for the purpose of cooking, while our butchers were killing and dressing our meat.[163]

Meanwhile, the besiegers failed to make the rapid progress that Wellington had hoped for. An initial success when the San Miguel hornwork was taken was followed by a failed escalade of the outer wall of the defences. Also, it was becoming increasingly obvious that 'the fire from our cannon did not make much impression on the place, and were so much injured that some of them could not be used. It was determined to make our approaches by mining, and the engineers with their assistants had an arduous task to accomplish.'[164] Nevill, of course, was engaged in this arduous task.

On 4 October, a lodgement was made in the lower line of the French defences. Two days later a working party from the 5th Division, who had been making gabions and fascines, was ordered to serve as covering troops for a further attack. This proved dangerous work. 'Out of [blank] Offrs: belonging to that party, four were Wounded, one of which has since Dead [sic]. The Off: Com'g: (Capn of the Royals) was wounded & received a visit next day from Lord Wellington who expressed himself highly pleased with the behaviour of this Party.'[165]

The siege finally reached a point where any hope of success depended on the effectiveness of the mining that was taking place, while the conditions for the covering troops steadily deteriorated.

> Rain and cold winds roused us pretty early from our Beds, for the sake of warming ourselves near a large fire…and what comes hard upon us is that our Stock of Tabacco is nearly out and good is not to be procured here. A pound of common Tea is sold here for Four Dollars and a pound of corse brown Sugar 1/9d: and we are glad to procure it at that rate.[166]

Le Mesurier also noted that of 67 men sent to the rear, 17 died on the road. Burgos was fast becoming what Wellington would later call it, his worst scrape.

At Burgos itself, the 5th Division was taking further casualties. On 2 October Captain Kenny, who had volunteered against Cameron's wishes, was killed by a French sharpshooter, while on the 10th Lieutenant Dumaresque suffered a grape shot wound to his thigh. Nevill was also a casualty. On the 4th, during the attempt to form a lodgement,

---

163 Hale, *Journal*, p.96.
164 Nevill, *Some Recollections*, p.23.
165 Greenwood (ed.), *Through Spain with Wellington*, p.135.
166 Greenwood (ed.), *Through Spain with Wellington*, p.136.

…the enemy made a most determined sortie, upsetting our gabions and in part driving us back; but we speedily rallied, and had a regular stand-up fight, in some cases hand to hand. I felt suddenly paralyzed and became unconscious, until a hand pulled me out of some rubbish; it was a sergeant of the 79th. A ball had struck me on the left shoulder, passing out through the blade-bone.

The kind sergeant carried me to my quarters, refusing to take my watch as a present.[167]

Nevill was distressed to learn when he made further enquiry that the sergeant was killed soon afterwards.

The siege was finally brought to an end not by Dubreton's resistance but by Souham's decision to advance, coupled with disturbing news from further south. On 18 October, the day of the final Allied assault, Souham sent Maucune's division to drive in the Allied forward posts near Santa Olalla, which were manned by the 7th Division, and then to take possession of the high ground at Monasterio de Rodilla. Maucune was successful, including taking a Brunswick Oels picquet. This advance by the Army of Portugal was an obvious threat to the covering force, which in turn jeopardised the continuation of the siege. Wellington reacted by bringing the outposts back to Quintanapala and Olmos, while the rest of the covering troops were positioned in battle order, the line extending from San Palaccio on the left to Ibeas on the right. At the same time, the working parties at Burgos were warned to be ready to march if a French attack materialised. Souham did indeed sent two divisions forward but it was information that Joseph, meaning Joseph and Soult, had left Valencia for Madrid, thus putting Hill under severe pressure, which persuaded Wellington to abandon Burgos.

Souham, meanwhile, attacked the troops at Olmos, but met strong resistance from the Chasseurs Britanniques. When the 1st and 5th Divisions came up under the command of the recently arrived Lieutenant General Sir Edward Paget, Maucune was forced back to Monasterio. Nevertheless, this was further evidence, if evidence were needed, that the French were on the offensive, while a communication from Hill, received on the 19th, confirmed that the French were concentrating against him. Wellington was forced to raise the siege.

Retreat

The retreat commenced as darkness fell on the 21st. In orders received from Colonel James Willoughby Gordon, the Quartermaster General, Gomm was instructed that

> The 5th Division with their guns are to march to the left this evening as it becomes so dark that the movements cannot be seen by the enemy. The above mentioned troops are to proceed by Quintana Dueñas to Villalon – hence by Badajos [Tardajos] across the Urbel river, there they are to halt. Lieutenant-Colonel Gomm is to conduct the columns. The two Spanish divisions to follow the 5th division with their infantry.

---

167 Nevill, *Some Recollections*, p.24.

Lieutenant-Colonel Gomm to place the above troops in column of battalions as soon as they arrive on their ground; he will take care that these orders are duly communicated to the Spanish division. Care must be taken to make fires previously to their march.[168]

Thus, the 5th Division and the Galicians would form the right of the retreating force.

According to Hale, the division set off at about 7:00 p.m. and marched until 4:00 a.m. Having been granted two hours to rest, they then had to stir themselves because the French were reported to be making a rapid advance. Souham had finally reached Burgos on the 22nd, and immediately responded to the raising of the siege by sending Curto's light cavalry forward to ascertain the Allies' line of retreat. This led to a clash with Anson's cavalry, who were driven in, but this did not alter the fact that Wellington had stolen a day's march on the French.

It had been a hard march, however. The persistent rain had saturated the ground, with the result that the infantry found themselves struggling against the conditions. Major General Pringle, in a letter written on 5 November, described it as 'a most disagreeable and harassing march'.[169] Others were more specific. Le Mesurier referred to ploughed fields and ditches, with the men up to their knees in mud. This produced an inevitable result. As the division covered eight leagues on bad roads, an immense number of stragglers fell behind and had to be abandoned.[170]

On 23 October the 5th Division and the Galicians marched to Cordovilla, which placed them northwest of the rest of the Allied troops, who had headed for Torquemada. Before either destination was reached, first the cavalry and then the 7th Division had to fight off the French pursuit from Celada del Camino to Venta del Pozo. At Torquemada, it was not long before the troops found the wine vats, so that in a very short time a state of drunken chaos reigned. There were no wine vats at Cordovilla, however. Somewhat confusingly, in his diary Captain Robert Lawson, who was attached to the 5th Division, but had followed the main army to Torquemada because the route taken by his division was unsuitable for artillery, not only described the drunkenness, 'which would have disgraced a Billingsgate rabble' but noted that on the 24th 'the division arrives at Torquemada & I join it & we march to Villamuriel.'[171] This suggests either that the 5th Division marched from Cordovilla to Torquemada or that Lawson joined them somewhere in the region of that town as they now brought up the rear of the Allied force. Certainly, no other writers connected to the 5th Division make any reference to Torquemada and the drunkenness there.

On the morning of the 24th the division once again stood to arms at 4:00 a.m., and then continued the retreat until sunset, which brought them beyond Palencia to Villamuriel, where they took position on the left of an Allied line along the Carrion downstream to Dueñas. According to Le Mesurier it had been another hard march, 'Seven Leagues (the road was strewed on both sides with men completely knocked up) and we arrived about

---

168 Carr-Gomm (ed.), *Letters and Journals*, vol.I, p.288, footnote.
169 Pringle to Aylmer Haly, 5 November, private collection.
170 Greenwood (ed.), *Through Spain with Wellington*, p.137.
171 John H. Leslie (ed.), *The Dickson Manuscripts* (Huntingdon: Ken Trotman, 1987), vol.IV, p.712.

dark at Villa Muriel, a village situated on the Carrion River between Dueñas and Palencia. We were buoyed up with the hopes of a halt on the 25th:' a hope that would be realised but not in the form that Le Mesurier anticipated. It started well, however. 'On our arrival at this place I was ordered on Guard at the Town to protect the property of the Inhabitants and was comfortably lodged in a house that night with plenty of forage for my Poney, which he seemed to enjoy greatly, having fared hard since the commencement of the Retreat.'[172]

One divisional development that none of the letter writers made note of was the arrival of Major General John Oswald on the morning of the 25 October to take command of the division. His appointment to the staff in the Peninsula had been noted in a general order of the 7th, and he had been at headquarters since the 22nd. Either late on the 24th or very early on the 25th, he received the order to take command of the 5th Division in Leith's continuing absence. Douglas does make some reference to him in his retrospective account of the day's events in which echoes of Napier's account may be detected. The change of command, though, must have given Gomm the hope that he would now be working with a man very different from one 'who is liked by all the world in private life, and respected by no one in public.'[173] In a later memorandum, he described how during the first day of the retreat Pringle constantly badgered him with the question, '"Now, Gomm, are you sure you are right?"' as Gomm, definitely less than sure, conducted the division and the Galicians 'over some miles of waste country, trackless save by private landmarks of my own previous establishing.'[174] Oswald was an unknown quality, however, and only time would reveal whether he was an adequate substitute for Leith.

While one of the Galician divisions, Francisco Javier Losada's, joined the 5th division at Villamuriel, the other, Francisco Cabrero's, was sent to Palencia, supported by the Royal Scots. Douglas, having described the difficulty of crossing the bridge because of the mass of 'men, baggage, guns and every species of trumpery attendant on an army', then depicted Palencia as 'a beautiful town situated at the foot of a mountain. A dry canal ran nearly parallel with the river, to near the town. A dilapidated bridge over the canal led to a beautiful green, ere you reached the town, where a noble bridge crossed the river leading in to it.'[175] This description was not incidental, since Wellington had sent an order that the 5th Division should blow up the bridge at Palencia. Although this order had been sent on the evening of the 24th, the dragoon who carried it lost his way in the dark, with unfortunate consequences.

In his dispatch to Bathurst of 26 October Wellington merely wrote: 'I had directed the 3rd battalion of the Royals to march to Palencia to protect the destruction of the bridges over the Carrion at that place, but it appears that the enemy assembled such a force at that point, that Lieut. Colonel Campbell thought it necessary to retire upon Villa-muriel.'[176] Douglas's account elaborates on this brief statement. Because the dragoon lost his way, the message did not reach the Royal Scots until 8:00 a.m., by which time the bridge should have been

---

172 Greenwood (ed.), *Through Spain with Wellington*, p.137.
173 Carr-Gomm (ed.), *Letters and Journals*, vol.I, p.287.
174 Carr-Gomm (ed.), *Letters and Journals*, vol.I, p.292.
175 Monick (ed.), *Douglas's Tale*, pp.56–57.
176 Gurwood (ed.), *Dispatches*, vol.IX, pp.516–517.

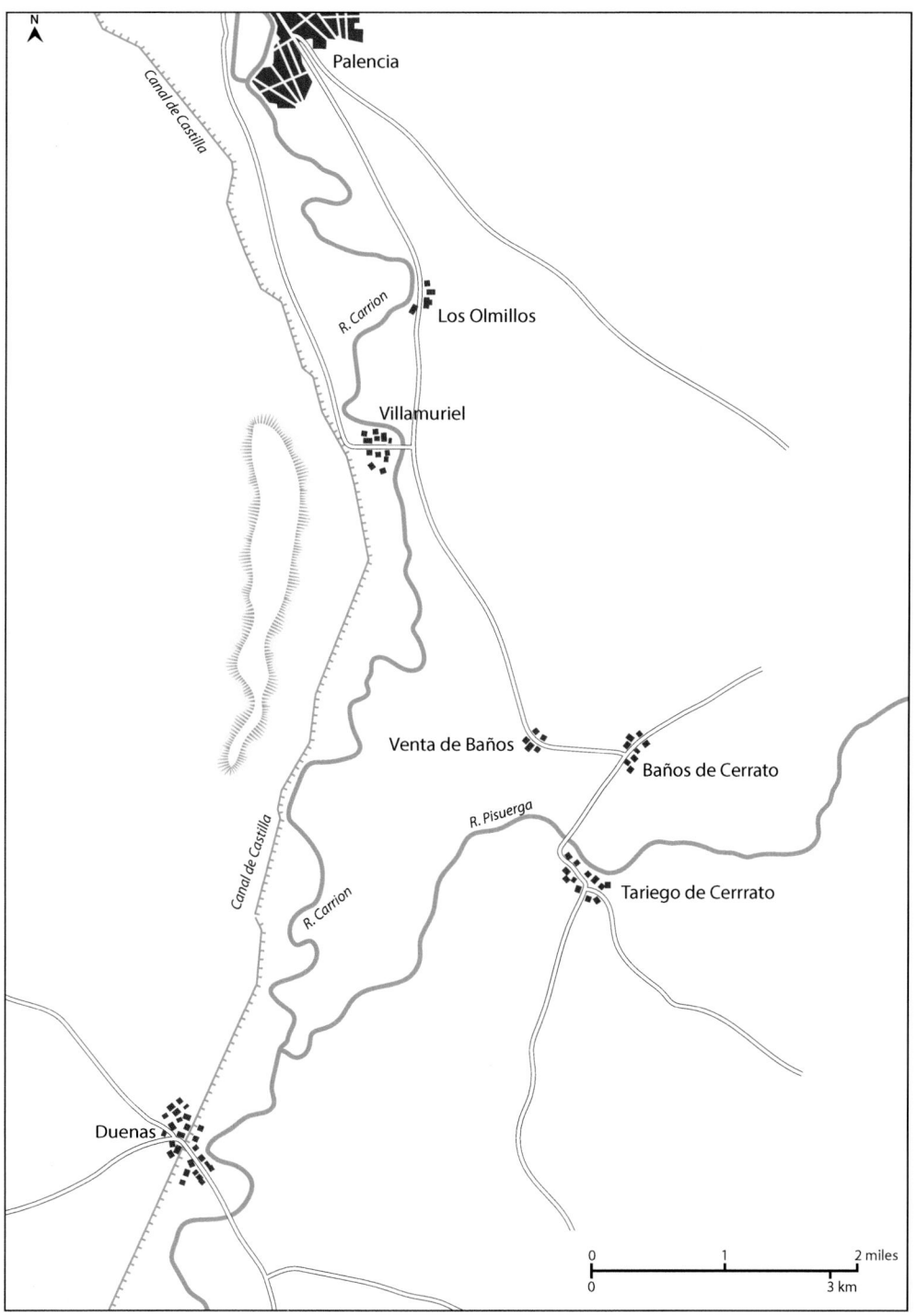

The area around Villamuriel.

destroyed. Whatever the time, though, in Douglas's opinion 'this accident was the sole cause of the disasters of the day.'[177]

Villamuriel

Souham, now well aware that he had over-estimated the size of the Allied force, was ready to go on the offensive. He was somewhat hindered by his own soldiers' discovery of the wine that still remained at Torquemada but he was able to establish his headquarters at Magaz and give orders to Foy and Maucune for an attack on Palencia and the Allied position on the Carrion. Foy, with his own division and *Général de brigade* Michel Louis Bonté's, previously Thomière's, was to take Palencia and its all-important bridge, while Maucune, again with his own division and *Général de brigade* Jean Pierre Gauthier's, formerly Bonnet's, was to force the bridges at Villamuriel and San Isidro. For this purpose, Maucune sent Gauthier to San Isidro and focused his attack on Villamuriel.

At Palencia, the artificers and miners were sent to the bridge to work upon its destruction under the supervision of Lieutenant William Reid R.E, while the Royal Scots, the Galicians and two squadrons of dragoons covered. The atmosphere seems to have been surprisingly relaxed: 'We were formed on a delightful green close to the river, which separated us from the town, in open column of companies, not expecting the enemy to be so convenient.'[178] After all, with the exception of the cavalry, the French had been keeping their distance and it was easy to become over-confident. This is instanced by the way the battalion's shoemakers went into the town to acquire leather.

Having ascribed some desultory fire to stragglers shooting pigs, the Allied troops were taken completely by surprise 'when all of a hurry our leather merchants came running down the lines and spread alarm of the enemy being in the town. Scarcely had they reached the column when some close firing took place on the bridge, and the enemy got possession of it. The Engineer Officer comes running to Col Campbell and says, "Col Campbell, the bridge is taken. You are to act as you please with your Battalion."'[179]

In order to understand what had happened at Palencia it is necessary to consider the French perspective. According to Foy, he found Palencia 'closed and barricaded, a regiment of Spanish cavalry around the ramparts, a part of the English 5th division and Brigadier Francisco Cabrera's troops of the army of Galicia in the town.' The cavalry was soon put to flight, whereupon the Galicians said they would open the gates if the general approached. When Foy sent an aide and a trumpeter forward, the Spanish fired on them, killing a horse. Not surprisingly, Foy retaliated with artillery, which stove in the gates. 'Brigadier Cleminceau, at the head of the 2nd battalion of the 69th, entered the town with the bayonet and knocked over the English in the streets and, despite a lively fusillade, took the bridge over the Carrion, which the enemy tried to blow up; the powder for the explosion was in place.'[180]

---

177 Monick (ed.), *Douglas's Tale*, p.57.
178 Monick (ed.), *Douglas's Tale*, p.57.
179 Monick (ed.), *Douglas's Tale*, p.57.
180 Girod de L'Ain, *Vie Militaire*, p.381.

In Foy's account, written to Souham on the 25th, the French pursued the enemy, who had cannon, but the French guns did great damage, with one shot taking out three dragoons. The pursuit lasted to the entrance to Paramo. This is an exaggeration, for the only Paramo in the area, implying a moorland plateau, is well beyond Villamuriel. He further claimed to have taken 100 prisoners, with 60 men killed, while in Palencia his troops found a great store of biscuit. Douglas, however, conceded a loss of 10 men, while the dragoons lost one man and two horses to French round shot. Douglas also referred to grape shot as they hurried to cross the dry canal on the narrow bridge, which was in a bad state of repair, but 'almost every shot flew over the column'. Once the bridge had been crossed, the French cavalry were deterred from pursuing by the well-directed fire of two 'Spanish grasshoppers', which seems to refer to the light guns used by Spanish guerrillas. Having reached open ground, the Royal Scots made their way back to Villamuriel as best they could. Here they discovered that 'since our departure in the morning the face of affairs had considerably changed. The enemy had now occupied the dry canal in great numbers, which General Oswald ought to have done.'[181]

At the time, Douglas was very unlikely to have been aware of the arrival of Major General Oswald, or of the dispositions of the division. The source for this comment is easy to locate, however. According to Napier,

> The left of the position was equally strong [compared to San Isidro], yet general Oswald, who had just arrived from England and taken the command of the fifth division on the instant, overlooked the advantages to be derived from the dry bed of a canal with high banks, which, on his side, run parallel with the Carion, and he had not occupied the village of Muriel in sufficient strength.[182]

Napier was not at Villamuriel, of course, and he gives no source for this observation, which, as will be seen, was based on a false premise, that Oswald was present when the 5th Division was deployed.

In Villamuriel the day had started for Le Mesurier when

> About Seven o'Clock in the morning of the 25th: the Adjt: Genl: of the Division passed by the Guard and astonish'd me a little by an Order to go and support the Picquet on the Bridge, about 200 Yards from the Village. On my arrival there I found the Picquet lining the Bridge and preparations making for Blowing it up. We had not been there long when some Spanish Dragoons told us the French were coming on with One Thousand Cavalry and 600 Infantry, but soon we found our information was false. Artillery made their appearance, took a position and oppened [sic] a heavy fire of round and Grape on the Artillery that was supporting the Bridge. A short time after, a Gun moved to their right and took post in a situation which raked us completely. They then opened on the Bridge with Grape and round, and wounded Three of our Men.[183]

---

181 Monick (ed.), *Douglas's Tale*, pp.58–59.
182 Napier, *History of the War*, vol.V, p.300.
183 Greenwood (ed.), *Through Spain with Wellington*, p.137.

This seems to be the point at which Oswald arrived.

According to Hale, the 9th had already been ordered to defend the bridge the previous evening. Soon after dark on the 24th a party of engineers started boring the bridge, in order to blow it up. There was no further disturbance, however, until about 9:00 a.m. on the 25th when a French division was discovered to be advancing on Villamuriel. As a result two hundred of the 9th were positioned by the bridge, while the rest of the battalion 'extended along the banks of [the] River to the left of the Bridge in light infantry order.'[184] He also referred to two companies which had been detached to the right, and of which they had no information.

As for the rest of the division, Pringle had been responsible for their deployment. While the two battalions of the 1/4th seem to have held the village, and extended back to the canal, the other British battalions and the two Portuguese line battalions were in the dry canal. The evidence for the position of the 15th Line comes, rather bizarrely, from the sad incident of a British major, Edward Ovens, who was serving with the battalion, being killed by round shot as he was sitting in the canal, reading a newspaper.[185]

The 8th Caçadores, being light infantry, were probably nearer the river, guarding one of the several fords. There is also a suggestion that Pringle called in the light companies from his own brigade and one of the two Brunswick Oels companies and led them across the river under his direct command, although, if so, they were driven in soon after the Royals began their march to Palencia. As for the Galicians, they 'were taking their position on the heights in the rear of Villa Muriel and appeared to us to be in great confusion, every one trying who could reach the Top first, but formed on the Hill as soon as the whole had got up.'[186] This confusion, of course, had been caused by Foy's irruption into Palencia.[187]

Twenty-five years later, Oswald wrote that upon his arrival, most of the division

> …was admirably disposed of about the village as also in the dry bed of a canal running in its rear, in some places parallel to the Carrion. Certain of the corps were formed in columns of attack, supported by reserves, ready to fall upon the enemy, in consequence of the mine failing, he should venture to push a column across the narrow bridge.[188]

In the usual French fashion, Maucune commenced his attack with his guns, which took out two of Lawson's. Then,

> …seeing so small a party to defend the bridge, they made a grand push for that place, but fortunately, before they could make their object, the bridge blew up, which put a stop to their pursuit; so then they extended themselves along the river,

---

184 Greenwood (ed.), *Through Spain with Wellington*, p.138.
185 Bannatyne, *History of the Thirtieth Regiment*, p.286.
186 Greenwood (ed.), *Through Spain with Wellington*, p.138.
187 See Garry Wills, *Wellington at Bay* (Warwick: Helion, 2020), pp.88–93, for a full discussion of the allied deployment.
188 Quoted in Wills, *Wellington at Bay*, p.90.

in about the same direction that we were, by which a smart skirmishing immediately took place, and continued about four hours.[189]

By this time, Wellington was aware that Foy was in possession of Palencia, with its bridge intact, and ordered a change of front, throwing back the left, including the Spanish on the high ground, against Foy's likely advance while the right continued to hold off Maucune at the Carrion. This enabled both the 3/1st and the Cabrera's Galicians to re-form. As for. Maucune, his priority was to find a way across the river, which was in flood after the heavy autumn rains. Napier claimed that he succeeded with a *ruse de guerre*, when a French cavalryman, claiming to be a deserter, sought the help of the troops on the Allied side. They (very likely the 8th caçadores) indicated the ford, thereupon the Frenchman kissed his hand in derision and galloped back to share his information with Maucune.[190] Again, Napier gives no source for this story. It is certain, however, that by whatever means the French located the ford. They were then able to overwhelm the Allied troops lining the banks, including taking prisoner a whole company of the 1/9th who were posted in a grist mill and fighting their own battle against French tirailleurs. They then pushed further forward until the they reached the dry canal, where Pringle's brigade was posted.

According to his own account, Wellington now 'made Major General Pringle and Brig. General Barnes attack these troops, under the orders of Major General Oswald; in which attack the Spanish troops co-operated, and [the French] were driven across the river with considerable loss.'[191]

In Napier's version, Brigadier General Edward Barnes proceeded to attack the main body of the French, with the support of the Galicians and one of the Brunswicker companies to their left, while Pringle's brigade cleared the dry canal. Douglas presents a slightly different scenario as far as Barnes' brigade was concerned, claiming that his battalion and the 1/38th cleared the canal with the bayonet. He then claimed that

> …if Wellington's orders had been obeyed, our loss would have been trifling, as we were to halt and take possession of it and then it would have been impossible for those dispossessed of their lodging to have escaped, as they became exposed to two fires. But, instead of occupying this post, we were ordered to follow the fugitives to the river's brink, exposed to a front and flanking fire of round and grape shot with occasional shells.[192]

Significantly, Hale remembered being ordered to stand to arms and then charge – no mention of the dry canal. The charge drove the French back to the river, with considerable loss.

As for Pringle's brigade, it may be assumed that one of his battalions, the 1/4th which had been on the right, supported Barnes brigade, while the other two, the 2/30th and the 2/44th, cleared the canal before extending, where the Galicians were in considerable disarray.

---

189 Hale, *Journal*, p.98.
190 Napier, *History of the War*, vol.V, p.301.
191 Gurwood (ed.), *Dispatches*, vol.IX, p.517.
192 Monick (ed.), *Douglas's Tale*, p.59.

Fortunately, the Spanish liaison officer, *General de brigada* Miguel Álava, was able to restore order and lead them forward against the French. As for the two British battalions, according to Lieutenant Alexander Hamilton of the 2/30th, 'The 30th and the 44th did rather a dashing thing when they advanced in line against seventeen pieces of cannon, cleared the adjoining village and took more prisoners than their own force was composed of.'[193]

Gomm put the divisions losses at 600, and summed up the day's action as doing all that was required of them. Pringle was rather more informative in a letter written to Haly on the 5 November.

> On the 25th the army halted and they attacked the part where the 5th Division in which I am, was placed. After an action which lasted almost all day we succeeded in repulsing them with considerable loss, but we suffered also a great deal, the division losing 40 officers and 600 men killed and wounded, which is a great deal to lose you may say for nothing, as we retired next day. My brigade lost a good many. I had my usual good fortune and was not touched, tho' I had another horse shot under me and a shot through my coat. I am very unlucky about my horses, for the loss of two good ones in one campaign is a very serious loss.[194]

Eventually, those French still able to do so crossed the river, leaving the Allies, battered and exhausted, in possession of Villamuriel. Despite some intermittent firing during the night, the 5th Division remained in position until the morning of the 26th. A very cold night without shelter, according to Douglas, during which the sufferers from the recurrent Walcheren fever felt the effects of the ague. They were also aware of the guns and the baggage moving off, so it was no surprise when, at first light, the picquets were called in and the division was soon on the march, still in the rear because the rest of the army had moved on after the situation at Villamuriel was known to be secure. On the 27th the division crossed the Pisuerga and camped about four miles from Valladolid. The following day they crossed the Duero at Tudela. They then moved towards Rueda, with the French pursuit slowed by the need to repair bridges, a task which eventually required a six-day halt.

The Allies were now themselves able to halt for several days, during which the 3/1st acquired new uniforms. Their quartermaster had been trying for some time to bring men and uniforms together, which finally happened at Arevalo, where the refit took place. Not before time, this refit 'being 2 years in arrears; so that in 19 cases out of 20 it would have required judges of no ordinary capacity to determine the original colour of either coat or trousers.'[195] It is doubtful if the other battalions of the division were in any better state but Wellington did not expect parade ground smartness in troops that had fought a year-long campaign.

The fullest account, from the perspective of the 5th Division, of what happened once the retreat was resumed, comes in a letter Le Mesurier wrote on 15 November and continued 10 days later. He had already informed his family in an earlier letter of the 2nd, written when

---

193 Bannatyne, *History of the Thirtieth Regiment*, p.287. Hamilton's words were recorded verbatim by a friend.
194 Pringle to Aylmer Haly, 5 November 1812, private collection.
195 Monick (ed.), *Douglas's Tale*, p.61.

the division was encamped near Tordesillas, that they had no wood and had to forage for several miles to find any. They were also still short of officers fit for duty, while there were too frequent sales of the possessions of dead and missing officers, always a melancholy affair. Not surprisingly, nine days later, when they were once again on the Heights of San Cristoval, their position remained

> ...not very pleasant. We have no good water within two Miles. We are obliged to use water from a large Pool which serves almost for meat and drink, and our Wood is brought from Villages when parties are sent to pull down houses, and of that we are obliged to be sparing. Forage for our Animals is not to be had within Two leagues, so that it has very little to recommend it, the Strength excepted which His Lordship says is equal to Twenty Thousand men.

The battalion had received reinforcements of both officers and men, but Le Mesurier was also being paid for a company since Villamuriel. Some of the newcomers, who were senior to him, wanted the company for themselves, but Lieutenant Colonel Cameron had ignored their demands, regarding it as unfair that Le Mesurier should lose the extra pay the moment that the battalion was out of danger.[196]

As Pringle informed Haly in his letter of the 5 November

> General Hill has abandoned Madrid and is come up towards us with his army which makes us tolerably strong but I think our situation by no means a pleasant one with Soult manoeuvring with a very strong army on our right flank, and this army of the North [Portugal] quite close on our left. I own I fear the consequence will be our being obliged to fall back into Portugal.

Thinking of how the British public would respond, he commented: 'I fear John Bull will not like the news from this country, after all our losses this year.'[197]

To return to Le Mesurier, there were other causes for complaint. His impression of Major General Oswald, as well as the newly arrived Brigadier General Barnes, was not favourable. They 'anoy [sic] us greatly. They wish to parade us continually. We have not one single day we can call our own. Immediately after a March, instead of rest we have a Parade. They are to be removed to the 6th Division as soon as Genls: Leith & Hay arrive, so that we shall be comfortable again in a Short time.'[198] Barnes did, indeed, soon leave the 5th Division, as did Pringle some months later, but Oswald remained.

Positioned as they were, there was keen anticipation among the Allies of another Battle of Salamanca. Soult and Souham had made contact on 7 November, enabling joint French operations. With the former in command, his would be the decision whether to accept the invitation that Wellington seemed to be offering. It is certainly open to question whether there was ever much likelihood of another battle, however. As early as the 8th, in a dispatch to Bathurst, Wellington rehearsed the reasons why his and Hill's troops were in no fit state

---

196 Greenwood (ed.), *Through Spain with Wellington*, pp141–142.
197 Pringle to Aylmer Haly, 5 November 1812, private collection.
198 Greenwood (ed.), *Through Spain with Wellington*, p.142.

for action, having been 'in the field, and almost constantly marching since the month of January last; their clothes and equipments are much worn, and a short period in cantonments would be useful to them. The cavalry likewise are weak in numbers, and the horses low in condition.'[199] He might have added that sickness was rife, particularly dysentery and rheumatism.

As for Soult, according to the advice he supposedly left for his successor in the Peninsula, he cautioned: 'Whenever you find the British army in retreat, let them alone, and they will go to the devil in their own way; but if you go near them, they will get into their places, and give you such a drubbing as you never had before.'[200] Memories of Albuera lingered. It was better, therefore, to harry the enemy out of Spain.

There was a rapid realisation among the Allies that they were once more in retreat. Le Mesurier opened the continuation of his letter of 15 November thus:

> I had proceeded this far when the word 'Stand to your arms!' passed through the Camp, and in a moment the Tents were struck [the officers' tents, presumably]. We encamped that night near the Zamora Gate, Salamanca, and on the 16th passed the Tormes about Daylight and halted about 500 Yards from Salamanca. We expected every moment to be ordered to take up our old position on the Arapiles but about Two in the afternoon we moved on the Road to Ciudad Rodrigo. The weather had been Cloudy all day and we were deluged with torrents of rain.[201]

Wellington now set out details of the three routes back to Ciudad Rodrigo that his troops should follow. On the left were the 2nd, 3rd and 4th Divisions under Hill. Paget commanded the centre column, which marched in the order 1st, 6th, 5th, 7th and Light Divisions. The Galicians were on the right, following the usual route to Ciudad Rodrigo. Le Mesurier noticed, as they crossed a rivulet near a place he named as Treguas, that Wellington had taken position to watch the departure of his troops and that he appeared rather pale. The commander, like his troops, would not have wanted such an ending to a year's campaigning that had initially been so successful.

The next four days were to test every last man as the Allies trudged back to Ciudad Rodrigo, the scene of the year's first victory. They were cold, wet and hungry because the Quartermaster General, presuming the route Wellington would follow, had sent supplies in the wrong direction. They also had French cavalry snapping at their heels, the only pursuit that Soult mounted. On the 17th,

> ...the Enemy Vedettes made their appearance and we expected to have something to do. We moved off slowly (fast it was impossible) over ploughed ground the Cavalry protecting our retreat. About Four we halted near Salmonita where some Skirmishing took place between the Light Division and the Enemy. Sir Ed'd: Paget

---

199 Gurwood (ed.), *Dispatches*, vol.IX, p.544.
200 Quoted in Charles Cadell, *The Slashers; the Campaigns of the 28th Regiment of Foot during the Napoleonic Wars by a Serving Officer* (Driffield: Leonaur, 2008), p.91.
201 Greenwood (ed.), *Through Spain with Wellington*, p.142.

was taken by the French that day, a circumstance of which they will, no doubt, boast greatly, he being Second-in-Command of the Army.[202]

As Wellington explained to Bathurst,

> …the fall of rain having greatly injured the roads, and swelled the rivulets, there was an interval between the 5th and 7th divisions of infantry. Sir Edward rode alone to discover the cause of this interval, and as the road passed through a wood, either a detachment of the enemy's cavalry had got upon the road, or he missed the road, and fell into their hands in the wood.[203]

It was, as Le Mesurier's comment suggests, a serious loss to the Allied army.

If anything, the nights were worse than the days. Le Mesurier referred to being 'obliged to shift with our Boat Cloaks on the damp ground with nothing to Eat and no drink,' because the baggage had been sent ahead.[204] While Douglas, recalling the experience from several decades back, remembered how 'If inclined to sleep we were obliged to repose like so many turkeys on the branches of trees, to keep us out of the water and mud.'[205] Gomm, who had experienced the retreat to Corunna, noted how

> …during the last few days it revived many recollections of the dreadful race to Corunna. In some respects the hardships were greater, for on that occasion the troops were generally under cover, such as it was, during the night; but here the only resting-place… was a bleak, swampy plain, with more temptation in it to watch than sleep, and to look out with patience for the break of the following morning.[206]

On the 18th they received no attention from the enemy but 'had to retreat through horrible roads. Baggage Animals were strewed on it by half Dozens. Even Greyhounds could not stand it. Our loss, I am afraid, has been very great from the state of the roads and weather. I assure you it is not at all agreeable to sleep in the Open Air in the month of November.'[207] This is echoed by Gomm in his letter of the 22nd. 'During the last five days of our march the rain fell in torrents; so that we waded with difficulty through rivers where scarcely the trace of a watercourse was observable when we came up the country.'[208] Yet Douglas remembered that those who had the strength to continue, many having fallen out, might be 'not only mid-leg but knee-deep in mud, yet the men plodded on this cheerless way with cheerfulness.'[209]

---

202 Greenwood (ed.), *Through Spain with Wellington*, pp.142–143.
203 Gurwood (ed.), *Dispatches*, vol.IX, p.561.
204 Greenwood (ed.), *Through Spain with Wellington*, p.143.
205 Monick (ed.), *Douglas's Tale*, p.62.
206 Carr-Gomm (ed.), *Letters and Journals*, vol.I, p.290.
207 Greenwood (ed.), *Through Spain with Wellington*, p.143.
208 Carr-Gomm (ed.), *Letters and Journals*, vol.I, p.290.
209 Monick (ed.), *Douglas's Tale*, p.62.

What none of the eyewitnesses from the 5th Division mentioned was the misdirected march that some of the divisions in the centre column undertook when their divisional commanders under the instigation of Lieutenant General William Stewart decided against a route that took them across flooded fields and chose instead to march their troops to the right, which brought them onto the route the Galicians were following. As a result, the men had to stand, shivering in the rain, while the Spanish crossed the bridge at Castillo de Yeltes. Wellington subsequently wrote to Colonel Henry Torrens, Military Secretary to the Duke of York, the Commander-in-Chief, on 6 December, requesting that Stewart should be moved to a position where he was 'under the particular charge of somebody'. His reason was that

> ...he and certain other General officers commanding divisions (new comers) held a council of war to decide whether they would obey my orders to march by a particular road. He, at the head, decided he would not: they marched by a road leading they knew not where, and when I found them in the morning they were in the utmost confusion, not knowing where to go or what to do.[210]

Fortescue identified the other two generals as Dalhousie and Clinton but Oman, picking up on 'new comers', decided that one of them was Oswald.[211]

The conditions were worse for some than for others. The women and children always suffered when physical hardship intensified. Douglas, however, remembered another group who proved particularly vulnerable to the harsh conditions. 'On our first march from Salamanca we received a draft of 250 men. Poor wretches! I pitied them. Being unaccustomed to such work, they stood in mid-leg shivering with cold, not knowing what to do.' And then there were the sights that could not be forgotten. In Douglas's case,

> ...a woman a little to the right of the column had sunk under the hardships and expired, but her infant was still alive, and a little further on the left a Portuguese soldier, worn with hunger and fatigue, had also sunk in the mud and was totally unable to extricate himself. Though not more than 50 yards off no assistance could be given as the means of conveyance on our front was as far off as Ciudad Rodrigo. Our adjutant made an attempt to rescue him by riding up and taking hold of his hand, but to no purpose. There he was left, and most likely it was his grave...

For, as Douglas concluded, the French would probably 'expend a ball upon him rather than a biscuit.'[212]

Finally, 'On the last day's march we plunged through the river Huebra; just in time as the enemy's guns opened on us in great style, while a host of skirmishers extended along the rugged banks, keeping up a very sharp fire.' Others would become engaged in a more intense firefight, but for the 5th Division this was the last they saw of the enemy. 'The French followed no further, and we reached the hills near Ciudad in peace, on the 19th November.' This was fortunate for Douglas, because on the final day 'the sinews of my right

---

210 Wellington (ed.), *Supplementary Despatches*, vol.IX, p.494.
211 Oman, *The History of the Peninsular War*, vol.VII, fn p.151.
212 Monick (ed.), *Douglas's Tale*, p.62.

foot protruded through the skin, which would have been the means of my being made an inmate of a French prison, had the retreat continued another day.'[213]

Table 3.1: The Retreat from Burgos: Casualties from 19 September – 24 December 1812

	Died	Died of wounds	Killed	Deserted	Missing	Prisoner of War	Total
3/1st	59	1	0	7	35	9	111
1/4th	37	1	4 (6)	0	4	36	82
2/4th	60	0	0 (1)	1	76	0	137
1/9th	79	0	7 (7)	2	32	0	120
2/30th	42	0	1 (4)	0	33	0	76
1/38th	116	8	3 (7)*	0	0	31	158
2/38th	27	3	1 (2)*	0	6	3	40
2/44th	30	2	3 (6)*	1	0	35	71
Divisional Totals	350	15	19	11	186	114	795

Notes:
1. These are the casualty figures as given in the battalion casualty returns, or in the case of the 1/4th (who only recorded natural deaths in the casualty returns) in the musters. Garry Wills has established that the number killed (all on 25 October) is considerably higher than official figures suggest. His figures are given in brackets. It is likely that in the confusion of the day's action some were later posted as missing or prisoners of war.
2. The seven men given as having deserted from the Royal Scots, all on 25 October are almost certainly the seven fatalities identified by Wills in *Wellington at Bay*.
3. The 2/38th were by this time a very depleted battalion.
4. The casualty returns for the 2/44th include only the men who subsequently formed the provisional battalion with the 2/30th.
5. It is interesting to note that five of the eight battalions have chosen to identify absent men as either missing or prisoners of war.
6. The 'Killed' marked with an asterisk include officers, three in the case of the 2/44th, who are not included in the casualty returns.
7. The company of the Brunswick Oels lost three men, two of them officers.

Aftermath

The army that finally crossed into Portugal was bruised, battered and dispirited. Between 22 October and 19 November, the period of the retreat, the 5th Division suffered 795 casualties, including deserters and those taken prisoner. (See Table 3.1). Furthermore, any assumption that losses would now decrease proved over-optimistic. An examination of the reports which James McGrigor, the Inspector General of Hospitals, received on a monthly basis from the general hospitals, makes clear why this should be when the troops were no longer suffering from the weather conditions, hunger and exhaustion. The reports reveal a host of diseases: typhus, dysentery, typhoid fever and an intermittent fever, which was probably malaria. McGrigor concluded from these findings, that 'the sick were exposed to severe weather,

---

213 Monick (ed.), *Douglas's Tale*, p.63.

heavy rain, [which] in their protracted journeys occasioned Simple Continued Fever and Intermittents, to degenerate into Typhus and Dysenteries and to assume so malignant a character as to baffle the skill of the medical officer, the case frequently proving fatal within a few days sometimes after being committed to his care.'[214] The weather, therefore, coupled with the exigencies of retreat, could be identified as one cause of the disturbingly high sickness rates, and the consequent fatalities. Another was the state of the men's lice-ridden uniforms. The nits carried typhus; and typhus, as has been noted, was prevalent in all units, including the Portuguese. Taken together, the state of the uniforms and the extreme conditions of the long retreat explain why the sickness rate was so slow to decrease.

It was inevitable that there would be criticism of the decision to attack Burgos. Gomm offered a particularly even-handed judgement in a letter written on 22 November. On the one hand, Wellington's conduct of the retreat

> …has been masterly; he has withdrawn the army upwards, I believe, of 200 miles, the greater part of the time before a superior force, which has never once found him in a situation to attempt anything serious, except upon the Carrion, where they failed; and he has reached the point upon which, from the beginning, he directed himself, with his army unbroken, except by the elements and their own indiscipline.

On the other hand,

> I will say, that from the moment the siege of Burgos Castle was seriously undertaken it has appeared to me that there was more fondness than firmness, or even obstinacy, in the conduct of an enterprise which all the world saw (and it is absurd to suppose that he himself did not see) was entered upon with means inadequate, and carried on, certainly, many days after the success of it was more than doubtful.[215]

Gomm's use of the word 'indiscipline' is significant in relation to a memorandum of 28 November that Wellington addressed 'To Officers Commanding Divisions and Brigades'. Although written out of frustration, it might have been specifically designed to set his officers against him. It also suggested that Wellington had not appreciated the actual conditions the troops suffered during those last days of the retreat.

> The discipline of every army, after a long and active campaign, becomes in some degree relaxed, and requires the utmost attention on the part of the generals and other officers to bring it back to the state in which it ought to be of service; but I am concerned to have to observe that the army under my command has fallen off in this respect than any army with which I have ever served, or of which I ever read. Yet this army has met with no disaster; it has suffered no privations which but trifling attention on the part of the officers could not have prevented, and for which there existed no reason whatever in the nature of the service; nor has it suffered

---

214 Aberdeen Medico-Chirurgical Society Library: Undated commentary, James McGrigor.
215 Carr-Gomm (ed.), *Letters and Journals*, vol.I, p.291.

any hardships excepting those resulting from the necessity of being exposed to the inclemencies of the weather at a moment when they were most secure.

Having claimed that the officers lost control of the men, thus leading to a situation where 'Irregularities and outrages of all descriptions were committed with impunity, and losses have been sustained which ought never to have occurred', he placed the blame firmly on their shoulders.

> I am far from questioning the zeal, still less the gallantry and spirit of the Officers of the army; and I am quite certain that if their minds can be convinced of the necessity of minute and constant attention to understand, recollect and carry into execution the orders which have been issued for the performance of their duty, and that the strict performance of this duty is necessary to enable the army to serve the country as it ought to be served, they will in future give their attention to these points.

This haranguing continued in the same vein, implicitly criticising senior officers for not enforcing the need for frequent inspection and superintendence of the junior officers under their command, and the junior officers for not giving enough attention to both the behaviour and the welfare of the men. He concluded: 'But I repeat that the great object of the attention of the General and Field Officers must be to get the Captains and Subalterns of the regiments to understand and perform the duties required from them, as the only mode by which discipline and efficiency of the army can be restored and maintained during the next campaign.'[216]

Wellington had not intended that his memorandum should go beyond the senior officers, but such things have a habit of becoming more widely disseminated. Needless to say, it provoked widespread outrage, both for its generalised nature, no distinction having been made between units that preserved a state of discipline and those that did not, and the commander's apparent ignorance of what both officers and men had suffered. Perhaps the most damning assessment was written retrospectively by Captain William Grattan of the 88th, the Connaught Rangers, in the 3rd Division.

> Blame and praise, if properly employed, make a great change in the actions of a young man – so they do if improperly employed; and this letter of Lord Wellington, directed chiefly against the junior officers of his army had a bad effect. Those officers asked each other, and asked themselves, how or in what manner they were to blame for the privations of the army endured on the retreat? The answer uniformly was, in no way at all. Their business was to keep the men together, and, if possible, to keep up with their men on the march, and this was the most difficult duty they had to perform; for many, very many, of these officers were young lads, badly clothed, with scarcely a shoe or boot to their feet – some, attacked with dysentery, others with ague, and more with a burning fever raging through their system, had scarcely

---

216 Gurwood (ed.), *Dispatches*, vol.IX, pp.582–583.

strength left to hobble on in company with their more hardy comrades, the soldiers. Nothing but a high sense of honour could have borne them on, and there were many who would have remained behind, and run all risks as to the manner in which they would be treated as prisoners, were it not for this feeling.[217]

One such lad from the 5th Division was Ensign Thomas Kelly, who had only joined the 2/30th immediately after Villamuriel and had no previous experience of campaigning. Having been sent to the rear during the final days of the retreat, his death was reported on 2 December, with the detail that he had died in a hospital waggon.[218]

One officer from the first brigade whose possible outrage was assuaged by the way his brigadier handled the generalised nature of the memorandum was Peter Le Mesurier. On 29 December, in his first letter for over a month, he wrote home that,

> Some time ago the Offrs: were called together to hear a Circular Letter from Lord Wellington to Genl: Offrs: of Divisions, to be by them communicated to the Offrs: of the several Regts: under their command, the substance of which was to impress on the. mind of Offrs: the exertions they ought to make on a Retreat to keep their Men in Order, and stating that in the Retreat from Burgos some Regts: were in the utmost state of insubordination, that Offrs: lost all command over their Men, in consequence of which a great number were taken by the Enemy, straggling, and recommended the greatest Discipline and regularity during our Stay in Winter Quarters. The Brigadier, in transmitting the Letter to Col'l: Crawford, said that he would leave it to himself to make the necessary remarks on the Letter, though he was convinced it did not at all apply to the 9th; We have only lost one Man during the retreat straggling, and that Villain had leave from an Offr: to fall out and put another pair of shoes on.[219]

The casualty returns suggest that the battalion lost rather more than one man, but, as Le Mesurier was at pains to inform his family, the other seven men reported missing had been severely wounded at Villamuriel, and had been left in the hospital station behind the village by the waggon train. As he somewhat sardonically commented, 'it would not have looked well in a dispatch to have said that our wounded were left on the field.'[220]

There followed a period of rest which both officers and men needed and (it may be felt) deserved. The 5th Division's headquarters were at Lamego, a fine town high above the Douro, while the battalions were in quarters in the various villages that surrounded the town. Gomm wrote on 28 December, 'We are at present in very good quarters, and close to our stores, so that it is presumed we shall grow fat. There are some pleasant families in

---

217 William Grattan, *Adventures of the Connaught Rangers from 1808-1814* (London: Henry Colburne, 1847), vol.II, p.141.
218 TNA: WO 17/138: Monthly Returns, 30th Foot.
219 Greenwood (ed.), *Through Spain with Wellington*, p.146. The brigadier in question may be either Barnes or Hay, depending on when the meeting took place, since Hay returned from leave three weeks before Le Mesurier wrote his letter home.
220 Greenwood (ed.), *Through Spain with Wellington*, p.146.

the town and neighbourhood, who pay us attention enough to make us also grow saucy.'[221] In other words, the staff, at least, found themselves in ideal circumstances for a period of respite.

Ensign Woodward of the 4th Foot took a very different view. He was disenchanted not just with his present circumstances but with military life in general and in a letter of 3 December urgently warned his brother, 'Do not run yourself into utter ruin as I have done in entering the Army and particularly the miseries attending a Person that has but little or no Money excluding of his Pay…' The then referred his brother to a poem he had copied from a newspaper, which was an extended and exaggerated version of John Allen's Lament, as published in *The Military Chronicle*. He was confident that, after reading it, 'you will never attempt to encounter with a life so burthened with such a Multitude of difficulties.'[222]

If Hale is typical, then the men might also have felt that they had grievances to complain of. Not only did the Portuguese live 'in a very dirty, beastly way', but also

> Most of the house, that belong to the lower class of people, are very mean, mostly only a ground floor, and perhaps no light than what comes in at the door, or at least at a hole made in the upper part of it… In many of these poor habitations the fire is placed in the middle of the house, their seats are some rough-made stools or blocks of wood. Some of the natives, perhaps half naked, and as yellow with smoke and dirt as a parcel of tawnies, some covered in vermin, in this manner will huddle round a bit of fire, to all appearance as comfortable as that live in a palace.

On the other hand,

> While we remained in this place, we got good provisions, and very regular, also, some other articles that were needful, in particular shoes and shirts, for at that time we were got very bare of both these articles, and in a few days after we were supplied with every thing that was necessary, we received the balance of six months arrears of pay that were due to us, for during this campaign, we never received any money whatever.

As a result, 'having good provisions, rest and a little. Money to purchase a few bottles of good wine, all past fatigues were smothered.'[223]

---

221 Carr-Gomm (ed.), *Letters and Journals*, vol.I, p.294.
222 Woodward, 3 December 1812, private collection.
223 Hale, *Journal*, pp.103–104.

4

1813

Recovery

At the start of 1813 the Allies were still in no state for action, and the early months of the year were spent rallying from the hardships of the last months of the previous year, as well as restoring order and discipline. This took the form of drill, reviews, and the inevitable courts martial, 92 across the 5th Division.[1] There were also field days, such as the one described by Le Mesurier at the beginning of April.

> We had a Field Day last Monday, the Caçadores' as French attacking a Bridge, and our light companies, supported by the Royals and 9th: British, 3d: & 15th: Portuguese, defending. I am happy to say we did not suffer quite so much as last time we had any thing to do, though, had it been in earnest, our Light Comp'ys would have been cruelly mauled by about 50 of their opponents placed in ambush on their flank.[2]

As the different battalions recovered their strength and some received reinforcements, one decision pleased everyone, from the officers down to the most inexperienced recruit. As Le Mesurier explained to his sister:

> Orders have been given for the issue of Tents for the Men, which Tents are to be carried on Mules formerly appropriated for the carriage of Camp Kettles but now done away with, a thin camp Kettle substituted, which the men are to carry and which I think will be highly beneficial to the health of the Men. Formerly they were exposed to the Broiling heat of the sun by Day, and to heavy dews by night, which certainly caused great sickness.[3]

There were also some significant changes in the composition of the division, the first coming at the end of 1812 when a general order of 6 December saw all the fit men of the 2/4th and 2/38th transferred to their senior battalions, while the officers, NCOs and unfit men

---

1 TNA: WO 27/111 & 112: Inspection Returns
2 Greenwood (ed.), *Through Spain with Wellington*, p.160.
3 Greenwood (ed.), *Through Spain with Wellington*, pp.155–156.

would return to England. This brought the 1/4th and the 1/38th up to strength. Other weak battalions, however, presented a different problem. The 1/30th were in India and although it was not involved in any active service, the depot company in England, whose purpose was to recruit and train, was observing the normal practice of sending these recruits to the senior battalion. Consequently, the junior battalion had received no reinforcements since the summer of 1810. The 1/44th was serving in the Mediterranean, moving between Sicily and Malta, and once again was receiving the available reinforcements. Only the scope of the present wars had forced the War Office to send so many second battalions to the Peninsula. Wellington's practical solution was to pair these weak battalions into provisional battalions. The weakest troops in each of the combined battalions, along with surplus officers and the staff of the junior regiment, would return to England, while the remaining troops were formed into eight companies, four from each battalion. As a result, Lieutenant Colonel Hamilton took command of the 4th Provisional Battalion. Since the two battalions knew each other well, there were unlikely to be any problems. Furthermore, Hamilton had a good reputation as a trainer of men, so he should soon have been able to bring them to a state where they worked well as a single unit.

The Duke of York, however, as commander-in-chief of the army was unhappy with the arrangement, particularly as he had units available to replace the weakest battalions. As he informed Wellington in a letter of 13 January:

> Experience has shown that a skeleton battalion composed of officers, non-commissioned officers, and a certain foundation of old and experienced soldiers can be reformed for any service in a short time: but if a corps reduced in numbers be broken up by the division of its establishment, such an interruption is occasioned to its interior economy and *esprit de corps*, that its speedy recompletion and reorganization for foreign service is effectually prevented.[4]

Wellington saw things differently.

> I am of opinion, from long experience, that it is better for the service here to have one soldier or officer, whether of cavalry or infantry, who has served one or two campaigns, than it is to have two or even three who have not. Not only the new soldiers can perform no service, but by filling the hospital they are a burthen to us. For this reason, I am so unwilling to part with the men whom I have formed into provisional battalions; and I never will part with them as long as it is left to my discretion.[5]

Eventually, Wellington agreed to send the weakest of the four provisional battalions back to England, that being the 4th, although the order was not issued until 10 May, by which time the men of 2/30th and 2/44th must have been keenly anticipating the new campaign. The remnants of the two battalions received the thanks of Wellington and of their brigadier,

---

4   Wellington (ed.), *Supplementary Despatches*, vol.VII, p.524.
5   Gurwood (ed.), *Dispatches*, vol.X, p.77.

Frederick Robinson, who particularly commented on the state of readiness into which Hamilton had brought the troops. The order coincided with the arrival of the 59th (2nd Nottinghamshire), the second brigade having already been strengthened at the end of 1812 by the 2/47th (Lancashire).

The former had been with Moore and then at Walcheren; the latter had come up from Cadiz but had been with Hill during the retreat of 1812. Robinson was particularly gratified by the promise of the 59th, informing his sister that 'His Lordship has flattered me exceedingly lately by adding the 59th Regt (a thousand fine fellows) to [the brigade], so I shall have a little army to commence the campaign with, and am perfectly satisfied with it.'[6] He had previously dismissed the brigade on first sight as one of the worst brigades in the army, although he had been impressed by the company of Brunswickers, commanded by Captain Ludwig von Nassau, which was attached to the brigade.

Brigadier General Robinson, an American Loyalist, had been in the Peninsula since the autumn of 1812, but Wellington had been reluctant to employ him, possibly because Robinson had never commanded a unit larger than a company. He finally appointed him to the 5th Division on 13 March and Robinson arrived at Lamego a month later, having travelled up from Lisbon by way of headquarters at Freineda, where Wellington seems to have changed his view of the American.

Hay, upon his return from leave at the end of 1812, commanded the division until April in the absence of both Leith and Oswald. The return of the latter meant that he was now back with his brigade, while the Portuguese remained under Spry's command. This was the formation of the division when the new campaign finally commenced: a new brigadier and two new battalions, but without the general that officers and men alike most respected.

A letter that Gomm to his sister, dated 11 April, suggested that plans were already in place for the new campaign. He had received an order from headquarters to reconnoitre the Tras-os-Montes for the second time, which suggested that Wellington was considering an advance across country generally perceived as too challenging. Gomm had spent three weeks exploring the area and on his return informed his sister that

> The mountaineers are a kind people, and there are some 'happy valleys' as unconnected with the great world, and almost as inaccessible, as that in which the 'Father of Waters' begins his course, and that have not suffered so much alarm for many a day, as when I held out to them the prospect of my being shortly forced to conduct a band of locusts over their possessions.

Indeed, Gomm was already speculating that 'Part of the army, including this division, will perhaps cross the Douro here, and march through the mountains upon Zamora and Valladolid. I shall like it, for the beaten path is rather a tedious one.[7]

His speculation proved accurate. Wellington intended that a large proportion of his troops would march north across this supposedly inaccessible hinterland. Lieutenant General Thomas Graham, upon his return from a period of leave for the recovery of his

---

6 Nicholas Fogg, *Wellington's American General: the Oldest serving Soldier in the British Army* (Stroud: Amberley, 2022), p.145.
7 Carr-Gomm (ed.), *Letters and Journals*, vol.I, pp.297–298.

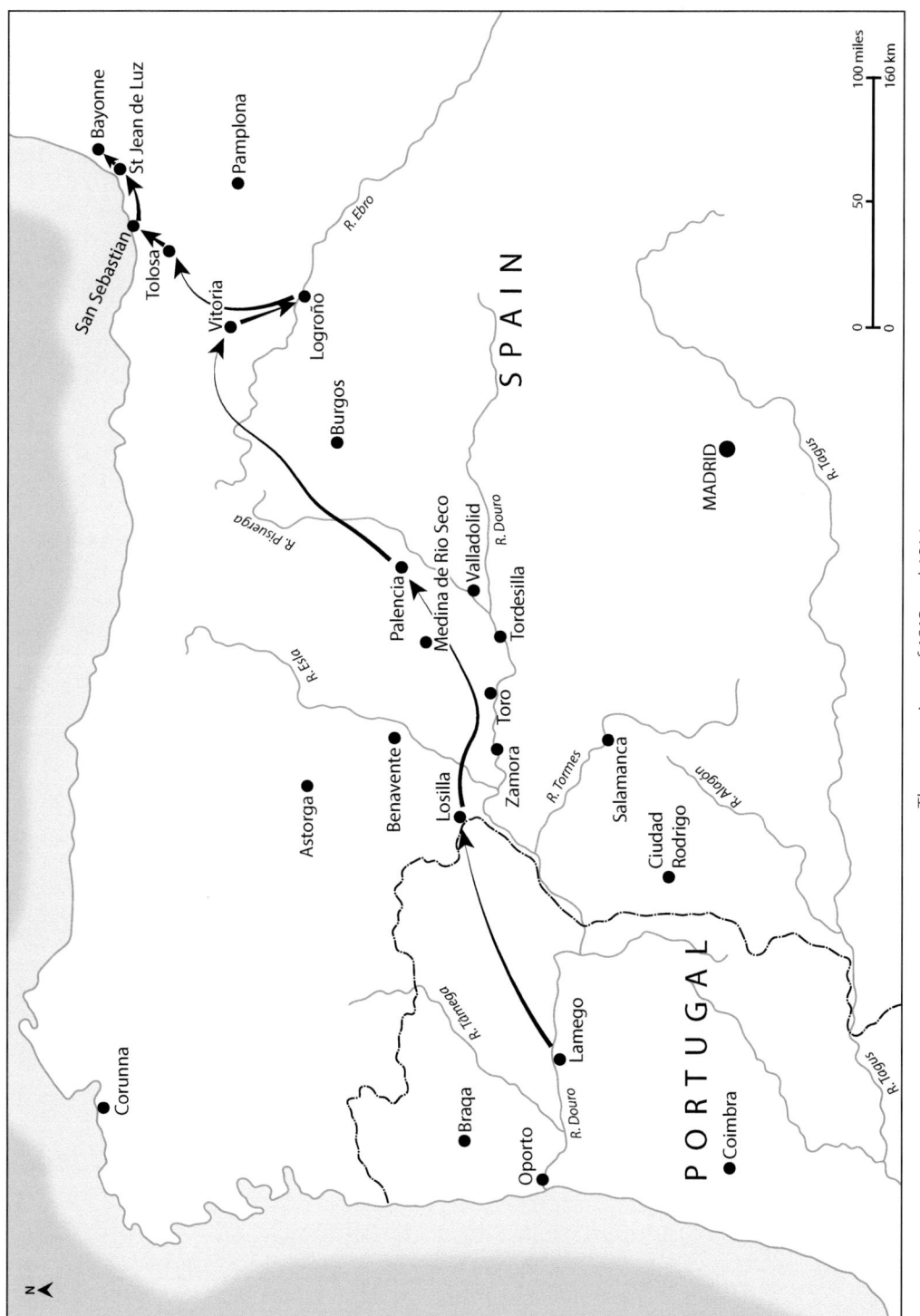

The campaigns of 1813 and 1814.

health, would have all but the 2nd and Light Divisions under his command, as well as Pack's and Bradford's Portuguese, a force 52,000 strong. This certainly pleased Gomm.

> We compose part of the left column, under the immediate command of Sir Thomas Graham. Next to Lord Wellington's self, there is no one who will take so good care of us. He is looking remarkably well, and, although he has not quite recovered the use of his sight, there are no fears entertained of his suffering in this respect from fatigue.[8]

Despite being in his sixty-fifth year, Graham was to demonstrate the energy of a much younger man.

Over the hills…

On 14 May, a fortnight later than Wellington had planned due to a shortage of forage, Graham's troops were on the move. The 4th, 6th and 7th Divisions had already left their cantonments and were advancing towards the Douro. The 3rd and 5th Divisions, being closer to the river, started on the 14th, while the First division marched on the 18th. With barges and boats already assembled for the purpose, the 3rd Division crossed at São João de Pesquiera, the 1st and 5th Divisions at Peso de Regua, and the other divisions further upstream. Then, with all his troops across the river, Graham began his advance into Spain along country roads, following a route which remained completely unsuspected by the French but also proved a challenge to the Allies.

On 21 May Le Mesurier wrote home,

> This day a week [ago] we commenced our Campaign for this year and crossed the Douro near Lamego in boats. The Day was wet and it was near Six o'Clock before we could get under cover. Our Baggage was left on the Lamego side as well as our riding Animals, and on the 15th we started with out either for Villa Real through a most beautiful Country; for an immense tract nothing but Vineyardes can be seen, to the very tops of the Mountains. The country Houses appear comfortable and decent, but to counterbalance this the Roads are most abominable and we have to ascend two very high hills before we are blessed with the sight of Villa Real, which is a very pretty Town and the largest in Tras os Montes. Our Baggage joined us here late at night, which I assure you was very agreeable for we were in a miserable plight (Crotté jusqu'aux Genoux) [Muddy up to the knees], and without meat or drink. We then proceeded on the road to Mourza. [Murça][9]

Whatever the problems faced by the officers of the 9th, Gomm would undoubtedly have claimed that his, as quartermaster to the division and responsible for keeping the troops to

---

8   Carr-Gomm (ed.), *Letters and Journals*, vol.I, p.301.
9   Greenwood (ed.), *Through Spain with Wellington*, p.166.

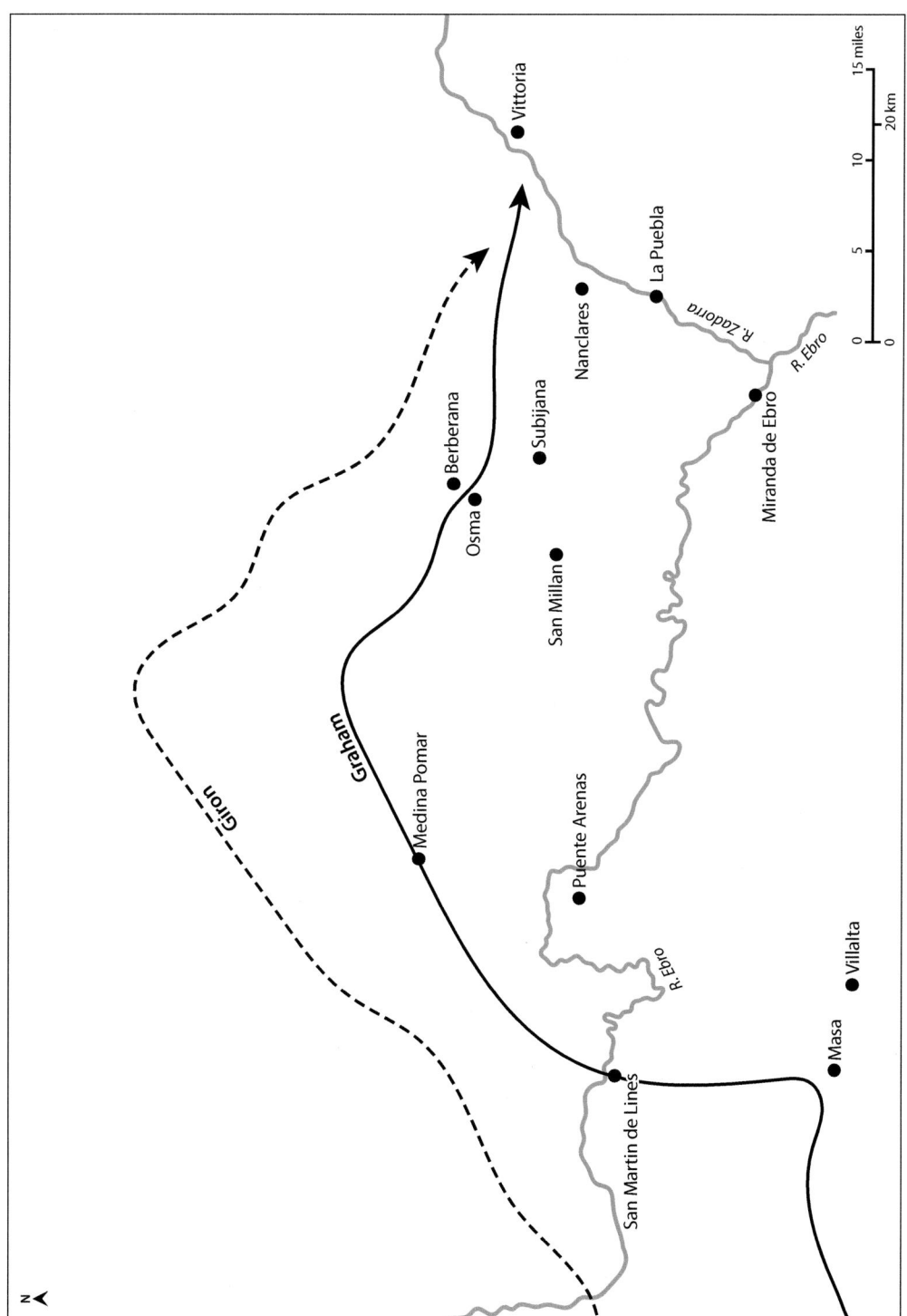

The advance of the 5th Division.

their given routes, were greater. Writing from Outeiro on the 24th, he remarked sardonically, 'My guns behaved very well, but their officer required more driving than their horses; and had I not been more interested than they in the success of the enterprise, there was, on more occasion than one, opposition enough to have turned an obstinate man from his opinion.'[10]

As Graham's divisions approached their given objectives, the 5th Division's being Losilla, the only French troops who might have intervened were *Général de division* Honoré Charles Reille's seriously depleted Army of Portugal, three of his divisions having been detached to serve with the Army of the North and with only *Général de division* Jean Barthélemy Darmagnac's division from the Army of the Centre to compensate for their absence. Furthermore, Reille's principal task was to watch the Esla and stop a Galician advance. Reille did later report that there appeared to be Allied cavalry on the Esla and at Braganza, but these were mistakenly thought to be searching for supplies.

The French, in fact, were more concerned by Hill's advance from Estremadura and the junction effected between his troops and those Wellington was bringing from Portugal. When the French under *Général de division* Eugène-Casimir Villatte were driven out of Salamanca, this setback only confirmed that Wellington was following his usual route into Spain and on to the Duero. Hill remained six days in Salamanca, but Wellington was able to slip away undetected and join Graham, whose command was becoming more concentrated as the different divisions reached their destinations. They were now able to march as three columns, never more than 12 miles apart. On the left, the 1st Division, Pack's Portuguese, with Anson's light and Ponsonby's heavy cavalry, was making for Tabara; in the centre, the 3rd and 5th Divisions, Bradford's Portuguese, and Bock's German heavy cavalry (later joined by D'Urban's Portuguese cavalry) marched for Losilla; on the right, the remaining four divisions had Caravajales as their objective. The left column had a further task, to make contact with *Teniente general* Pedro Augustín Girón and his Galicians, who were supposed to have left Astorga on 26 May. He had already received orders to cross the Esla at Benevente.

The 5th Division reached Losilla on 28 May. The following day all Graham's troops were in position to cross the Esla and were awaiting the arrival of the pontoon train, which had been lumbering its way from Lisbon for several weeks. On the 30th, Wellington joined Graham at Caravajales and finally, on the 31st, the first crossings were made without the pontoons, in order to drive off some French dragoons on the opposite bank. This was a dangerous undertaking which resulted in some loss of life, although the French dragoons were persuaded to withdraw. The pontoons were then put in place, an operation that was completed within two hours, and the infantry began to cross, which took until the following day. Even before all the troops were across, the French abandoned Zamora and Wellington was welcomed into the town by cheering crowds. Hill was now summoned to join the main army and the campaign to drive the French beyond the Ebro could commence.

By 4 June the Allied infantry was in and around Toro. The French had been joined by *Général de division* Jean François Leval and the encumbrance of an enormous baggage train from Madrid, and were now at Palencia, Magaz and Dueñas. They had to extend their line in order to forage for food but were still uncertain about their next move. Joseph was hoping

---

10 Carr-Gomm (ed.), *Letters and Journals*, vol.I, p.300.

that Clarke would order Clausel, now in command of the Army of the North, to join him. He received a dispatch from Paris on the 5th, written several weeks before, but it made no reference to Clausel. Instead, on the false presumption that Wellington was detaching troops, Joseph was instructed to threaten Portugal, the one thing he could not do from his present position, and also to send more troops to Clausel. To add to their problems, although the French were aware of Allied cavalry probing their lines, they were uncertain of Wellington's exact whereabouts. This was solved when a message about an exchange of officers was answered in four hours, which demonstrated Wellington's proximity. There was no choice. They would have to continue their retrograde movement to Burgos. Then, on 9 June, Joseph finally took the decision to disobey his brother and summon Clausel to join him.

Meanwhile, Wellington had been reorganising his troop formations. Orders issued on 3 June for the following day regrouped his forces into three columns. Graham, on the left, had command of the 1st and 5th Divisions, Pack's and Bradford's Portuguese, and Anson's and Bock's cavalry. They were to march at daybreak for Medina del Rio Seco. The headquarters column in the centre comprised the 3rd, 4th and Light Divisions, D'Urban's and Ponsonby's cavalry and the reserve artillery. Their immediate objective was La Mota. Hill was on the right, with his own command, brought up from Salamanca, the 6th and 7th divisions and the rest of the cavalry. Further to the right was Julian Sanchez, while Girón continued as an outlier on the left. The Galicians, however, were seriously short of ammunition and thus of little use in any action, although they continued to advance in parallel with the main Allied force. Nor was there any immediate likelihood of a major action, contact between the two armies being restricted to cavalry skirmishing.

By 7 June, Graham's column was encamped near Palencia, having also stopped at Medina de Rio Seco, where, Le Mesurier informed his family, they were received

> …with much cheering' and 'a great number of very pretty Signoras came in spite of wet weather and Waltzed in the camp ground with the Offrs: of the Brunswick Oels Corps. I am afraid we shall not be favoured to night by the Ladies from Palencia as we are about Two Miles from the Town and the weather is not very tempting being windy and wet.[11]

Far from the broiling heat that Gomm had anticipated when they began their march across the Tras-os-Montes, the weather was more like November. An advancing army, however, is less troubled by inclement conditions than one in retreat.

By 11 June Hill's and the headquarters columns were moving towards Burgos, and the following day the right column launched an attack on Reille's still depleted Army of Portugal, which was posted on the Espejar Heights above Hormaza, less than 20 miles from Burgos. Reille was forced into the first of several fighting withdrawals. Meanwhile, Graham was marching well to the left of the Great Road, making for the upper waters of the Ebro. Jourdan had, in fact, suggested that troops should be dispatched to guard this stretch of the river but Joseph had insisted that the Allied artillery could not cross such challenging

---

11   Greenwood (ed.), *Through Spain with Wellington*, p.170.

terrain. Because communications had now been restored with Clausel and all but Foy's of Reille's detached divisions had joined or were about to join, Joseph was confident that he could make a stand. Not at Burgos, though, because the civilian convoy, sent ahead, had seriously depleted the city's stores. Having mined the defences, the French departed towards Vitoria. The subsequent explosions caused considerable casualties, including among the departing French. Had the men of the 5th Division been closer, they would no doubt have shared the general relief that there was not to be another siege of Burgos.

Graham's column had problems of its own. The 5th Division had been without bread since 1 June, while the 1st Division was on half-rations. Le Mesurier somewhat facetiously reported that

> ...it is not fashionable to serve out Bread as usual, but, as we had a little hard marching, they tried to accustom the Troops to do without that article. The Commissary Department not being able to keep up, and money so scarce, that they cannot pay ready money and the Spaniards do not like paper, in consequence of which they hide their Bread and Flour and we do as well as we can.[12]

They were not alone in suffering these privations. On the 12th the whole army halted so that the supply train could catch up, Graham's troops then being within one day's march of the Ebro. Tomkinson of the 16th Light Dragoons, who were attached to Graham's command, wrote in his journal that the commissaries were ordered to have four days' supply of bread by 7:00 a.m. on the 13th. He also noted that it was the rapid advance of the army, rather than dereliction on the part of the Commissary, that had led to the problem.[13]

For Gomm, any delay at this point was frustrating because he was 'anxious to cross the Ebro, and to know something more than we do at present of the French positions. They seem to be quite unprepared to meet the force Lord Wellington has collected, and to meet it in the way in which he has disposed of it.'[14] In other words, he and, probably, many others were anxious to strike a blow against the enemy, particularly as their position so far to the left had kept them out of contact with the French.

Wellington was able to report to Bathurst on 13 June that he expected Graham and Girón to cross the Ebro at Rocamunde and San Martin, which meant that he was about to turn the French right, using Graham's column to do so. With Burgos no longer a problem, he could concentrate on getting all his troops (except the 6th Division, which remained to cover the supply line) across the Ebro. This was completed by the 16th, and brought the centre column into contact with the left. Kincaid of the 95th recalled that

> After following the course of the river for nearly two miles the rocks on each side gradually expanded into another valley, lovely as the one we had left, and where we found the fifth division of our army lying encamped. They were still asleep, and the rising sun, and a beautiful morning, gave additional sublimity to the scene; for there was nothing but the tops of the white tents peeping above the fruit trees and

---

12 Greenwood (ed.), *Through Spain with Wellington*, p.171.
13 Tomkinson (ed.), *Diary of a Cavalry Officer*, pp.239–240.
14 Carr-Gomm (ed.), *Letters and Journals*, vol.I, p.303.

an occasional sentinel pacing his post that gave any indication of what a nest of hornets the blast of a bugle could bring out of that apparently peaceful solitude.[15]

Had Kincaid returned 24 hours later he would have witnessed a very different scene. The camp of the Royal Scots (and probably other battalions as well) was pitched on gravel and during the night of the 16th

> …it commenced to rain and blow most tremendously… the tent pegs were uprooted and down came our house on top of us. Each man was eager to have a sleep, and each and all wished to have the tent pitched again. Yet no-one would stir, so there we lay; the water soaking through left both men and accoutrements in a miserable plight on the bugles calling us to renew our labour at daylight. The sight of the men encamping from under the tents exceeded anything, almost anything, that could be conceived in the shape of misery. Benumbed with cold, drenched to the skin, hungry as wolves, without the means of any kind of comfort, or the most distant hopes of relief unless providence would intervene and send us a little provisions, at the conclusion of the day's march we had the good fortune to have about half a pound of wheat per man, which was a welcome guest.[16]

While Wellington was making what was in effect a detour in order to turn the French position, Joseph was heading for Vitoria by the most direct route. He was still slowed down by the baggage train, loaded with the loot of five years' occupation of Spain; and then disturbed by the news that the whole allied army was now on the left bank of the Ebro. He was at Miranda del Ebro by this time, about 25 miles from Vitoria, and his three armies were close enough to concentrate at short notice. The arrival of Sarrut's division of the Army of Portugal had increased the French strength to 60,000, enough to make a stand. Reille had been using his cavalry to locate the Allies and on 17 June, Maucune, who was at Frias, reported the presence of Allied cavalry at Puentes Areñas. For the first time, the French command appreciated that Wellington had successfully completed a wide turning movement.

Joseph now ordered Reille to Osma, from where he could advance to whatever route Wellington chose to follow. While Girón was marching in the direction of Bilbao in order to disrupt French communications, the three Allied columns were all heading towards Orduña, and then the Great Road. Reille sent Sarrut's and *Général de division* Thomas Lamartinière's divisions towards Osma, while Maucune was about to withdraw from Frias to re-join the Army of Portugal. At the same time, Wellington issued a general order for the movements of his troops on 18 June, most significantly, that the Light Division would march for San Millan, the 4th Division would follow a route to Osma, while Graham would 'put the troops under his orders in motion at 4 A.M., and will march in two columns to Orduña, the left column moving by Villafio and Peña Vieja; the right by Villalba, Peña Nueva and Tartanga. The whole of the artillery will move with the right column.'[17]

---

15 John Kincaid, *Adventures in the Rifle Brigade in the Peninsula, France and the Netherlands from 1809 to 1815* (London: Leo Cooper, 1997), p.100.
16 Monick (ed.), *Douglas's Tale*, p.71.
17 Wellington (ed.), *Supplementary Despatches*, vol.VII, p.641.

The result would be two sharp actions.

Graham set off in a northerly direction towards Orduña but veered from his given route to follow a shorter although more difficult advance by way of Murguia, which brought him into contact with Reille's two divisions at a crossroads near Osma, forcing them to make a stand. The 5th Division took up the fight. 'The French appeared to be in good heart and played their part well, but getting flanked by our taking the village of Orma [sic], they cut off the engagement and made for Vitoria after a very light skirmish.'[18] A rather different perspective on the action is offered by Lieutenant Colin Campbell of the 9th, one of the officers who had come up from Gibraltar in January.

> Through Astri to Osma, where a large body of the enemy was met unexpectedly. This meeting was as great a surprise to them as to us. They placed themselves on the heights of Astalitz, evidently with a view to effect their retreat. The light companies of the 1st brigade, with a portion of the 8th Caçadores, were employed against the enemy, and were supported in the first instance by the fire of a brigade of Royal Artillery. Colonel Cameron sent a battalion company to support his own light company. This being our first encounter this campaign, the men were ardent and eager, and pressed the French most wickedly. When the enemy began their movement to the rear, they were constrained to hurry the pace of their columns, notwithstanding the cloud of skirmishers which covered their retreat. Lord Wellington came up during the day about half-past three. We continued the pursuit until dark, when we were relieved by the light troops of the 4th division… The ground on which we skirmished was so thickly wooded, and so rugged and uneven, that when we were relieved by the 4th division, and the light companies were ordered to their respective regiments, I found myself incapable of further exertion from fatigue and exhaustion, occasioned by six hours of almost continuous skirmishing.[19]

At much the same time, Maucune's division came up against the Light Division and were put to flight, with the result that not all of Maucune's troops had made their way to Vitoria by 21 June. Consequently, when early that morning Joseph was looking for a unit to escort the civilian convoy well away from Vitoria, he chose Maucune's division, a decision that would leave Reille somewhat thinly stretched.

The French command now recognised how effectively Wellington had turned their position, once more forcing them to consider alternative options. They could make a stand at Vitoria or, as Reille suggested, they could continue their retreat into Navarre, call in Clausel and even Suchet, and offer battle on ground of their own choosing. Joseph adopted the first option because the second meant losing direct communication with France, abandoning the civilian convoy, and endangering Clausel. Vitoria would be the chosen battlefield, and taking up their ground the first requirement. Reille was to cover the Puebla defile so that the rest of the French forces, the Army of the Centre followed by the Army of the South, could pass into the valley that led to Vitoria.

---

18   Monick (ed.), *Douglas's Tale*, p.72.
19   Lawrence Shadwell, *The Life of Colin Campbell, Lord Clyde* (Edinburgh: Blackwood, 1881), pp.13–14.

Wellington had issued his own orders for 19 June. Specifically, Graham was ordered to march to Orduña via Berberana, thus opening up a route for the rest of the army to follow towards Vitoria. Both the French and the Allied forces initially moved as instructed. When Reille found himself threatened by the 4th and Light Divisions, however, he had no choice but to conduct another fighting withdrawal. As for Graham's corps, it proved a very frustrating day. On the march for 14 hours in continuous rain, which made bad roads impassable, they covered only 12 miles across wooded and mountainous terrain.

The French were now ready to offer battle. There was still a chance that Clausel would arrive in time, since he was known to have left Pamplona and be making his way to Logroño, but the crucial question remained unanswered. What were Wellington's intentions? If he meant to attack, it was safe to assume that he would be slowed down by the difficult tracks his troops would have to follow, which suggested that he could not arrive before 22 June, time enough for Clausel to join the main army. On the 20th, however, Wellington had his troops in position for an advance to the battlefield, and also had time to reconnoitre before making his final arrangements.

Vitoria

The town of Vitoria sits at the head of a valley which extends about 12 miles from the town to the Puebla defile, and is six miles across at its widest point. The town itself

> ...is situated on rising ground, surrounded, at a considerable distance, by an amphitheatre of mountains. With the exception of the height on which the city is built, the country in its immediate neighbourhood is level, and of slight elevation. Extending along the north-west front of the town, at the distance of a mile, runs the Zadorra, a considerable stream, over which there are erected several bridges; to the south-west the lofty and extensive heights of Puebla communicate with the high grounds domineering the route leading to Pamplona; while on the directly opposite side of the valley, which in that particular part becomes more widely displayed, rise the eminences above the villages of Gamarra Mayor and Abucheca [sic].'[20]

This last was the part of the battlefield where Graham's troops would be engaged. Gamarra Mayor was on the Zadorra, along with Durana, both giving access to the Great Road that led eventually to Bayonne, the route that Joseph had been ordered to protect. Abechuco was situated on the Bilbao to Logroño road and, although some way back from the river, guarded yet another bridge. Both roads would be crucial to Graham's advance, and a French retreat if the battle went against them.

Obviously, the disposition of the French troops was crucial to their success. It was unfortunate, therefore, that Jourdan should have been taken ill on the 20th, so that the task fell to Joseph, whose battlefield experience was minimal. Essentially, he kept the troops in the positions they had taken up as they passed through the Puebla defile on the 19th (or early

---

20   Leith Hay, *A Narrative*, vol.II, pp.184–185.

on the 20th in the case of the Army of Portugal). Thus, Gazan's Army of the South formed the front line, d'Erlon's Army of the Centre, the second, and the Army of Portugal, the third, Reille's corps still being the weakest of the three. By the 21st he had only two infantry divisions, Sarrut's and Lamartinière's, the cavalry of Boyer, Mermet and Digeon, and 30 guns. Also under his command were Joseph's Spanish Guards and a force, 2,000 strong, of Spanish afrancesados. Significantly, neither Wellington nor Graham were certain of Reille's total strength, and erred on the side of caution.

On the evening of 19 June, Wellington was making his own arrangements for the following day, so that the Allied army would be in position for an attack on the 21st. Any hope of launching a surprise attack had been lost because of Reille's stand at the defile. It was still possible, though, to surprise the French with the form the attack would take. Wellington also knew that Clausel had left Pamplona, which meant that time was of the essence. Thus, Hill was to advance to the Puebla defile, while the 3rd and 7th Divisions, under Picton and Dalhousie, would take up positions two miles northwest and four miles north of Hill. The 4th and Light Divisions were to remain in their present positions. Graham was to advance to the Bilbao road, while Pack and Bradford would take position at Murguia. This meant Graham's troops were well to the north and remained detached from the main army. Girón, called in some time before, was to advance to Orduña as a reserve.[21]

The 20th was another excessively wet day. 'The left column marched three leagues on the banks of the Bayas to Marginia. The brigade was pushed a league on the main road, and occupied for the night Olano, and adjacents. The Spanish infantry, under Longa, are a league in our front, and one league only from Vittoria. The enemy made a reconnaissance on them this evening, in which they kept their ground, and a battalion of Caçadores was ordered up close to us in consequence of firing. I think we are pushed too far, as the enemy may be aware of our advance on this road, which is the main one from Bilbao to Vittoria, and I fear have seen the officers who went to look at the affair.'[22]

Coronel Francisco de Longa, a blacksmith by trade, had been an active guerrilla leader in Cantabria before his troops were subsumed into the Spanish regular army. He had been called in by Wellington, who seems to have been impressed by his energy and effectiveness, and attached to Graham's command. On the 20th, his troops had been sent forward to create the impression that only guerrillas were advancing along the road from Bilbao but, as Tomkinson commented, some British officers could not resist the temptation to witness the skirmish between Longa's men and the reconnoitring French, thus defeating the purpose of Longa's forward movement. That Tomkinson was correct in his assumption is demonstrated by Reille's decision to change the disposition of his troops. He seems to have doubted the likelihood that only guerrillas were advancing along the Bilbao road, particularly as the dragoons sent forward by *Général de division* Alexandre Digeon reported that they had encountered a sizeable Spanish force. In the middle of the night, he changed position so that his troops were protecting the road to Bilbao. This meant that Lamartinière was on the left of the Zadorra, defending the bridges at Gamarra Mayor and Menor, and at Durana. Sarrut, with *Chef d'escadron* Jean-Baptiste Curto's light cavalry from *Général de brigade*

---

21 Wellington (ed.), *Supplementary Despatches*, vol.VII, p.648.
22 Tomkinson (ed.), *The Diary*, pp.243–244.

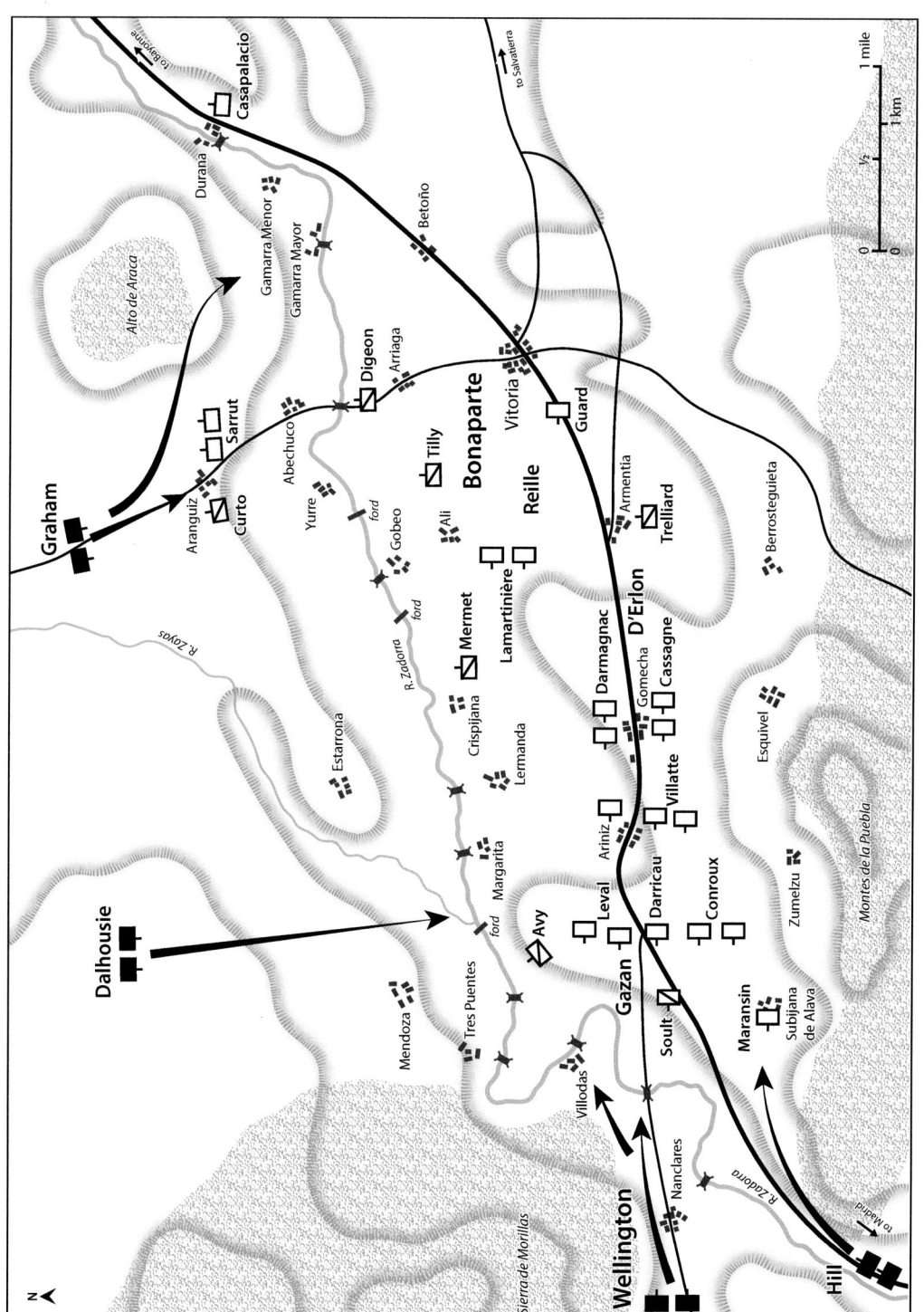

The Battle of Vitoria.

Julien Augustin Mermet's brigade, crossed the river and advanced to Aranguiz, the infantry taking up positions in the town while the cavalry manned the outposts.

It was now obvious that a battle would be fought on the morrow. As far as Graham's command was concerned, their orders were that

> The left column of the army (divisions moving by their left) will move from Murguia towards Vitoria.
>
> Sir T. Graham will put himself in communication as soon as possible with the column of the 3rd and 7th divisions [to his right] at Los Guetos towards Murguia to facilitate their communication.
>
> The movements of the Earl of Dalhousie and Sir Thomas Graham's columns are to be regulated from the right; and although those columns are to make such movements in advance as may be evidently necessary to favour the progress of the two columns on their right [the 4th and Light Divisions], they are not, however, to descend into the low grounds towards Vitoria or the great road, nor give up the advantage of turning the enemy's positions and the town of Vitoria by a movement to their left.

As for *Coronel* Longa, he was 'to move his corps to Murguia, and to receive further instructions.'[23]

Co-ordination between the various Allied columns was obviously vital to the success of Wellington's overall strategy, but there were implicit problems in the orders that Graham had received. His advance was along major roads, making it relatively easy in comparison with Dalhousie's longer advance over challenging terrain. The inevitable result was that Graham would reach the Zadorra well before Dalhousie. The even more problematic final order seemed to suggest that, if the opportunity arose and it would be advantageous to the columns on his right, Graham could push forward, but not too far nor into a situation where his whole corps was involved in an action against Reille, since his main purpose was to turn the enemy right and sever the Great Road. This begged the question, what was too far?[24]

Wellington's orders were for senior officers. Douglas had a more immediate and familiar problem to contend with, lack of bread. The halt on the 20th, he understood, was 'to allow the commissary to come up if possible, but no, and as a last shift we were obliged to send out parties through the country to try to collect a little grub. This day was spent in gloomy forebodings and many a long look out for rations, but in vain.' Finally, on the morning of the 21st the party 'which had been sent to collect bread…brought a timely supply which accounted to nearly a pound a man.'[25] It was much easier to fight on a full stomach.

Hale was more concerned with discomfort.

> The night previous to the battle, we formed our camp about two leagues from Vittoria, on a sort of wilderness place, among brambles, thorns, &c and to my thinking, all sorts of vermin, but nevertheless, in the evening, after we had got our

---

23 Wellington (ed.), *Supplementary Despatches*, p.653.
24 See Oman, *A History*, vol.VI, pp.396–397, for a full discussion.
25 Monick (ed.), *Douglas's Tale*, p.72.

bit of meat and cooked it, which was not long about, for most of us broiled it on some fire coals, having nothing to eat with it, we laid ourselves down, two or three in a place, where it was most convenient, but hearing such music with the vermin crawling and running about among the leaves, and sometimes running over us, caused our rest to be middling that night.

According to Hale they had been three days without bread, which explains Douglas's comments. On the 21st, the 9th, like the Royal Scots, finally received some. There was nothing else, 'but however, that with a drop of good water was very acceptable'.[26]

Since the action was to start with Hill's advance on the right of the Allied position, his troops were the first to move, leaving their bivouacs at 7:30 a.m. Their objective was to take the Puebla Heights, both the summit and lower slopes, in order to convince the French that the Allied attack would come from the west and draw them to that side of the valley. As a result, *Général de division* Louis Victorin Cassagne's division of the Army of the Centre was actually sent with *Général de division* Jacques-Louis-François Tilly's cavalry to check against an Allied approach along the road from Logroño. Fighting fiercely, Hill's troops established themselves on the Heights and in possession of the lower ground, by which time the Allied centre right had come into action. Crossing the Zadorra was a serious challenge, with bridges barricaded and armed. When Wellington was informed by a local peasant of an undefended bridge at Tres Puentes, he sent Kempt's brigade of the Light Division to take possession. Having crossed the river, however, they could advance no further, held in check by *Général de division* Jean-François Laval's strongly posted troops. The centre left should now have made its appearance. Picton was there, fuming at the lack of orders, but there was no sign of Dalhousie, one of whose brigades had lost its way in the wild country it was traversing. Picton, though, was not the man to stand about waiting and on his own initiative he crossed the bridge at Mendoza and then continued the advance towards Margarita. By this time, the main body of the centre right had finally managed to take the heavily defended bridge at Nanclares and the increasing strength of the Allies was putting the French under considerable pressure.

On another stretch of the Zadorra, however, there had been only cautious interaction between Graham and Reille. The latter had established a defensive line that extended from Ariaga to Durana. Acting as the French reserve, his principal purpose was to protect the French line of retreat along the Great Road. In the event of a defeat, if the bridges at Gamarra Mayor or Durana had fallen into Allied hands, the French would be forced to retreat across difficult terrain towards Salvatierra. To guard against this Reille, as noted, had posted Sarrut's division and Curto's light cavalry in a forward position at Aranguiz to protect the bridge at Ariaga while Lamartiniére's division, with *Général de brigade* Pierre Boyer's heavy cavalry, guarded the crossing at Gamarra Mayor and also held the now heavily defended village on the right bank of the river. The Spanish troops under *Mariscal de campo*, le marquis de Casalpalacios and some stray troops from the Army of the North who had been on garrison duty, were at Durana with a half-battery of guns. Reille's force consisted of about 13,000 infantry and 3,500 cavalry, in addition to Digeon's cavalry, about

---

26 Hale, *Journal*, p.107.

800 strong, which had been operating with the Army of Portugal since the beginning of the campaign. Yet he was in a situation where he needed more troops, both because of the scope of the ground he was supposed to be holding and because Graham had about 17,000 troops, infantry and cavalry, as well as Longa's 3,000 men. Had Maucune not been sent as escort to the civilian convoy, Reille would have had something like the strength he needed.

Early on the 21st Reille sent Curto forward to reconnoitre along the Bilbao road and, as a result of Curto's report and his own observation when he also rode forward to assess the situation, Reille had sent an urgent dispatch to Jourdan, informing him that two 'English' divisions, as well as the Spanish troops of Longa and Girón were bearing down on him.[27]

Reille realised that Sarrut, with 6,000 men at lightly defended Aranguiz, was particularly vulnerable in his forward position. Reille had no more intention of starting a full-scale action, which risked dangerously weakening his inadequate forces, than had Graham, conscious of Wellington's ambiguous order. Should the Allies continue their advance, he would bring Sarrut back to the river. Had he but known it, Graham's caution was not only in response to the unclear orders he had received; but there was also nothing to indicate that Dalhousie's troops, with whom he was supposed to be co-ordinating, had come into action.

According to Campbell, it was not until midday that Graham's corps, with the 1st Division and Bradford's Portuguese on the right and the 5th Division, and Pack's Portuguese, led by Longa's Spanish on the left, moved from Murguia and Vitoriano along the Bilbao road towards Vitoria. This timing definitely seems too late. Hale remembered them starting their advance at five o'clock, while Tomkinson timed it as eight o'clock, this being the most likely. By noon Graham was able to see Hill's troops on the Puebla Heights and, although there was still no sound of Dalhousie's advance, he decided to move on Aranguiz, only to discover that the French were withdrawing. *Général de brigade* Jean-Baptiste Menne took position at Abucheco, while *Général de brigade* Joseph Fririon retired back to the river. The cavalry crossed to the south bank, the heavy cavalry behind Fririon and Lamartinière and the light cavalry protecting the flanks.

Graham now sent Longa forward to Gamarra Menor and then on to Durana. Unlike the other villages along the Zadorra, Durana was on the left bank, making its bridge a more feasible objective for Longa's small force. Pack's Portuguese and the 8th Caçadores were also sent forward, to clear the high ground above Gamarra Mayor ready for the advance of the 5th Division. At the same time, the 1st Division and Bradford's Portuguese were preparing to advance on Sarrut at Abucheco. Longa quickly gained possession of Gamarra Menor, facing only limited opposition from the French battery holding the place. He then moved on to Durana and soon became involved in a much tougher fight, Spanish against Spanish, for the bridge. After several hours he was able to cross the Zadorra, but could advance no further because of the enemy guns and Mermet's cavalry. Nevertheless, the road to Bayonne was now effectively closed to the French, since if Reille sent more troops to dislodge Longa he would be unable to hold the Gamarra Mayor and Ariaga bridges.

By the time the 1st Division reached Abucheco, again the French were withdrawing to the Ariaga bridge. The 1st Division then remained inactive until much later in the day. Reille

---

27　Jean-Baptiste Jourdan, *Mémoires militaires du maréchal Jourdan (guerre d'Espagne)* (Paris: Ernest Flammarion, 1899), pp.478–479.

judged the situation to have reached a stalemate and felt confident enough to bring Fririon back to Betonia, while Menne's brigade remained to guard the bridge.

Gamarra Mayor

It was a very different story for the 5th Division at Gamarra Mayor, which saw some of the hardest fighting of the day. To backtrack somewhat,

> ...before approaching the village of Abechuco, the 4th Caçadores of Pack's brigade and the 8th Caçadores of the 5th division moved towards the hills on the left of the road in extended order against the enemy on the heights in front of Gamara Mayor. They were supported by two battalions of Pack's brigade, followed by our division and Anson's brigade of cavalry, having their left covered by Longa's division of Spaniards, which moved towards Gamara Menor.[28]

The cavalry were very much spectators at this stage of the action and Tomkinson observed that 'the attack made on the hills to our left by Major-General Pack's brigade, supported by the 5th Division and the Spaniards under Colonel Longa, had succeeded, the 4th Caçadores belonging to General Pack's brigade having distinguished itself, charging the enemy from the heights with the bayonet.' He then noted that 'The possession of these heights placed us within a mile of the Zadorra, and gave us the command of the plain from them to the river. A squadron from the 12th Light Dragoons had been detached with the troops making the attack on the heights, and the enemy showing two or three of theirs at the foot of the hill, mine of the 16th were ordered to that point.'[29] The French cavalry retired before Tomkinson could reach them but it left him in an ideal position to witness the attack on Gamarra Mayor.

Another spectator was Captain William Hay, of the 12th Light Dragoons. Although the dragoons were occasionally the target for a salvo of artillery,

> ...the attention of the batteries was directed principally against the moving columns of infantry, either contending for the passage of the river, or directed to clear the ravines of the French troops in possession; hence we were not much molested and had fair time for observation. Nothing could exceed the magnificent sight or the excitement with which one viewed the progress of our gallant men.[30]

Private Adam Reed of the 2/47th, the regimental surgeon's soldier servant, had originally been posted to guard the surgeon's baggage. Sent forward by the adjutant, he found himself gazing down on

---

28 Shadwell, *The Life of Colin Campbell*, pp.14–15.
29 Tomkinson (ed.), *The Diary*, pp.247–248.
30 S.C.I. Wood (ed.), *Reminiscences 1808-1815 under Wellington* (London: Simpkin, Marshall, Hamilton, Kent & Co. Ltd., 1901), pp.111–112.

> ...a beautiful plain about 6 or 8 miles long and 3 or 4 broad. There also appeared a large army of the French and likewise a town called Vitoria. The officers and men were all surprised to see such an army. The plain was covered with men and guns. We never had to engage such an army before, for they appeared like ants on an anthill. While we were on the top they were scuttling about and forming ready for action.[31]

By this time, Tomkinson had joined the 12th Light Dragoons. He

> ...remained in the rear of Gamarra Mayor, whilst the 5th Division, under Major-General Oswald, attacked and carried the village at the point of the bayonet. The leading brigade was the 2nd Brigade, under Major-General Robertson [sic], consisting of the 4th, 47th and 59th, and they were moving in an echelon of regiments from the left. There was either some shyness in the two leading regiments, [47th and 58th] or some misunderstanding of orders; but Colonel Brooke, perceiving it, called: 'Come on, Grenadiers 4th!' passed the other two with his battalion, and carried the place, taking 2,000 prisoners and three guns.'[32]

This was the version of events as described to Tomkinson by Lieutenant Colonel Brooke. The 4th certainly took very heavy casualties, but so did the other two battalions, as they struggled for possession against a determined foe in a strongly defended and barricaded village, the whole covered by artillery. Adam Reed of the 2/47th makes clear that it was more of a struggle than Brooke suggested to Tomkinson. Reed recalled:

> The French having a great many guns in the village as soon as they saw us they fired them at us. The first round they fired made great havoc in our regiment for to hear the deadly groans of some of the men that were hit was horrible.
> Immediately we were ordered to fire a volley, come to port and commence double quick time and charge. By that village runs a river and over it is a bridge that led us from the village to the town. The enemy having their guns in the village and we pushing upon them with our charge so rapidly caused them to leave 5 behind.
> Having gained the village Gamarra Maior, a number of serious attacks were made to gain control of the bridge, but neither side could gain success and the number of casualties mounted rapidly. We charged at them four successive times but was beat back by superior numbers that some were forced to jump into the river up to their necks and we kept the village. There we stood for four hours and could not get a foot of ground on the other side...[33]

During one of the forays onto the bridge, Lieutenant Francis Maguire, bearing the colour of the 4th, in an attempt to encourage an even greater effort, rested it on a parapet of the bridge. It was then shot to pieces in his hands and the bridge remained untaken.

---

31 Glover (ed.), *The Napoleonic Archive Volume 1*, p.106.
32 Tomkinson (ed.), *The Diary*, p.248.
33 Glover (ed.), *The Napoleonic Archive Volume 1*, pp.107–108.

Fighting in the village of Gamarra Maior, by James Beadle. (Nuneaton Museum and Art Gallery)

Another who found himself in the thick of the fighting was George Freer of the 38th. 'Part of the Action, led the Grenadiers – the latter part. The Artillery and Engineers becoming scarce, and I having been accustomed to act as Engineer, was called to that post, for a while directing and loading the guns – then again called to my Company and advanced in a charge three times, wondrously escaping even a scratch.'[34]

The light companies of the first brigade and the Portuguese line battalions were now called in.

> We reached the village, which we named Gomorrah, as it was a scene of fire and brimstone. The enemy was driven through the village, and over the River Zadorra. One wing cleared the house and gardens on the right and then lined the bank of the river, keeping up a heavy fire on the advancing supports. The light company entered a house at the end of the bridge, from the windows of which a very destructive fire was then kept up, while as many as could pushed across and formed as they arrived close to an old chapel.

This is an interesting claim, as is Douglas's further assertion that they would have held the position 'had the regiments which entered the village been pushed across the bridge at the time we crossed,' and would actually have separated the right wing of the French army from

---

34 Freer, *The Thirty-Eighth*, p.305.

the left, which would have led to the wreck of the French.[35] Other eye-witnesses agree with Reed that although the 5th Division prevented the French from retaking the village they were unable to cross the bridge, which became so full of corpses that they began to roll into the river. As a result, according to Campbell,

> We were not long in the village before we were ordered to the left, to cover the flank of the village. We moved through and occupied the bank of the river, upon the opposite side of which was the enemy. During our stay the enemy relieved his skirmishers three times. After three hours' hard fighting the enemy retired, leaving his guns in our possession. Crossing the Zadorra in pursuit, we proceeded about a league after them and encamped near Metauco.[36]

Interestingly, both Douglas and Hale, in their accounts create the impression that they were the leading troops when Gamarra Mayor was attacked, rather than coming up in support of Robinson's brigade. Hale even claimed that 'we advanced in double quick time, and gave them a grand charge, by which we got full possession of the village in a few minutes'.[37]

Elsewhere on the battlefield, the French were being driven back towards Vitoria. This forced Reille to abandon the Zadorra. Longa had finally gained possession of Durana at about 5:00 p.m., and Reille needed to block any advance by Graham (who at this point was about to move the 1st Division forward) so that the rest of the French army could effect a retreat towards Salvatierra which Joseph had now ordered. The Army of Portugal was safe as long as the retreat was conducted in good order but after d'Erlon's position had been turned, Reille had to focus on the safety of his own troops. He had been instructed to wait until the Army of the Centre had passed behind him, but with the rest of the French in growing disorder, he decided to retire without waiting for D'Erlon's troops.

His immediate problem was how to withdraw Lamartinière from Gamarra Mayor and Casapalicios from Durana, the latter already under pressure from Longa and the former vulnerable as soon as he moved his guns from the bridge. Nor was Menne's position secure. Although there was still no movement from Abucheco, Allied troops were advancing towards him along the Zadorra. By using Digeon's cavalry, which launched several attacks, to hold these troops back, Reille enabled Menne to withdraw, although the division had to leave behind their guns and the mortally wounded Sarrut. The rest of the cavalry was at Betonia with Fririon's brigade and they constituted a rallying point both for Menne and for Larmartinière, who was hotly pursued by the 5th Division. Casapalacios's troops had taken to the hills, hounded by Longa, and Lamartinière's were already in disarray when they reached. Betonia. Reille, however, was able to restore some kind of order and bring his whole force back to Zubana, where they came under attack from Graham's light cavalry. They stood their ground and it was only the arrival of the guns of the Royal Horse Artillery which forced them to retreat. Unlike the rest of the French forces, Reille ignored Vitoria, which was in a state of chaos, and brought the Army of Portugal safely to Salvatierra after a long and difficult march.

---

35 Monick (ed.), *Douglas's Tale*, p.72.
36 Shadwell, *The Life of Colin Campbell*, pp.16–17.
37 Hale, *Journal*, pp.108–109.

As for the 5th Division, 'After so warm and well contested a race, it may be easily imagined that a halt became indispensable to renew the wind in our exhausted bellows.' In other words, Douglas and his fellows

> ...started to look for something in the shape of eatables. A small village was close at hand, but the principal houses were occupied by the General Officers and their staff. Yet even this protection was not proof against hunger. One house in particular was occupied by General Hay (who had just lost his son, a fine young man, Captain of our light company and aide-de-camp to his father; he was mortally wounded by grape shot in crossing the bridge at Gamarra Mayor.) Into this house the prowling wolves entered, and finding some wheat and flour, a light became necessary. But the struggle was so severe as to who would get most that the light was unheeded and, making contact with some rubbish, the house was in flames in a few minutes. The old general, running out, exclaims, 'What would I think of it but my own Regiment to set fire to the house over my head.' However, house or no house, the point in question was the belly.[38]

Hale's repast started with beans, a field of them having been found 'very convenient to us. Something was needed to go with it, and 'at this place we were not refused of getting something to eat if we could find any, although we had never been favoured with such a liberty before'. The result was 'a great quantity of good flour', and 'having plenty of flour and green beans, we all made a noble supper.' There is a pattern to Hale's after-battle reminiscences: first one needed to eat and then 'we amused ourselves over what had passed during the day'. On this occasion the conversation was more protracted than usual because 'our commissary arrived with a pint of wine for each man.'[39]

Le Mesurier made an ironic comment on this self-indulgence when he wrote home two days after the battle.

> We have been on short allowances since I wrote [15 June]. The Men, however, found plenty of Flour on the 21st: and treated themselves to such a degree that they were unable to March yesterday, and were Obliged to stop often to discharge their over loaded Stomachs – something like the Emigrant in Guernsey, who enjoyed la Preparation, la Fete & la Purification.[40]

Gomm was more concerned with reputation:

> The 5th Division have again had their full share of employment. We carried by storm the village of Gamarra Mayor, on the flank of the French army, and thereby cutting off their retreat by the Bayonne road. It was a post of the utmost importance to the enemy, and they knew it; for they defended the village obstinately, and charged the bridge over the Zadora river repeatedly after we had taken possession

---

38   Monick (ed.), *Douglas's Tale*, pp.74–75.
39   Hale, *Journal*, pp.110–111.
40   Greenwood (ed.), *Through Spain with Wellington*, pp.175–176.

of it… judges say we have added to our reputation, and we are given to understand that Lord Wellington thinks we performed a very important service at that moment.

There was also a word of praise for Longa. 'His people behaved well, and were of much service… I thought his behaviour admirable, in falling in so readily as he did with our plans – sometimes very opposite to his own.'[41]

As for the Portuguese, Spry reported that 'Concerning the 8th Caçadores, I can only tell you that Lieutenant Colonel Hill and all the battalion distinguished themselves during the day. I believe that General Pack, under whose orders the battalion was, will praise the corps in his report', which he did. As for the two line regiments, 'Nothing could exceed the steadiness of the 3rd and 15th Regiments, both when advancing to attack the village under artillery and musketry fire, and when for several hours under a heavy artillery fire, they remained in support of the brigade that was attacking the enemy.' Having been forced to deploy them in extended order in the absence of the caçadores, Spry added, 'These officers and men, from the 3rd and 15th, distinguished themselves under the command of Major A. Campbell, 15th Regiment, to my greatest satisfaction and to the applause from all who observed their conduct throughout the day.'[42]

The aftermath of the battle is as infamous as the victory is famous. Account after account describes the chaos in Vitoria and the Allied looting of the abandoned French baggage, which led Wellington to castigate his troops, yet again. There are no references to this chaotic free-for-all in the accounts from the 5th Division, for the simple reason that they had no chance to join in the plundering. Halting at Zurbano with Pack's Portuguese, they and the rest of Graham's command were nowhere near Vitoria.

Of the total 5,158 Allied casualties, 577 were taken by the 5th Division, 352 by Robinson's brigade. Among the officers who died or were mortally wounded was Lieutenant Colonel Charles Fane, in command of the 2/59th. Having survived a serious head wound received at Corunna, he had only re-joined in March 1813. At Vitoria he 'had his leg and part of his thigh carried off, but survived the wound some days. He wrote to some of his relations after he had received his wounds. His last moments were easy and quiet. He was buried at Vittoria, the scene of his latest glory and death', aged 32. He was also described as 'one of the most promising officers in the service.'[43] According to Robinson, having seemed likely to survive his wounds, he then died of tetanus.

On 23 June, Graham sent Wellington his report on the battle. He was characteristically generous in his praise: '…the village of Gamarra Maior was most gallantly stormed by Brigadier-General Robinson's brigade of the 5th Division (formed in three columns of battalions, which advanced under heavy fire of artillery and musketry, without firing a shot), assisted by two guns of Major Lawson's brigade.' Having described events at Abechuco, he then continued:

---

41   Carr-Gomm (ed.), *Letters and Journals*, vol.I pp.304–305, 307.
42   Gaudêncio & Burnham, *Fighting Cocks*, p.100.
43   *The Gentleman's Magazine*, July 1813, p.94.

Victory of Vitoria, by John Massey Wright, illustrating the aftermath of the battle.
(Anne S.K. Brown Military Collection)

During this operation on the right, the enemy made the greatest efforts to repossess themselves of the village of Gamarra Maior by a heavy fire of artillery and musketry, and having at least two divisions of infantry in reserve on strong ground behind. But the enemy's repeated attacks were successfully repulsed. It was, however, evidently impossible to push a column across the river by this bridge in the face of such a force so posted. Too much praise cannot be bestowed on Major-General Oswald for the disposition he made to defend this village, and he speaks in the highest terms of the conduct of Brigadier-General Robinson and the troops of his brigade, which suffered severely in maintaining the post they had so gallantly won, and of that of Major-General Hay and Major-General Spry, successively called to support the second brigade.[44]

Wellington now intended to force the French to cross the border, including Clausel's troops and Foy's division of the Army of Portugal. Clausel finally left Spain on 11 July, by which time the main army and Foy's division had already crossed into France. On the same day,

---

44 Alex M. Delavoye, *The Life of Thomas Graham, Lord Lynedoch*, (London: Richardson & Co., 1880), pp.661–662.

Gomm wrote to his sister from Mondragon: 'Sir T. Graham has driven Foy and his division across the Bidasoa river, so that the country is clear on this side. We have had a dance meanwhile after Clausel, who I believe has gone down to Zarragoza, and there joined Suchet. We are going tomorrow towards Tolosa, to rejoin Sir T. Graham.'[45] This information was not quite accurate, however. There were still troops on 'this side', the garrisons at Pamplona and San Sebastian, the latter having been strengthened by 3,000 troops under *Général de Brigade* Emmanuel Rey. As for 'dancing after Clausel', as Gomm termed it, on 23 June the 5th Division remained in Salvatierra while the rest of Graham's corps were sent to Guipuscoa. Three days later they marched to Logroño with the 6th Division, which had been brought up to Vitoria, and D'Urban's and the heavy cavalry. Their task was to intercept Clausel and his 14,000 troops. The division continued its march beyond Logroño, almost to Laguradia, but Clausel, having received news not just of the French defeat but also the nature of that defeat, was already on the road to Zaragoza. The 5th Division then received an order to counter-march towards Vitoria and take the Great Road to Tolosa via Mondragon. From there they advanced on San Sebastian, which Graham was in the process of investing.

The First Siege of San Sebastian

Reaching San Sebastian,

> We pitched our camp on the slope of a hill within gunshot of the town, but hid from view of San Sebastian as we were now on the sea coast. We had abundance of rations. The sight of the sea was so novel that the men could with difficulty be restrained from ascending the hill to look at it, and would sit enjoying the sight as if looking at their native shore. Here the vegetables were pretty plentiful and good, and though not regularly served out we were not always short of a little mutton, so that I may say we lived like what we were – fighting cocks.[46]

If Douglas had a complaint, it was that the French fired at the Allied sentries, which he obviously considered unwarranted, if not unsporting

Having harried the main French army out of Spain, Wellington next needed to secure his own position before he could contemplate an advance into France. Assuming that Suchet could be kept occupied by Lieutenant General John Murray's Anglo-Sicilian army and the Spanish (despite the aborted siege of Tarragona), the fortresses of Pamplona and San Sebastian were the immediate problem. Both were under blockade, the former by Hill's forces, the latter by a Spanish force under *Teniente general* Gabriel de Mendizábel. Since he lacked the resources to besiege both fortresses, Wellington decided to continue the blockade at the former, substituting Spanish troops for Hill's, and besiege the latter.

A contemporary elucidation of San Sebastian by an engineer officer described it as a town of nearly 10,000 inhabitants

---

45   Carr-Gomm (ed.), *Letters and Journals*, vol.I, p.308.
46   Monick (ed.), *Douglas's Tale*, p.76.

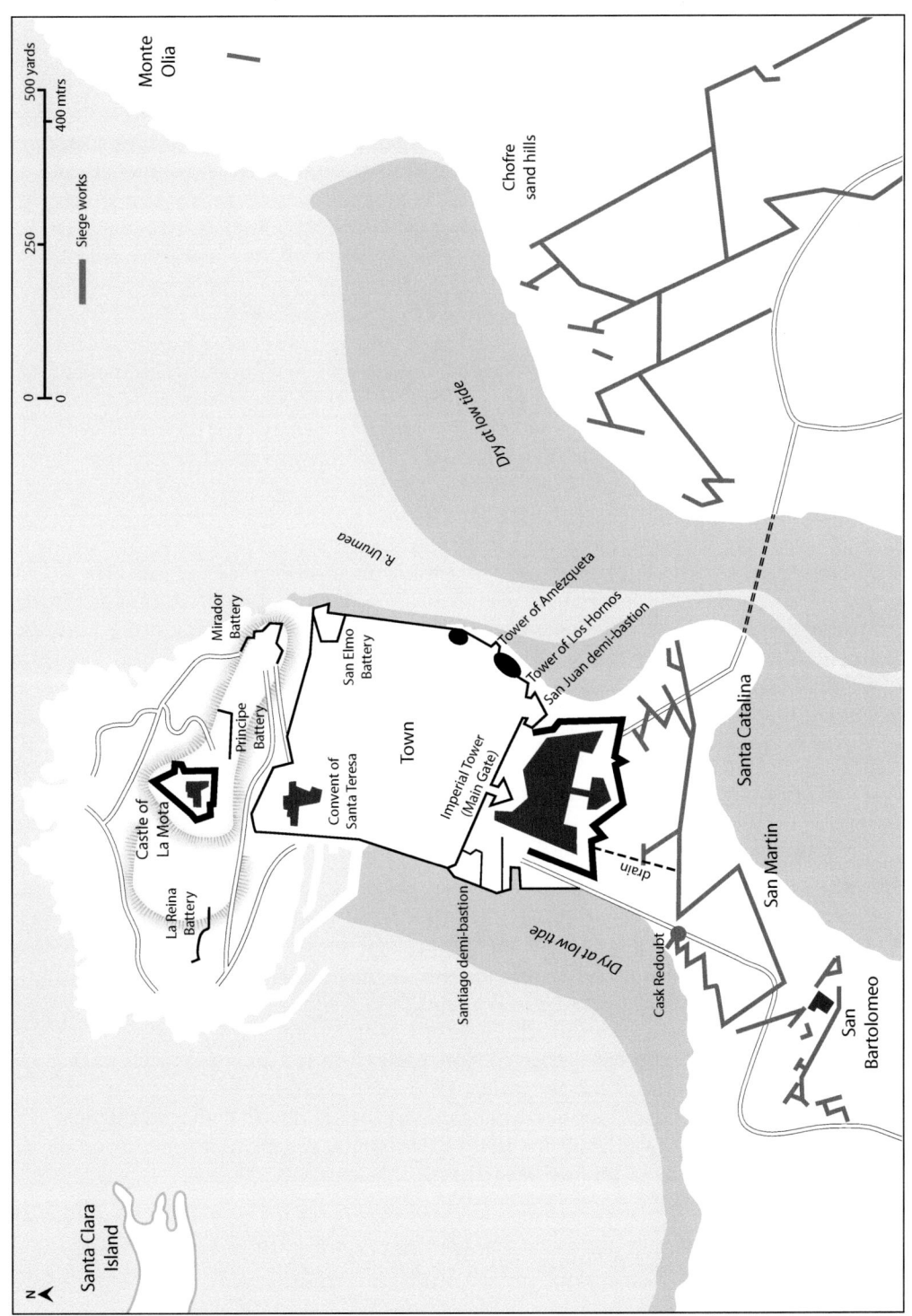

The Siege of San Sebastion.

> …built on a low peninsula, running north and south; the defences of the western side being washed by the sea, and those on the eastern side by the river Urumea, which, at high water, covers four feet of the masonry of the scarp.
>
> The works of the land front across the isthmus consist of a single front of fortifications, exceeding 350 yards in length, with a flat bastion and cavalier in the centre, covered by a hornwork, having the usual counterscarp, covered-way, and glacis; but the defences running lengthwise of the peninsula consist merely of a simple rampart wall, indifferently flanked, without either ditch, counterscarp, glacis or other obstacle in its front; and further, this naked scarp wall, on the eastern side, is seen from its summit to its base, from the Chofre range of sand-hills, on the right of the Urumea, at distance from five hundred to a thousand yards.
>
> At the extremity of the peninsula, a rocky height called Monte Orgullo, of the considerable base of 400 yards by 600 yards, rises steeply to a point, which is occupied by a small work called Fort la Mota. The whole of this promontory is cut off from the town by a defensive line near its foot and its southern face is covered with batteries which plunge into the lower defences of the place, and add materially to their powers of resistance…[47]

Jones wondered why the eastern defences had been left without cover or a second obstacle, all the more surprising when it transpired that the Urumea was fordable at low tide.

When *Général de brigade* Rey reached San Sebastian the day after the action at Vitoria, he immediately rid himself of the convoy he had been escorting, and any other non-residents, by sending them on to France. His position was strengthened by the detachment that *Général de division* Foy left at San Sebastian as he made his way to the frontier, as well as by a further 300 troops from Gueteria and a detachment of gunners brought south from St Jean de Luz. In addition, he also had some sappers and miners, giving him a garrison of over 3,000 men. San Sebastian had been used as a depot rather than a defensive point, so the defences had been allowed to fall into disrepair. Rey now set to work repairing and strengthening them, including the construction of a redoubt in the graveyard attached to the convent of San Bartolomeo.

Despite Rey's efforts, or because he was not aware of them, Wellington anticipated a rapid and successful siege. On 12 July he informed Bathurst that 'we are in a good position here. I hope we shall soon have San Sebastian; and if we get well settled in the Pyrenees, it will take a good reinforcement to the French army to drive us from thence.'[48] This was dangerously optimistic. On 4 July Wellington had told Graham that

> From the account which I have received from Major Smith [R.E.] of the state of San Sebastian, and in a view to the general situation of our affairs, I feel very anxious to attack that place. Although our train, which was framed with a view to the siege of Burgos, is not quite sufficient for that of Pamplona, it appears to me, from all accounts, that it is fully so for San Sebastian.[49]

---

47 Jones, *Journals of Sieges*, vol.II, pp.14–16.
48 Gurwood (ed.), *Dispatches*, vol.X, p.523.
49 Gurwood (ed.), *Dispatches*, vol.X, p.510.

San Sebastian, by Andrew Leith Hay. (*A Narrative of the Peninsular War*)

Four days later, he wrote: 'Upon consideration, I think you had better give General Oswald charge of the siege of San Sebastian, with the 5th division, and either Pack's or Bradford's brigade; and as many Spanish battalions as you may think fit should assist.'[50] Graham had arrived two days earlier and now proceeded to dispose his troops in accordance with this order.

San Sebastian had already been under blockade since 27 June. Mendizábel had also made several weak assaults, all of which had failed. As Graham now set about positioning his own troops from his own command, he received yet another memorandum from Wellington which requested him 'to order such troops as he may think proper, of the 1st and 5th divisions, and General Pack's and General Bradford's brigades to invest and carry on the operations of the siege of San Sebastian'.[51] Initially, Graham chose to follow the original plan and give the 5th Division and Bradford's Portuguese responsibility for the conduct of the siege, with some support from Pack's brigade.

In 1719, during the war of the Quadruple Alliance which saw Britain and France acting together, the Duke of Berwick, in command of the French forces, successfully laid siege to San Sebastian by placing his guns on the Chofre sandhills to breach the eastern wall while also placing batteries on the isthmus to counteract fire from the south side of the town. It was this plan that Major Charles Felix Smith, Graham's senior engineer, advocated, culminating in ballistic fire to destroy the castle. Smith had been present at none of Wellington's sieges, having been with Graham at Cadiz, but he had the support of Lieutenant Colonel

---

50   Gurwood (ed.), *Dispatches*, vol.X, pp.512–513.
51   Gurwood (ed.), *Dispatches*, vol.X, p.525.

Alexander Dickson R.A., and of Wellington when he arrived on 12 July to reconnoitre and supervise. It was decided, 'as a preliminary to drive the enemy from the Convent and redoubt of San Bartolomé, where they had established a strong post about 800 yards in front of the town'. This having been effected, it would then be possible 'to raise batteries in that situation to aid the main attack, and to oblige the enemy to withdraw from the circular work on the causeway'.[52] This was another redoubt, referred to as the cask redoubt because it had been strengthened with casks filled with sand.

As a further limitation on French operations, a naval blockade, comprising a frigate, a corvette and two brigs under Vice Admiral Sir George Collier, and some local boats, was put in place. The French, however, were still able to run the blockade with supplies from Bayonne and St Jean de Luz, including the gunners mentioned above, and carry off the wounded. The island of Santa Clara in the harbour proved invaluable to the French in the conduct in these operations.

Graham followed the advice of the engineers and tried to reduce the convent by fire from a Portuguese battery, but it proved too solid, demonstrating the need for heavier guns. At the same time, the French continued to strengthen their position. On 14 July the batteries on the left, opposite the convent, opened fire, including two 18-pounders which sent hot shot against the building. It did not catch fire, however, despite the use of shells and carcasses. The following day, further pounding brought down the roof and part of the walls, although the defenders managed to contain the fires that broke out. Rey also positioned two battalions to hold both the convent and the adjoining suburbs of San Martin.

Graham now sent the 4th Caçadores from Pack's brigade, attached to the 5th Divison, to storm the position but the French proved too strong, and the Portuguese took some loss, including two officers. The bombardment continued on the 16th, demolishing most of the front of the building. Further firing the following morning meant that by 9:00 a.m. the convent had effectively been breached. An hour later troops were in position for a more concentrated attack. On the right were 150 men from the 13th Portuguese (Bradford's brigade), three companies from the 9th, under Major Henry Crauford, with three companies from the Royal Scots in reserve, all under the command of Major General Hay. On the left 200 men from the 5th Caçadores (Bradford's brigade), a further 200 from the 13th Portuguese, and the rest of the 9th, under Cameron's command, advanced on the convent under Bradford's overall command. Hay's target was the cemetery and the houses which had been fortified, and Bradford's, the main convent buildings.

Under cover of two allied guns that were training their fire on the redoubt, the signal was given for the advance. Hale was on the left.

> Between the enemy and us was a narrow lane, with a high growing hedge on each side, and as soon as the enemy found of our approaching, they placed themselves along the hedge on their own side, and the Portuguese in like manner placed themselves along this side of the hedge, and commenced firing through both hedges: there they continued firing in that way, for about a quarter of an hour, without making any sort of attempt any further. But at length Lieutenant Colonel Cameron,

---

52   Leslie (ed.), *Dickson Manuscripts*, vol.V, p.959.

who commanded our regiment, got quite out of patience in waiting, upon which he ordered the regiment to advance by the Portuguese, and make an attack.[53]

In a letter written many years later to Lieutenant Colin Campbell, as he was in 1813, Cameron gave his own account. Ordered by Bradford to make the assault,

> …in the first instance I had to halt under cover of a stone wall within fifty yards of the convent until a signal should be observed from the right attack. In a few moments I perceived the enemy running from the redoubt towards the convent though *no signal yet*. We sprang over the wall and moved rapidly against a strong body of the enemy posted outside of the convent, and on seeing these a very galling fire opened upon us from the adjacent buildings which I ordered to be forced. Woodham entered the largest in which he was killed after gaining the first floor at the point of the bayonet. The row was now at its height, some charging those posted at the convent, others clearing the houses of which the windows and other outlets the enemy availed themselves of to escape and all uniting in full chase to the village of San Martin.[54]

The result was that both the convent and the redoubt were taken, the French offering limited resistance once the Allied troops were upon them, abandoning the redoubt and joining the troops posted at San Martin. Here they made a more determined defence and a fierce struggle ensued. Eventually, they were driven out and retired to the town, pursued by some of the 9th, who pressed too far forward, towards the cask redoubt, with the result that casualties were higher than they might have been with a little more circumspection. The Allies lost 207 officers and men, the 9th losing 70, killed or wounded, including two officers killed, and five wounded, one of whom died of his wounds that night. The French recorded 230 casualties.[55]

Significantly, Cameron in the letter quoted above, noted how 'I beheld some of your people running in breathless haste by the right of the convent towards the Cask Redoubt and I truly reported the circumstances and also what would probably be the consequences.'[56] This comment seems to be in response to his recent reading of Graham's dispatch, which he believed to be based on Hay's report to Oswald. That there was some animosity between the two officers is borne out by an earlier comment. 'It is sufficiently manifest by the note of General H to General O that the pen of the former was guided by a feeling that I shall not name.'[57] Yet Hay actually praised Campbell for his 'gallant and exemplary conduct', while hoping that he should be 'but a short time deprived of the services of this excellent officer Lieutenant Colonel Cameron, 9th, by the severe concussion he has received.'[58]

---

53 Hale, *Journal*, p.113.
54 Glover (ed.), *The Napoleonic Archive Volume 1*, p.51.
55 Oman, *The History of the Peninsular War*, vol.VI, p.572.
56 Glover (ed.), *The Napoleonic Archive Volume 1*, p.52.
57 Glover (ed.), *The Napoleonic Archive Volume 1*, p.51.
58 Gaudêncio & Burnham, *Fighting Cocks*, p.126.

Both the French and the Allies now focused on the cask redoubt, the former to strengthen it by constructing a parapet and the latter to weaken it ready for an assault. The Allied engineers had established a lodgement in a forward position and the troops were set to work preparing the ground for

> ...a battery of 15 twenty-fours, 6 mortars and 2 howitzers. During these preparations the enemy were not idle in letting us have plenty of shot and shell. The trenches commenced at the gate of the convent, and ran in a zig-zag fashion towards a fieldwork, called the half-moon battery, of field pieces. These, though small, annoyed us most unmercifully, as all out approaches had to be thieflike in the dark.

Even so, the smallest spark from a spade or other implement would attract the attention of the French, with the result that 'a great many were killed and wounded.'[59]

At the same time further batteries were established on the Chofre Heights, while the French were observed to be erecting traverses on the land front of the town.

On the 20th the Allied guns opened fire on the cask redoubt, while the French concentrated on what they had identified as the breaching battery on the Chofre Heights, putting some of the Allied guns out of action and killing one of the engineer officers. By the evening, though, Rey had accepted the vulnerability of the redoubt and withdrew the defending troops. That night 700 men from Spry's brigade were designated to start work on the parallel across the isthmus, but the weather was wild and stormy, with the result that most of them took shelter in the ruins of San Martin. As a result, by the following morning the work was only a third of its intended length. At daylight on the 21st the Allied guns opened fire again but went quiet at 10:00 a.m. when Graham invited Rey to surrender. Not surprisingly, Rey refused even to accept the letter. Napoleon had ordered his garrison commanders to refuse all offers to surrender and to do so without even a breach being made would have been a serious offence, sufficient to end any officer's career.

The battering continued until 24 July, by which time the parapets and embrasures were collapsing. The previous day 50 yards of the curtain wall between Los Hornos and Amezqueta had been brought down, thus creating a practicable breach. The parallel was complete and a drain had been discovered. This was explored by Lieutenant Reid R.E. who established that it led to the west of the hornwork counterscarp. Thirty barrels of powder were then placed at the far end to create a mine. On the following day a smaller breach was made, only 50 yards wide at low tide, but sufficient to serve as a distraction.

As for the French, when not toiling to repair as much of the damage as possible they continued to strengthen the defences, particularly at the hornwork where the guns on Monte Olia were putting the garrison under pressure. Furthermore, although supplies were still coming into the harbour, it was noted that the French appeared to be husbanding their resources by not firing on the working parties and using minimal powder to fire shells.[60]

With everything set for an assault, Wellington now ordered that it should take place in daylight. Early on the 24th, the troops that were going to carry it out were already in

---

59 Monick (ed.), *Douglas's Tale*, p.77.
60 Jones, *Journals of Sieges*, vol.II, p.33.

position, waiting for a half ebbing tide. It was then observed that the houses nearest to the breach were burning so fiercely that they presented a formidable obstacle and the assault was called off. Jones pertinently observed that, combined with the difficulties the troops would face as they advanced, this countermanding 'created an unlucky impression on the troops that they were about to be employed on a desperate service without a probability of success.'[61]

Although the French had been steadily losing guns, Rey was still able to improve his defences. He was helped by the simple fact that the stones at the breach had fallen outwards while the inner rampart remained undamaged. This meant there was a drop of as much as 20 feet, making ladders necessary. Rey increased the difficulties the Allies would face by demolishing the houses that were built against the walls and blocking the streets that led away from the breaches, while the previously constructed traverses prevented sideways movement. As for the burnt-out houses, they became shelters for the defenders. The Allied artillery also detected that the defenders had moved 10 guns into position, ready to target the attackers. Since they would have to be run out, the Allied gunners were confident that they could soon put them out of action.

Low tide was crucial to the attack. On 25 July it occurred at 5:00 a.m., before clear daylight. There were also two practical problems: the narrowness of the parallel, which allowed no more than three men to go abreast; and the nature of the ground when the tide receded. Neither complication was allowed to delay the assault. The right wing of the Royal Scots under Major Peter Frazer was to lead, followed by Lieutenant Lancelot Machell R.E. directing a ladder party drawn from all three battalions of Hay's brigade, with support from a detachment of the 1/9th under Lieutenant Colin Campbell, and finally the left wing of the Royals. This column would attack the main breach. At the same time, the 1/38th would advance between the leading troops and the water's edge before heading for the lesser breach. The third battalion of the brigade, the 1/9th, was to give support where it was needed, while the 8th Caçadores would take position in front of the parallel and in the ditch to pick off the French sharpshooters who would be firing from the east flank of the hornwork. These troops were faced with a challenging advance. Having emerged from the parallel, they would then have to cover 300 yards across ground that was broken, with pools of water and exposed rocks covered in seaweed, thus slowing their progress and inevitably causing loss of order. Beyond these natural obstacles were the French, lining the flanking parapets, still intact. In addition, the French held the damaged towers at each end of the breach.

The signal for the attack was the firing of a mine, which caused an unexpected amount of damage to the counterscarp wall and glacis of the hornwork. The French actually abandoned their left flank for a brief while and this enabled the head of the Allied column, which had rushed forward in response to the explosion, to reach the foot of the breach. While the left wing of the Royal Scots halted near the hornwork to restore order, the right wing, led by Frazer and Lieutenant Harry Jones R.E., attacked impetuously. They soon found themselves under heavy French artillery fire which killed Machell and dispersed the ladder party, but the men of the 3/1st persisted in their attack, taking heavy casualties. Nor could they proceed further. Not only were they without ladders but they were also deterred by the

---

61 Jones, *Journals of Sieges*, vol.II, p.40.

smoke that still filled the burnt buildings. This gave the French the chance to recover. Heavy musketry fire increased the Allied casualties as did the hand grenades being lobbed from the two towers. Despite some more uncoordinated attacks it was obvious that the assailants could advance no further and a withdrawal was ordered. Frazer had been killed and although Jones continued to hold his ground with a handful of men, still hoping for the arrival of the ladders, they all eventually fell into French hands. By this point, the left wing, recognising a hopeless situation, had withdrawn to the trenches. As for the 1/38th, they never reached the lesser breach because there was insufficient width of dry ground to pass the Royal Scots. They then witnessed the retreat and returned to the trenches.

Although Colin Campbell recorded the day in his journal with just a single word, 'Storm!', in a letter which formed part of his correspondence with Cameron in 1836, he had more to say on this fiasco. He placed himself 'in the centre of the Royals with twenty men of our light company' and was accompanied by the ladder party.

> It was dark, as you know, when ordered to advance. All before me went willingly enough forward, but in a very straggling order, arising, in the first instance, from the order of formation previous to attack, it being extended the whole length of the parallel in a front of fours, which it (the parallel) would admit of by packing when halted, but was not of sufficient width for troops to maintain that front when in movement… The space we had to traverse between this opening [of the parallel] and the breach – some three hundred yards – was very rough and broken by large pieces of rocks, which the falling tide had left wet and exceedingly slippery, sufficient in itself to have loosened and disordered an original dense formation; and the heavy and uninterrupted fire to which they were opposed in the advance, increased this evil.

Campbell then found himself behind a crowd of men at the demi-bastion on the left. They were 'returning a fire directed at them from the parapet above, and which was sweeping them down in great numbers.' There was also 'a heavy firing at the breach; and as the larger portion of the right wing appeared to be collected, as I have described, opposite the demi-bastion, it was very manifest that those who had gone forward to the breach were not only weak in numbers for the struggle they had to encounter, but it was apparent that they were unsupported.'

In consultation with Lieutenant Samuel Clarke, who commanded the light company of the Royal Scots (and was killed soon afterwards), Campbell decided to lead his detachment past the right of the men engaged in the firefight with the French on the parapet, his hope being that they would stop firing and follow him. Most of them stayed, however, which he ascribed to their having kept close to the retaining wall of the hornwork as they advanced and then 'on arriving at the opening into the main ditch, mistook it in the dark and in their ignorance for the main breach, and imagined it to be an opening through which they might find or force a way into the place'.

When he arrived at the main breach, Campbell observed that 'There were a few individual officers and men spread on the face of the breach, but nothing more. These were cheering, and gallantly opposing themselves to the close and destructive fire directed at them from the round tower and other defences on each flank of the breach, and to a profusion of hand-grenades which were constantly rolling down.' At this point he was twice wounded but noted that 'A good deal of firing was kept up by our unwounded men from the bottom of the breach during the period of which I am giving an account.'

Captain Lawrence Arguimbeau of the Royal Scots now brought up

> ...some eighty or ninety men, cheering and encouraging them forward in a very brave manner through all the interruptions that were offered to his advance... Seeing, however, that whatever previous efforts had been made had been unsuccessful – that there was no body of men nor support near him, while all the defences of and around the breach were fully occupied and alive with fire, and the party with him quite unequal in itself, – seeing, also, the many discouraging circumstances under which the attempt would have to be made, of forcing its way through such opposition, – he ordered his party to retire, receiving, when speaking to me, a shot which broke his arm. I came back with him and his party, and on my way met the 38th, whose advance became interrupted by the wounded and others of the Royals returning.[62]

That the assault had become a debacle could not be denied and was inevitably followed by an outbreak of what may be described as a blame-game.[63] Campbell believed 'that the main cause of our failure was the narrow front and consequent length and thinness of the columns in which we advanced. This necessarily became more loosened and disjointed by the difficult nature of the ground it had to pass over in the dark – a disadvantage which the heavy fire it was exposed to in that advance augmented – so that it reached the breach in driblets and never in such body or number to give the mind of the soldier anything like confidence of success, or such as would be in the least likely to shake the firmness of the defenders.' He also ascribed the failure to its being undertaken before daylight, which prevented the men from seeing their officers, whereas in daylight officers would have been able to inspire their men into action.

This seems a fair assessment, to which it might be added that attacking in the dark caused a further problem. 'Arrangements had been made by Colonel Dickson for the batteries on the Chofre sand-hills to direct their fire during the assault on the high curtain, the barrack under the Mirador, and the enemy's artillery generally'. This would definitely have aided the troops but, although the guns were primed and ready to fire and had the measure of their targets, 'it was so perfectly dark that the officers could not distinguish objects to direct their fire: indeed it did not become sufficiently light till after the return of the troops into the trenches, to enable the Artillery to ascertain what had occurred.'[64]

Gomm, who admitted to a dread of sieges, believed that success at both Ciudad Rodrigo and Badajoz,

> ...owing to the almost miraculous efforts of our troops, has checked the progress of science among our engineers, and perhaps done more; for it seems to have inspired

---

62 Shadwell, *The Life of Colin Campbell*, pp.25–29.
63 Oman, *A History*, vol.V, pp.583–584.
64 Jones, *Journals of Sieges*, vol.II, p.43.

them with a contempt for as much of it as they had attained. Our soldiers have on all occasions stood fire so well that our artillery have become as summary to their proceedings as our engineers; and, providing they can make a hole in the wall by which we can claw up, they care not about destroying its defences, or facilitating in any degree what is, under the most favourable auspices, the most desperate of all military enterprises.

This is a harsh judgement (which defenders of the engineers and artillery would be quick to question),[65] but it comes from his distress that 'In a very few minutes five hundred of the flower of the army were cut down – the Royals, which was the pride of the division, the 38th, an excellent corps. The 9th, fortunately, had not time to suffer much; but they lost nearly as many heads as they showed. Most fortunately, the troops behaved as they always have done.'[66] The actual casualty figure for the whole assault was 571, of which 330 were taken by the Royal Scots. This explains the anger that Gomm obviously felt. It might also be suggested that the lack of direct connection between the engineers (in particular) and the artillery on one hand and the infantry officers on the other meant there could be little mutual understanding between the two scientific arms and the cannon fodder, the fault for which lay on neither side.

Interestingly, one of the artillery officers implicitly castigated by Gomm, Lieutenant Colonel Augustus Frazer R.H.A., had a very different opinion of the men's behaviour. In a letter written on the 26th he told his wife that 'The troops did not behave well, according to present appearances.'[67] He made clear in a later letter, however, that neither he nor the other artillery officers had witnessed anything of the actual assault and had thought that only a false attack was being made until they were able to discern the returning troops and the dead and wounded they were leaving behind. In contrast, Graham, in a dispatch to Wellington, insisted that, 'notwithstanding the distinguished gallantry of the troops employed, some of whom did force their way into the town, the attack did not succeed.' Further on, he wrote: 'Though this attack has failed, it would be great injustice not to assure your Lordship, that the troops conducted themselves with their usual gallantry, and only retired when I thought a further perseverance in this attack would have occasioned a useless sacrifice of brave men.'[68] Graham, of course, was always generous to his troops.

There was one positive note in the midst of this disaster, somewhat surprisingly struck by the French. As Frazer described it to his wife,

> In a little while one or two of the enemy appeared on the beach, and one sergeant, with a gasconading humanity, ran down among the wounded, raising some, and speaking to others. We stopped our fire, which till then had been continued

---

65 See, Mark S. Thompson, *Wellington's Favourite Engineer: John Fox Burgoyne: Operations, Engineering, and the Making of a Field Marshal* (Warwick: Helion, 2020), p.287.
66 Carr-Gomm (ed.), *Letters and Journals*, vol.I, pp.311–312.
67 Edward Sabine (ed.), *Letters of Colonel Sir Augustus Simon Frazer, K.C.B. Commanding the Royal Horse Artillery in the Army under the Duke of Wellington written during the Peninsular and Waterloo Campaigns* (London Longman, Brown, Green, Longmans, & Roberts, 1859), p.199.
68 Delavoye, *The Life of Thomas Graham*, pp.669–670.

occasionally over the breach. More of the enemy appeared: a kind of parley took place between them and three of our people at the head of the trenches: then a white flag was hoisted, by whose authority I know not. We, of course, ceased firing. The Urumea to our left prevented communication, and during the time the truce lasted the enemy carried away into the town such of our wounded as could be moved... After this strange interval, which lasted about an hour, we recommenced firing, but without any definite object.[69]

Wellington had heard the guns, which led him to anticipate the fall of San Sebastian. By 11:00 a.m. he had heard a suggestion of failure and an hour later he received confirmation, whereupon he rode to San Sebastian to discover why the assault had failed. While he was on his way back, he received news of actions at the passes of Maya and Roncesvalles as Soult launched an attack on the Allied positions there in order to force them back and allow him to relieve Pamplona and San Sebastian. These actions, followed by the two battles at Sorauren on the 28th and 30th, obviously required Wellington's full attention. He had previously told Graham that the battering of San Sebastian must continue, so that the same plan could eventually be implemented more successfully. At 10:00 p.m. on the 25th, however, he wrote:

> As the siege is now in that state that we can do no more till the ammunition, &c., arrives from England, it will render your force much more disposable, and it will be desirable, that you should have embarked all the carriages, wheels, &c., and everything else not absolutely necessary. The guns ought likewise to be returned to the *Surveillante*, and the others moved out of the batteries to the landing place, excepting two on the right to keep up a fire on the breaches, and the other 18 pounders to be on the left. Two howitzers might be left on the hill.[70]

Thus, the siege was converted to a blockade as Wellington waited for the supplies from England that he had been promised. During the night of the 26th the troops were engaged in dragging the guns away. Early on the 27th Rey launched a sally from the hornwork. Hay was returning from the trenches, which he had been inspecting, preparatory to making a verbal report to Oswald, when

> ...on looking over the old 18-pounder battery, my attention was called by a discharge of musketry in the trenches, when I saw the enemy there and advancing in considerable force along the causeway from the town, and in another body from the right of the ditch.
> The covering party, consisting of 600 of the 3rd and 15th regiments, and 100 of the 9th and 38th British, under Major O'Halloran [4th Foot], were leaving the trenches and scattering over the low ground.

---

69 Sabine (ed.), *Letters*, pp.205–206.
70 Gurwood (ed.), *Dispatches*, vol.X, p.566.

> I directed a working party of the 9th and 38th regiments, who were near me, to follow me to the trenches, and with their assistance, Major O'Halloran rallied the Portuguese of his party and drove the enemy back to town.
>
> The distance between the right of our trenches and the entrance, where our men principally rallied, made it easy for the enemy to carry off a considerable number of prisoners whom they had taken in the night.

Hay was quick to cover himself, insisting in this report to Oswald that he had ordered Major George O'Halloran to ensure that every fifth man was standing sentry. He had also stressed to the officers, both British and Portuguese, that they must ensure by constant vigilance that the sentries remained alert, since this was obviously an ideal moment for a French sortie. In his own account, O'Halloran detailed the steps he had taken, including an order that the officers should report to him every half-hour. The French had attacked the Portuguese end of the trench and at the gap between the Portuguese and the British. In his opinion, the subsequent panic had occurred despite the best efforts of the officers to prevent it. He estimated the loss as up to 30 British and 100 Portuguese. O'Halloran was subsequently court martialled but was found not guilty and honourably acquitted.[71]

Soult's first attack at Sorauren on the 28 July led to the transports with the battering train being instructed to put to sea at Passages, although this order was rescinded on 5 August, when it was clear that the French were withdrawing. Wellington now appreciated that he needed more resources to take San Sebastian, and those resources were still at sea, not having set sail until the 27th. Worse still, they did not include what was most desperately needed, more shot. Graham's command at San Sebastian had been expanded to include the Guards brigade and a brigade comprising the 76th, 2/84th and 85th under the command of Major General Matthew Whitworth Aylmer, Lord Aylmer. These troops and the three lines of earthworks constructed between the Bidassoa and Oyarzun covered San Sebastian against any attempt to relieve it.

The Second Siege of San Sebastian

At San Sebastian itself all was quiet between 27 July and 19 August, apart from a second sally by Rey on 1 August, which took more prisoners, and French fire on any movement in the trenches. The Allies strengthened the works on the San Bartolomeo Heights and returned some of the re-landed guns to their former positions. On the 19th, the first transports arrived from England with part of a battering train, followed by others over the next few days which brought with them the first-ever British company of sappers and miners, 92 men strong. On the 23rd, the long-awaited shot arrived. Manpower from both the navy and the army helped with the unloading, as did the local Basque women, who were rewarded with a dollar a day for their efforts. Once the extra guns had reached San Sebastian, they were used to replace any damaged guns and extend the scope of the batteries or create new batteries. Eventually, there were 48 guns on the Chofre sandhills and 13 on the San

---

71 Wellington (ed.), *Supplementary Despatches*, vol.VIII, pp.157–158.

Bartolomeo Heights. These last were to target the San Juan bastion and the curtain wall, as well as to create a wider breach. Yet there remained the one insoluble problem, that the assailants could only offer a limited front because of the tidal pattern.

On the French side, Rey was taking advantage of the lull both to stock up with stores brought in by the small boats and to further strengthen his position. This included the construction of a thick 15-foot-high, loopholed wall from the ruins of the burnt-out houses which, in effect, functioned as an inner rampart. He also scarped the inner walls at the breaches, thus creating a sheer drop, repaired the damage from the mine and created retrenchments at the hornwork. There was more work on the barricades in the town, which would enable the defenders to effect an orderly withdrawal to La Mota, should they be overwhelmed, while the batteries in the castle were better protected. He also sent yet another sortie into the Allied trenches at midnight on 24–25 August, which damaged the sap and took a few prisoners but was then driven off before there was any further harm done.

At 9:00 a.m. on 26 August the Allied guns once more opened fire. The 48 guns on the Chofre sandhills targeted the towers of Los Hornos and Amezqueta, which would enable the first breach to be extended, and also the San Juan demi-bastion, while the 15 guns on the San Bartolomeo Heights were aimed at the hornwork. These last were less successful than those on the right because of the distance from their target, which inevitably lessened the precision of their fire. Nevertheless, some damage was done to the flank of the hornwork. Wellington, however, was not satisfied when he came to inspect the progress being made and ordered that a further battery of six 24-pounders should be constructed to the right of the parallel across the isthmus, in front of the ruins of San Martin. Lieutenant Colonel Sir Richard Fletcher R.E., who was in overall command of the operation, subsequently modified the battery to four guns since he did not wish to weaken the fire from San Bartolomeo, which could sweep the rear of the sea line.[72]

The garrison, meanwhile, had continued to be supplied with ammunition by a fleet of small boats. In order to cut off this supply, on the night of 26–27 August an attack was launched on the islet of Santa Clara, Allied possession of which would prevent further incursions into the harbour. Furthermore, a battery established there could direct its fire against the castle. The islet was held by a small garrison. The boats of the naval blockade, under the command of Lieutenant James Arbuthnot, carried 200 Allied infantry, Captain Hector Cameron of the 9th in command, to the islet, where they quickly overwhelmed the garrison. In this operation they lost Lieutenant Chadwick R.E. and two privates killed, while six were wounded.[73] On the 27th, after another day of sustained Allied fire, Rey chanced a third sortie but it was quickly beaten back with the bayonet by Lieutenant Colonel John Cameron and men of the 9th.

The bombardment continued for the next few days, achieving the degree of damage the engineers felt necessary before another assault could be made. There was also a false attack on the breach on the 29th by Lieutenant Macadam and 17 men of the Royals, with the intention of making the French fire any mines they had laid, and also to discover what kind of fire the French would mount against an assault. No mines were exploded but the Royals came

---

72 Jones, *Journals of Sieges*, vol.III, p.61.
73 Jones, *Journals of Sieges*, vol.III, p.61.

under fire and only Macadam returned unwounded. Nevertheless, Graham seems to have shared the concern of the senior officers of the 5th Division that the breach might actually be where the French defences were strongest.

Frazer, writing to his wife early on the 30th was able to report:

> All going on well. The wood and rubbish of the right breach of the former siege is in flames, and a mine near it has just blown up. We are directing part of our fire at the Mirador battery, so as to silence the guns for to-morrow. The enemy fire but little, chiefly at the advanced battery on the other side of the river.

He might have added that the sea wall had been mined by the engineers. It would be fired the following day, bringing down 70 feet of wall. Continuing the letter in mid-afternoon, Frazer informed her that 'To-morrow the attack will be at 11 A.M. A lodgement only is to be made in the first instance.' An hour later, he added the information that Soult was on his way to relieve San Sebastian.[74] This would lead to the battle of San Marcial, fought as the second assault on the town took place, and where the troops of Freire and Mendizabel would hold the French at bay.

There can be little doubt that after the disaster of 25 July, the men of the 5th Division developed a strong sense of grievance. They were convinced that they had been victims of poor planning rather than any lack of determination on their own part. This view may well have percolated from the senior command, because Gomm was not alone in his resentment of the artillery and engineers. Oswald and Robinson had voiced similar criticism. On 22 August, Graham conveyed to Wellington the poor morale of the division. Wellington responded:

> I am very sorry to hear the indiscretion of the principal officers of the [5th Division]. It is impossible to stop people's mouths if they are so indiscreet as to deliver their opinions on such a subject as the practicality of storming a breach, where those opinions can be of no use, excepting to render success quite unattainable by the inferior officers and troops who hear such opinions. There are some very valuable officers, and some of the best regiments in the army, in the [5th Division]. And I shall be very sorry that the officers and troops of other [divisions] may storm the place. I must do so, however, and also make clear the cause for this necessity.[75]

Five days later he again wrote to Graham,

> It will be necessary to prepare immediately for the assault of the place, and I shall be obliged to you if you would let me know whether you still doubt the troops of the [5th Division], as, if you do, we must send over some others who, with the [redacted], will show the [5th Division] that they have not been called upon the perform what is impracticable.[76]

---

74 Sabine (ed.), *Letters*, pp.231–232.
75 Gurwood (ed.), *Dispatches*, vol.XI, p.33.
76 Gurwood (ed.), *Dispatches*, vol.XI, p.46.

Not surprisingly, Oswald and the brigadiers vehemently protested when they realised what was intended, since it would reflect both on them personally and on the troops they commanded. It was not the need for reinforcements that Oswald resented but the suggestion that his troops were cowards who could only follow those who had more backbone. Graham certainly agreed that a reserve was needed. Whatever he wrote to Wellington in response to the dispatch of the 27th, it provoked an order that:

> 300 men of the 4th and Light divisions should march to Oyarzun to-morrow morning; and I shall be obliged to you if you will order 400 of the 1st division to assemble at the same place. I should hope these, and some of Lord Aylmer's brigade would be enough to show the way to the breach, if it should be practicable to storm it.[77]

In response, 750 men from the 1st, 4th Division and Light Divisions (rather less than the number that actually volunteered) comprised the force that would teach the 5th Division how to assault a breach. Or would have done but for one fortuitous event, the arrival of Lieutenant General Leith on the 29th. When he was informed that his division was to take a secondary role, he was 'deeply offended and would not suffer [the volunteers] to lead the assault.'[78] Nor would they be chosen for the forlorn hope. That honour would be given to the Irish daredevil, Lieutenant Francis Maguire, whom Robinson had described in a letter of reassurance to the young man's mother as 'a fine fellow' whose conduct 'has already brought him very much within my notice and regards.'[79]

Graham agreed with Leith, who then set about acquainting himself with the situation. He also willingly accepted Oswald's offer to act as an aide-de-camp. As for the volunteers, they had the good sense to keep well apart from the men of the 5th Division and their simmering resentment.

Rey, meanwhile, had been continuing to strengthen his defences. His troops removed as much debris as possible from the breach, although while doing so they took casualties from the Allied mortars. The sheer drop was 30 feet deep in places and the only practicable exit was at each end of the breach, although even there traverses meant that further progress would be difficult, particularly as the assailants would come under fire from the Almezqueta tower at one end and Los Hornos at the other. Three concealed guns, two in the casements of the curtain wall and one behind the hornwork could enfilade but the mines would inflict even greater damage. The Allied engineers were, in fact, aware of these, particularly one positioned between the breach and what remained of Los Hornos, loaded with 12 hundredweight of powder. This would certainly be sufficient to take out the head of an advancing column. When it came to the actual assault, each defender would be armed with three muskets, as well as bombs and live shells.

Graham had decided that he should take position on the Chofre Heights, from where he would be able to direct the general pattern of the assault, while Leith would assume immediate command, giving him control over the disposition of the troops. He decided that Robinson's brigade should lead the assault in two columns, one of which would advance to

---

77 Gurwood (ed.), *Dispatches*, vol.XI, p.50.
78 Napier, *History of the War*, vol.VI, p.198.
79 Fogg, *Wellington's American General*, pp.195–196.

the old breach, and the other to the San Juan bastion, from which it might be possible to reach the high curtain and thus outflank and fire down on the French defenders in the hornwork. Spry's brigade and the 5th Caçadores from Bradford's brigade would follow Robinson's three battalions, while Hay's brigade and the volunteers would remain as supporting troops. Most significantly, bearing in mind the failure of the first assault, this attack was to take place in daylight, low tide being at midday.

Douglas described how, the previous evening,

> A number of non-commissioned officers of the brigade met at sunset under some apple trees, for the purpose of bidding goodbye. The liquor went round in full bumpers, to the health of distant friends. With a few good songs and jokes, we parted, with hearty wishes for each other's safety, but this was our last meeting, as nearly all were either killed or badly wounded.[80]

Lieutenant Maguire was equally fatalistic on the morning of the assault, which coincidentally was his 21st birthday. Having dressed with great care 'as if for some great occasion', he was asked why. He responded, 'When we are going to meet all our old friends, whom we have not seen for many years, it is natural to look as well as possible'. He was wearing a bicorne into which he had fastened a white plume, thus making himself conspicuous to the enemy, to the 30 volunteers from 4th which formed the forlorn hope and the further 65 volunteers from the 5th Division, 45 from the British battalions and 20 from the two Brunswick-Oels companies, comprising the storming party.

Frazer, from his position on the Chofre Heights, wrote to his wife at 8:00 a.m.

> The tide is fast receding. The enemy has fired musketry, but hitherto no cannon, this morning. The day will be a broiling one: the sun has just forced itself through the fog, and a gentle sea breeze assists in clearing the fog away. It seems arranged that 1200 men only are to attack: this is too few – it may fail. The stake is serious, and should not be left subject to the least accident or to any chance over which we might have control.

At 10:15 a.m., he continued,

> The assault is momentarily expected to take place… It is curious at such moments to watch the countenances, and endeavour to read the minds of men. Hope, solicitude, anxiety are to be seen; frequently, apathy and indifference, the effects of a continuance of scenes of danger; and now and then, though rarely, open fear. But most have the address to conceal this last acquaintance, of whom all are ashamed.[81]

Frazer then made notes in pencil of the sequence of events and timings, which have been used in the following account.

---

80   Monick (ed.), *Douglas's Tale*, p.82.
81   Sabine (ed.), *Letters*, pp.233–234.

The Allied guns opened up as soon as the fog had cleared sufficiently to make their targets visible, and continued firing until 10:55 a.m. Although they inflicted little further damage to the defences, they severed the saucisson (fuse) of a large mine under Los Hornos, which was positioned to destroy large numbers of the advancing Allied troops. Then, as Frazer wrote, 'It begins! They reach the top of the breach. A mine springs, but behind them! All seems well. They reach the top and halt; – if they are supported it will do.'[82]

The forlorn hope had already passed beyond the play of the mine, and now speeded along the strand amidst a shower of grape and shells, the leader, Lieutenant Maguire of the 4th Foot, conspicuous from his long white plume, his fine figure and his swiftness, bounded far ahead of his men in all the pride of youthful strength and courage.'[83] He reached the breach, but just as he waved the men forward, he was shot, leaving the rest of the forlorn hope and the head of the column, led by Lieutenant Francis le Blanc with the light ocmpany to rush past his body. Later, a fellow officer who found him among the dead and wounded commented that 'His face had the classic beauty of sculptured marble.'[84]

Almost immediately there was a deafening explosion as the French fired a mine under the sea wall opposite the hornwork. A sergeant and 12 men had been sent forward by the engineers to sever the saucisson, and fell victims to the mine. The advancing troops, however, had been warned to keep clear of the sea wall, so that there were no more than 30 further casualties.[85]

Frazer, watching as an intelligent spectator, was concerned that too many of the assailants were making for the old breach and not enough for the demi-bastion and high curtain. Even those that reached the breach were confronted by the sheer drop; and all the while they were under attack from French guns firing canister and from musketry. As a result, it looked as if the assault had stalled, although the bugles were sounding the advance. At the same time, the 300 volunteers from the 13th Portuguese Line and six companies from the 24th Line were advancing with great determination, despite being attacked with grape and suffering heavy casualties. The 13th Line headed for the lesser breach and, although initially repulsed, succeeded in establishing themselves there at the second attempt. They then had to deal with the traverse which initially prevented further progress. The 24th Line, meanwhile, joined Robinson's brigade at the Amezqueta Tower. There were sappers with them but it was impossible to create a lodgement because the stones and blocks of concrete making up the rubble were too large and heavy.

Then something happened that Frazer had not expected. Reinforcements were being brought up and would continue to be fed into the attack, thus sustaining the momentum of the assault. Later he commented in his notes: 'This duty is well performed whoever may direct it.'[86] The answer to that, of course, was Leith who, like Frazer, had realised that 1,200 men were not enough to take the place.

About midday Graham gave a surprising order to the artillery. All the guns on the Chofre Heights were to open fire over the heads of the stormers. This was sustained for 20 minutes,

---

82   Sabine (ed.), *Letters*, pp.234–235.
83   Napier, *History of the War*, vol.VI, p.199.
84   Fogg, *Wellington's American General*, p.203.
85   Jones, *Journals of Sieges*, vol.II, p.74, says 20 or 30.
86   Sabine (ed.), *Letters*, p.237.

taking out a large number of the defenders. At 12:40 p.m. Frazer observed that some Allied troops seemed to be descending from the breach into the town, and were also waving their hats from the terrepleine of the curtain

Despite some of the French still holding the curtain nearest the cavalier, by 1:00 p.m. it was clear to the watchers on the sandhills that troops were entering the town, most of them by way of the end of the old breach by the Amezqueta Tower. Some volunteers had gained access through a ruined house that abutted the tower, and others quickly followed, while some of the Portuguese had found their way in by using the old foundations of a wall built by Berwick. About the same time, as both Graham and Rey noted, bombs and musket cartridges on the traverse below the cavalier exploded, killing 60 of the French. This happened just as Leith was sending in the final reinforcements, from Hay's brigade. The Royal Scots were able to take possession of the traverses but were then halted by French resistance at the cavalier and forced back. They pushed forward again and soon overwhelmed the defenders. The Allies were also advancing along the rampart from the Amezqueta Tower to the lesser breach, where they quickly drove back the defenders. At this point, the Allies were flooding into the town.

Leith had chosen to take position on the beach beyond the sea wall, opposite the advanced trench. It was dangerously exposed to French fire, which became apparent when Lieutenant Colonel Fletcher was killed beside him, this being in Frazer's opinion, an irreparable loss. Not long afterwards Oswald was wounded. Another casualty was Robinson, who was severely wounded in the face as he accompanied his brigade to the breach.

Leith lasted two hours, during which time the pattern for judiciously sending in reinforcements had been established to keep the French under constant pressure. Then a shell splinter broke his arm and he had to be carried behind the lines. Douglas, with the Royal Scots, had just entered the trenches when 'we met our old General Leith, being carried up wounded, lying on a blanket... Some of the men cried out, "Oh" at this sight, and, "There's the old General"; others, "We'll have revenge for that." In a feeble voice he exclaimed, "I would not doubt you."'[87] The Royal Scots pressed forward under showers of grapeshot and Douglas received a shot in his right leg

> ...when within a few yards of the top of the breach. The scene before me was truly awful. Here you might observe a leg fastened between the ruins of the wall, legs and arms sticking up, some their clothes in flames; numbers not dead, but so jammed as not to be able to extricate themselves, and of course had to remain exposed to the fire of the enemy, which was so thick that you would think it impossible for any living thing to escape. Indeed, I never expected to reach my trench with my life, for not content with depriving me of my limb, the fire shot away my crutch [his firelock] also.[88]

Ensign Freer of the 38th, who had been an acting engineer throughout both sieges, and who had also brought up troops.

---

87 Monick (ed.), *Douglas's Tale*, p.82.
88 Monick (ed.), *Douglas's Tale*, p.82.

Remained on the breach full half an hour exposed to every species of Missile. Ordered to lie low, Artillery firing over our heads. Observing a window from the houses on the breach which had been lately stopped up with green or yellow mortar, drove it in – *first* entered the town and displayed my pocket handkerchief [elsewhere called 'the English flag']. Held a house for a time – rushed up the street; in so doing, severely wounded in the knee and fell, but the work was done.'[89]

He subsequently learnt that his friend and mess-mate, Captain Thomas Willshire, was mortally wounded in the assault.

At 1:20 p.m. Frazer recorded hearing heavy firing in the town, and 15 minutes later French prisoners were bring brought out. Then he heard the Allied bugles in the town sounding the advance. By 1:50 p.m. he was able to scribble: 'With judgement the town is securely ours, according to all appearances. Our men are pulling prisoners out of the breaches. The enemy retire. Many enter the Mirador [La Mota].'[90] The 9th were sent in to help them on their way.

Within San Sebastian the situation was chaotic. According to Hale, 'By some means or other, in this attack the town caught fire, in consequence of which a great part of it was burnt to ashes before it could be extinguished.'[91] Gomm wrote home on 5 September:

With the exception of ten or twelve fortunate buildings there is nothing left of San Sebastian but the walls of its houses, and these are falling every instant with a tremendous crash. How the fire was communicated in the first instance is uncertain, but I think there is little doubt of its having been intentionally done by the enemy. (The Spanish, however, claimed it was deliberate Allied arson.) …Never surely was there a more complete picture of devastation than this place presents. I do not know whether it is more distressing in its present quiet state than even when the fire was raging at its height, and every effort was making, not only by the people to save their property, but by all ranks and conditions to rescue some hundreds of wounded, French as well as English, from the flames, which were every instant gaining ground upon them, and many decrepid [sic] and venerable inhabitants, who were ill prepared, from their age and infirmities, to meet such a visitation.[92]

John Harley, paymaster of the 1/47th, ventured into the town on the evening of the 31st, passing through the breach

…which was filled with dead bodies, so that I could scarcely get over them. The scene that presented itself to me was horrifying – the dead lying in heaps in the streets – the French and British lying side by side; and not infrequently a drunken soldier of ours was seen amongst them fast asleep; plundering parties, too, women

---

89 Freer, *The Thirty-Eighth*, p.306.
90 Sabine (ed.), *Letters*, p.239.
91 Hale, *Journal*, p.117.
92 Carr-Gomm (ed.), *Letters and Journals*, vol.I, pp.319–320.

as well as men, were very active in every direction; breaking, not only into private houses, but into the churches and theatres.[93]

Oman connected the disorder in the town to the losses the 5th Division had suffered, which were indeed horrific. The worst affected was Robinson's brigade which lost 72 percent of its officers and 57 percent of the brigade overall amounting to 865 killed, wounded and missing. Hay's brigade, although late on the scene, took 33 percent casualties, 495, and Spry's 25 percent, 408. The two Black Brunswicker companies suffered 15 casualties. From this it might be deduced that an absence of officers would be a contributory factor in the disorder, as was the state of mind of men who had come through an experience that can only be described as hellish. Oman also makes the point that the ratio of killed to wounded was 664:1,047, which was exceptionally high. Despite Napier's claim that the volunteers lost a similar proportion to the 5th Division, Oman also makes clear that only the Guards brigades, with 122 casualties, came anywhere near the losses of the 5th Division, to which must be added all the losses taken earlier in the siege.[94] Among those whose wounds took them out of the war were Douglas and Hale, both of whom were eventually repatriated to Britain.

Bearing in mind his criticism of the troops after the failure of 25 July, Frazer now conceded that 'The breaches have proved more difficult (as I now believe) than I had apprehended, since in many places it was necessary to apply scaling ladders in the inside to get down from the breach into the town'.[95] On the 25th, of course, the ladder party had been dispersed before reaching the breach. This second assault benefitted, not so much from ladders, as from the constant flow of reinforcements, which kept the French under pressure. Leith was in command of the 5th Division for the last time, so it was fitting that 'The mural crown will be well established upon his head by this last exploit.'[96]

One of the most generous comments on the success at San Sebastián came from that fierce critic, Ensign Aitchison of the 3rd Foot Guards:

> Whatever may have been the discredit which the British Army suffered by the defeat at San Sebastian, it has been most fully recompensed by the success there today – in no instance since the commencement of the Peninsular War has it had more obstacles to encounter and in no instance – not even in the capture of Badajoz – have they been more gloriously overcome. The conduct of every man engaged was so truly admirable, that no words in our language can do them justice – it required to be seen to be conceived; and when history should give to future ages the simple narrative of the day's deeds – they will excite admiration rather than belief. Portuguese troops acted their part excellently, and they are well entitled to participate in all the praises that can be bestowed.[97]

93　Gareth Glover (ed.), *The Veteran or Forty Years' Service in the British Army: the Scurrilous Recollections of Paymaster John Harley 47*th *Foot – 1798-1838* (Solihull: Helion, 2018), p.212.
94　Oman, *The History of the Peninsualr War*, vol.VII, pp.529–530.
95　Sabine (ed.), *Letters*, p.241.
96　Carr-Gomm (ed.), *Letters and Journals*, vol.I, p.318.
97　Thompson (ed.), *An Ensign*, p.264.

Rey and the surviving members of the much-depleted garrison had withdrawn to the castle once it was clear that the town was lost. On 5 September, Gomm judged that 'The French still hold the castle, but they hold it like people that are anxious for an opportunity of surrendering with a good grace; and I fully expect that the opening of our batteries upon the castle wall, and preparations for a fresh assault; there is little *acharnement* left among them.'[98] His anticipation proved accurate.

> We opened a fire upon him [Rey] from sixty *bouches à feu* on the 8th, and in less than two hours after he proposed to capitulate. The day following, the garrison laid down their arms, and today they are embarking for England; their strength is about fifteen hundred, the remains of three thousand six hundred when we came before this place. We are not at all sorry to get rid of them so soon; they are a disgusting set of fellows.

San Sebastian had cost the 5th Division dear, but Gomm was certainly not alone in his view that 'Here, then, ends our siege, which we have all longed so heartily to bring to a conclusion, but in which, I believe, we need not regret our having been employed.'[99]

Soult's defeat at San Marcial had persuaded him to return to France, even though Pamplona was still holding out. Wellington did not choose to move his own troops forward in response. There had been some idea of crossing the Bidassoa immediately after the fall of San Sebastian, but a misdirected order concerning the pontoon train, his recognition that the Spanish troops would almost certainly plunder once on French territory, and some suggestion of Allied defeats in central Europe were sufficient to keep him in his present position. 'However, I shall put myself in a position to menace a serious attack, and to make one immediately, if I should see a fair opportunity, or if I hear that the Allies have been really successful, or when Pamplona should be in our possession' he wrote to Bathurst.[100]

Soult, meanwhile, had been taking up an extended defensive position. Guarding the estuary of the Bidassoa on the right of the French line was Reille's corps. Maucune was in command of the first line of defence. Five miles back was Boyer's division, formerly Lamartinière's, but that general had died of wounds received during action at Vera on the 31 August. Reille's force, without Foy's detached division, totalled only 10,000 men, which suggested that Soult expected his centre and left, under d'Erlon and Clausel, to be the focus of any Allied attack. He had placed a reserve force behind his centre, but also much closer to his left than his right. Without realising it, Soult had positioned his troops just as Wellington had hoped he would.

The 5th Division needed a period of recuperation, with the less seriously wounded returning to the colours in pleasing numbers, thanks to what Gomm considered a particularly healthy climate. Unfortunately, there was then an outbreak of typhus, once again due to the louse-ridden uniforms, although the 5th seem not to have suffered as severely as the 1st Division. And reinforcements were arriving for the 2/47th, seriously depleted by this stage of the year's campaigning, as well as men seconded from the 2/84th. The division remained

---

98 Carr-Gomm (ed.), *Letters and Journals*, vol.I, p.318.
99 Carr-Gomm (ed.), *Letters and Journals*, vol.I, pp321–322.
100 Gurwood (ed.), *Dispatches*, vol.XI, p.124.

Crossing of the Bidassoa, by William Heath. (Public Domain)

at San Sebastian until 25 September, when they were relieved by a Spanish garrison and marched about eight miles to Oyarzun, taking up a position in the second line.

One alteration that would affect them when they next went into action was a change of command of the Allied left. Graham was about to return to Britain, because of his persistent eye problem and possibly because he was also, as Robinson suggested, feeling his age. Sir John Hope, a veteran of the West Indies (1796), Egypt (1801) and the war in the Peninsula until Corunna, took command on 5 October, leading Gomm to observe: 'We are fortunate in being always under men who have particularly distinguished themselves.'[101]

Across the Bidassoa

By the beginning of October, when the pontoon train finally arrived, Wellington was ready to take the war to the southwest of France. He planned to make a surprise attack with his left column, covered by a more overt attack with his centre and a demonstration on his right that would disguise his actual objective. He had even made a point of being visible at Roncesvalles on 1 October to create the impression that the attack would come from

---

101 Carr-Gomm (ed.), *Letters and Journals*, vol.I, p.325.

that direction. On 5 October the 2nd and 6th Divisions at Roncesvalles and Maya were ordered to hold their position while the second line was to move west. The Light Division and Girón's and Longa's Spanish would threaten both the east and west fronts of La Grande Rhune, in readiness for action two days later.

The French, knowing the Bidassoa was fordable at Béhobia, downstream from the apparent Allied positions and near a wrecked bridge, had constructed a redoubt on their side of the river. Further downstream, although the river was 1,000 yards wide at the highest tides, at the lowest it became a narrow stream snaking its way through sandbanks. Only a few locals were familiar with the depth of the stream and Wellington intended to make use of this local knowledge. He learnt that there were three fords at Irun and three more nearer the sea at Fuenterabia, these last being virtually unknown. Because of Reille's shortage of troops to cover a long front, there were only a few picquets covering the last three miles to the sea, leaving Maucune's weak division dangerously exposed to a flank attack.

The next low tide was on 7 October and Hope received orders for that day by which the 5th Division would advance under cover of darkness, then conceal themselves in the ruins of Fuenterabia, one brigade in the ditch of the old enceinte and two behind another ditch, south of the walls. At 7:15 a.m. when the fords would be only three feet deep, they were to make a rapid advance across the sands towards Hendaye. They would be followed by the divisional guns and a squadron of the 12th Light Dragoons. Once across, they would then take possession of the Heights of Hendaye, before advancing along the higher ground to take Croix de Bouquet, which was a French rallying point. The 1st Division would be upstream at Irun, under cover of a low ridge, and would take their cue to advance from the movements of the 5th Division, using the other three fords. They would then storm the hill opposite with support from Brigadier John Wilson's Portuguese and two squadrons of the 12th Light Dragoons. Once the troops were safely across, the engineers were to use the pontoons for the guns. Further upstream *Teniente general* Manuel Freire, with the Army of Galicia, was to use six fords above the broken bridge, while Aylmer's brigade was to act as a reserve to the 1st Division and Bradford's, to the Spanish. They would cross if the situation allowed.

The 5th Division began their final forward movement in the early hours of the 7th, with Robinson's brigade on the left, supported by the light dragoons and the guns and hidden behind the ruined walls of Fuenterabia. On their right was the Portuguese brigade under the command of *Coronel* Luis do Rego Barreto in the absence of Spry, who was sick. On the right, Hay's brigade, commanded by Greville in place of Hay, who was once again in command of the division, was in the ditch with embankments in front, and a white convent building behind. Each brigade had a local guide, procured by Robinson. Once the tide had dropped sufficiently, all three brigades would advance in line.

A violent storm broke out about midnight on the night of 6–7 October, just as the troops were getting into position. Despite the noise and turmoil, the French subsequently claimed that their picquets had still heard the sound of continuous movement. If they had, Maucune's failure to respond must be judged irresponsible. As planned, although 10 minutes later than intended, at 7:25 a.m. the 5th Division were on the sands as the fords became passable. They then waded into the water, in the case of the second brigade led by their commanding officer. A rocket was fired from Fuenterabia, which was a signal to the guns that Wellington had ordered to San Marcial during the storm, to fire a further signal. This instructed the 1st Division to begin their crossing, followed in turn by Freire's Spanish.

The 5th Division, up to their waists in mud and water, had crossed the channel before the French opened fire. The left column made for a sand spit which jutted out from the heights while the centre and right columns headed for the ground in front of Hendaye. According to Robinson, 'With hearty cheering we greeted the French shore',[102] having been helped on their way by the regimental bands playing the National Anthem and the applause of crowds of Spanish at Fuentarabia. With only one picquet at Hendaye the enemy was soon overwhelmed and the division then moved towards Croix de Bouquet in three columns. Robinson's brigade kept close to the coast in case French reinforcements arrived from San Jean de Luz. They took a shore battery that lay in their path and then met a single French battalion, the 2/105e. 'We let them come very near and then, with the Gamarra War whoop rushed forward to the charge, which had the effect of proving that Frenchmen can run faster that the English when they have a mind to try.' The French formed up on the next high ground. When the light companies failed to dislodge them, Robinson then sent in the 4th. As ordered, 'they charged as soon as they could with effect, which was done in the usual gallant style of that regiment.'[103] The arrival of the guns finally caused the French to retreat in some haste. Robinson then received a message from Wellington to advance no further.

At the same time, Greville's brigade and de Rego Barreto's Portuguese marched south along the high ground above Hendaye. Here the French gave them

> …a warm reception, but were driven from Hill to Hill, beyond the village of Irun where the business ended for the day, which I humbly conceive would have been a most glorious one for England if the Cavalry and Artillery could have been up, but for the want of it we were unable to do more than drive them without taking prisoners.

Le Mesurier did not escape unscathed, however. Having joined up with the 1st Division at Croix de Bouquet, some of the 9th and some Germans continued the attack but eventually had to halt

> …as they were much too strong to think of cutting them off, when a Musket ball hit me in the Right shoulder, but so civilly and gently that it only cut the Skin without lodging. The thing that vexed me most was my Epaulet [sic] and Coat suffering; it cut two or three Bullion off and made a hole in the coat and shirt.[104]

As for the Portuguese, de Rego reported that they too had overcome the enemy's attempt to resist and all their movements 'were executed with great regularity and promptitude, until, achieving our goals we were ordered to halt.'[105]

Wellington was a witness to the conduct of all three brigades and generous with his praise. 'Well done, 5th Division. By heavens, they are gallant fellows. I never saw anything

---

102 Fogg, *Wellington's American General*, p.212.
103 Fogg, *Wellington's American General*, p.213.
104 Greenwood (ed.), *Through Spain with Wellington*, p.198.
105 Gaudêncio & Burnham, *Fighting Cocks*, p.173.

so bravely or so well performed.'¹⁰⁶ He came down from the high ground as the 9th were on the charge. The battalion gave him three cheers and then continued the attack.

On the French side, Reille had been trying to hold off the 1st Division and Wilson's Portuguese, seemingly unaware of the threat the 5th Division posed. He was waiting for Boyer, whose leadings troops only arrived as the two brigades of the 5th Division made their appearance. As a result, Boyer had to cover a retreat rather than take part in a counter-attack. He was helped on his way by the 9th, but when Reille decided to stand his ground at Urugne, the Allied troops were ordered not to attack. Wellington had achieved what he intended and since Freire had also crossed successfully he now held all the high ground north of this stretch of the Bidassoa. For the 5th Division the cost had been 136 British casualties, 122 of them from Hay's Brigade, who had run up against Boyer's troops, as well as an unknown number of Portuguese and Brunswickers. Overall, the Allied loses were 815, including the Spanish, against French losses of 1,676.¹⁰⁷

On 9 October Wellington wrote to Bathurst to report the success of the crossings of the lower Bidassoa.

> ...The operations of both bodies of troops succeeded at every point... I had particular satisfaction in observing the steadiness and gallantry of all the troops. The 9th British regiment were very strongly opposed, charged with bayonets more than once, and have suffered; but I am happy to add, that in other parts of these corps, our loss has not been severe.¹⁰⁸

He also reported the success of Alten and the Light Division and Longa's Spanish at Puerta de Vera, and Girón's attack on the French defences on La Grande Rhune with the army of reserve of Andalusia, although it took until the following day to eject and finally drive the French back to their camp at Sarre.

Soult had been outmanoeuvred, helped by some subterfuge on Wellington's part. Had Reille, in particular, but also Clausel been given more troops to hold a 12 mile front, the crossing of the Bidassoa would have been a greater challenge for the Allies. As it was, on the 7th Reille was attacked by 25,000 troops, with more than 5,000 in reserve, while Clausel was also heavily outnumbered. Nevertheless, the blame was placed on Reille and, to an even greater extent, Maucune, who certainly was found wanting. His dilatory response earned Soult's sharp criticism and, as a result, he was relieved of his command.

A pressing concern for Wellington, now part of his army was on French soil, was the future conduct of his troops. On 8 October he wrote to Hope:

> I have sad accounts of the plunder of the soldiers yesterday, and I propose again to call the attention of the officers to the subject. I saw yesterday many men coming in from Olague [sic], drunk and loaded with plunder; and it cannot be prevented unless the General and other officers exert themselves. If we were five times stronger

---

106 Fogg, *Wellington's American General*, p.213.
107 Oman, *The History of the Peninsular War*, vol.VII, pp.534–535.
108 Gurwood (ed.), *Dispatches*, vol.XI, p.176.

than we are, we could not venture to enter France, if we cannot prevent our soldiers from plundering.

Since Hope had with him many of the Cavalry Staff Corps, which might be described as the first British military police unit, Wellington instructed him to 'order them out, in order to bring all soldiers, of all nations, found straggling from their corps.'[109]

A month later Gomm placed the 5th Division as still at Camp des Sans Culottes. Wellington had been waiting for the surrender of Pamplona, more certain news from central Europe and better news from the east coast. Writing to Vice Admiral Sir William Sidney Smith on 12 October, he had pointed out that 'the enemy has still possession of all the strongholds in Valencia and Catalonia, with the exception of Tarragona. Furthermore, although the left of his army was firmly established on French soil, only the fall of Pamplona would set his right at liberty.'[110]

Six days later he wrote to Bathurst that he was

> ...very doubtful indeed about the advantage of moving any further forward here at present. I see that Buonaparte was still at Dresden on the 28th; and unless I could fight a general action with Soult, and gain a complete victory, which the nature of the country would scarcely admit of, I should do but little good to the allies; should hardly be able to winter in France; and, in retiring, should probably incur some loss and inconvenience.[111]

Nevertheless, on 25 October Hope was informed by Murray that he was to receive some additional artillery, while the 14th Light Dragoons and Bock's cavalry brigade would be brought nearer the front. In addition,

> The pontoon train at Irun should likewise be put in a state to move along with the troops under your command, in case circumstances should require it to be used for the passage of the Nivelle. I beg that you will ascertain when it can be prepared to move, and give any orders regarding its preparation that may be necessary.[112]

Two days later, Hill received an order from Murray to ensure that all the paraphernalia, such as tents and baggage, that might impede the operations of the army was out of the way and in a secure position.

On the same day, 'Arrangements preparatory to an intended forward movement of the Army' were also published. If implemented, these would have brought the 5th Division up the coast towards St Jean de Luz, although Hope and Freire, who was in support, were instructed not to turn their forward movements into a real attack unless the enemy abandoned his ground as a result of what was happening further right. Pamplona finally surrendered on 31 October, yet a week later the 5th Division, instead of advancing, was still at

---

109 Gurwood (ed.), *Dispatches*, vol.XI, pp.169–170.
110 Gurwood (ed.), *Dispatches*, vol.XI, p.188.
111 Gurwood (ed.), *Dispatches*, vol.XI, p.207.
112 Quoted in F.C. Beatson, *Wellington: the Bidassoa & Nivelle* (London: Tom Donovan, 1995), p.127.

the Camp des Sans Culottes. Gomm ascribed their failure to move to 'the extreme badness of the weather. A great deal of snow has fallen about Roncesvalles, and unless the season favours us more than it promises to do, I am afraid we shall find it difficult to establish our winter quarters upon the Adour.'[113]

Meanwhile, Soult was maintaining his policy of linear fortification. Although his first line had been overwhelmed, he had merely retired to his second line of strengthened defensive points which extended from St Jean de Luz to the Petite Rhune, and on to St Jean Pied-de-Port. There was also a third line and Soult was confident these lines would deter Wellington from attacking, while further back was Bayonne, where two entrenched camps were under construction.

The Battle of the Nivelle

Wellington now needed to decide on his next move. He could not maintain his current position during the winter and must either advance deeper into France or withdraw to Spain. The government wanted him to remain on the offensive, thus sending a pertinent message to the Sixth Coalition powers in central Europe that Britain intended to continue the war. He also knew how his troops would react to what would seem like a retreat; the last months of the previous year had made that clear. He decided, therefore, that it would be both politically expedient and the best means of maintaining morale to take the war to the French.

The speediest approach to Bayonne, which needed to be taken before making any advance deeper into France, required the overthrow of the French right, which guarded the Great Road. Bayonne, though, was the most strongly defended part of the French position. Furthermore, if Wellington were to concentrate his own forces on the left, the enemy would recognise the vulnerability of his right. He decided, therefore, to make his strongest attack on the French centre, the defences of which were easily visible to the Allied troops holding the higher ground at La Grande Rhune. They could see that Clausel's strongest positions were about Sarre and La Petite Rhune. Further left, d'Erlon was short of troops, although he could call on Foy's detached corps if necessary. Wellington intended that Hill would make a demonstration against d'Erlon, just as Hope would against Reille. The Allied forces were already appropriately disposed. In the centre Beresford commanded four British divisions, the 3rd, 4th, 7th and Light, as well as Bradford's Portuguese, and Girón's and Longa's Spanish. On the right, Hill had command of the 2nd and 6th divisions, Hamilton's Portuguese and Morillo's Spanish, while Hope on the left had the 1st and 5th divisions, Aylmer's brigade, Wilson's Portuguese and Freire's two Galician brigades.

One practical problem was the shrinking hours of daylight, so that any action would have to start early. Consequently, the first movements, across difficult terrain, would be made before sunrise, which necessitated a full moon, the next being due on 7 November. Hill, being furthest back at Roncesvalles, should have started his advance in the early hours of the 8th, but was thwarted by heavy rain. The early morning of the 10th, however, was bathed in moonlight. By sunrise the Allied troops were in position for the forthcoming action.

---

113 Carr-Gomm (ed.), *Letters and Journals*, vol.I, pp.325–326.

The Battle of the Nivelle.

Hope's corps had commenced their advance between 3 and 4:00 a.m. Once the troops had reached their allotted position and the sun had risen, Captain Robert Cairnes' RHA troop opened fire against the defences which the French had constructed around a ruined chapel at Socorry. Then the outposts moved forward, followed by the main body of troops. On the left, closest to the coast, were the 5th Division, with the second Guards brigade from the 1st Division to their right and Aylmer's brigade on the extreme right, close to the Bayonne road. To the south Major General Heinrich von Hinüber's German brigade, the First Guards Brigade and Wilson's Portuguese formed a right column. The corps also had the extra support of the 16th Light Dragoons. As the columns drew closer to the target, the 2nd Light Battalion KGL moved to the left of the redoubt in order to attack from the rear while the picquets of the Second Guards Brigade charged directly at the French position. The defenders were soon overwhelmed and withdrew to Bordagain. Meanwhile, the 85th, from Aylmer's brigade, was able to take Urrugne.

Once the French had abandoned Socorry, the 5th Division advanced along the Croix-des-Bouquets heights, carrying the defences that the French had constructed and driving the defenders back to Socoa, just south of St Jean de Luz. Private Adam Reed of the 2/47th recalled that

> ...We had several skirmishes in the course of the day but none of them heed [sic] long for we pushed upon them desperately. We kept advancing (finding no object to oppose us) till we came to a village called St Jean de Luz being the first seaport we had yet seen in France and there the enemy made a stand but were forced to retreat in about an hour towards Bayonne.[114]

Hope in obedience to orders had resisted the temptation to push on against Reille, but his advance made it impossible for the French right to come to the aid of the embattled troops in their centre, thus enabling the Light Division and Longa's and Girón's Spaniards to take possession of La Petite Rhune, while the 3rd, 4th and 7th Divisions were overwhelming a sequence of French defensive positions. It is no surprise, considering their role in the battle, that the 5th Division took only 38 of the 2,526 British and Portuguese casualties, while even the 1st Division took just 193.[115]

Once the French had been forced from their strongholds, Soult issued orders for a general withdrawal. Reille was to send Boyer's and Leval's divisions across the Nivelle along with their field artillery, then onto the high ground at Bidart, thus covering the direct road to Bayonne. Detachments would remain to spike the heavier guns and destroy ammunition. The bridge between Ciboure and St Jean de Luz was also to be destroyed. By 6:00 a.m. the following day, the bulk of Reille's troops had crossed the Nivelle, having abandoned the guns at Bordagain, Ciboure and Secoa. An advance by Hope also prevented them from completely destroying the St Jean de Luz bridges, although they were damaged. They finally reached the Bidart Heights three hours later. Similar movements were made by Clausel's and d'Erlon's corps, while Foy's detached division made for Cambo, on the Nive.

---

114 Glover (ed.), *The Napoleonic Archive Volume 1*, p.118.
115 Oman, *The History of the Peninsular War*, vol.VII, p.542.

Wellington had recognised that Soult would either have to retreat or stand and fight another battle and he predicted that Soult would choose the first option, which created an opportunity to isolate and cut off Reille's two divisions. Hope's advance was in response to an order to cross the Nivelle as early as possible on the 11th, as part of a general advance in battle order. He was then to pursue Reille, so that no bridges were destroyed, with possession of the high ground at Guethery his final objective.

Hope's advance was hindered by the damage to the Ciboure-St Jean de Luz bridge and a trestle bridge further upstream, meaning that time was wasted on the construction of pontoon bridges. At low tide several fords became passable but it was still past noon when Hope's two divisions finally crossed the river, and another two hours before they reached Guethery, where they bivouacked. This unavoidable delay meant that Wellington had also had to hold back his centre, so that darkness was falling as they finally moved into position.

Somewhat belatedly, Soult became aware of the Allies' forward movement and his own need to pull back deeper into France. A new line from Bidart to Ustaritz was feasible, but harder to defend in terms of terrain and fortifications than his previous positions. Furthermore, the morale of his troops did not invite a commander's confidence in them, and was likely to worsen once the news of Napoleon's defeat at Leipzig, which had just reached Soult, became common knowledge. He decided, therefore, to withdraw the main body of his troops to Bayonne, having already urged the governor, *Général de brigade* Pierre Thouvenot, to finish the entrenchments as quickly as possible and to post a small force on the Nive. Should Wellington advance, the French would be in position to attack on either side of the river.

Wellington, meanwhile, was concentrating on forming his own new line north of the Nivelle and parallel to the French outposts as of 11 November. Hope occupied ground from St Jean de Luz, which was also Wellington's headquarters, to Cibourne, Bidart (5th Division headquarters), Guethary and Ahetze. Beresford, with the centre, continued the line from Arrauntz, and Hill, to Suraide, with a flank-guard watching Foy at Cambo. These, in fact, were to be the Allies' winter quarters, although it took Soult (and some of the Allied troops) time to appreciate Wellington's intentions. Wellington also decided to send all the Spanish troops except Morillo's back to Spain. They were still not being supplied by the Spanish government, and starving troops were likely to prey on the local population. Wellington was determined to avoid this, even if it reduced the Allied force to 30,000 British, 23,000 Portuguese, and 4,500 Spanish, while Soult's total forces amounted to 54,500.

The army remained in these cantonments until 9 December. On 15 November there was a minor encounter between Foy and Hill at Cambo, which the former was abandoning, while eight days later the Light Division, in the process of throwing forward an advance line, came up against the French and took considerable losses. Meanwhile, the 5th Division was enjoying a period of rest, although in atrocious weather. This was one of the reasons that Wellington had chosen not to advance. The attitude of the local population was another. Some reports suggested that they were sick of the war and ready to turn against Napoleon, but Wellington was reluctant to trust such reports, particularly as most of them emanated from the Bourbon cause.

Battle of the Nive

On 8 December Wellington received the government's authorisation for a further advance into France, although he had actually been waiting for an improvement in the weather to restart his campaign, and had already planned how he would proceed. His present position, bounded as it was by the Pyrenees, the sea and two rivers, the Nive and the Adour, into which the Nive flowed at Bayonne, severely limited his options. He also knew that although Bayonne might represent the obvious target, it was too strongly fortified to be attacked. The old Vauban citadel was protected by flooded ground to the south and west, while redoubts and other armed points had been constructed beyond the inundation. This was in addition to the entrenched camps to the south and east, and gunboats on the Adour.

Any advance towards Bayonne by Hope's corps would take them over 'a chaos of hills separated by steep ravines and gullies.' The terrain was further divided 'into innumerable small enclosures by hedges and banks, and dotted all over in all directions by little coppices of oak',[116] while water courses flowed to east and to west. The watershed was the obvious route to follow. It carried the main road to that town, but was inevitably rendered narrow in places by the nature of the ground and even more so at Barrouillet by the encroachment of an estate known as the Mayor's House.

On 8 December Wellington issued his orders for the following day. Hill, on the right, was to cross the Nive at Cambo, then send Morillo upstream as a flank guard, while his other troops advanced towards Bayonne, using the main road to the left of his position. This would bring him to the flank and rear of any French troops that were watching the river. He would then take position from Villafranque to Petit Mouguerre. Beresford, in the centre, was to set a pontoon bridge at Ustaritz, ready to send his troops across on the 9th. Having cleared the ground of any French, he would advance to link up with Hill. The 7th and 4th Divisions, in reserve, would then move forward, concealing themselves around Arrauntz. Hope's troops and the Light Division were to advance across the wooded ground that lay between Biarritz and Bassussary, clearing it of French troops, then halt when they reached the entrenched camps at Bayonne.

Soult, for his part, was confident that Wellington would have to divide his troops to cross the Nive. The French could then pounce on one part or the other and inflict a signal defeat.

The action began early on 9 December. The first to cross the Nive was the 6th Division at Ustaritz, while Hill at Cambo was putting sufficient pressure on Foy to force him to withdraw. The waterlogged terrain, however, hindered any further advance in this area. This allowed d'Erlon to occupy the ground between Villafranque and Petit Mouguierre until an attack by the 6th Division in the middle of the afternoon forced the French out of Villafranque. Then the fog came down, making further action impossible.

On the left, where Hope's corps was once again making a feint, a five-hour march brought the 1st Division to the high ground at Barrouillet, while the 5th Division advanced past Bidart and then towards Anglet. At about 8:00 a.m., Hope turned the two divisions half-right and sent his skirmishers forward, only to discover that there were three French battalions at Anglet. A bayonet charge dislodged them but not before Robinson's brigade had

---

116 Fortescue, *British Army*, vol. IX, p.449.

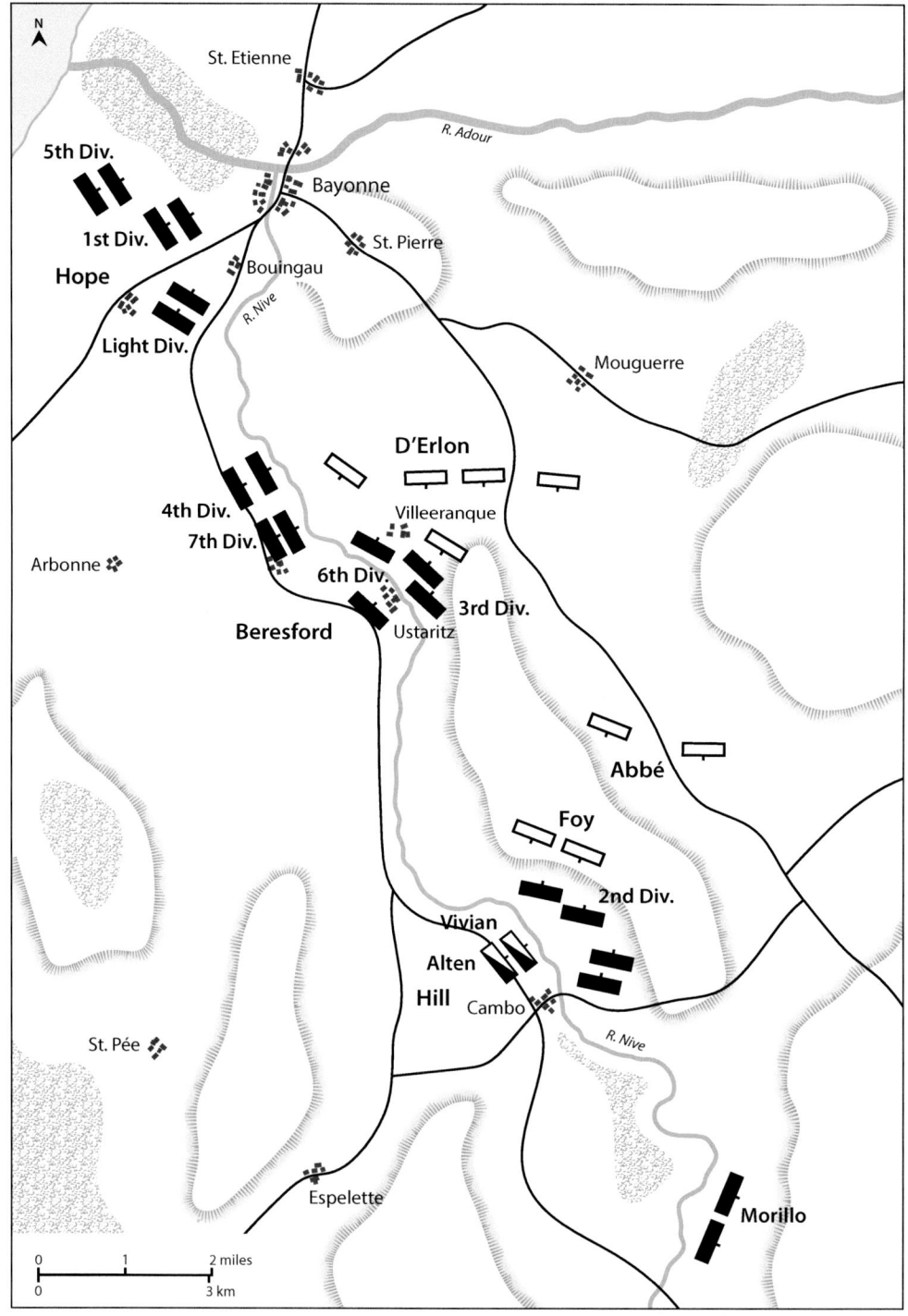

The Battle of the Nive, 9 December 1813.

taken heavy casualties. By early afternoon the 1st and the 5th Divisions were threatening the entrenched camp to the west of Bayonne. Meanwhile, the Light Division had been advancing from Bassussary to Plaisance. Meeting no opposition, they reached the entrenchments at Monréjau. The three divisions engaged in reconnaissance under cover of darkness to discover the strength of the entrenchments and to establish whether Wellington would be able to bridge the Adour near the sea. Hope then pulled his divisions back in accordance with Wellington's orders. His corps had suffered 292 casualties, the 5th Division taking 186 losses, 108 of them in Robinson's brigade.[117]

With Wellington's troops on either side of the Nive, Soult now decided to go on the offensive. At midnight d'Erlon, having first sent Foy to Reille, moved his four divisions, with sappers and artillery, from the entrenched camp that lay beyond Bayonne and the river to support two of Clausel's divisions, which were at Boudigau. D'Erlon's target was the Allied left, while Clausel focused on the centre. Soult also had nine divisions available to attack the Allied right on the right bank of the Nive.

Having withdrawn from the forward positions they established on 9 December, Hope's corps was posted with the 1st Division back at St Jean de Luz, and the 5th Division and Bradford's Portuguese holding a line from Bidart to Barrouillet, while the 8th Caçadores from Luis do Rego Barreto's (formerly Spry's) brigade held the advanced posts. Orders had been sent that the position should be entrenched but it seems that little more than a few abattis were constructed. On their right, the Light Division had withdrawn to Arcangues, with an order to move to Arbonne. Further right still, one brigade from the 7th Division was posted on the Nive at the Urdains bridge and another was behind Sainte Barbe, three miles away. The 4th Division was even further back. In other words, the 5th Division, Bradford's Portuguese and the Light Division were dangerously exposed. The situation was made even worse because communication between Hay, in command of the 5th Division, and Alten, of the Light Division, was hampered by difficult terrain. Furthermore, Hope was with the 1st Division at St Jean de Luz, while Wellington, Beresford and Hill were all on the right bank of the Nive. It may be assumed that Wellington did not anticipate a French attack.

Soult had originally intended a bayonet attack, but heavy rain during the night made movements difficult. Indeed, the Allies could have been forgiven for failing to recognise that the French commander was about to attack, with the French troops (visible to the Light Division) in no apparent hurry to take position. One of the brigades was about to march to Arbonne, but the order was rescinded when the French inaction began to cause suspicion.

At about 9:30 a.m. French skirmishers began an advance on the Light Division, which was soon under serious attack. Some took post at the church of Arangues and others at the nearby chateau, while the rest of the division strengthened their position. The French did not push their attack, however, so that by 1:00 p.m. it had become little more than a rather desultory cannonade. Further right the brigade of the 7th Division at Urdains also came under attack, but again without the French seeming inclined to force the issue. As a result, the Light Division took no more than 140 casualties, and the brigade of the 7th Division, none at all. Thus, a division and a brigade occupied four French divisions, one of which never came into action.

---

117 Oman, *The History of the Peninsular War*, vol.VII, p.545.

The Battle of the Nive, 10 December 1813.

At about 9:00 a.m. Reille sent Leval's division along the great road to Barrouillet while Boyer's marched on his left. He then waited until he could see Clausel at Boussassary and received confirmation that Foy was approaching. In fact, Leval's advance had been held up by the strong resistance of the 8th Caçadores, who were holding a defile. This enabled Hay to bring up Robinson's brigade, which took position at Barrouillet, using the walls of the Mayor's House and a coppice to its front, where the company of Brunswickers was posted, to establish a strong defensive position.

By midday, Boyer, with his division in column of battalions, had pushed forward towards Barrouillet, with Leval in reserve, while Foy was advancing from the east. Boyer's troops were particularly hampered by the broken ground, wooded in places, which caused the column to lose cohesion. The result was a somewhat confused encounter, small groups of French against small groups of Allies, until the French were eventually repulsed. Soult then ordered Reille to renew the attack, but by this time Hay had both Bradford's Portuguese and Aylmer's brigade in reserve, and could also call up Greville's brigade to reinforce Robinson. Nor did the French find it any easier to maintain cohesion, particularly as they advanced into the garden and orchard of the Mayor's House. They persisted, however, despite taking considerable losses, until they found themselves under a counter-attack on their rear ranks by the 9th on the right and de Rego's Portuguese on the left. The 3rd Portuguese Line was ordered 'to charge the enemy by the right of the main road, which was done by the whole regiment with great gallantry driving the enemy before them. The conduct of the regiment, of its commander and officers, was very brave and conspicuous.'[118] At the same time, the 15th of the line was protecting the artillery.

A large number of prisoners were taken, while the rest of the French retreated. It was now about 2:00 p.m., and the 1st Division could be seen coming up from St Jean de Luz. Soult, however, decided to make a third effort to dislodge the Allies. This time, one of Leval's divisions was brought forward, while Foy's was to turn the Allied position from the east. In the event, though, there was no attack. An urgent message from Clausel reported that large numbers of Allied troops were coming up and threatening his position at Urdains. These were the 3rd and 6th Divisions, while the 4th Division marched towards Arcangues and Arbonne, thus restoring communication with Hope. By nightfall, all Reille's units had been called back except Leval's division, which remained in front of Barouillet.

At Arcangues the Light Division had taken 224 casualties, while Hope's corps suffered 550 losses, over 500 from the 5th Division.[119] Among the officers killed was Lieutenant Peter Le Mesurier,

> …who received two shots in the breast, one through the heart. He died without a pang; it may be some consolation to know this.
>
> Cameron desires me to add that in him he has lost a most gallant officer, and a worthy young Man. He is deplored by the whole corps with whom he was deservedly a very great favourite. I had only been introduced to him three or four days

---

118 Gaudêncio & Burnham, *Fighting Cocks*, p.212.
119 Oman, *The History of the Peninsular War*, vol.VII, p.546.

before he was kill'd. Will you make this known to his friends in Cameron's name? He would have written himself but his time has been completely occupied on duty.[120]

French casualties were considerably fewer, but Soult suffered a further loss when three German battalions crossed to the Allied lines. Forced to disarm the remaining Germans, he deprived himself of 1,200 troops.

As the day's action unfolded, Wellington recognised the need for a bridge opposite Villafranque in order to protect Hill, should Soult cross the river. Although there were two bridges at Ustaritz, only one of them was usable for military purposes. Consequently, he then ordered Beresford to construct another bridge, which was finished by the evening of the following day. At this point Hill was his principal concern, particularly as he did not know how many French divisions had been moved to the left back and how many were free to attack the Allied right.

The morning of 11 December was densely foggy, particularly on the high ground around Barrouillet. Wellington, at St Jean de Luz, ordered Hope to clear the enemy outposts that occupied the heights towards Boussassury, only to discover that the French had already withdrawn. This allowed the Allied picquets to re-establish themselves on the ground they had occupied on the 10th. It also convinced Wellington that there would be no further attack on his left and he rode off to inspect the pontoon bridges at Ustaritz. At about the same time, the 9th Foot were sent towards Pucho to reconnoitre, only to be attacked when they ventured into the village. Fortunately, there were Portuguese troops to hand who covered the battalion's withdrawal.

For the rest of the 5th Division rations were being served out, and many of the troops were searching for fuel so that the food could be cooked, not aware that Reille had been ordered to force the forward Allied troops back to Barrouillet. Once again, Boyer advanced along the Great Road while Foy marched on his left. At about 2:00 p.m. French sappers were spotted cutting gaps in the hedges at Barrouillet in order to bring up the guns. Those gathering fuel made a hasty retreat as Boyer's troops rushed forward, their spirited attack giving them possession of the outbuildings attached to the Mayor's House and the wood in front of it after yet more confused fighting. Hope personally rallied his troops, managing to restore some sort of order, while flanking fire deterred the French from further advance.

Once order had been fully restored, the 5th Division, Bradford's Portuguese and part of Aylmer's battalion formed a first line while behind Barrouillet the Guards brigade of the 1st Division and the rest of Aylmer's brigade formed a second line. In this formation the troops were able to repulse the French attack and once again occupy the forward posts of the morning. A sustained cannonade was maintained for the rest of the day to prevent any further French encroachment. Although the 5th Division had eventually succeeded in holding their ground, it was at a heavy cost, another 323 casualties, while the Light Division took five at Arcangues.[121] It had definitely been a touch-and-go situation and Hope could be criticised for over-confidence. Nevertheless, he proved his mettle when the attack came. He was a large man and personally brave, thus setting an example to his troops. He was

---

120 Greenwood (ed.), *Through Spain with Wellington*, p.213. Note, written by Lieutenant George Brock to his brother, the Brocks being, like the Le Mesuriers, a Guernsey family.
121 Oman, *The History of the Peninsular War*, vol.VII, p.547.

severely wounded in the ankle, as well as taking shots to his hat and clothes, but refused to leave the field. Wellington later commented, having noticed how carefully he concealed his sharpshooters while ignoring any danger to himself, 'We shall lose him if he continues to expose himself as he did on the last three days.'[122] He felt unable to advise him to be more careful, however, since such behaviour was obviously a point of honour.

Another of the casualties was Major General Robinson, although it is not clear when during the three days of fighting he was wounded. Even Gomm, who had seemed to lead a charmed life, was slightly wounded when he 'was struck early on the 9th' but 'was not only able to keep my place during the whole of that day, but to return to it on the following days, which were much more trying ones…' He gave his sister an account of the three days' fighting, writing with some pride that 'During these last two days [when the fighting had been most severe] the 5th Division, alone with two Portuguese brigades, sustained every attack upon the great road.' The cost, however, had been severe and

> …to tell you the truth, I never have been exposed to so many risks as during the 10th and 11th. We fought with very little interruption on both of these days from sunrise until dark. I think the loss of the division amounts to nearly 1,400 men. We marched on the 9th with 3,700, so that we have lost considerably over a third of our force.[123]

For this reason, the 1st Division now replaced the 5th in the front line.

There had been no attack from either Clausel in the French centre or d'Erlon on the left of the line, but the presence of these two corps meant that the Allies had to hold their positions rather than manœuvre. The only movement on the French left was some reconnaissance carried out by *Général de division* Pierre Soult's cavalry, and even that was conducted with minimal commitment. Nor had the French seemed to register the construction of a bridge opposite Villafranque, which would allow Wellington to bring more troops to the right bank of the Nive.

As the 12th dawned, the Allied troops on the left were already expecting another attack, and the French right, for their part, seem to have been equally uneasy. When Major General Edward Pakenham, the adjutant general, arrived with his staff to inspect the outposts, Reille interpreted it as a threat. The French prepared to defend themselves, which caused the nearest Allied troops to react similarly. The result was a severe exchange of fire between the outposts. In response, Wellington moved the 7th Division to Arbonne as a precaution, which Soult decided was preparation for an attack on the 13th. By noon, though, both sides realised that there was no threat and the firing died down, although not before both sides had suffered about 200 casualties. On the Allied side they were mainly taken by the 1st Division, although there was also a cavalry action at Hasperran.

Wellington now had reason to be concerned about his right. During the night of the 12th the pontoon bridge at Villafranque was swept away, isolating Hill and Morillo on the right of the Nive. Although Wellington sent two divisions to undertake the much longer march

---

122 Gurwood (ed.), *Dispatches*, vol.XI, p.370.
123 Carr-Gomm (ed.), *Letters and Journals*, vol.I, pp.328–330.

to Ustaritz, it was Hill's corps that on the 13th defended a line from Petit Mouguerre to the Nive and, although heavily outnumbered, held off the attack launched by Clausel, with four French divisions. The approach of the 6th and 7th Divisions finally led to a French withdrawal.

The exact total of Allied losses during the five days of fighting is difficult to establish. Wellington put it at just over 5,000, while regimental returns suggest perhaps 500 fewer. The French seem to have lost just under 6,000. It is clear, however, that despite the 2nd Division's 904 casualties on the 13th at St Pierre, in what was a fierce and bloody fight, and 914 in total, the smallest division in the Allied army, the 5th, their ranks unfilled since San Sebastian, took proportionately the highest casualties, 1,292 British and Portuguese.[124] This explains the limited role they would play in the remaining months of the war.

The actions on the Nive brought the 1813 campaign to an end. Bad weather created impassable roads which, in turn, prevented any further manoeuvres. The Allied troops went into cantonments from the right bank of the Nive to the coast. The 5th Division remained on the left with the 1st Division, stationed between Biarritz and St Jean de Luz, where Wellington once again established his headquarters and where he intended to remain until Soult started to withdraw troops from the entrenched camps at Bayonne. For his part, Soult's main objective was to prevent the Allies from establishing themselves on the Adour, which would enable them to block supplies reaching Bayonne. He set up defensive posts on the right bank, but the Allied positions prevented him from doing the same on the left. As a result, this would be the situation at the beginning of 1814.

---

124 Extrapolated from Oman, *The History of the Peninsular War*, vol.VII, pp.545–548.

5

1814

After the actions on the Nive, Soult's main concern was protecting access to Bayonne. He was confident that downstream from the town both the strength of the fortress and the width of the Adour would prevent an Allied crossing. Reille remained at Bayonne with four divisions, but in order to strengthen the French defences upstream Foy was ordered to extend his position to Port de Lanne, to link up with Boyer and Darmagnac, while the French left wing, under Clausel, was south of the Adour, flanking the Allied right.

With his troops in cantonments, Wellington initially focused on little more than strengthening his front line. The unremitting wet weather made any other action impossible, although he already had his next move in mind. There was a more immediate problem, however. As had so often been the case during the war in Spain and Portugal, he was short of specie. Although the government found a considerable amount, it was still not enough for Wellington's purposes. He needed gold and silver coinage if he were to pay the local peasants. To complicate matters, they would accept only Spanish and Portuguese gold coins. The result was one of the more bizarre subterfuges of the war. A call was put out for coiners to volunteer their services (with the reward of extra pay) to melt down Iberian silver dollars and turn them into French five-franc pieces. More than 40 coiners were found and put to work. Unfortunately, their names were never revealed, so it is impossible to know whether any men from the 5th Division were among the number.

In the wider world, after his defeat at Leipzig in October, Napoleon had returned from central Europe with the remains of his army. He needed more troops, and the best of them were the veterans of Soult's and Suchet's armies. He decided, therefore, to take Spain out of the war by restoring the imprisoned Ferdinand VII. The plan was simple. As the price to be paid for gaining his crown, Ferdinand would sign a treaty which, among other conditions, would eject all British and Portuguese troops from Spanish soil. Having played for time, Ferdinand finally put his signature to the Treaty of Valençay on 10 December. Before it could be implemented, however, it needed to be presented to the Cortes for ratification. It was only on 10 January that Wellington became aware of the treaty, and he could think of only two reasons why the Cortes might not ratify it, one being the existing Anglo-Spanish treaty and the other, the cost of the financial arrangement for the dethroned Charles IV.[1] To

---

1   Gurwood (ed.), *Dispatches*, vol.XI, p.434.

his satisfaction, the Cortes refused to ratify Napoleon's treaty, and persisted in this decision for several months, their justification being that Ferdinand was still a prisoner in France.

The emperor had been so confident that the Treaty of Valençay would result in Spanish neutrality that he had already instructed Soult to send some of his troops north. The *Maréchal* responded by detaching half his cavalry but it was not until 21 January that he reluctantly sent two of his best divisions, Boyer's and Leval's, comprising some 10,000 men, to join the Napoleon. Coupled with the inevitable wastage of war, his force was now reduced to about 60,000 troops, instead of the 87,000 he had initially possessed. His call for volunteers produced only a minimal response and what conscripts he had were not only unsatisfactory as soldiers but also had a tendency to disappear. Against this, Wellington had 67,000 men, and the Spaniards were still just over the border.

Despite some limited encounters, none of which involved the 5th Division, it was not until mid-February that Wellington resumed his campaign, giving Soult time to alter his dispositions to cover the departure of Boyer's and Leval's divisions. The result was an eastwards movement which actually worked to Wellington's advantage, since he was planning to cross the Adour near the mouth of the river and then invest Bayonne. Firstly, though, he intended to force the French so far east that relieving the garrison of Bayonne would be impossible. All his divisions except the 1st and the 5th were involved in this preliminary operation. Hope's command still comprised these two divisions, along with Aylmer's independent British brigade, Bradford's and Campbell's independent Portuguese, and Vandeleur's cavalry. These 18,000 troops would be the ones to cross the Adour and invest Bayonne. They would be thinly stretched, however, so Wellington called up de España's and Freire's troops, which added 16,000 Spanish to Hope's command.

All this while, the 5th Division were lying south of the Adour near the estuary in conditions that prompted Thomas Woodward to write to his brother:

> I suppose more dreadful weather was never knowen on this Coast than has been this Winter we have had for the last ten days most wretched weather Snow & Rain & blowing as if it would level very House and Tree to the Ground … our regiment is Quartered in the new front of our collum. I am quartered in a very prity Cottage with four Brother Officers not a quarter of a Mile from the French Pickets & we fully expect to be surprised & taken in our Beds one of these Cold mornings as the coldness of the weather induces us sometimes to indulge ourselves an hour longer than we ought our Regiment is under Arms an hour before Day light every morning to prevent surprise if possible so don't be surprised if I write to you from Verdune some fine morning.[2]

Verdun, of course, was where captured British officers were held.

The result of the main Allied army's sustained pressure on Soult was a victory at Orthez on 27 February. Shortly before this, though, Hope's corps had been carrying out the other part of Wellington's plan. When Wellington rode to St Jean de Luz on the 19th, he had hoped to find everything in place for the crossing, thanks to the co-operation of Rear

---

2   Woodward, letter to his brother, 31 January 1814, private collection.

Admiral Charles Penrose. His orders had been carried out up to a point. More than 50 small craft had been assembled in the local harbours, along with the cables and extra wood that would be needed to construct a bridge across an estuary a quarter of a mile wide. A crossing point had already been decided upon; artificers were ready to do the work; and guns had been concealed amongst the conifers that overlooked the mouth of the river. The weather, however, had been as obstreperous as ever, which meant the small boats could not be brought from their present shelter. Thus, it was possible to plan with Hope what should be done, but impossible to implement the decisions made.

By 21 February Wellington felt he could no longer remain away from the main army and rode off to re-join Hill, leaving Hope to superintend the crossing as soon as the weather allowed. His corps was presently distributed from the front of Bayonne, where the 5th Division had replaced the 6th, almost to Anglet, where the 1st Division was posted, closest to the crossing point since they would be the first to cross. Linking the two divisions were Aylmer's, Campbell's and de España's brigades, while Bradford's Portuguese were behind the 1st Division, along with the pontoon train.

The immediate problem was how to bring the small craft, the *chasse-marées*, needed for the crossing over the bar at the mouth of the Adour, as well as the gunboats which would ward off any attack by French armed vessels. It was also vital to secure a landing point on the north bank, and that meant ferrying men across. In this respect the Allies were fortunate because the governor of Bayonne, *Général de division* Pierre Thouvenot, like Soult, had convinced himself that any river crossing would be attempted above Bayonne, where the Adour was narrower, rather than near the tidal estuary. Consequently, he had pulled back the guns which were posted close to the estuary. For his part, Hope sent Aylmer's, Campbell's and de España's brigades further forward, as if to prepare for an attack on French outposts.

The plan was to lay the bridge on 23 February. On the previous day, Rear Admiral Penrose organised the removal of the local craft from the harbours but was thwarted when the wind changed and the boats were blown out to sea. Hope also brought the 1st Division, the guns and the pontoons to the river mouth under cover of darkness and the dense forest of Bayonne. At daybreak, the French picquets were attacked and retreated to the entrenched camp. As Hope brought one of the Guards brigades closer to the mouth of the river it was attacked by French gunboats, which were then forced to move upriver when they came under rocket fire, an armament the enemy had not experienced before. There was no sign of the small craft, however, while conditions made crossing the bar impossible. Nevertheless, Hope was determined to establish a lodgement. He initially tried to get the troops across using rafts, but the turbulence made that an impracticable solution. He had five small boats attached to the pontoon train at his disposal, though, and used them to ferry six to eight men at a time to the north bank. Eight companies finally crossed the river by this means and established a defensible position, while at the same time Aylmer, Campbell and de España launched a demonstration that convinced Thouvenot his defences were about to be attacked.

On 24 February, despite swamped boats and lost sailors, two naval boats managed to cross the bar. Although the wind freshened, Penrose continued to send in boats, which occasioned yet more drownings, but by the end of the day the 1st Division was across the Adour, to be followed the next day by Campbell's and Bradford's troops. On the 26th, de España's brigade reached the north bank and then advanced on the citadel, while the 5th Division and Friere's Spaniards, who had now come up, demonstrated against the entrenched camp to the west of Bayonne. The bridge was completed by the afternoon, which meant that Vandeleur's brigade and two troops of the Royal Horse Artillery were able to cross on the 27th. Hope then advanced in three columns, with the 1st Division on the left towards St Etienne, which was quickly taken, and de España towards Mousseroles, the 5th Division having moved to a position between the Nive and Anglet.

Once Hope's corps had invested Bayonne, there followed a period of inaction. On 3 March Gomm wrote home from Arcangues:

> Lord Wellington has been making considerable progress with the right and the centre of the army, and has gained some brilliant advantage over Soult. You will, I have no doubt, receive accounts of many sanguinary conflicts that have never taken place, before the authentic reports reach you; but I must warn you that on these occasions not to consider us as being implicated, for they seem disposed to give us a very easy time of it during the siege, and I am not sorry for it. So much has fallen to our share lately that another siege at this moment would almost exterminate our little division.[3]

Although Gomm was making an assumption in his reference to a siege, because Bayonne was actually under blockade, Wellington did indeed give orders on 6 March for the siege guns to be brought up from Passages. He also sent Hope a memorandum: 'Plan for collecting the Stores for the Siege of Bayonne'. Hope believed that Bayonne could be taken by blockade, based on the supposition that supplies were limited, so that the garrison could soon be starved into surrender. Food was indeed limited, but nowhere near starvation level, and as Wellington somewhat caustically wrote to Hope on the 18th:

> The inhabitants may be distressed, but that the French officers will not mind; and, at all events, our blockade is not sufficiently close to keep them in if they wish to come out.
>
> I have reason to believe they have provisions for the troops for six months. Under these circumstances, I would recommend that you should attack the citadel at all events. Success will make the subsequent blockade more easy, and we may be able to keep it by Spanish troops.[4]

Furthermore, Thouvenot was a devoted supporter of the emperor and was not likely to surrender unless he found himself in desperate straits. Nevertheless, there was a steady stream of deserters from the garrison which suggested that not all his troops shared the governor's loyalty.

Gomm might have mentioned other changes affecting the 5th Division in his letters home. In December a new commander was appointed to the division, although it was some time before Major General Charles Colville was able to join it, needing to spend several weeks in St Jean de Luz recovering from a severe attack of rheumatism which, in a letter to

---

3 Carr-Gomm (ed.), *Letters and Journals*, vol.I, pp.334–335.
4 Gurwood (ed.), *Dispatches*, vol.XI, p.591.

a relative, he blamed on 'the constant wettings I had to endure so frequently in course of the season, cause enough to account for it, but my former experience of the disease has not made me bear this with better spirit...' He was not alone in suffering the painful effects of rheumatism, as a survey of discharge papers proves.

In the same letter he explained that he was now 'as a permanent command, appointed to the 5th Division in the room of Sir James Leith who goes to the West Indies. They are reduced at present as low as 3,600 firelocks having been very much under fire this campaign, but they have the debris of some good regiments who are likely to recruit well from the Militia...' He took up active command early in February, finally being able to 'pay my compliments to my new Divn.'[5]

Leith, now recovered from his San Sebastian wound, had been offered the position of Commander of the Forces in the West Indies at the beginning of December and on the 7th had written to Wellington to inform him of this change in his circumstances. In response, Wellington wrote:

> I can assure you that nothing can at any time give me more satisfaction than that to find that the Government attend to the claims and interests of the officers of this army; and I am quite delighted that they have given you the appointment which you mention. Nobody could expect you to decline to accept it in order to return to your division with this army; and if I could have advised you before you accepted the offer, my advice would have been by all means to accept; and I now most sincerely congratulate you.[6]

On 3 March Colville wrote that he was not pleased by what he described as the '*désagrément*', or inconvenience

> ...of being with the 5th Division, forming part of the left column devoted to the investment and probably a place in the siege of Bayonne, instead of the more animated service of the field. For a week I occupied the ground between the Nive and Adour and now being relieved by Don Carlos D'Espana's Spanish Division (not a desirable exchange for the unfortunate inhabitants) do occupy that, with the addition of Lord Aylmer's weak Brigade, from the Nive to the sea, a long line for so small a force, (not above 4,000 duty men), were the strength or energies of the enemy calculated for vigorous sorties.
>
> After nine days of fine weather which our noble chief knew so well how to take advantage of, we must not grumble for some time at the reverse, but for the last three days it has been as bad as bad can be, with snow, hail, rain, wind, thunder and lightning. It is severely felt by the troops on duty and the state of the clay soil is much against the operations of a siege.[7]

---

5   John Colville, *The Portrait of a General: A Chronicle of the Napoleonic Wars* (Wilton: Michael Russell, 1980), pp.157, 165.
6   Gurwood (ed.), *Dispatches*, vol.XI, p.383.
7   Colville, *The Portrait of a General*, pp.167–168.

While the right and centre of the army continued their harassment of Soult to the gates of Toulouse, the left waited for the arrival of the siege train, and while they waited the officers on both sides observed a virtual armistice. Hope saw no reason to intervene. He even informed Wellington that he did not intend to start siege operations until 27 March. Thouvenot, for his part, justified his inaction by ascribing it to the adverse weather conditions and the need to further strengthen his defences. He did plan a sortie for 4 April but was thwarted by the weather. Soon afterwards Hope learnt of the abdication of Napoleon from messengers who were on their way to carry the news to Soult in Toulouse. Allied officers inevitably shared the news with their French counterparts, who, it must be assumed, carried it to the governor. Hope, however, decided to wait for a specific order from Wellington before officially informing Thouvenot.

The Battle of Toulouse, fought on 10 April, was an unsatisfactory action from the Allied point of view, but it served to persuade Soult to abandon the city the following evening and then take himself to Paris to establish the truth of the message he had received, that a provisional government was now in power. This might well have been the final Allied bloodshed of the war, except that Thouvenot had not abandoned his plan for a sortie. He decided upon an attack in the early hours of the 14th, in order to drive the Allied troops away from the important junction of the Bordeaux and Toulouse roads, which Bayonne guarded. Nearly 6,000 men were to attack in three columns, with the village of St Etienne, the most forward of the Allied positions, the objective of the right column, and the road junction, of the left. The centre column would follow up once the other two columns were closing in on their targets, its purpose being to clear and hold the junction.

The Allies were positioned with Bradford's brigade on the left at Hayet, then the 1st Division, with the King's German Legion brigade on its left and the two Guards brigades in its centre and right, extending to St Etienne. Hay's brigade of the 5th Division had been brought across from the south bank to Bocau to act as a reserve, although the picquets from this brigade were at St Etienne. Hay himself was general officer of the day. A deserter had warned the Allied command of Thouvenot's intentions, with the result that the 1st Division was under arms by 3:00 a.m. The French attack, however, was initially successful, partly because of a feint towards Anglet but mainly because of its sheer momentum which carried the assailants beyond the Allied picquets and into a position from which they could attack St Etienne. This first onrush led to Hay's death, killed as he rallied the troops at the church in St Etienne. Hope, riding to investigate, was wounded and then trapped under his horse when it was killed by French fire. He was taken prisoner along with his two aides-de-camps, who were trying to free him. The picquets were either killed or taken prisoner.

A state of Allied confusion was the inevitable corollary of the attack, helped by the darkness of the night and the gunfire from the citadel. As a result, the only initial Allied resistance was offered by a party of the 38th, under Captain Matthew Forster, who were holding a house in St Etienne and another party in the walled Jewish cemetery to the right of the junction.

Only when Major General von Hinüber brought his KGL brigade to St Etienne, with Bradford's Portuguese in support, were the French finally driven out. Major General Kenneth Howard then ordered the two Guards brigades to attack the French troops holding the junction from the east and the west. The French soon buckled under the pressure and had no choice but to effect a rapid withdrawal to the citadel under the fire of the Allied guns. By 7:00 a.m. all firing had ceased.

The following day, Woodward wrote a personal view of events.

> They made a most desperate sortie yesterday morning from the Citadel about two hours before day light and drove in our advanced Pickets, & as they advanced they had men on purpose with combustible stuff to set every house they got near on fire they burnt to the ground about thirty beautiful Houses we had about three hours most desperate hard fighting – I am sorry to inform you they wounded & took Prisoner our Brave Commander Lieut Genl Sir John Hope & three of his staff Sir Johns horse was killed under him & fell with his leg under the Horse so as he could not extricate himself & the French dragged him about in a most cruel manner & its just this instant reported that he died last night [news that proved false] the General of our First Brigade died just as he was given the Field Officer of the Pickets his orders to defend his post to the last moment several Generals wounded twenty one Officers and Seven Hundred Rank & file killed wounded or taken Prisoner Lt Marshall of our Regiment was taken Prisoner he being on Picket they surrounded him before they fired a Shot & we hear he is wounded but I hope not I must consider myself very fortunate as I was on Picket the night before…[8]

The Allied losses were heavy, heaviest in the 1st Division, who took 706 casualties, killed wounded or missing. The 5th Division, although only peripherally involved, suffered 97 losses, and the Portuguese, 29. Four gunners and engineers were also wounded.[9] Among the wounded was George Freer of the 38th. 'Before Bayonne; had scarcely recovered from my former wound, again wounded, ball passing through my left thigh, slightly splintering the bone in its passage… Suffered much from this wound, lay on my back for nine months when I was able to be brought to England. "Oh! War, War, when wilt though be commanded to cease?"'[10]

As for the French, what was a pointless gesture in terms of the wider situation, cost them about 900 casualties. Not surprisingly, Thouvenot has been castigated for this loss of life. It can be argued in his defence that he had received no official confirmation of Napoleon's abdication and, as the French were themselves much given to subterfuge in their conduct of affairs, he may well have identified the unofficial news as a deceptive device to bring about his surrender. On the other hand, though, he showed no regret for the loss of life in an escapade that had achieved nothing, and may simply have been determined upon a final gesture in pursuit of *la gloire,* or, as Clerc termed it: 'The sortie of April 14th was an affair of *amour propre* [self-esteem].'[11]

Gomm's account suggests that Thouvenot excused himself with a reference to proper form. On the 17th he communicated the good news that the governor of Bayonne had proposed

---

8 Woodward, letter to his brother, 15 April 1814, private collection.
9 Oman, *The History of the Peninsular Wars*, vol.VII, pp.561–562.
10 Freer, *The Thirty-Eighth*, p.307.
11 Charles Clerc, *Campagne de Maréchal Soult dans les Pyrénées Occidentales en 1813–1814* (Paris: Libraire Militaire de L. Baudois, 1894), p.458.

>...a suspension of hostilities until a further confirmation of all the great events that have recently taken place in Paris shall have reached him; and address to him from the Provisional Government is hourly expected. He adds that it is to be regretted that we did not communicate to him earlier the information that had reached us officially several days ago, as it would have prevented the sortie made from the town on the morning of the 14th.
>
> Would to God it had been communicated in spite of form, although a most proper form; for there are cases, extraordinary ones, which justify and dictate the breach of order, and this was one. We should not have then had to lament Sir John Hope wounded and made prisoner, poor Herries wounded by his side, and also a prisoner, General Hay killed – the man who had so often commanded us on fortunate occasions, and for whom I had so high a respect and regard, whose wife and three daughters had just completed a journey overland from Lisbon, and had arrived at this place only three days before. Upwards of 600 men and an unusual proportion of officers of distinction killed, wounded and prisoners.[12]

The previous day, Wellington had written to Hope to inform him of events at Toulouse and in Paris, with an instruction to send Thouvenot an official communication to the same effect. He then received a letter from Colville, who had taken command when Hope was wounded, with news of the French sortie and a report of what happened. He also mentioned Hay's death. 'I have much lament to have to mention the death of Major General Hay, General Officer of the night. His last words were (a minute before he was shot) an order to hold the church of St Etienne, and a fortified house adjoining it, to the last extremity.'[13] This, of course was the order that Captain Forster obeyed. He also informed Wellington that he would receive a further report from Major General Howard, since he himself had been with the 5th Division throughout.

In response, Wellington instructed him to maintain his

> ...fortified posts in the neighbourhood of the garrison, giving at the same time free ingress to the provisions which it will be settled shall enter, and egress to whatever it may be wished to send out; and you will canton or encamp the troops in such situations as may be most convenient to you till I shall send further orders.[14]

He also send him a copy of the 'Convention of Toulouse', which he was to pass on to the governor, in order to expedite his surrender. This did not happen until 27 April when Thouvenot received specific orders from Soult.

Four days later Gomm felt able to write:

> So these big wars are finally drawing towards their close. I do not know whether everyone has been affected in the same manner with myself by late events, but I declare that from the moment I heard of the detailed turn affairs had taken in Paris,

---

12 Carr-Gomm (ed.), *Letters and Journals*, vol.I, pp.335–336.
13 Gurwood (ed.), *Dispatches*, vol.XI, p.661.
14 Gurwood (ed.), *Dispatches*, vol.XI, p.658.

> I felt as if some great piece of good fortune had befallen me, something that was to brighten the prospect of all my future life.[15]

There followed the protracted task of dismantling the military machine that had so successfully created Napoleon's Spanish ulcer before taking the war over the border and onto the sacred soil of France. The Portuguese returned to their own country, having proved that England's oldest ally was a steadfast friend. The British needed transports to return to theirs and Gomm was probably not alone in becoming increasingly impatient. On 12 June he wrote from Biarritz: 'The army is embarking; we expect our turn will come about July 1. We are then to start from Passages. We are passing a stupid time of it *en attendant* [in the meantime].'[16] Eleven days later, there was still the same sense of frustration.

> I suppose the troops here will be embarking in about a fortnight; there is but little chance, I am afraid, of their point of embarkation being changed to Bordeaux, and as my crusty chieftain [Colville] is determined to keep me at his elbow till they do embark, I shall probably go up to Bordeaux after seeing then off at Passages, and likely be in England before them; for the voyage from Passages is generally long.[17]

Colville, who became 'a very kind and good man' and 'began at last to think we were leading a very sluggish life,' finally gave Gomm leave to do as he pleased, which turned out to be a journey to Bordeaux, followed by a visit to Paris. As for the troops, when they finally sailed, some from Passages and some from Bordeaux, their destinations were as varied as the dates on which they finally left France. While the 1/4th and 1/9th sailed to North America, where the War of 1812 was still being waged, the 1/38th and 2/59th were sent to Ireland, the 2/47th to Liverpool and the 3/1st, the last to leave France, finally sailed to Cork in September.

The returning heroes, as they undoubtedly thought of themselves, did not always get the welcome they had good reason to expect. As Reed of the 2/47th describes it:

> We arrived safely in Portsmouth on the 18th [August] and landed the same day. We unfurled our colours and the drums and fifes played as we marched through the town and thus we landed in happy England the harbour of all peace and safety.
>
> While we were marching through the town same of the inhabitants said 'Look at those dirty colours full of holes and all rags more like dishcloths than colours'. The officers who were carrying them said 'Yes and, if you had been where they have, you perhaps might have been full of holes and all rags, but we count these colours, or dishcloths as you call them, an honour to our regiment.'

It was a different story, though, when they reached Sandhurst, where Sir Alexander Hope, their colonel, was governor. When they unfurled their colours in his presence, 'he pulled off his hat and said, "Well done my brave lads. I have heard of your fame in the Peninsula

---

15   Carr-Gomm (ed.), *Letters and Journals*, vol.I, p.337.
16   Carr-Gomm (ed.), *Letters and Journals*, vol.I, p.342.
17   Carr-Gomm (ed.), *Letters and Journals*, vol.I, p.342.

although I had not the honour to be with you. But now I witness it with my own eyes by your colours what you have been through.'"[18]

This might have been the end of the Peninsular War but it was certainly not the end of the war against Napoleon, while across the Atlantic the War of 1812 was still raging. Three of the battalions that served with the 5th Division were subsequently posted to North America, The 1/4th fought at Bladensburg, where Thomas Woodward was amongst those killed, and then at New Orleans, while the 1/9th and the 2/38th were sent to Canada to hold off American encroachment across the border. Two of the battalions served in the Netherlands under Graham in 1814, the 2/30th by way of Jersey and the 2/44th from home service. These two battalions were still in Belgium when Napoleon returned to France, so it is no surprise that they formed part of Wellington's 'infamous' army, along with the 3/1st who had been on home service since their return from the Peninsula. The 2/59th had been in Ireland but were also sent to Belgium in response to the threat Napoleon posed. They saw no action at Waterloo, however, being out at Halle on the right as part of a covering force. As for the 2/47th, they were the first to suffer the fate of all the junior battalions, being disbanded in 1814, more or less upon their return to Britain. The last to go was the 3/1st in 1818.

---

18 Glover (ed.), *The Napoleonic Archive Volume 1*, p.125.

6

Inside the Division

The evolution of the 5th Division has already been discussed in the context of the campaign that embraced Bussaco and the retreat to the Lines of Torres Vedras. Leith Hay was present from the beginning.

> At this period the author of these pages quitted the Spanish army [with which he had been liaising], returned to General Hill's head-quarters, and from thence proceeded to Lisbon, where he again became aide-de-camp to General Leith, recently arrived from England to join the army… On the 14th July, General Leith assumed command of ten thousand infantry and cavalry at Thomar. The corps, destined in the first instance to observe the lines of the river Zezere, was in reserve to that of General Hill.[1]

Leith's command, with its preponderance of Portuguese troops, was officially acknowledged as the 5th Division on 8 August. The British brigade, later the first brigade, would retain the same regiments (if not the same battalions) until the end of the war. The Portuguese, under Brigadier General William Spry, comprised the two Portuguese line regiments that again would remain with it until 1814. Attached to the brigade was the Thomar militia, while the Loyal Lusitanian Legion was attached to the division.

On 30 September the division was joined by the recently arrived Major General Andrew Hay, who took command of the British brigade, a command he retained throughout, except for an extended period of leave in 1812 and two brief periods of acting divisional command. Similarly, Spry would have command of the Portuguese until ill health forced him to surrender it in 1813.

Having brought his army safely back to the Lines of Torres Vedras, Wellington (as he now was) could indulge in some reorganisation. A further division, the 6th, was officially established early in October, to be followed by a 7th Division in November. There were also sufficient troops for the 5th Division to acquire a second British brigade. 'The corps hitherto commanded by General Leith, formed principally of Portuguese, was broken up, and the 5th division, composed of the brigades of Generals Hay and Dunlop, with the Portuguese troops of General Spry, placed under his orders. The British regiments of this division were,

---

1   Leith Hay, *A Narrative*, vol.I, pp.211–212, 219.

the Royal, 4th, 9th, 30th, 38th, and 44th.' The three new battalions were acclimatised, the 1/4th having been at Ceuta and the 2/30th at Gibraltar and Cadiz, and the 2/44th, Cadiz. 'The 3d and 15th Portuguese infantry of the line and 8th Caçadores formed the brigade of General Spry. To each of the British brigades of this division was attached a company of the Brunswick Oels corps.'[2]

The addition of light troops was deliberate on Wellington's part. He had already attached companies of the 5/60th Rifles to most of the British brigades and caçadores (or hunters) to most of the Portuguese brigades, while the British brigades of the 7th Division, when finally formed, were predominantly light infantry battalions. For the 5th Division, the most interesting development was probably the arrival of the two companies of Black Brunswickers, another light infantry unit. Leith Hay described the division's first encounter with these German troops during the withdrawal to the Lines.

> On the 6th, General Leith's corps marched to Quinta de Torres, on the 7th to Ribaldiera. Soon after leaving the former very early in the morning, we for the first time saw the Brunswick Oels regiment, which, on its route to join the army, had bivouac'd on the line of march, a short distance in advance of the Quinta. A dense fog covered the face of the country, dispersing at intervals, so as to make objects discernible when not far removed. The appearance of the Brunswick corps under these circumstances was peculiarly novel and picturesque. The long black clothing of the men, - their schakos, bearing in front the emblems of mortality, – and waving horse-hair that streamed in the wind, were increased in magnitude and effect by the misty curtain that at times admitted to view these unusually gaunt figures.[3]

Divisional and Brigade Commanders

The man most associated with the 5th Division was, and is, James Leith (1763–1816). When the amount of time he actually spent with the division is examined, less than two years, the strength of this association might be considered unexpected; but it is obvious from the many references to his presence or his looked for return after a period of absence, that he was very much their commander in the eyes of his troops, officers and men alike.

Born in 1763, James Leith was the oldest of Wellington's divisional commanders, with a wealth of experience before he took command of the 5th Division. He was a Scot, a younger son of John Leith of Leith Hall in Aberdeenshire, who died when James was only a few months old. Having been well educated according to the Scottish system, which including in his case attendance at Elgin Grammar School and one of the two universities of Aberdeen, Marischal College, he then decided on a military career and was sent to study at the Military College, Lisle.

Returning to Great Britain, he was commissioned into the 21st Foot before transferring to the 81st Foot as lieutenant, and then captain. When this latter regiment was disbanded

---

2   Leith Hay, *A Narrative*, vol.I, p.254.
3   Leith Hay, *A Narrative*, vol.I, p.247.

in 1783, he transferred to the 50th Foot, stationed in Gibraltar, where he held several staff appointments, including as aide-de-camp to the governor, Sir Robert Boyd. When Lieutenant General Charles O'Hara succeeded Boyd, Leith became his aide-de-camp. As a result, he accompanied O'Hara to Toulon in 1793, when British ships and troops were sent to aid the Royalist cause against the Revolutionaries. Here he would have encountered the talents of a Corsica-born French artillery officer, a certain Napoleone Buonaparte, which led to the evacuation of Toulon.

Back in Gibraltar, Leith served as town major and was given command of an independent company of foot. In October 1794, he returned to Scotland and was granted authority to raise a fencible regiment, the Aberdeenshire Fencibles. The following year, now colonel by brevet, he took his regiment to Ireland, where he remained until 1808. This meant that he was inevitably involved in the rebellion of 1798, and the disturbed period that followed. According to his nephew,

> During the Rebellion he was conspicuous for his activity and firmness of mind, and those qualities that found full scope for development in the mercy and forgiveness extended to many of the unfortunate objects of mistaken feeling, whom circumstances placed in his power; – and it is no slight eulogium, that, during scenes where so much bloodshed was inevitable, Colonel Leith's humanity never became in the slightest degree questioned.[4]

There is nothing in his uncle's subsequent career to suggest that Leith Hay exaggerated his uncle's humane instincts.

In 1801 Leith received the permanent rank of colonel, and after the fencibles regiments were disbanded in 1803 he served as colonel of the 13th Battalion of Reserve. The following year he was a brigadier general on the staff in Ireland.

His career took a new direction in 1808 when, as a newly appointed major general, he headed a delegation to the Asturias. His task was to reconnoitre, with the assistance of four engineer officers, and establish the means to prevent Napoleon using a route that would enable him to send more troops into Spain. He was also required to convince the local junta to mobilise against the French, with the result that a force, 10,000 strong, was raised and sent to join the main Spanish army. Leith then joined Lieutenant General John Moore's army and commanded a brigade throughout the campaign and at the battle of Corunna, as part of Lieutenant General John Hope's division.

Before he returned to the Peninsula, at Wellington's express wish, and after a brief period on the home staff, Leith served in the Walcheren campaign which had such a detrimental effect on his health, being appointed to the command of a brigade comprising the 11th, 59th and 79th regiments. Towards the end of the campaign, he developed the fever which so decimated the British forces. '...rendered incapable of serving, he embarked and was conveyed to Harwich in a state of dangerous illness, which although overcome for a moment, shook a constitution not naturally strong, and had a baneful effect throughout his future life.'[5]

---

4 Leith Hay, *Memoirs*, pp.10–11.
5 Leith Hay, *Memoirs*, p.32.

To pick up his career after his period of command in Spain and Portugal, in February 1814 Leith was appointed governor and commander-in-chief of the Leeward Islands. Soon after he arrived, news reached him of Napoleon's return to France, news which inspired French troops on Martinique and Guadeloupe to indicate their support for the emperor, although the French governors of both islands remained loyal to the monarchy. Leith's intervention, which was welcomed on Martinique but resisted on Guadeloupe, prevented either island sinking into revolution.

Leith returned to his headquarters on Barbados in April 1816. Six months later he suffered an attack of yellow fever and died on 16 October 'to the regret of the army, and all who had known him.'[6]

The inevitable consequence of Leith's frequent and often protracted absences was that the men of the 5th division found themselves under the command of many different officers, sometimes in an acting capacity, sometimes appointed as replacements for Leith. That the longest serving of these last, John Oswald, was with the division for little over 10 months, makes it easy to understand why Leith remained so obviously the man the division considered their true commander.

All the officers appointed only in an acting capacity were brigadiers with the division, and will be considered as such. That leaves four who were appointed from outside the division, the first being Major General Sir William Erskine, 2nd Baronet, of Torrie, Fife (1770–1813). Wellington, when informed that Erskine was to join his army, is supposed to have queried Erskine's sanity, to which he received the famous reply from Horse Guards: 'No doubt he is sometimes a little mad, but in his lucid intervals he is an uncommonly clever fellow; and I trust he will have no fit during the campaign, though he looked a little wild as he embarked.'[7] Although Erskine was appointed to command of the division on 6 February 1811, he did not join until 23 April. His previous command, of the Light Division, had suggested that his actions were often erratic. It is fortunate, therefore, that the 5th Division was so minimally engaged at Fuentes de Oñoro. On 10 May, the French garrison escaped from Almeida and on 11 May, Major General Dunlop was appointed to acting command of the division. Erskine was removed to the command of the 2nd Cavalry Division attached to Hill's troops, but in 1812 he was declared insane and the following year he was widely believed to have committed suicide when he fell from a window in Lisbon.

The next appointment, after Leith was seriously wounded at Salamanca, was that of Major General Richard Hulse (1770–1812), acting from the day of the battle, and appointed to full command on 31 July. The son of a Hampshire baronet, he first saw action in Flanders in 1794. He had commanded various brigades in the Peninsular before his appointment to the 5th Division, but his time with them was brief. On 7 September he died of typhus fever. As already noted, the officer who had the longest permanent command of the division after Leith was Major General John Oswald (1771–1840). He was appointed to the division on 25 September 1812, joined them at Villamuriel, and was nominally in command until December 1813. This period of command was punctuated by two periods when Hay was acting commander, and Leith was, very briefly, with the division. Oswald came from Fife,

---

6   Leith Hay, *Memoirs*, p.162.
7   Michael Glover, *Wellington's Army in the Peninsula 1808-1814* (Newton Abbot: David and Charles, 1977), p.347.

born into a political family, his father being the member of parliament for Dysart Burghs. When he was about 14, he was sent to study at the military academy at Brienne-en-Château, with the result that he became a Francophile, and enjoyed an enduring friendship with Louis-Antoine Fauvelet de Bourrienne, later Napoleon's secretary. On his return to Britain, he was commissioned as an ensign by purchase in the 23rd Foot, transferring the following year into the 7th Foot with the rank of lieutenant. Two years later, he acquired a captaincy in the 35th Foot. At the outbreak of the French Revolutionary War he saw action in the West Indies, in command of a detachment of local troops. Having returned to Britain and purchased a lieutenant colonelcy in the 35th, he again saw action in the Helder campaign (1799) and Graham's conquest of Malta (1800). After the collapse of the Peace of Amiens he saw more action in Calabria (1806), in the failed expedition to Egypt (1807) and in the Ionian Islands (1809). Three years later, with the rank of major general, he was attached to the general staff in the Peninsula, and given command of the 5th Division. His active career ended at San Sebastian. He then returned to Scotland in order to manage the family estates, to which he eventually succeeded. He was colonel of the 35th and, eventually, a full general.

The last of the four appointments was Major General Charles Colville (1770–1843). He was a younger son of the 8th Lord Colville of Culross, and began his active military career in 1787. During the Revolutionary Wars he served in the West Indies and Egypt, and in 1808 was once more in the West Indies. In 1810, having been promoted to major general, he sought a post in the Peninsula and was given command of a brigade in the 3rd Division. Whenever Picton was absent, Colville took command of the division and was also given acting command of the 6th Division in the autumn of 1813. On 5 December he took command of the 5th Division, remaining with them until the end of the war, although again this gave them only a brief acquaintance with one of Wellington's most well-respected generals. At Waterloo he commanded one of the divisions on the Allied right, at Halle. He subsequently served in India and Mauritius, being promoted to full general in 1837.

The Senior Staff

Just as at army headquarters, so at divisional headquarters a complement of staff officers enabled the efficient functioning of the division. The general order of 18 June 1809 had allocated an assistant adjutant general attached to the commanding officer and an assistant provost attached to the division. The commanding officer was also allowed an aide-de-camp, although he was permitted to increase the number at his own expense. As the divisional system developed, other staff officers were attached, the most important being an assistant quartermaster general. Both the AAG and the AQMG might also have deputies. There would also be an assistant commissary general, a civilian, who had a clerk, and a brigade major, attached to each brigade. In other words, the administration of a division was mirroring the headquarters system.

When Major Charles James was compiling his *Universal Military Dictionary*, he defined an adjutant-general as

> ...an officer of distinction, who aids and assists the general in his laborious duty: he forms the several details of duty of the army, with the brigade majors, and keeps

an exact state of each brigade and regiment, with a roll of the lieutenant-generals, major-generals, colonels, lieutenant-colonels and majors. He every day at head quarters receives orders from the general officer of the day, and distributes them to the majors of brigades, from whom he receives the number of men they are able to furnish for the duty of the army, and informs them of any detail which may concern them. On marching days he accompanies the general to the ground of the camp. He makes a daily report of the situations of all the posts placed for the safety of the army, and of any changes made in their posts.[8]

It is significant that James refers to brigades rather than divisions, because once Wellington had organised his army on a divisional basis, most of what he defines as the responsibilities of the adjutant general at army headquarters applies equally to the assistant adjutant general attached to a division. The adjutant general and his assistants were crucial to the chain of command, being the conduit through which orders and information passed in both directions.

The assistant adjutant general attached to the 5th Division from its inception was George Henry Frederick Berkeley (1785–1857), who was socially very well-connected. He was the eldest son of Admiral Sir George Cranfield Berkeley, whom Wellington respected, worked well with and valued as a personal friend, and the grandson of the 4th Earl of Berkeley. His mother was Emilia Lennox, granddaughter of the 2nd Duke of Richmond. Educated at Harrow, he was appointed cornet in the Horse Guards by purchase in January 1802. By May 1805 he was a captain in the 35th Foot and a major three years later. In 1811 he became its lieutenant colonel. His active career began when he joined the 35th in Sicily upon appointment and then accompanied them to Egypt in 1807. Although his regiment saw no service in the Peninsula, Berkeley was there from 1809, having been appointed an assistant quartermaster general. His attachment to the 5th Division as assistant adjutant general was interrupted by only one brief period when he was attached to the newly formed 7th Division (March–December 1811). He was present at Waterloo, where he liaised with the Prince of Orange. He later rose to general and commanded the Army of Madras in 1848. He spent the last three years of his life as member of parliament for Devonport.

Major James' definition of the duties of a quartermaster general again serves to suggest the responsibilities that the divisional assistant quartermaster general held. He was

> …a considerable officer in the army, and should be a man of great judgement and experience, and well-skilled in geography; his duty is to mark the marches, and encampments of an army; he should know the country perfectly well, with its rivers, plains, marshes, woods, mountains, defiles, passages, &c. even to the smallest brook. Prior to a march, he receives the orders and route from the commanding general, and appoints a place for the quarter-masters of the army to meet him next morning, with whom he marches to the next camp; where, after having viewed the ground, he marks out to regimental quarter-masters the space allowed each

---

8 Charles James, *An Universal Dictionary in English and French, in which are explained the Terms of the Principle Sciences that are necessary for the information of an officer* (London: T. Egerton, 1816), p.5.

regiment for their camp: he chuses [sic] the head quarters, and appoints the villages for the generals of the army's quarters: he chuses a proper place for the encampment of the train of artillery: he conducts foraging parties, as likewise the troops to cover them against assaults, and has a share in regulating the winter quarters and cantonments.[9]

James might have added that the quartermaster's department also dealt with equipment, although not with the responsibility of supplying it, and intelligence.

William Maynard Gomm (1784–1875), who served as deputy assistant and assistant quartermaster general throughout the existence of the 5th Division, was the son of Lieutenant Colonel William Gomm, who was killed in 1794 during Lieutenant General Charles Grey's expedition to Guaadeloupe. It was Grey who wrote suggesting that, for services rendered, the lieutenant colonel's nine-year-old son should be given an ensigncy in the 9th Foot. The boy was being educated at a private school in Woolwich at the time but in 1799 he went with the regiment to Den Helder, and in the following year to Ferrol, under Lieutenant General Sir James Pulteney. By this time a captain, he then continued his military education by attending the Royal Military College at High Wycombe. This was briefly interrupted in 1806 by the expedition to Stralsund. He finally left the college in 1807, in time to be involved in the expedition to Copenhagen, when he was appointed to his first staff post, as AQMG. He held the same position in Wellington's first Peninsular army and in Moore's army, as well as the force Lord Cathcart took to Walcheren. He returned to the Peninsula with the 9th in 1810, bringing with him the lingering effects of Walcheren fever. He was initially appointed DAQMG, and then AQMG, serving through to 1814, by which time he was a major in the 9th. Following his return to England, he transferred to the Coldstream Guards, but at Quatre Bras and Waterloo he once more served on the staff, as AQMG attached to Picton's 5th Division. Gomm lived more than half his life after Waterloo. Among other appointments, he was governor of Jamaica in 1839 and Mauritius in 1842. Seven years later, as lieutenant general, he was commander-in-chief in India and in 1868 he was appointed field marshal.

Gomm's letters to his sister and his aunt inevitably reveal something of the challenges facing an AQMG. There seems little doubt that the failure of the 5th Division to come into action at Valladolid on 7 September 1812 has to be ascribed to Gomm. Against this, though, are the two thorough reconnaisances to Tras os Montes which proved crucial to the success of the Vitoria campaign. And then there was the difficulty of conducting the division away from the position at Burgos, in the dark and with a panicking commanding officer.

Brigadiers

The brigade commanders were the next link in the chain of command, and there can be no doubt that the dominant brigadier in the 5th Division was Major General Andrew Hay (1762–1814), who was appointed to the staff in the Peninsula as a brigadier general (his rank

---

9   James, *Universal Dictionary*, p.69.

at this point was brevet colonel) and then, on 30 September, to the command of the British brigade, later the first brigade of Leith's division. He held the command until his death at Bayonne, except for an extended period of leave in 1812, which he had been seeking since the previous year, and some periods when he was in acting command of the division.

Hay was the son of a Banffshire laird whose first commission, in 1779, was as ensign in the 1st Foot, the Royals. There followed a career which was, as much as anything, distinguished by the propensity of the regiments he served with to be disbanded, leaving him on half-pay. At the same time his rank rose steadily to major by 1794. Four years later he received official permission to raise a fencible regiment, most of the men coming from the family estates. This gave him the temporary rank of colonel. Originally posted to Guernsey, the Banffshire Fencibles were then transferred to Ireland, where they saw action during the rebellion. The Treaty of Amiens in 1802, however, brought about another disbandment. When the treaty collapsed in May 1803, Hay was given command of the 16th Battalion of the Army of the Reserve which subsequently joined the regular army as the 2/72nd, with Hay promoted to lieutenant colonel, having previously held the rank by brevet. Then his career turned full circle when in March 1807 he was given command of the 3rd battalion of the Royals.

Hay and the 3/1st were sent to the Peninsula in October 1808, serving under Sir David Baird, who was moving in support of Sir John Moore. As a result, the Royals shared in the retreat to and Battle of Corunna. They were then part of the force sent to Walcheren, with its consequent health issues, although there is no evidence that Hay was affected. Finally returning to Britain in December 1809, the Royals had just a brief period to bring the battalion up to strength before returning to the Peninsula, landing at Lisbon on 1 July 1810.

Hay seems to have been a somewhat divisive character. Gomm praised him posthumously as 'the man who had so often commanded us on fortunate occasions, and for whom I had so high a respect and regard'[10] while an obituary in *The Gentleman's Magazine* described him as 'a most zealous and able officer, whose whole life was spent in the service of his country, and who in every situation entitled himself to the esteem of his commanders, to the friendship of his brother officers, and to the care of his men.'[11] Major General Robinson, however, described him as 'an arrant coward… That he is a paltry, plundering old wretch is established beyond doubt – That he is no officer is clear, and that he wants spirit is firmly believed, ergo he ought not to be a General.'[12] This harsh judgement, however, seems to be an exaggerated response to Hay's claim that it was the Royal Scots who successfully assaulted San Sebastian rather Robinson's brigade, who were written out of Hay's report to Graham. No doubt, there was also a strong element of personal dislike.

Before Hay arrived to join the 5th Division, the nascent first brigade was under the command of Lieutenant Colonel James Stevenson Barnes (d.1823, sometimes Burnes). Unlike Hay, Barnes spent almost the entirety of his military career with the 1st Foot. He joined the second battalion as an ensign in 1792, rising to lieutenant two years later, captain in 1796 and major in 1803. He served with the Royals at Toulon and Corsica, 1793–1794, Den Helder in 1799 and Egypt two years later. There then followed a period in the West Indies from 1803 to 1807. In November 1806 he was promoted to lieutenant colonel in the Fribourg

---

10 Carr-Gomm (ed.), *Letters and Journals*, vol.I, p.336.
11 *The Gentleman's Magazine*, May 1814, p.517.
12 Fogg, *Wellington's American General*, p.209.

Regiment, and when it was disbanded seven months later he was appointed to the Chasseurs Britanniques. Less than a year later he was back with his original regiment, but as lieutenant colonel of the 3rd battalion. He seems not have joined them until the Walcheren campaign and was with them when they returned to the Peninsula. In relation to Hay's report on San Sebastian, mentioned above, Graham later wrote to Wellington: 'Major-General Hay speaks most highly of the conspicuous gallantry of Lieut. Col. Barnes, in the successful assault of the curtain, with his brave battalion of the Royal Scots.'[13] On 4 June 1814 Barnes was appointed full colonel by brevet.

During Hay's six-month period of leave in 1812, the first brigade came under the command of Lieutenant Colonel the Honourable Charles John Greville (1780–1836), a younger son of the second Earl of Warwick. Having served as a junior officer in the Warwick Fencibles, he was commissioned as lieutenant in the 10th Foot in 1796 and gained his captaincy in 1799. He saw action with the 10th in Egypt, 1801. Two years later he was appointed major in the 38th, and lieutenant colonel of the 1st battalion in 1803. He served in the Peninsular, first under Wellesley and then under Moore, being present at the battles of Roliça, Vimeiro and Corunna. The battalion was then sent to Walcheren and suffered severe losses from the local fevers. Consequently, it was the second battalion that joined Wellington in 1810 while the first battalion remained in Britain for recovery and recruitment. By 1812 the senior battalion was considered fit for action and returned to the Peninsular, joining the army shortly before the Battle of Salamanca where, in Hay's absence, Greville led the first brigade of the 5th Division into action. He remained in command of the 1/38th until the end of the war, and in 1815 was colonel commanding the 12th British Brigade in Paris. Although he was appointed major general in 1819, he had already exchanged the military for a political life, being elected member of parliament for Warwick in 1816, a seat he held with only a brief interruption until 1835, when he resigned because of his failing health.

The second brigade had a sequence of four commanders, the first being James Wallace Dunlop (1759–1832), the son of an Ayrshire laird, John Dunlop of Dunlop. James was the fifth son but received the Dunlop estates from his father in 1786, becoming the 21st of that ilk. By this time, as an ensign in the 82nd Foot, he had served in the American colonies, where he survived a shipwreck and a period as a prisoner of war, as well as overseeing the. British withdrawal from Wilmington at the end of the war. He re-joined the 82nd at Halifax in 1782 with the rank of captain. Upon his return to Scotland and the disbandment of his regiment he spent a period on half-pay before being appointed captain in the newly raised 77th in 1787. He then saw service in India in both the Third and the Fourth Mysore Wars, including fighting at Seringapatam, where he was seriously wounded. He returned to Scotland in 1800 and three years later was a colonel in the Army of Reserve and in the newly raised second battalion of the 77th. In 1804 he exchanged into the 59th, who were manning defences in Kent. The following year he was sent to Cornwall to command a brigade. On his second period of command in the Peninsula, Wellington requested Dunlop, whom he probably knew from India, and appointed him to the command of the second brigade in the newly formed 5th Division. Dunlop was also put on the general list in July, although it was November 1809 before he arrived to join his brigade. In Leith's absence he commanded the

---

13   Gurwood (ed.), *Dispatches*, vol.XI, p.64.

division at Sabugal and Fuentes de Oñoro. In October 1811, however, he chose to end his military career, having already decided to contest the parliamentary seat of Kirkcudbright, which he held from 1812–1826. Wellington described his departure as a real loss. Dunlop was appointed lieutenant general in 1814 and colonel of the 75th in 1827.

Dunlop's successor was George Townshend Walker (1764–1842), who requested a regular command in the Peninsula. The son of Major Nathaniel Walker, his was not a moneyed background, which explains why none of his promotions were by purchase and he accepted every opportunity he was offered to make a name for himself. He joined the army in 1782, but his first two regiments, the 95th and the 71st, were disbanded soon after he joined them, although he had already been promoted lieutenant while still with the 95th. He then joined the 36th in 1784, and served in India. Two years later he was appointed Deputy Quartermaster to the King's troops. The following year he was invalided home, suffering from a fever. Upon recovery, he served as aide-de-camp to Major General Thomas Bruce in Ireland before joining the 14th Foot in 1790 as captain lieutenant. The same year he travelled to Germany, both to learn the language and to study German military tactics. Upon his return he was appointed captain in the 60th Foot but remained at the depot as his battalion was in North America. When the war with France broke out in 1793, Walker went to Flanders as a volunteer, taking with him the new recruits from the depot. His next post was Inspector of Foreign Corps, in which capacity he was instrumental in the setting up of the de Roll's Regiment. By 1797. having reached the rank of major, he went with de Roll's to Portugal, but once again ill health brought him back to Britain, where he was appointed Inspector of Recruiting for the Manchester District. His next promotion, in 1799, was as lieutenant colonel in the 50th Foot. Not only did he accompany them to den Helder, but he also served as Military Commissioner to the Russians. And so it went on: commander of garrisons in Malta and Ireland; the expedition to Copenhagen; the Peninsula, where he served with the 50th at Vimeiro before the battalion took on garrison duties; and Walcheren.

In 1810 he was appointed brigadier general and was sent to liaise with the Spanish in Galicia and the Asturias. The following year his request for a regular command was granted when he was appointed to the second brigade of the 5th Division and also promoted to major general. His period of command was relatively brief, from October 1811 to June 1812, but was distinguished by his leadership at Badajoz. Not until May 1813 was he judged fit for another command, the first brigade of the 2nd Division, and even then he did not join the division until August, when he briefly took over as acting commander in place of the wounded commander, Sir William Stewart, before taking command of his brigade at the Nivelle. He then transferred to the 7th Division, as acting commander, and led them at the Nive and Orthez, where he took another serious wound, at which point he resigned his command,

Walker subsequently served as Governor of Grenada (1815–1817), Commander in Chief of the Madras army (1826–1830) and finally as Lieutenant Governor of the Royal Hospital, Chelsea, a position he held to his death. He was also made a baronet in 1835.

The effect of Walker's protracted period of recovery (it was four months before he could be moved from Badajoz) led to the appointment of William Henry Pringle (c.1772–1840) as commander of the second brigade. There is some uncertainty about the year of his birth, in Dublin, and his education. He might have attended Drogheda Grammar School or have been privately educated, followed by Trinity College. He certainly came from a military background, being the son of Major General Henry Pringle, and in 1792 was commissioned into the 18th Light Dragoons. In 1793 he was a lieutenant in the 16th Light Dragoons, with whom he served in Flanders. By 1795 he was a major and had transferred to the 111th Foot. During the Den Helder campaign of 1799 he was taken prisoner. In the same year he inherited estates in Ireland from an uncle, and was appointed lieutenant colonel in the 4th Foot. Three years later he was captain and lieutenant colonel in the Coldstream Guards. He was involved in the 1805 Hanover expedition and was at Copenhagen in 1807. The following year he exchanged into the 1st Foot. In 1809 he was appointed colonel and made Inspector of Forces in Canada. He also pursued a political career, becoming the member of parliament for St Germans in 1812, the same year that he rose to major general and was appointed to the staff in the Peninsula. He commanded the second brigade from June 1812 to March 1813, although from early September until Villamuriel he was acting commander of the division. He was then transferred to the 2nd Division, commanding its third brigade until the end of the war, although a wound taken at Garris (Saint-Palais) in February 1814 rendered him *hors de combat*. He remained the member of parliament for St Germans until 1818, after which he represented Liskeard.

The last commander of the second brigade was the American Loyalist, Frederick Philipse Robinson (1763–1852). Robinson was the fourth son of Colonel Beverley Robinson, himself the son of the President of the Council of Virginia, while his mother's family were prominent landowners. The family's attitude to the agitation for independence was made clear when in 1776 Robinson's father raised the Loyal American Regiment, in which the son served as an ensign. A year later he was appointed to the 17th Foot and in 1779 was in garrison at Stoney Point. When the revolutionaries attacked, Robinson was wounded and taken prisoner. In his absence he was promoted to lieutenant in the 60th Foot and then, in 1781, transferred to the 38th Foot, by which time he had been released on Washington's specific order, seemingly because of a boyhood friendship with Robinson's father. In 1783 Loyalists were proscribed and their property confiscated, so Lieutenant Robinson accompanied his regiment to England, landing at Portsmouth in January 1784. Nine years later they formed part of Grey's expedition to the West Indies but in 1794 Robinson, now captain of the grenadier company, had to return to England for the recovery of his health. Soon after his return he was appointed major in the 127th Foot, and then exchanged with the same rank to the 32nd, but when this regiment was ordered to the West Indies he exchanged again, to the 134th, only for his new regiment to be disbanded within six months of his joining it. He was placed on half-pay, but also took on his first staff appointments, Inspecting Field Officer for the Bedford Recruiting District and then Inspecting Field Officer for the London Recruiting District. So effective was his discharge of his duties in the latter that he received a valuable piece of plate from the Bank of England. Meanwhile, he had been appointed lieutenant colonel in the army in 1800 and colonel in the army in 1810. He had also been requesting to serve under Wellington in the Peninsula.

His request was finally granted in the autumn of 1812 and he was in the Peninsula by 21 October, although his arrival was not welcomed by Wellington, possibly because of his lack of command experience. It was only in March 1813 that he was finally given command of the second brigade of the 5th Division. He was subsequently praised by Graham for his conduct at Osma and at Gamarra Major. He had also been appointed major general by this time. He was then wounded in the face at San Sebastian and severely wounded at the Nive.

He was subsequently given a staff appointment in Canada as commander of the fourth brigade, followed by the provisional governorship of Upper Canada, and then served as Governor of Tobago from 1816–1821.

The third, or Portuguese brigade had just two commanders, one British, one Portuguese. William Frederick Spry (1770–1814), son of Lieutenant General William Spry, was first commissioned in 1782, as an ensign in the 70th Foot. Two years later he was a lieutenant in the 73rd Foot, on half-pay before transferring the following year to the 64th Foot, still a lieutenant but on full pay. He changed regiments again in 1786, joining the 77th Foot as captain lieutenant, advancing to captain the following year. He served in India with this regiment, including at the Battle of Seringapatam, rising to major by 1797, brevet lieutenant colonel three years later, and brevet colonel in 1810, he and the regiment having returned to Britain in 1807. Two years later the regiment was involved in the Walcheren campaign. Spry was one of the British officers commissioned into the Portuguese army, in his case in August 1810, as a brigadier general. He was then given command of the Portuguese brigade under Leith, soon to be the third brigade of the 5th Division. In 1813 he was promoted to major general in both the British and the Portuguese armies. As commander of the third brigade he took part with the 5th Division in all the major engagements through to San Sebastian. By this time, though, he was in poor health and had to return to Britain to recover. There was no recovery, however, and he died in January 1814.

He was succeeded by Luis de Rego Barreto (1777–1840), the illegitimate son of an army officer who later legitimised him, presumably so that he could serve as an officer in the Portuguese army. De Rego began his military career as a cadet, aged 13, in the Viana infantry. He was appointed *alferes* (ensign) in 1802 and *tenente* five years later, just as the French began their invasion of Portugal. A year later he was asked to resign as the Portuguese army was being re-organised. He went to Viana de Castello, where he set up a provisional government which, in turn, promoted him to *major*. He also raised the Beira Caçadores, later the 4th Caçadores, of which he became the *tenente-coronel*. In 1812, he became *tenente-coronel* of the 15th Line, also in Spry's brigade. Because of the impressive behaviour of both his regiments, he soon attracted favourable attention, even from Wellington. In October 1813 he was appointed commander of the third brigade upon Spry's departure to England.

After the war, *Marechal de Campo* do Rego (as he soon became) went to Brazil, where he held several staff positions and also, as Governor of Pernambuco, suppressed all signs of separatism with considerable brutality. He returned to Portugal in 1821 and was appointed Military Governor of the Minho. The rest of his life was spent in and out of favour, although in 1835 he was created Visconde de Geraz do Lima.

Brigade Majors

The other officers who were a link in the command system were the brigade majors. Although a brigade major was

>...an officer appointed by the brigadier, to assist him in the management of his brigade... According to the regulations published by authority, a brigade-major is attached to the brigade, and not to any particular brigadier-general, as an aide-de-camp is. Brigade-majors must be taken from the regular forces, and must not be effective field-officers. If they are subalterns, they take rank in the brigade or garrison, in which they are serving, as junior captains.[14]

His duties may best be compared to those of a regimental adjutant, but obviously carrying much greater responsibility.

According to Gomm, whose brother, Henry, serving with the 6th Foot, had just been appointed brigade-major to the third brigade of the 2nd Division, 'The pay and rank are the same as those of an aide-de-camp: the officer has the rank of major during the time he holds the appointment, and he is not considered as generally belonging to the general's family so much as the aide-de-camp. The situation is more independent.'[15]

The first officer to be appointed a brigade-major in what would later be the 5th Division was Captain Selwyn Smith of the 3/1st Foot, the appointment dated 7 July 1810.[16] He was attached to the British brigade, later the first brigade and held the position for two years. In July 1812 Captain William Taylor of the 38th was appointed to Hay's brigade. The first brigade major in the second brigade, appointed on 11 October 1810, as the brigade was being formed, was Captain Richard Machell of the 2/30th. He was severely wounded during the escalade at San Vincente and finally resigned in October 1812, being forced to return to England for recovery of his health. On 9 October, Captain Robert Anwyll of the 1/4th was appointed in Machell's place. Interestingly, Anwyll had also been wounded during the escalade but had obviously made a speedier recovery. One point of interest in passing is that although all the above brigade majors belonged to regiments serving in the 5th Division this was not necessarily the case. Captain William Stewart of the 2/30th was appointed brigade major to a brigade in the 2nd Division and remained with them until seriously wounded at Pamplona.

Wellington's general order of 18 June 1809 included in its arrangements that each division should have an assistant provost marshal. The provost marshal, of course, is probably the oldest staff position, since it can be dated back to the thirteenth century. His function was 'to secure deserters, and all other criminals; he is to often go round the army, hinder the soldiers from pillaging, indict offenders, execute the sentence pronounced, and regulate the weights and measures used in the army, when in the field.'[17] The assistant provost marshals would replicate these essential duties within the division. According to general orders, four sergeants were appointed assistant provost marshals (or assistant provosts) to the 5th Division: Sergeant Richard Newman of the 3/1st in July, 1810; Sergeant James Johnson of the 1/9th in March, 1811; Sergeant Williams of the 1/4th in September 1813; and Sergeant Barber of the 1/9th in November 1813. Since there were 24 assistant provosts by the end of the war, these appointments may not all have been sequential. In accordance with an order

---

14   James, *Universal Dictionary*, pp.67–68.
15   Carr-Gomm (ed.), *Letters and Journals*, vol.I, p.105.
16   See Anon., *General Orders*, vols.II–IV.
17   James, *Universal Dictionary*, p.688.

by Sir John Moore in 1809, and continued by Wellington, APMs received the pay and allowances of ensigns.

General Orders also reveal other personnel attached to the division, although not military. There is a reference in general order of the 11 October 1811 to Deputy Assistant Commissary General St Remy, who was attached to the second brigade of the 5th Division. Obviously, the first and third brigades would also have a DACG attached to them. There is also just one reference to a medical appointee. Staff Surgeon Emery, attached to the 5th Division, was instructed in March 1811 to travel to Condeixa to care for the sick and wounded.

There are passing references in various journals and memoirs to Sunday prayers, so it is no surprise to discover that chaplains were attached to the division. The Reverend Edward C. Frith was appointed chaplain to the forces and attached to the 5th Division in July 1811, and then transferred to the 2nd Division the following month. He was succeeded by the Reverend Frederick Harvey Brown, acting chaplain, who joined the 5th Division in September 1811. Finally, the Reverend Mr Cracroft was attached to the division in September 1813. That prayers might take place without a divisional chaplain, however, is borne out by an entry Lieutenant William Stewart of the 30th made in his journal on 24 February 1811: 'Ensign N. read divine service to the Battn.'[18] Ensign Neville was a vicar's son, which undoubtedly explains why he performed this duty.

One of Wellington's concerns was the spread of Methodism in the army, for whereas the Church of England had a hierarchical system like the army, Methodism preached a more individual relationship between God and man which did not require the authority of bishops and even vicars. On 28 February 1811 Stewart recorded: 'Lt Killet & Balfour of the 1st Foot with us in the evening after we had all attended prayers at a House where two officers of the 9th Regt preached every night – one named Lt Watson the other Ensign Whitley.' That Wellington regarded these two officers as a cause for concern is demonstrated in a letter to Henry Calvert, the Adjutant General, in which he expressed his concern about the spread of Methodism. 'In the 9th regiment there is one [meeting] at which two officers attend … and the commanding officer of the regiment has not been able to prevail upon them to discontinue this practice.'[19]

And then there was the large number of Irish soldiers in the division (see Table 6.1), most of whom would be Catholic, to say nothing of the inevitability of some Irish Catholic officers. In 1811 the Duke of York, as Commander in Chief of the army, issued a general order, aimed at the Militia, that no Catholic soldier should be penalised for not attending divine worship, and should be permitted to worship according to his own beliefs when the situation allowed. That such was the case in the regular army in the Peninsula is born out by an entry in Ensign John Carter's journal. On 1 December 1811, the division having heard divine service, a Portuguese approached Major General Hay with a claim that Lieutenant Brisac owed him 17 dollars. '…the general was very angry & asked for him. He was told that he had been sent to mass with the Catholics, the general made reply that he would have him even if he was on the altar.'[20] It remains a moot point whether Brisac himself was Catholic, since the religious persuasion of officers was not recorded until 1826.

---

18 NAM: 6112-33: Journal of Captain William Stewart, 28 February 1811.
19 Gurwood (ed.), *Dispatches*, vol.VII, p.131.
20 Glover (ed.), *Ensign John Carter's*, p.5.

Table 6.1: Nationality of NCOs and other ranks of the 5th Division, January 1813

	English	Scottish	Irish	Foreign	Total
3/1st	317	150	562	4	1,033
1/9th	375	3	65	1	444
1/38th	693	25	274	7	999
1/4th	612	4	135	2	753
2/30th	362	17	361	2	742
2/44th	24	1	429	0	454
Total, January	*2,383*	*200*	*2,153*	*16*	*4,425*
2/47th	453	17	329	0	799
2/59th	415	20	468	0	903

Table 6.2: Nationality of Officers

	English	Scottish	Irish	Foreign	Total
3/1st	16	13	17	1	47
1/9th	26	10	20	0	56
1/38th	23	5	14	0	42
1/4th	32	6	15	1	54
2/30th	18	5	26	0	49
2/44th	14	6	15	0	35
	129	45	107	2	283
2/47th	14	2	21	0	37
2/59th	20	11	17	0	48

Inspection, January 1813

For a final impression of the 5th Division, as it was at the beginning of 1813, there is no better place to look than at the half-yearly inspections, carried out by Major General Hay over three days in and around Lamego.[21] From the tabulated material, various conclusions can be drawn. Starting with the nationality of the NCOs and other ranks, (Table 6.1) it would be accurate to describe the division as Anglo-Irish with only a small Scottish presence, despite the 3/1st notionally being a Scottish regiment. Focussing on NCOs and other ranks, one battalion, the 2/44th, can be described as an Irish unit, a reflection of their having been raised in Ireland in 1803 according to the Army of Reserve and Additional Forces Acts, two government measures to bring the army up to strength after the collapse of the Treaty of Amiens in May of that year. They had then been posted briefly to the Isle of Wight before moving on to Guernsey and then, in 1810, to Cadiz, so that there had been no occasion to recruit in England. The 2/30th, who were almost a perfect balance of English and Irish, had moved in the opposite direction from the 2/44th, having been raised from the Army

---

21 TNA: WO 27/112: Inspection Returns.

of Reserve in England and then, along with the senior battalion, transferring to Ireland and taking in considerable numbers from the Irish Militia regiments. The third battalion of the Royal Scots, about two thirds Irish, was originally raised in Hamilton, along with a fourth battalion, in 1804. Two years later, the second battalion was sent to India, taking about 500 men from the third and fourth battalions. In 1807 the third battalion was sent to Ireland to recruit, thus creating its Irish predominance. Nevertheless, it did have the highest Scottish presence, limited though it was. As for the other three battalions, the 1/38th was a third Irish, having spent time in Ireland before the outbreak of the war in the Peninsula and again after the Walcheren campaign. The other two battalions, the 1/4th and the 1/9th, were about a fifth Irish. Taken together, therefore, the six battalions of the 5th Division at this point in its history had an Irish presence considerably higher than the estimated 30 percent of Wellington's Peninsular army, being closer to 50 percent. The Scottish presence, in comparison, was minimal. There were also 16 men identified as 'foreign' in the division, one sergeant and 15 privates. This does not include the two Brunswick companies, which were not inspected.

The 2/47th had not yet been incorporated into the 5th Division but were quartered near Lamego at the time of the inspections and were also inspected by Hay. As can be seen, their arrival as the third battalion in the second brigade, the 2/30th and 2/44th being a provisional battalion, of course, increased the proportion of English to Irish. The departure of the virtually Irish 2/44th, coupled with the arrival of the 2/59th, like the 2/30th a balance of English and Irish, had the same effect.

As for the officers, (Table 6.2) the situation was rather different when it came to commanding officers. To start with, three of them were Scottish: Lieutenant Colonels Thomas Campbell of the 3/1st (in place of the absent Lieutenant Colonel Barnes, also Scottish), Cameron of the 1/9th, and Hamilton of the 2/30th. Lieutenant Colonel Brooke of the 1/4th was Irish, and Lieutenant Colonels Greville of the 1/38th and George Carleton of the 2/44th (who was absent sick on the day of the inspection) were English. As far as the other officers were concerned, a similar pattern to the NCOs and other ranks emerges, although with a higher Scottish presence: 129 English, 107 Irish, 45 Scottish and two identified as foreign. Despite its overwhelmingly Irish presence in the ranks, the 2/44th had 14 English officers, 15 Irish and six Scottish, a reminder that an officer's progress in the army was more random than that of NCOs and other ranks. The 3/1st showed more of its Scottish origins with 13 Scottish officers against 16 English, 17 Irish and one foreign. The 1/4th, 1/9th and 1/38th all had more English officers than Irish, although the Irish presence was still notable. The only battalion with more Irish officers than English was the 2/30th, with 26 Irish against 18 English and five Scottish. This came about because when the first battalion left Ireland, eventually to be posted to India, it comprised a large number of officers transferred from the second battalion. As the junior battalion's ranks were filled with Irish volunteers, so the officer cohort took in Irish officers. The 2/47th also had more Irish officers than English and Scottish combined, having also been sent to Ireland soon after being raised in 1803.

It needs to be noted at this point that two of the battalions pose particular problems when it comes to analysis of their inspection returns. The 1/9th are not consistent in whom they count, thus creating considerable discrepancy between the various returns, while if the 2/30th had all the men they have counted, they certainly would not qualify as a weak battalion. A check in the muster rolls immediately demonstrates that they included men who had been sent back to England and, seemingly, men of the depot company.

Table 6.3: Length of Service

	Up to 2 yrs	3–5 yrs	6–9 yrs	10–13 yrs	14–20 yrs	21 yrs+
3/1st	307	775	118	4	16	3
1/9th	30	176	117	80	19	1
1/38th	310	287	130	223	17	25
1/4th	91	217	147	268	27	3
2/30th	265	240	248	79	25	4
2/44th	120	213	96	15	5	3
2/47th	41	521	173	30	14	5
2/59th	507	403	44	9	7	2

Table 6.4: Ages

	Under 20	20–24	25–29	30–34	35–39	40–50	50+
3/1st	72	390	443	188	84	41	1
1/9th	27	72	97	71	27	22	2
1/38th	54	235	260	310	82	53	5
1/4th	17	24	227	277	37	18	2
2/30th	81	146	214	132	107	30	0
2/44th	41	20	180	122	74	5	0
2/47th	61	259	234	153	50	32	5
2/59th	137	310	299	196	45	41	2

As might be expected (Tables 6.3 and 6.4), the experience of the NCOs and men in the ranks varied between battalions. The 3/1st and the 1/38th had a particularly high proportion of men who had served less than five years, as had the two battalions that were soon to join the division. The 2/30th and 2/44th, in comparison, had a larger proportion of men that had served for 10 years, while the 1/4th and the 1/38th, despite the latter having a large number of less experienced men, also had a good many who had served for up to 13 years. As far as age goes, it is no surprise that the highest proportion of men were in their 20s and early 30s. Only the 2/30th had a proportionately high number of men over 35, many of whom were amongst those who had been sent back to England.

A further section of the inspection return that sheds an interesting light on the division is the list of regimental courts martial carried out by each battalion, ranging from the 1/38th with 32 to the 2/44th with six, since the last inspection. The 3/1st and 2/30th each had 19 men stand a court martial, although in the case of the latter seven were tried together for disposing of their blankets. The 1/4th and the 1/9th each had eight. The most prevalent offences were theft and drunkenness, including being drunk on guard, while disposing of necessaries or, more seriously, ammunition were also notable in their frequency. Other offences were straggling, disrespect to an officer and unsoldierlike conduct. The average sentence was 200 lashes, but this ranged from 100 to 400, 300 being the most actually inflicted. The degree of punishment definitely varied from battalion to battalion. The 2/30th, for example, although usually sentencing the miscreant to 200 lashes, never inflicted more than 50 while the 3/1st inflicted 150–400.

As for the men themselves, in Oman's opinion, unless they were volunteers from the Militia, whom he identified as more committed, they were likely to be 'the usual raw stuff swept in by the recruiting sergeant – all those restless spirits who were caught by the attraction of the red coat, country lads tired of the plough, or town lads who lived on the edge of unemployment, and to whom the full stomach had been for some time a rarity.'[22] These are sweeping generalisations, of course, just as was Wellington's judgement of his troops as 'the scum of the earth. The English soldiers are fellows who have enlisted for drink – that is the plain fact: they have *all* enlisted for drink.'[23] The contemptuous description of his troops as scum had initially been provoked by the disorder and plundering that followed the Battle of Vitoria. In his much later conversation with Lord Stanhope he added: 'it really is wonderful that we should have made them the fine fellows they are.'

There were undoubted some king's hard bargains in the ranks, just as there were men who, having proved themselves outstanding NCOs, were rewarded with a commission. It may be assumed, however, that the majority lay between these two extremes.

As for the lives of the men of the 5th Division before they enlisted, the pension records and casualty returns provide useful data for establishing their previous occupations. An examination of the records of just one battalion in the division, the 2/30th, creates a clear picture, although with one important proviso, the significance of where the regiment was recruiting. In the case of the 30th, this was the western part of Lincolnshire, extending into Leicestershire and Nottinghamshire, and the area around Cambridge in England, and the West Coast of Ireland. Of the men whose occupations have been identified, 65 percent were labourers. This is a catch-all term for those with no identifiable craft or profession, but in the case of the 30th the vast majority would almost certainly be agricultural workers, who rarely seem to have been recognised as craftsmen. For example, a sergeant killed at Waterloo was described in one document as a labourer and in another as a thatcher, which is a highly skilled occupation.

The next largest group of workers also connects with the regiment's recruiting grounds, being the 15 percent who were textile workers. Apart from a handful of cotton-spinners and a silk worker, they were either hosiers or framework knitters from the East Midlands or Irish weavers. Other sizeable groups were cordwainers (or shoemakers) and tailors, seven percent, and those with building skills, five percent. Then there are the unexpected occupations like tutors or silversmiths, whose motives for joining the army were likely to have been something more than the lure of a red coat or a hungry stomach. There were also 13 butchers whose presence, when meat was on the hoof, must have been most welcome.

Whatever their age and experience, whatever their conduct, whatever reason they had for leaving their previous occupation, these were the men whom Leith Hay praised so highly, and it can be assumed that he would have included the Portuguese who had proved themselves as motivated and effective as their British allies. Nor should the two companies of

---

22   Charles Oman, *Wellington's Army 1809–1814* (London: Arnold, 1913), p.211.
23   Quoted in Oman, *Wellington's Army*, p.42.

Black Brunswickers be forgotten. When the light companies went into action their numbers, never less than 120 men, added to the division's skirmishing efficiency. Taken altogether, when 'commanded by a general possessing the confidence of his army, as Lord Wellington did, and led as they invariably had been, there is nothing within the scope of human powers which might not have been accomplished by the 5th division.'[24]

---

24   Leith Hay, *A Narrative*, vol.II, p.412.

Appendix

5th Division – Battle Casualties

Action	Unit	Killed		Wounded		Missing		Total
		Officers	Men	Officers	Men	Officers	Men	
Buçaco	1/9th		5	1	18			24
	2/38th		5	1	17			23
			10	2	35			47
Fuentes de Oñoro	3/1st				9			9
	1/9th				4			4
	2/30th				4			4
	2/44th				4			4
					21			21
Badajoz[1]	2/38th	1	12	3	26			42
	1/4th	2	40	15	173			230
	2/30th		38	6	86			130
	2/44th	2	37	7	88			134
		5	127	31	373			536
Salamanca	3/1st		23	8	129			160
	1/9th		3	1	42			46
	1/38th	2	24	12	115			143
	2/38th		9	2	40		1	52
	1/4th			1	17			18
	2/4th		2		23		6	31
	2/30th		3	1	22		1	27
	2/44th	2	4		23			29
	3rd Line		17	1	52		20	90
	15th Line	2	12	2	99			115
	8th Caçadores			3	22		3	28
		6	87	31	584		31	739

---

1   No separate return for Spry's brigade.

APPENDIX 249

Action	Unit	Killed		Wounded		Missing		Total
		Officers	Men	Officers	Men	Officers	Men	
Vitoria	3/1st		8	7	96			111
	1/9th	1	9		15			25
	1/38th			1	7			8
	1/4th	1	12	6	72			91
	2/47th	2	18	4	88			112
	2/59th		11	8	130			140
	3rd Line		2	3	8			14
	15th Line		6	3	19			28
	8th Caçadores		13	2	25			40
		4	79	34	460			577
San Sebastian[2]	3/1st	1	46	5	142			179
	1/9th	4	47	7	102		6	166
	1/38th	4	32	10	86		3	135
	1/4th	5	114	6	153		3	281
	2/47th	7	88	10	127			232
	2/59th	8	110	12	222			352
	Brunswick Oels		2	1	6	1	5	15
	3rd Line	4	67	10	47			128
	15th Line	3	101	8	85			197
	8th Caçadores	1	31	1	49			83
		37	638	70	1,019	1	18	1,783
The Bidassoa	3/1st		1		19			20
	1/9th		8	10	64			82
	1/38th		1		19			20
	1/4th			1	5			6
	2/47th				5			5
	2/59th				3			3
	3rd Line		1		4		1	6
	15th Line				2			2
	8th Caçadores			2	12		5	19
			11	13	102		6	163
The Nivelle	Greville's Brigade		3	3	10			16
	Robinson's Brigade		1		2			3
	De Regua's Brigade		9	1	9			19
			13	4	21			38
The Nive (9th)	Greville's Brigade		7	3	64		4	78
	Robinson's Brigade		15	11	80		2	108
	Brunswick Oels		2		1		1	4

---

2   Second storm.

Action	Unit	Killed		Wounded		Missing		Total
		Officers	Men	Officers	Men	Officers	Men	
	3rd Line				11			11
	15th Line		2		20		1	23
	8th Caçadores		1	2	12		12	28
			27	16	188		20	252
The Nive (10th)	3/1st		1	1	30	1	12	45
	1/9th	2	10	4	65			81
	1/38th		6		37			43
	1/4th		6	3	45		2	56
	2/47th		12	2	50	1	50	115
	2/59th		6	2	56		10	74
	2/84th	1	16	2	54	3	18	94
	Brunswick Oels			1	2			3
	3rd Line	2	26	6	70		85	104
	15th Line		19	4	26		85	134
	8th Caçadores		4	3	16	1	10	34
		5	50	28	451	6	187	783
The Nive (11th)	Greville's Brigade		16	2	91		10	119
	Robinson's Brigade	1	14	11	172		3	201
	Brunswick Oels		1	1	1			3
	De Regua's Brigade		19	8	71		89	187
		1	50	22	335		102	510
Bayonne	3/1st		8	1	12		21	42
	1/9th		2		8			10
	1/38th		2	2	5			9
	2/47th		3	2	11		10	26
			15	5	36		31	87

Notes

The two Brunswick Oels company have their casualties subsumed in the total for the whole battalion. Some conclusions may be drawn, however. The three detached companies (including the one serving with the 4th Division) took 35 casualties at Badajoz, while at Salamanca the three detached companies and the rest of the battalion took 49 casualties. In contrast, there were only six losses across the battalion at Vitoria.

There are no official returns for Villamuriel and the first storm of San Sebastian. Garry Wills, however, has identified eight officers and 38 men, British, German and Portuguese, who were killed at Villamuriel or died of wounds.[3] William Gomm gave the 5th Division's losses on the 25 July 1813 as over 500.

---

3   Wills, *Wellington at Bay*, Appendix V, pp.198–199.

Bibliography

Archives

Aberdeen Medico-Chirurgical Society Library
James McGrigor, unpublished papers

National Library of Scotland (NLS)
Adv 46-4-16-126 & 127, Correspondence and Papers of General Sir George Murray

National Army Museum (NAM)
6112-33, Journal of Captain William Stewart

The National Archives (TNA)
WO 12 Pay Lists and Muster Rolls
WO 17 Monthly Returns
WO 25 Casualty Returns
WO 27 Inspection Returns
WO 97 Men discharged and awarded Chelsea pensions
WO 119 Men discharged and awarded Kilmainham pensions

Unpublished Documents
Pringle, William, unpublished letters to Aylmer Haly, private collection
Woodward, Thomas, unpublished letters, private collection

Published Sources

Allen, John 'Journal of an officer of the Royals in the seat of war', *The Royal Military Chronicle,* November 1811 pp.9–13, December 1811 pp.124–126, April 1812 pp.419–425, May 1812 pp.39–44
Allen, John, 'The Subaltern's Complaint', *The Royal Military Chronicle,* March 1812, pp.341–343
Anon. (ed.), *General Orders: Spain and Portugal* (London: T. Egerton, 1814)
Anon. (ed.), *Papers on Subjects Connected with the Duties of the Corps of Royal Engineers* (London: Weale, 1839)
Aspinell-Oglander, Cecil, *The Story of Thomas Graham, Lord Lynedoch* (London: The Hogarth Press, 1956)

Bamford, Andrew, *Sickness, Suffering and the Sword: The British Regiment on Campaign, 1808-1815* (Norman: University of Oklahoma Press, 2013)

Bannatyne, Neil, *History of the Thirtieth Regiment now the First Battalion East Lancashire Regiment 1689-1881* (Liverpool: Littlebury Bros, 1923)

Beatson, F.C., *Wellington: the Bidassoa & Nivelle* (London: Tom Donovan, 1995)

Beatson, F.C., *Wellington: The Crossing of the Gaves and the Battle of Orthez* (London: Tom Donovan, 1994)

Beatson, Major General F.C., *Wellington and the Pyrenees Campaign: From Vitoria to the Bidassoa* (Driffield: Leonaur, 2007)

Belmas, Jacques Vital, *Précis des Campaignes et des Sièges d'Espagne et de Portugal de 1807 à 1814* (Paris: A. Leneveu, 1839)

Boutflower, Charles, *The Journal of an Army Surgeon during the Peninsular War* (Stroud: Spellmount, 1997)

Brett-Jones, Antony, *Life in Wellington's Army* (London: Tom Donovan, 1994)

Bruce, Robert B., Iain Dickie, Kevin Kiley, Michael F. Pavkovic, Frederick C. Schneid, *Fighting Techniques in the Napoleonic Age 1792-1815* (London: Amber Books, 2008)

Buckley, Roger Norman (ed.), *The Napoleonic War Journal of Thomas Henry Browne 1807-1816* (London: The Bodley Head for the Army Records Society, 1987)

Buttery, David, *Wellington against Massena* (Barnsley: Pen & Sword, 2007)

Cadell, Charles, *The Slashers; the Campaigns of the 28th Regiment of Foot during the Napoleonic Wars by a Serving Officer* (Driffield: Leonaur, 2008)

Carr-Gomm, Francis Culling (ed.), *Letters and Journals of Field-Marshal Sir William Maynard Gomm, G.C.B.* (London: John Murray, 1881)

Carter, Thomas, *Historical Records of the Forty-Fourth or the East Essex Regiment* (Chatham: Gale & Polden, 1887)

Chartrand, René, *Bussaco 1810: Wellington Defeats Napoleon's Marshals* (Oxford: Osprey Publishing, 2001)

Chartrand, René, *Fuentes de Oñoro: Wellington's Liberation of Portugal* (Oxford: Osprey Publishing, 2002)

Clerc, Charles, *Campagne de Maréchal Soult dans les Pyrénées Occidentales en 1813–1814* (Paris: Libraire Militaire de L. Baudois, 1894)

Collins, Bruce, *Wellington and the Siege of San Sebastian 1813* (Barnsley: Pen & Sword, 2017)

Colville, John, *The Portrait of a General: A Chronicle of the Napoleonic Wars* (Wilton: Michael Russell, 1980)

Delavoye, Alex M., *The Life of Thomas Graham, Lord Lynedoch* (London: Richardson & Co., 1880)

Divall, Carole, *Redcoats against Napoleon: the 30th Regiment during the Revolutionary & Napoleonic Wars* (Barnsley: Pen & Sword, 2009)

Divall, Carole, *Wellington and the Vitoria Campaign 1813* (Barnsley: Pen & Sword, 2021)

Divall, Carole, *Wellington's Worst Scrape: The Burgos Campaign 1812* (Barnsley: Pen & Sword, 2012)

Fletcher, Ian (ed.), *The Peninsular Wars: Aspects of the Struggle for the Iberian Peninsula* (Staplehurst: Spellmount, 1998)

Fletcher, Ian, *Badajoz 1812: Wellington's Bloodiest Siege* (Wellingborough: Osprey Publishing, 1999)

Fletcher, Ian, *In Hell Before Daylight* (Tunbridge Wells: The Baton Press, 1984)
Fletcher, Ian, *Salamanca 1812: Wellington Crushes Marmont* (Oxford: Osprey Publishing, 1997)
Fletcher, Ian, *Vittoria 1813: Wellington Sweeps the French from Spain* (Oxford: Osprey Publishing, 1998)
Fogg, Nicholas, *Wellington's American General: the Oldest serving Soldier in the British Army* (Stroud: Amberley, 2022)
Fortescue, J.W., *A History of the British Army* (Uckfield: The Naval and Military Press, 2004)
Freer, William J., *The Thirty-Eighth Regiment of Foot, now the First Battalion of the South Staffordshire Regiment* (London: Harrison & Sons, 1915)
Gaudêncio, Moisés, and Robert Burnham, *In the Words of Wellington's Fighting Cocks* (Barnsley: Pen & Sword, 2021)
Girod de L'Ain, Maurice, *Vie Militaire de Général Foy* (Paris: E.Plon, Nourrit et Cie, 1900)
Glover, Gareth (ed.), *Ensign John Carter's Journal 1812* (Huntingdon: Ken Trotman, 2006)
Glover, Gareth (ed.), *The Napoleonic Archive Volume 1: British Line Memoirs* (Godmanchester: Ken Trotman Publishing, 2021)
Glover, Gareth (ed.), *The Veteran or Forty Years' Service in the British Army: the Scurrilous Recollections of Paymaster John Harley 47*th *Foot – 1798-1838* (Solihull: Helion, 2018)
Glover, Michael, *Wellington's Army in the Peninsula 1808-1814* (Newton Abbot: David and Charles, 1977)
Glover, Michael, *Wellington's Peninsular Victories* (Gloucestershire: The Windrush Press, 1996)
Grattan, William, *Adventures of the Connaught Rangers from 1808-1814* (London: Henry Colburne, 1847)
Greenwood, Adrian (ed.), *Through Spain with Wellington: the Letters of Lieutenant Peter Le Mesurier of the 'Fighting Ninth'* (Stroud: Amberley, 2014)
Grehan, John, *The Lines of Torres Vedras: the Cornerstone of Wellington's Strategy in the Peninsular War* 1809-12 (Staplehurst: Spellmount, 2000)
Gurwood, John (ed.), *The Dispatches of the Duke of Wellington during his Various Campaigns* (London: John Murray, 1837)
Hale, James (transcribed by Peter Catley), *The Journal of James Hale late sergeant in the Ninth Regiment of Foot* (Windsor: IX Regiment, 1998)
Hall, John A., *A History of the Peninsular War Volume VIII: the Biographical Dictionary of British Officers Killed and Wounded 1808-1814* (London: Greenhill Books, 1998)
Harding-Edgar, John, *Next to Wellington: General Sir George Murray* (Warwick: Helion, 2018)
Hayman, Sir Peter, *Soult, Napoleon's Maligned Marshal* (London: Arms and Armour Press, 1990)
Haythornthwaite, Philip J., *The Armies of Wellington* (London: Arms and Armour, 1994)
Hunter, Archie, *Wellington's Scapegoat: the Tragedy of Lieutenant Colonel Charles Bevan* (Barnsley: Leo Cooper, 2003)
James, Charles, *An Universal Dictionary in English and French, in which are explained the Terms of the Principle Sciences that are necessary for the information of an officer* (London: T. Egerton, 1816)
Jones, John T., *Account of the War in Spain and Portugal and the South of France from 1808 to 1814 Inclusive* (London: T. Egerton, 1821)
Jones, John T., *Journals of Sieges Carried on by the Army under the Duke of Wellington in Spain between the Years 1811 and 1814* (London: T. Egerton, 1827)

Jones, John T., *Memoranda Relative to the Lines Thrown up to Cover Lisbon in 1810* (Uckfield: Naval and Military Press, 2006)

Jourdan, Jean-Baptiste, *Mémoires militaires du maréchal Jourdan (guerre d'Espagne)* (Paris: Ernest Flammarion, 1899)

Kincaid, John, *Adventures in the Rifle Brigade in the Peninsula, France and the Netherlands from 1809 to 1815* (London: Leo Cooper, 1997)

Leith Hay, Andrew, *A Narrative of the Peninsular War* (Edinburgh: Henry Washbourne, 1831)

Leith Hay, Andrew, *Memoirs of the Late… Sir James Leith, with a Précis of Events of the Peninsular War, by a British Officer* (Barbados: printed for the author, 1817)

Leslie, John H. (ed.), *The Dickson Manuscripts* (Huntingdon: Ken Trotman, 1987)

Lipscombe, Nick, *Wellington's Eastern Front: the Campaigns on the East Coast of Spain 1810-1814* (Barnsley: Pen & Sword, 2016)

Macarthy, James, *Recollections of the Storming of the Castle of Badajos* (London: W. Clowes & Son, 1836)

Marmont, Auguste de, *Mémoires de Maréchal Marmont, Duc de Raguse* (Paris: Perrotin, 1856)

McGuigan, Ron and Robert Burnham, *Wellington's Brigade Commanders, Peninsular and Waterloo* (Barnsley: Pen & Sword, 2017)

Monick, Stanley (ed.), *Douglas's Tale of the Peninsula and Waterloo* (Barnsley: Leo Cooper, 1997)

Muir, Rory, Robert Burnham, Howie Muir, & Ron McGuigan, *Inside Wellington's Army 1808-1814* (Barnsley: Pen & Sword, 2006)

Muir, Rory, *Salamanca 1812* (New Haven: Yale University Press, 2001)

Muir, Rory, *Tactics and the Experience of Battle in the Age of Napoleon* (New Haven: Yale University Press, 1998)

Myatt, Frederick, *British Sieges of the Peninsular War* (Staplehurst: Spellmount/Book Club Associates, 1987)

Myatt, Frederick, *Peninsular General: Sir Thomas Picton 1758-1815* (Newton Abbott: David & Charles, 1980)

Napier, W.F.P., *History of the War in the Peninsula and in the South of France* (London: Constable, 1993)

Nevill, Percy Parke, *Some Recollections in the Life of Lieut.-Col. P.P. Nevill* (London: Cox & Wyman, 1864)

Oman, Charles, *A History of the Peninsular War* (London: Greenhill Books, 1995)

Oman, Charles, *Wellington's Army 1809-1814* (London: Greenhill Books, 1986)

Park,. S.J. & G.F. Nafziger, *The British Military: its System and Organization 1803-1815* (Cambridge: Tafm Co. Inc., 1983)

Philippart, J. (ed.), *The Royal Military Calendar or Army Service and Commission Book* (London: Egerton, 1820)

Robertson, Ian, *A Commanding Presence: Wellington in the Peninsula 1808-1814* (Stroud: Spellmount, 2008)

Robertson, Ian, *Wellington at War in the Peninsula 1808-1814: an Overview and Guide* (Barnsley: Pen & Sword, 2000)

Rogers, H.C.B., *Wellington's Army* (London: Ian Allen, 1979)

Sabine, Edward (ed.), *Letters of Colonel Sir Augustus Simon Frazer, K.C.B. Commanding the Royal Horse Artillery in the Army under the Duke of Wellington written during the Peninsular and Waterloo Campaigns* (London: Longman, Brown, Green, Longmans, & Roberts, 1859)

Sarramon, Jean, *La Bataille de Vitoria* (Paris: J.C. Bailly Editeur, 1985)
Shadwell, Lawrence, *The Life of Colin Campbell, Lord Clyde* (Edinburgh: Blackwood, 1881)
Thompson, Mark S., *Wellington's Favourite Engineer: John Fox Burgoyne: Operations, Engineering, and the Making of a Field Marshal* (Warwick: Helion, 2020)
Thompson, W.F.K. (ed.), *An Ensign in the Peninsular War: the Letters of John Aitchison* (London: Michael Joseph, 1981)
Tomkinson, James (ed.), *The Diary of a Cavalry Officer in the Peninsular War and Waterloo Campaign 1809-1815* (London: Swann, Sonnenschein & Co, 1895)
Tyler, R.A.J., *Bloody Provost* (London: Phillimore, 1980)
Ward, S.G.P., *Wellington's Headquarters: a Study of the Administrative Problems in the Peninsular 1809-1814* (London: Oxford University Press, 1957)
Weaver, Lawrence, *The Story of the Royal Scots: the Lothian Regiment* (London: Country Life, 1915)
Weller, Jac, *Wellington in the Peninsula* (London: Greenhill Books, 1993)
Wellington, 2nd Duke of (ed.), *Supplementary Despatches, Correspondence and Memoranda of Field Marshal Arthur, Duke of Wellington K.G.* (London: John Murray, 1860)
Wills, Garry, *Wellington at Bay* (Warwick: Helion, 2020)
Wood, S.C.I. (ed.), *Reminiscences 1808-1815 under Wellington* (London: Simpkin, Marshall, Hamilton, Kent & Co. Ltd., 1901)
Woolgar, C.M. (ed.), *Wellington Studies I* (Southampton: Hartley Institute, University of Southampton, 1996)
Young, Peter & J.P. Lawford, *Wellington's Masterpiece: the Battle and Campaign of Salamanca* (London: George Allen & Unwin, 1973)

Index

Abechuco 167, 169, 173, 178
Abrantes 10, 13, 15, 40, 80
Adour river 207, 211–214, 218–221, 223
Agueda river 51, 55, 64, 66, 69, 98, 100
Aldea del Obispo 16, 51, 53
Aldeia da Ponte 67, 75
Alfaiates 51, 60–61, 66–67
Allen, Lieutenant John 63–68, 70, 73, 78–79, 155
Almaraz 13, 63, 82, 97
Almeida 13, 17–18, 36, 40–41, 44–46, 50–51, 55–58, 60–62, 72, 80, 97, 232
Anson, Major General George 61, 83, 98, 106, 114, 122, 126–128, 131, 139, 162–163, 173
Arcangues 213, 215–216, 222
Arguimbeau 189
Ashworth, Major General Charles 45, 52–53, 60
Attalya 64

Badajoz 9, 16–17, 30, 36, 44, 51, 59–62, 64, 72, 74, 78–79, 103, 118, 135, 138, 189, 200, 238, 250
Badajoz, third siege of 80–95
Barba del Puerco 51, 55–58
Bayonne 159, 167, 169, 172, 177, 184, 207, 209–214, 218–225, 236, 250
Beckwith, Lieutenant Colonel Thomas 47–48
Beresford, *Marechal do Exército* William Carr 12, 44, 58–60, 83, 98, 207, 210–213, 216
Bevan, Lieutenant Colonel Charles 56, 58–59, 62–63
Biarritz 211, 218, 227
Bidassoa river 192, 201–203, 205, 249
Blake, *Teniente General* Joaquín 60–62
Bonnet, *Général de division* Jean Pierre 100, 102–103, 105, 110, 116, 119, 122, 142
Boyer, *Général de brigade* Pierre 114, 116, 168, 171, 201, 205, 209, 215–216, 219–220

Bradford, Brigadier General Thomas 83, 98, 101, 116, 118–119, 122, 125, 132, 160, 162–163, 168, 172, 183–185, 196, 203, 207, 213, 215–216, 220–221, 224
British Army, cavalry regiments of: **5th Dragoon Guards** 112, 119; **3rd Dragoons** 108; **4th Dragoons** 20; **12th Light Dragoons** 102, 173–174, 203; **14th Light Dragoons** 54, 98, 101, 118, 206; **16th Light Dragoons** 58–59, 115, 164, 209
British Army, infantry regiments of: **1st** 14, 24, 29, 55, 63, 66, 84, 87, 92–93, 118, 122–123, 130, 137, 140, 142–144, 145–146, 151, 156, 165, 171, 184, 187–190, 193, 198, 227–228, 236–237, 239, 241–246, 248–250; **2nd** 56–57; **4th** 32, 56, 58–59, 63, 73, 88–89, 91, 95, 97, 118, 125, 128, 123, 144–145, 155, 151, 156–157, 191, 197, 227–228, 230, 239, 241, 243–245, 248–250; **9th** 14, 23, 26, 27–29, 44, 55, 70, 84, 86, 93, 98, 118, 121, 135–136, 145, 151, 187, 216, 227–228, 235, 241–245, 248–250; **24th** 54; **30th** 29, 31–34, 37, 49, 55, 59, 73, 84, 87–89, 91–93, 95, 104, 118, 131, 135, 145–146, 151, 154, 157, 191, 228, 230, 241–246, 248; **32nd** 64, 239
36th 57, 238; **38th** 14, 26–27, 29, 44, 86, 89, 95, 97, 103, 111–112, 117–119, 123, 128, 145, 151, 156–157, 175, 187–192, 198, 224–225, 227–228, 230, 237, 239, 241, 243–245, 248–250; **43rd** 48; **44th** 29, 31, 49, 55, 73, 84, 88–89, 95, 104, 118, 131, 145–146, 151, 157, 228, 230, 243–245, 248; **45th** 22–24; **47th** 158, 173–174, 199, 201, 209, 227–228, 243–245, 249–250, **52nd** 13, 42, 77; **59th** 158, 174, 178, 227–228, 231, 237, 243–245, 249–250; **60th** 12, 22, 116, 230; **68th** 113; **71st** 31, 54, 238; **74th** 22–23, 54; **79th** 54, 138, 231; **88th** 21–23, 153; **95th** 42, 48, 58, 77, 115, 164, 238

British Army, foreign corps of: **King's German Legion** 20, 31, 98, 126–127, 209, 224; **Loyal Lusitanian Legion** 17, 20, 23, 28, 36, 229; **Duke of Brunswick Oels Regiment** 32, 55, 65, 91, 116, 138, 144, 151, 158, 163, 196, 205, 215, 230, 244, 247, 249–250
Buçaco, battle of 12, 19–21, 25–27, 52, 86, 229, 248
Burgos 74, 127, 132, 134, 151–152, 154, 159, 163–164, 182, 235
Burgos, siege of 135–138
Burgos, retreat from 138–142
Burne, Brigadier General Robert 56–57, 236

Caffarelli, *Général de division* Marie-François 100, 103, 132, 135–136
Cameron, Lieutenant Colonel John 10–11, 23–24, 27, 94, 98, 100, 121, 137, 147, 166, 184–185, 188, 193, 215–216, 244
Campbell, Brigadier General Alexander 12, 20
Campbell, Lieutenant Colin 166, 185, 187–188
Campo Maior 44, 82–83, 95
Carter, Ensign John 73, 75–76, 78, 131, 242
Cassagne, *Général de division* Louis Victorin 169, 171
Castaños, *Teniente General* Francisco Javier 63–64, 80, 100, 134
Castello Branco 13, 15–16, 18, 64, 95
Castello de Vide 64
Castrejon 106–107
Celorico 13, 36, 41, 45–46, 69, 73
Ciudad Rodrigo 13, 15, 17, 44–46, 50–52, 55, 61, 64–67, 69–71, 78–80, 82, 84–85, 92, 95, 98, 111–112, 115, 134–135, 148, 150, 159, 189
Ciudad Rodrigo, siege of 72–77
Clausel, *Général de division* Bertrand 108, 114, 116–117, 119, 122, 127–128, 131, 134–136, 163–164, 166–168, 179–180, 201, 205, 207, 209, 213, 215, 217–219
Coa river 47–50, 52, 60–61, 64, 67, 69, 98
Coimbra 10, 19, 26–28, 38–41, 50, 74, 159
Cole, Major General Lowry 21, 60, 107, 114, 116, 119
Colville, Major General Charles 49, 222–223, 226–227, 233
Condeixa 41–42, 242
Conroux, *Général de division* Nicholas François 53–54, 169
Crauford, Brigadier General Robert 20, 31, 54, 66, 77, 184

D'Erlon, *Général de division* Jean-Baptiste Drouet 31, 34, 36, 39, 41, 46, 50, 52, 54, 66, 72, 103, 168–169, 176, 201, 207, 209, 211–213, 217
D'Urban, Brigadier General Benjamin 100, 110–111, 114, 116, 118, 122, 128–129, 132, 162–163, 180
Darmagnac, *Général de division* Jean Barthélemy 162, 169, 219
Digeon, *Général de division* Alexandre 168–169, 171, 176
Dorsenne, *Général de divison* Jean-Marie 66–67, 69
Douglas, Sergeant John 24–25, 27, 29, 34, 49, 93, 103, 107–108, 111–113, 117–119, 122–123, 126, 129–131, 133, 136, 140, 142–143, 145–146, 149–150, 170–171, 175–177, 180, 196, 198, 200
Dubreton, *Général de division* Jean-Louis 135, 138
Dunlop, Major General James 32, 47, 49, 51, 56, 58, 68, 229, 232, 237–238
Durana 167–169, 171–172, 176

El Bodón 66–67
Elvas 16, 36, 40, 44, 51, 63, 69, 83
Erskine, Major General Sir William 42, 47–48, 50–51, 53, 56, 58–59, 232
España, Carlos de 64, 69, 79, 95, 101, 103, 111, 116, 118, 122, 132, 220–222

Ferey, *Général de division* Claude François 52–54, 114, 122
Fletcher, Lieutenant Colonel Sir Richard 193, 198
Fort Concepcion 51–52, 55–56
Foy, *Général de brigade* Maximilien Sébastien 22–24, 31, 36, 61, 66, 69, 105–106, 113–114, 122, 126–127, 131, 134, 142–145, 164, 179–180, 182, 201, 207, 209–213, 215–216, 219
Foz de Arouce 43–44
Freer, Ensign George 112, 117, 119, 123, 175, 198, 225
Freire, *Teniente general* Manuel 194, 203, 205–207, 220
French army, regiments of: **2e légèr**; 22; **4e légèr** 22; **17e légèr** 22; **31e légèr** 22; **19e de la ligne** 31; **36e de la ligne** 22; **47e de la ligne** 22; **70e de la ligne** 22, 122
Fririon, *Général de brigade* Joseph 172–173, 176
Fuente Guinaldo 50, 64, 66–67, 69, 76, 98
Fuentes de Oñoro 16, 40, 50, 232, 238
Fuentes de Oñoro, battle of 52–55

Gamarra Mayor 167–169, 171–179
Gamarra Menor 169, 172
Girón, *Teniente general* Pedro Augustín 162–165, 168, 172, 203, 205, 207, 209
Gomm, Captain William Maynard 14–18, 26–29, 32, 37–39, 47, 49, 51, 55–56, 58, 61–63, 76–77, 79–80, 82–83, 90–92, 95–97, 102–103, 105, 113, 117, 121, 124–125, 127–132, 136, 138–140, 146, 149, 152, 154, 158, 160, 163–164, 177, 180, 189–190, 194, 199, 201–202, 206–207, 217, 222, 225–227, 235–236, 241, 250
Graham, Lieutenant General Sir Thomas 98, 102–103, 158, 160, 162–172, 176, 178, 180, 182–186, 190–192, 194–195, 197–198, 202, 228, 233, 236–237, 239
Greville, Lieutenant Colonel James 118–119, 203–204, 215, 237, 244, 249–250
Guadiana river 16, 61–63, 82–85
Guarda 13, 18–19, 40, 45–47, 61, 68–69, 75, 95–96

Hale, Sergeant James 25–26, 34, 43, 57–58, 71, 76, 78, 82, 105, 112, 123, 126, 137, 139, 144–145, 155, 170–172, 176–177, 184, 199–200
Hamilton, Major General John 12, 21, 27, 30, 44, 63, 157–158, 207, 244
Hay, Major General Andrew 29, 49–50, 70, 86, 118, 147, 158, 177, 179, 184–185, 187, 191–192, 196, 198, 200, 203, 205, 213, 215, 224, 226, 229, 232, 235–237, 241–244
Heudelet, *Général de division* Étienne 21–23, 53, 55
Hill, Lieutenant General Sir Rowland 10–13, 15–23, 30–31, 60, 63, 72, 82–83, 95, 97, 102–103, 115, 121, 128, 132, 136, 138, 147–148, 158, 162–163, 168–169, 171–172, 181–182, 189, 206–207, 210–213, 216–218, 221, 229, 232
Hope, Lieutenant General Sir John 202–203, 205–207, 209–213, 215–216, 220–222, 224–226
Howard, Major General Kenneth 60, 63, 224, 226
Hulse, Major General Richard 56, 133, 232

Iremonger, Lieutenant Colonel William 57, 59

Joseph, King of Spain 69, 100, 103, 110, 127–129, 131–132, 138, 162–168, 176

Jourdan, *Maréchal* Jean-Baptiste 100, 129, 163, 167, 172
Junot, *Général de division* Jean-Andoche 22, 24, 30, 39, 46–47

Lamartinière, *Général de division* Thomas 165, 168, 176, 201
Lamego 74, 96–97, 154, 158–160, 243–244
Le Marchant, Major General John Gaspard 98, 107, 111, 119
Le Mesurier, Lieutenant Peter 70, 73, 75–77, 79, 86–87, 94–96, 98, 100, 116–117, 127, 130–132, 134–137, 139–140, 143, 146–149, 154, 156, 160, 163–164, 177, 204, 215
Leiria 27–28, 36, 39–40
Leith, Lieutenant General James 13–24, 26–28, 31–32, 37, 51, 56, 76, 79–80, 82, 85–94, 97, 104, 108, 114–115, 117–120, 124–125, 132, 140, 147, 158, 195, 197–198, 200, 223, 229–232, 236–237, 240
Leith Hay, Captain Andrew 9–10, 33, 46, 88, 90, 92, 98, 101–102, 106–107, 109–110, 112, 115, 117, 119–120, 124–125, 183, 229–231, 246
Leval, *Général de division* Jean François 162, 169, 209, 215, 220
Lisbon 12, 14, 17–18, 27–29, 31, 35–37, 40, 97, 104, 111, 158, 162, 226, 229, 232, 236
Loison, *Général de division* Louis Henri 21, 24, 45–47, 52

Mackinnon, Major General Henry 23, 54, 76
Madrid 69, 74, 100, 110, 125, 127–132, 138, 147, 159, 162, 169
Maguire, Lieutenant Francis 174, 195–197
Marchand, *Général de division* Jean Gabriel 21, 24, 42, 51, 53
Marmont, *Maréchal* Auguste Frédéric 51, 60–67, 69–70, 72, 76, 80, 83–84, 95–97, 100–103, 105–119, 127, 132
Masséna, *Maréchal* André 13, 16–19, 21–22, 24, 26–27, 29–34, 36, 38, 41, 43–47, 50–56, 59
Maucune, *Général de division* Antoine Louis de 114, 116–121, 124, 138, 142, 144–145, 165–166, 172, 201, 203, 205
Maya Pass 191, 203
Mendizábel, *Teniente General* Gabriel de 36, 180, 183
Menne, *Général de brigade* Jean-Baptiste 172–173, 176

Menor 168–169, 172–173
Merle, *Général de division* Pierre Hugues 21–24, 48
Mermet, *Général de brigade* Julien Augustin 21, 24, 53, 168–170, 172
Mondego river 18–20, 27, 38, 47
Montbrun, *Général de division* Louis-Pierre 30, 38–39, 41, 52–54, 67
Murray, Colonel George 56, 180, 206

Napoleon, Emperor of France 31, 36, 41, 45, 51, 69–70, 72, 80, 84, 186, 210, 219–220, 224–225, 227–228, 231–233
Nave de Haver 52–54, 60
Nevill, Lieutenant Percy Parke 73, 75–76, 84, 87, 92, 135, 137–138
Ney, *Maréchal* Michel, 13, 20–22, 24, 38–39, 41–43, 45
Nive, battle of the 209–214, 217–219, 222–223, 238, 240, 249–250
Nivelle, battle of the 206–210, 238, 249

O'Halloran, Major George 191–192
Orduña 165–168
Oswald, Lieutenant General Sir John 9, 140, 143–145, 147, 150, 158, 174, 179, 183, 185, 191–192, 194–195, 198, 232

Pack, Brigadier General Dennis 20, 24, 28, 30, 33, 39, 42, 45, 50, 56–57, 60–61, 67, 76, 83, 98, 101, 115, 118, 121, 132, 160, 162–163, 168, 172–173, 178, 183–184
Pakenham, Major General Edward 111, 114, 116, 118–119, 121, 217
Palencia 63, 74, 127, 139–145, 159, 162–163
Pamplona 159, 167–168, 180, 182, 191, 201, 206, 241
Philippon, *Général de brigade* Armand 83, 86
Picton, Major General Thomas 20–23, 27–28, 39, 42–43, 46–47, 49, 53, 66–67, 86–88, 98, 103, 111, 116, 168, 171, 233, 235
Pinhel 13, 18
Pombal 39–41
Portuguese army, units of: **3rd Line** 14, 215, 248–250; **8th Line** 26; **13th Line** 184, 197 **15th Line** 14, 29, 95, 118, 123, 144, 230, 240, 248–250; **21st Line** 23; **2nd Caçadores** 113; **4th Caçadores** 115, 173, 184, 240; **5th Caçadores** 184, 196; **6th Caçadores** 29; **8th Caçadores** 55, 95, 120, 144–145, 166, 172–173, 178, 187, 213, 215, 230, 248–250; **Tomar militia** 14, 20, 23–24; **Ordenança** 19, 29, 44
Portalegre 16, 40, 62–63, 82
Porto Velho 52, 54
Pringle Major General William 97, 104–105, 118, 132–133, 139–140, 144–147, 238–239

Redinha 39, 41
Reed, Private Adam 173–174, 176, 209, 227
Reille, *Général de division* Honoré Charles 162–172, 176, 201, 203, 205, 207, 209–210, 213, 215–217, 219
Rey, *Général de Brigade* Emmanuel 105–106, 180, 182, 184, 186–187, 191–193, 195, 198, 201
Reynier, *Général de division* Jean-Louis-Ebénézer 13, 16–23, 31, 38–39, 45–47, 49, 52–55, 58, 61
Robinson, Brigadier General Frederick 158, 176, 178–179, 194–198, 200, 202–204, 211, 213, 215, 217, 236, 239, 249–250
Romana, Marques de la 16–17, 30
Roncesvalles 191, 202–203, 207
Sabugal, battle of 46–50, 61, 64, 68, 238
Salamanca 9, 12–13, 50–51, 63–66, 69, 72, 74, 76, 80, 83, 95, 97–102, 104, 106, 111–112, 128, 136, 147–148, 150, 159, 162–163, 232, 237, 248, 250
Salamanca, battle of 113–127
Salvatierra 82, 171, 176, 180
San Sebastian 9, 180, 182–183, 191–192, 194, 199–202, 218, 223, 233, 236–237, 240, 250
San Sebastian, sieges of 180–202
Sanchez, Julian 50, 54, 64, 69, 72, 163
Santarém 16–17, 32–34, 37–38, 40
Sarrut, *Général de brigade* Jacques 22, 53, 111, 122, 165, 168–169, 171–172, 176
Sherbrooke, Lieutenant General John Coape 10–12
Sobral 29–31, 33
Solignac, *Général de division* Jean-Baptiste 52–53
Souham, *Général de division* Joseph, Comte 67, 69, 134–136, 138–139, 142–143, 147
Soult, *Maréchal* Jean 12, 31, 36, 38, 60–62, 64, 80, 83–84, 95–97, 102–103, 129, 131–132, 138, 147–148, 169, 191–192, 194, 201, 205–207, 209–211, 213, 215–222, 224, 226
Soult, *Général de division* Pierre 30, 217
Spencer, Lieutenant General Sir Brent 21, 51–53, 58, 60–62

Spry, Brigadier General William 14, 20, 23, 29, 31, 50, 118, 123, 158, 178–179, 186, 196, 200, 203, 213, 229–230, 240, 248
St Jean de Luz 159, 182, 184, 206–207, 209–210, 213, 215–216, 218, 220, 222

Tagus river 13, 15–18, 29–30, 32, 40, 59, 61, 63–64, 66, 80, 82, 95–97, 103
Thiébault, *Général de division* Paul Charles 63–64, 67, 72, 76
Thomières, *Général de division* Jean Guillaume 114, 116–119, 121
Thouvenot, *Général de brigade* Pierre 210, 221–222, 224–226
Tilly, *Général de division* Jacques-Louis-François 169, 171
Tomkinson, Captain William 58–59, 164, 168, 172–174
Torres Vedras, lines of 29–30, 34, 37–38, 229
Trant, Brigadier General Nicholas 36, 38, 42, 50

Valladolid 13, 31, 45, 76, 104, 126–128, 131–134, 146, 158–159, 235
Valverde 62, 65, 84
Villa Muriel 9, 140, 144, 232
Villa Velha 13, 15, 17, 61
Villafranque 211, 216–217
Villamuriel, battle of 139–144, 146–147, 154, 239, 250
Villatte, *Général de division* Eugène-Casimir 162, 169
Vitoria 9, 12, 135–136, 159, 161, 164–170, 172, 174, 176, 178–180, 182, 235, 246, 248, 250
Vitoria, battle of 167–180

Walcheren 14, 32, 34–35, 37, 66, 96, 128, 146, 158, 231, 235–238, 240, 244
Walker, Major General George 86–91, 94, 97, 238
Wellington, Field Marshal, the Duke of 9, 11–20, 22–23, 26–31, 33–39, 41, 43–44, 46–56, 58–72, 75, 78–80, 83–87, 89–90, 92–97, 100–104, 106–118, 122, 124–140, 145–154, 157–158, 160, 162–172, 178–180, 182–184, 186, 190–195, 201–207, 210–211, 213, 216–224, 226, 228–235, 237–242, 244, 246–247
Wilson, Lieutenant Colonel Sir Robert 17, 36, 104, 203, 205, 207, 209
Woodward, Ensign Thomas 125, 155, 220, 225, 228

York, Field Marshal HRH, the Duke of 10, 150, 157, 242

Zadorra 9, 161, 167–173, 175–176
Zamora 74, 100, 128, 131, 148, 158–159, 162
Zezere river 14–16, 18, 33, 60, 229

From Reason to Revolution – Warfare 1721-1815

http://www.helion.co.uk/series/from-reason-to-revolution-1721-1815.php

The 'From Reason to Revolution' series covers the period of military history 1721–1815, an era in which fortress-based strategy and linear battles gave way to the nation-in-arms and the beginnings of total war.

This era saw the evolution and growth of light troops of all arms, and of increasingly flexible command systems to cope with the growing armies fielded by nations able to mobilise far greater proportions of their manpower than ever before. Many of these developments were fired by the great political upheavals of the era, with revolutions in America and France bringing about social change which in turn fed back into the military sphere as whole nations readied themselves for war. Only in the closing years of the period, as the reactionary powers began to regain the upper hand, did a military synthesis of the best of the old and the new become possible.

The series will examine the military and naval history of the period in a greater degree of detail than has hitherto been attempted, and has a very wide brief, with the intention of covering all aspects from the battles, campaigns, logistics, and tactics, to the personalities, armies, uniforms, and equipment.

Submissions

The publishers would be pleased to receive submissions for this series. Please contact series editor Andrew Bamford via email (andrewbamford@helion.co.uk), or in writing to Helion & Company Limited, Unit 8 Amherst Business Centre, Budbrooke Road, Warwick, CV34 5WE

Titles

No 1 *Lobositz to Leuthen: Horace St Paul and the Campaigns of the Austrian Army in the Seven Years War 1756-57* (Neil Cogswell)

No 2 *Glories to Useless Heroism: The Seven Years War in North America from the French journals of Comte Maurés de Malartic, 1755-1760* (William Raffle (ed.))

No 3 *Reminiscences 1808-1815 Under Wellington: The Peninsular and Waterloo Memoirs of William Hay* (Andrew Bamford (ed.))

No 4 *Far Distant Ships: The Royal Navy and the Blockade of Brest 1793-1815* (Quintin Barry)

No 5 *Godoy's Army: Spanish Regiments and Uniforms from the Estado Militar of 1800* (Charles Esdaile and Alan Perry)

No 6 *On Gladsmuir Shall the Battle Be! The Battle of Prestonpans 1745* (Arran Johnston)

No 7 *The French Army of the Orient 1798-1801: Napoleon's Beloved 'Egyptians'* (Yves Martin)

No 8 *The Autobiography, or Narrative of a Soldier: The Peninsular War Memoirs of William Brown of the 45th Foot* (Steve Brown (ed.))

No 9 *Recollections from the Ranks: Three Russian Soldiers' Autobiographies from the Napoleonic Wars* (Darrin Boland)

No 10 *By Fire and Bayonet: Grey's West Indies Campaign of 1794* (Steve Brown)

No 11 *Olmütz to Torgau: Horace St Paul and the Campaigns of the Austrian Army in the Seven Years War 1758-60* (Neil Cogswell)

No 12 *Murat's Army: The Army of the Kingdom of Naples 1806-1815* (Digby Smith)

No 13 *The Veteran or 40 Years' Service in the British Army: The Scurrilous Recollections of Paymaster John Harley 47th Foot – 1798-1838* (Gareth Glover (ed.))

No 14 *Narrative of the Eventful Life of Thomas Jackson: Militiaman and Coldstream Sergeant, 1803-15* (Eamonn O'Keeffe (ed.))

No.15 *For Orange and the States: The Army of the Dutch Republic 1713-1772 Part I: Infantry* (Marc Geerdinck-Schaftenaar)

No 16   *Men Who Are Determined to be Free: The American Assault on Stony Point, 15 July 1779* (David C. Bonk)

No 17   *Next to Wellington: General Sir George Murray: The Story of a Scottish Soldier and Statesman, Wellington's Quartermaster General* (John Harding-Edgar)

No 18   *Between Scylla and Charybdis: The Army of Elector Friedrich August of Saxony 1733-1763 Part I: Staff and Cavalry* (Marco Pagan)

No 19   *The Secret Expedition: The Anglo-Russian Invasion of Holland 1799* (Geert van Uythoven)

No 20   *'We Are Accustomed to do our Duty': German Auxiliaries with the British Army 1793-95* (Paul Demet)

No 21   *With the Guards in Flanders: The Diary of Captain Roger Morris 1793-95* (Peter Harington (ed.))

No 22   *The British Army in Egypt 1801: An Underrated Army Comes of Age* (Carole Divall)

No 23   *Better is the Proud Plaid: The Clothing, Weapons, and Accoutrements of the Jacobites in the '45* (Jenn Scott)

No 24   *The Lilies and the Thistle: French Troops in the Jacobite '45* (Andrew Bamford)

No 25   *A Light Infantryman With Wellington: The Letters of Captain George Ulrich Barlow 52nd and 69th Foot 1808-15* (Gareth Glover (ed.))

No 26   *Swiss Regiments in the Service of France 1798-1815: Uniforms, Organisation, Campaigns* (Stephen Ede-Borrett)

No 27   *For Orange and the States! The Army of the Dutch Republic 1713-1772: Part II: Cavalry and Specialist Troops* (Marc Geerdinck-Schaftenaar)

No 28   *Fashioning Regulation, Regulating Fashion: Uniforms and Dress of the British Army 1800-1815 Volume I* (Ben Townsend)

No 29   *Riflemen: The History of the 5th Battalion 60th (Royal American) Regiment, 1797-1818* (Robert Griffith)

No 30   *The Key to Lisbon: The Third French Invasion of Portugal, 1810-11* (Kenton White)

No 31   *Command and Leadership: Proceedings of the 2018 Helion & Company 'From Reason to Revolution' Conference* (Andrew Bamford (ed.))

No 32   *Waterloo After the Glory: Hospital Sketches and Reports on the Wounded After the Battle* (Michael Crumplin and Gareth Glover)

No 33   *Fluxes, Fevers, and Fighting Men: War and Disease in Ancien Regime Europe 1648-1789* (Pádraig Lenihan)

No 34   *'They Were Good Soldiers': African-Americans Serving in the Continental Army, 1775-1783* (John U. Rees)

No 35   *A Redcoat in America: The Diaries of Lieutenant William Bamford, 1757-1765 and 1776* (John B. Hattendorf (ed.))

No 36   *Between Scylla and Charybdis: The Army of Friedrich August II of Saxony, 1733-1763: Part II: Infantry and Artillery* (Marco Pagan)

No 37   *Québec Under Siege: French Eye-Witness Accounts from the Campaign of 1759* (Charles A. Mayhood (ed.))

No 38   *King George's Hangman: Henry Hawley and the Battle of Falkirk 1746* (Jonathan D. Oates)

No 39   *Zweybrücken in Command: The Reichsarmee in the Campaign of 1758* (Neil Cogswell)

No 40   *So Bloody a Day: The 16th Light Dragoons in the Waterloo Campaign* (David J. Blackmore)

No 41   *Northern Tars in Southern Waters: The Russian Fleet in the Mediterranean 1806-1810* (Vladimir Bogdanovich Bronevskiy / Darrin Boland)

No 42   *Royal Navy Officers of the Seven Years War: A Biographical Dictionary of Commissioned Officers 1748-1763* (Cy Harrison)

No 43   *All at Sea: Naval Support for the British Army During the American Revolutionary War* (John Dillon)

No 44   *Glory is Fleeting: New Scholarship on the Napoleonic Wars* (Andrew Bamford (ed.))

No 45   *Fashioning Regulation, Regulating Fashion: Uniforms and Dress of the British Army 1800-1815 Vol. II* (Ben Townsend)

No 46   *Revenge in the Name of Honour: The Royal Navy's Quest for Vengeance in the Single Ship Actions of the War of 1812* (Nicholas James Kaizer)

No 47   *They Fought With Extraordinary Bravery: The III German (Saxon) Army Corps in the Southern Netherlands 1814* (Geert van Uythoven)

No 48 *The Danish Army of the Napoleonic Wars 1801-1814, Organisation, Uniforms & Equipment: Volume 1: High Command, Line and Light Infantry* (David Wilson)

No 49 *Neither Up Nor Down: The British Army and the Flanders Campaign 1793-1895* (Phillip Ball)

No 50 *Guerra Fantástica: The Portuguese Army and the Seven Years War* (António Barrento)

No 51 *From Across the Sea: North Americans in Nelson's Navy* (Sean M. Heuvel and John A. Rodgaard)

No 52 *Rebellious Scots to Crush: The Military Response to the Jacobite '45* (Andrew Bamford (ed.))

No 53 *The Army of George II 1727-1760: The Soldiers who Forged an Empire* (Peter Brown)

No 54 *Wellington at Bay: The Battle of Villamuriel, 25 October 1812* (Garry David Wills)

No 55 *Life in the Red Coat: The British Soldier 1721-1815* (Andrew Bamford (ed.))

No 56 *Wellington's Favourite Engineer. John Burgoyne: Operations, Engineering, and the Making of a Field Marshal* (Mark S. Thompson)

No 57 *Scharnhorst: The Formative Years, 1755-1801* (Charles Edward White)

No 58 *At the Point of the Bayonet: The Peninsular War Battles of Arroyomolinos and Almaraz 1811-1812* (Robert Griffith)

No 59 *Sieges of the '45: Siege Warfare during the Jacobite Rebellion of 1745-1746* (Jonathan D. Oates)

No 60 *Austrian Cavalry of the Revolutionary and Napoleonic Wars, 1792–1815* (Enrico Acerbi, András K. Molnár)

No 61 *The Danish Army of the Napoleonic Wars 1801-1814, Organisation, Uniforms & Equipment: Volume 2: Cavalry and Artillery* (David Wilson)

No 62 *Napoleon's Stolen Army: How the Royal Navy Rescued a Spanish Army in the Baltic* (John Marsden)

No 63 *Crisis at the Chesapeake: The Royal Navy and the Struggle for America 1775-1783* (Quintin Barry)

No 64 *Bullocks, Grain, and Good Madeira: The Maratha and Jat Campaigns 1803-1806 and the emergence of the Indian Army* (Joshua Provan)

No 65 *Sir James McGrigor: The Adventurous Life of Wellington's Chief Medical Officer* (Tom Scotland)

No 66 *Fashioning Regulation, Regulating Fashion: Uniforms and Dress of the British Army 1800-1815 Volume I* (Ben Townsend) (paperback edition)

No 67 *Fashioning Regulation, Regulating Fashion: Uniforms and Dress of the British Army 1800-1815 Volume II* (Ben Townsend) (paperback edition)

No 68 *The Secret Expedition: The Anglo-Russian Invasion of Holland 1799* (Geert van Uythoven) (paperback edition)

No 69 *The Sea is My Element: The Eventful Life of Admiral Sir Pulteney Malcolm 1768-1838* (Paul Martinovich)

No 70 *The Sword and the Spirit: Proceedings of the first 'War & Peace in the Age of Napoleon' Conference* (Zack White (ed.))

No 71 *Lobositz to Leuthen: Horace St Paul and the Campaigns of the Austrian Army in the Seven Years War 1756-57* (Neil Cogswell) (paperback edition)

No 72 *For God and King. A History of the Damas Legion 1793-1798: A Case Study of the Military Emigration during the French Revolution* (Hughes de Bazouges and Alistair Nichols)

No 73 *'Their Infantry and Guns Will Astonish You': The Army of Hindustan and European Mercenaries in Maratha service 1780-1803* (Andy Copestake)

No 74 *Like A Brazen Wall: The Battle of Minden, 1759, and its Place in the Seven Years War* (Ewan Carmichael)

No 75 *Wellington and the Lines of Torres Vedras: The Defence of Lisbon during the Peninsular War* (Mark Thompson)

No 76 *French Light Infantry 1784-1815: From the Chasseurs of Louis XVI to Napoleon's Grande Armée* (Terry Crowdy)

No 77 *Riflemen: The History of the 5th Battalion 60th (Royal American) Regiment, 1797-1818* (Robert Griffith) (paperback edition)

No 78 *Hastenbeck 1757: The French Army and the Opening Campaign of the Seven Years War* (Olivier Lapray)

No 79 *Napoleonic French Military Uniforms: As Depicted by Horace and Carle Vernet and Eugène Lami* (Guy Dempsey (trans. and ed.))

No 80 *These Distinguished Corps: British Grenadier and Light Infantry Battalions in the American Revolution* (Don N. Hagist)

No 81 *Rebellion, Invasion, and Occupation: The British Army in Ireland, 1793 -1815* (Wayne Stack)

No 82 *You Have to Die in Piedmont! The Battle of Assietta, 19 July 1747. The War of the Austrian Succession in the Alps* (Giovanni Cerino Badone)

No 83 *A Very Fine Regiment: the 47th Foot in the American War of Independence, 1773–1783* (Paul Knight)

No 84 *By Fire and Bayonet: Grey's West Indies Campaign of 1794* (Steve Brown) (paperback edition)

No 85 *No Want of Courage: The British Army in Flanders, 1793-1795* (R.N.W. Thomas)

No 86 *Far Distant Ships: The Royal Navy and the Blockade of Brest 1793-1815* (Quintin Barry) (paperback edition)

No 87 *Armies and Enemies of Napoleon 1789-1815: Proceedings of the 2021 Helion and Company 'From Reason to Revolution' Conference* (Robert Griffith (ed.))

No 88 *The Battle of Rossbach 1757: New Perspectives on the Battle and Campaign* (Alexander Querengässer (ed.))

No 89 *Waterloo After the Glory: Hospital Sketches and Reports on the Wounded After the Battle* (Michael Crumplin and Gareth Glover) (paperback edition)

No 90 *From Ushant to Gibraltar: The Channel Fleet 1778-1783* (Quintin Barry)

No 91 *'The Soldiers are Dressed in Red': The Quiberon Expedition of 1795 and the Counter-Revolution in Brittany* (Alistair Nichols)

No 92 *The Army of the Kingdom of Italy 1805-1814: Uniforms, Organisation, Campaigns* (Stephen Ede-Borrett)

No 93 *The Ottoman Army of the Napoleonic Wars 1798-1815: A Struggle for Survival from Egypt to the Balkans* (Bruno Mugnai)

No 94 *The Changing Face of Old Regime Warfare: Essays in Honour of Christopher Duffy* (Alexander S. Burns (ed.))

No 94 *The Changing Face of Old Regime Warfare: Essays in Honour of Christopher Duffy* (Alexander S. Burns (ed.)

No 95 *The Danish Army of the Napoleonic Wars 1801-1814, Organisation, Uniforms & Equipment: Volume 3: Norwegian Troops and Militia* (David Wilson)

No 96 *1805 – Tsar Alexander's First War with Napoleon* (Alexander Ivanovich Mikhailovsky-Danilevsky, trans. Peter G.A. Phillips)

No 97 *'More Furies then Men': The Irish Brigade in the service of France 1690-1792* (Pierre-Louis Coudray)

No 98 *'We Are Accustomed to do our Duty': German Auxiliaries with the British Army 1793-95* (Paul Demet) (paperback edition)

No 99 *Ladies, Wives and Women: British Army Wives in the Revolutionary and Napoleonic Wars 1793-1815* (David Clammer)

No 100 *The Garde Nationale 1789-1815: France's Forgotten Armed Forces* (Pierre-Baptiste Guillemot)

No 101 *Confronting Napoleon: Levin von Bennigsen's Memoir of the Campaign in Poland, 1806-1807, Volume I Pultusk to Eylau* (Alexander Mikaberidze and Paul Strietelmeier (trans. and ed.))

No 102 *Olmütz to Torgau: Horace St Paul and the Campaigns of the Austrian Army in the Seven Years War 1758-60* (Neil Cogswell) (paperback edition)

No 103 *Fit to Command: British Regimental Leadership in the Revolutionary & Napoleonic Wars* (Steve Brown)

No 104 *Wellington's Unsung Heroes: The Fifth Division in the Peninsular War, 1810-1814* (Carole Divall)